CHRISTIAN CLASSICS

BROADMAN PRESS
NASHVILLE, TENNESSEE

Early American Christianity

Bill J. Leonard

Editor

BROADMAN

Nashville, Tennessee

4265-78

ISBN: 0-8054-6578-2

Dewey Decimal Classification: 277.3

Subject heading: U.S.—CHURCH HISTORY

Library of Congress Catalog Card Number: 83-15244

Library of Congress Cataloging in Publication Data
Main entry under title:

Early American Christianity.

   (Christian classics)
   1. United States—Church history—Addresses, essays,
lectures.   I. Leonard, Bill.   II. Series.
BR515.E24   1984   277.3   83-15244
ISBN 0-8054-6578-2

Printed in the United States of America

To Stephanie Erin Leonard,
a gift of hope

Acknowledgments

This collection of materials is presented as an introduction to certain basic issues, movements, and controversies evident in the early years of the American religious experience. Hopefully, these documents will provide a context for further understanding the development of American religion in its pluralism, sectarianism, and other unique forms.

I am indebted to numerous persons for their encouragement in this endeavor. The students and faculty of the Southern Baptist Theological Seminary provided a community of affirmation and support. Professor E. Glenn Hinson, colleague and friend, recommended me for this assignment; and I am deeply grateful. Mrs. Kathy Melton provided invaluable assistance in the preparation of the manuscript. Her wry humor was also an important contribution.

I am also indebted to Frances Edith Henton, in her ninety-third year, who, as grandmother and teacher, introduced me to many aspects of American religion—revivals, hymns, and controversies—which she experienced firsthand.

Candyce C. Leonard was, as usual, the source of honest criticism, unfailing encouragement, and necessary patience. Her scholarship and literary insights are gratefully acknowledged.

Louisville, 1979

The editorial staff of this volume wishes to express thanks to the following publishers for the use of the material cited.

William Warren Sweet, *Religion on the American Frontier* (New York: Henry Holt and Company, 1931).

Ralph Waldo Emerson, "An Address Delivered to the Senior Class of the Harvard Divinity School, July 15, 1838," from *The Selected Works of Ralph Waldo Emerson* (New York: The Modern Library, 1950).

George Maclaren Brydon, *Virginia's Mother Church and the Political Conditions Under Which It Grew* (Richmond: Virginia Historical Society, 1947), pp. 426-439. Used by permission.

Thomas O'Brien Hanley, ed., *The John Carroll Papers* 1 (Notre Dame, Indiana: University of Notre Dame Press, 1976). Used by permission.

CONTENTS

Introduction

The earliest American colonists did not arrive on these shores to establish a democracy. Many were monarchists, loyal subjects of a variety of European sovereigns. In fact, Governor John Winthrop of the Massachusetts Bay Colony called democracy the "meanest and worst" of all forms of government.

Many of the colonial leaders repudiated any idea of religious liberty. While some colonies—Maryland, Rhode Island, and Pennsylvania—did extend varying degrees of religious toleration, others such as Virginia, New Hampshire, and Massachusetts promoted tax-supported churches and often dealt severely with nonconformists. Even after passage of the Bill of Rights, there remained an established church in Massachusetts until 1833.

Throughout the colonial era, only a minority of Americans held membership in any organized church. There was no "golden age" of religious dedication among great numbers of people. It is estimated that in 1700 no more than 10 to 20 percent of all Americans were affiliated with any church.

While many of the so-called "founding fathers" of the republic—John Witherspoon, James Madison, and George Washington—were practicing churchmen, others—Thomas Paine, Ethan Allen, and Benjamin Franklin—were not. Many early leaders considered themselves Deists—stressing belief in the God of reason and creation, rejecting belief in the deity of Christ. Still others held to no religious belief at all.

The above statements serve to illustrate the need for the study of American religion in order to dispel many popular myths regarding American beginnings. They remind us that it is difficult to generalize concerning religion and its relationship to American life and culture. This volume seeks to present certain basic aspects of the American religious experience during the years 1607-1840 as illustrated in representative source materials written during that significant period.

The religion that was brought to the New World was in many respects the religion of the Old. The earliest American Christians were the theological heirs of Martin Luther, John Calvin, the Radical Reformers, Thomas Cranmer, and the Council of Trent. Much of their theology and practice was written and worked out before they arrived. Many early Protestant settlers believed that Providence had prepared this new land as a place where the theology of the Reformation could be established in its ultimate expression.

The Catholics, however, were equally convinced of the reality of providential guidance in their discoveries in America; and the Catholics were the earliest European arrivals. Columbus actually did "sail the ocean blue in fourteen hundred ninety-two." He was seeking a shorter trade route to the Orient. As a God-fearing Catholic, Columbus believed he was a vehicle of divine guidance in his discovery of these new lands for their Catholic majesties, Ferdinand and Isabella of Spain, the Supreme Pontiff in Rome, and the Holy Catholic Church. As exploration continued, friars of the Jesuit, Franciscan, and other orders accompanied many expeditions. They sought to evangelize the native peoples discovered on these shores. The friars lived with the Indians, instructing them in faith and frequently incorporating indigenous religion into Catholic observances. The theology they brought was that of the Council of Trent, which by 1565 had formulated the basic expression of Catholic doctrine. It proclaimed the necessity of salvation through faith and works, known particularly in seven sacraments whereby the grace of God was mediated to humanity through the Church. It was a Catholicism concerned for clerical and church renewal, zealous in missionary spirit, and seeking to recover lost ground from the Protestant insurgents.

Those Protestants who first came to America were likewise on the offensive against Catholicism, concerned lest the "papists" would extend their influence politically as well as spiritually in the new land. The theology that these Protestants brought with them had some common characteristics but was also very diversified. A century after its eruption, the Reformation had become factionalized into numerous groups, many claiming to represent the only true church of Christ. Generally speaking, the traditions brought to America were founded on the following theological movements.

First, there was the theology of Martin Luther and the later German Pietists. Luther, the seminal figure of the Reformation, had introduced such doctrines as justification by faith alone, the supreme authority of Scriptures, and the priesthood of all believers. These concepts influenced all major Protestant bodies. His distinctive liturgical and doctrinal viewpoints were brought to America by German Lutherans who gave a specific ethnic expression to their faith, retaining many Old World traditions along with the German language long after their arrival.

During the 1600s, as Lutheran doctrine became more formal and dogmatic, a reaction developed which is known as Pietism. This movement was a reassertion of the importance of personal conversion, holiness, and heart religion. Its concern for devotional prayer and Bible study, laity-led small groups, and religious experience over doctrinal obscurity, has had a wide impact on American religious life. Elements of pietistic influence are evident in many major American denominations.

Another significant Old World influence on the religion of America was that of Puritanism. Developing out of the theology of the reformer of Geneva, John Calvin, it has also had a pervasive effect on American religious communions. Calvinism was built upon the doctrine of divine sovereignty. The chief duty of men and women was "to love God and enjoy him forever." Humanity, however, was totally depraved and without hope. Salvation was given to those whom God had elected "before the foundation of the world" to be recipients of his grace. Such grace was irresistible and all-sustaining. The church, Calvin believed, was where the Word was preached, the sacraments (baptism and the Lord's Supper) administered, and discipline applied. Calvinism expressed itself through Huguenots in France, Presbyterians in Scotland, Puritans in England, and the Reformed Church in Holland.

The Calvinism of Geneva did not come to America untampered with, however. It had been filtered through various interpretations, particularly those evident in that diverse English movement known as Puritanism. Puritanism developed within the Anglican Church as churchmen sought to purify the Church of England toward a more Calvinistic position. The Anglican Church of Henry VIII, the *Book of Common Prayer,* and later Elizabeth I was a via media, a middle way, between the ceremony and liturgy of Roman Catholicism and the theology of the Reformation. It sought to incorporate the best of both Catholic and Reformation traditions without divisive extremes on either side.

The Puritans desired to bring the English Church more clearly into the theology of the Reformation by abolishing elaborate ritual, vestments, and other "trappings of popery." But the Puritans themselves were divided on just how far to go in reforming the church. Some nonseparating Puritans felt that the Anglican Church was the true church and needed only to be purified and awakened to more biblical types of church order. Certain Puritans favored a church governed by a Presbyterian system with pastor, teachers, elders, and deacons as leaders. Other Puritans, known as Independents, favored a church government in which the congregation had the final word in church affairs, selecting two officers, pastors, and deacons.

Still others rejected the Church of England entirely, labeling it as a false church and urging true believers to separate from Anglicanism. They are known as Puritan Separatists, a group of whom came to Plymouth in 1620.

Each of these factions held to some type of Calvinistic theology while stressing the importance of a church of believers united by a covenant with God and one another. Puritanism expressed itself within such varied American communions as the Congregationalists, the Baptists, and the Presbyterians.

Another of the Old World influences on the religion of America is evident in that movement known as the Enlightenment. It is less a theological system than a philosophical one, representing a more optimistic view of human nature than that of the Reformers. The Enlightenment appealed to the God of nature and reason as the benevolent deity who endowed humanity with natural faculties for confronting life and truth. It was in many respects the religion of the intellectuals, many of whom shaped the directions of the Republic. Natural rights, God-given liberties, and human capabilities were prominent emphases of the Enlightenment in America.

While the religion of the American experience was formulated in Europe, it was shaped and adapted by the circumstances of life in the new land. The religion of the Old World took on new interpretations as it was applied to new situations and thereby developed uniquely American characteristics.

One of the most significant indigenous aspects of American religion is its pluralism. In spite of the existence of established churches in many of the colonies, the fact remains that there was never one American church. Indeed, the presence of multiple denominations, often competing for the souls of the constituency, became a major characteristic of American religion. As freedom of religion became the norm, membership in the churches became voluntary; and voluntary churches meant a diversity of groups, emphasizing varying doctrines and institutional structures.

Thus multitudes of new Christian bodies sprang up, developing programs, policies, and procedures for securing "volunteers" and proclaiming the gospel. This meant that another related quality of American religion was its sectarian nature. As denominations became institutionalized, formal, and staid, reactions frequently developed from those who believed that existing churches had forsaken true apostolic faith. These new sects often claimed to have reinstituted the primary doctrine of the New Testament church or to have been founded out of the continuing revelation of the Spirit. Because America provided a vast expanse of land, sectarians could find secluded locations where they could thrive and develop their new societies. Thus American religion often learned "to multiply by dividing."

The effort to secure these latter-day kingdoms also illustrates another quality of American religion: its utopian spirit. The new American land, so long unknown to Europeans, now appeared to be the place that Providence had preserved for the establishment of the kingdom of God on earth. Such terms as "a city upon a hill," "a New People in a New Land," and "the Holy Experiment" give evidence of the concept of election and chosenness which many believed to be inherent in the destiny of America. From New England Puritans to radical communitarians, to the Church of Jesus Christ of Latter-Day Saints, America seemed a land divinely prepared for the millennial age and the kingdom of God.

This sense of destiny was also an important influence in the religious interpretation given to another formative aspect of American religion, the frontier. The American people were a people moving west; and if the church was to keep pace with the nation, it had to follow the westward migration. On the frontier the traditions of the past were often swept away, and new practices developed to fit the frontier situation were instigated. With time, however, these practical responses were frequently crystallized into immovable traditions within the supposedly traditionless frontier churches.

On the frontier, revivalistic methods thrived as a means for securing converts and building churches. For many Protestant denominations the religion of the revivals reshaped the theology of conversion, ethics, and preaching.

Finally, the period 1607-1840 witnessed the triumph of Protestantism as *the* American religion. Protestant morality, politics, and doctrine dominated the American religious scene. American religion was shaped as the ideologies of the Old World were applied to life in the New. It was formed by persons who wrote and preached, worked and prayed, while seeking to establish the Kingdom in the wilderness.

I

COLONIAL BEGINNINGS

Tales of cities made of gold, lands of conquest, and bounty brought the first settlers to North America. Spanish and French explorers with such names as Hernando Cortez, Ponce de Leon, and Robert La Salle came in search of glory and riches. The first permanent colony was founded at Saint Augustine, Florida, in 1565. Catholic influence spanned the continent, shaping American culture particularly in the Southwest and West. Catholic missionaries, the friars, were forced to live within the tension of loyalty to European authorities and opposition to the exploitation of the Indians they had come to serve. The Catholics were not to have primary impact on the colonial period of American history, however. It would be Protestants, particularly English-speaking Protestants, whose initial efforts at colonization would have the greater influence on early American religion.

After a series of false starts and aborted attempts, they settled first at Jamestown in May 1607. Merchants, artisans, and gentlefolk were sent out by the Virginia Company to develop the economic benefits of the New World for settlers and investors alike. These colonists did not emigrate in order to practice a dissenting religion but to found a trading company. The religion they brought was important to most of them, but it was the religion of the Anglican Establishment founded on the episcopacy and the *Book of Common Prayer*. The first communion shared by the English in the New World was celebrated at Jamestown by an Anglican chaplain, Robert Hunt, under a sail strung between two trees. Hunt served faithfully, dying, no doubt, during the "starving time" which swept the colony in the first year.

The names of the founders of Jamestown have long been a part of American heritage and legend: Captain John Smith, John and Priscilla Alden, and John Rolfe, who was wed to the Indian princess Pocahontas. Most of the colonists were gentlemen and women ill prepared for the hardships of life in the wilderness. Jamestown itself was poorly located, and the settlers fell victim to diseases caused by bad water, mosquitoes, and climate. By 1610 they were ready to abandon the experiment until a new governor, Lord De La Warr, arrived bringing provisions, additional colonists, and better government. It was a long time, however, before Jamestown became a stable colony.

Religious life was difficult to maintain in the wilderness of Virginia. Clergymen were scarce, and many of those who did come to the colony died as a result of the harsh life. Many clergymen were of questionable character, creating problems in the New World similar to those which prompted their migration from England.

There were, however, a number of clergymen who helped bring stability to the church in Virginia. One early leader was James Blair, who came to the colony in 1685 as the first commissary or representative of the Bishop of London. He directed church affairs and was instrumental in organizing the College of William and Mary in 1693.

Anglican ministers in Virginia were supported from the revenues of "glebe" lands set aside for such purposes. Parishes were widespread, and plantation owners frequently built their own chapels for use by family and workers to avoid long trips to the central parish church. The tobacco economy and slave system soon helped make Anglicanism the religion of the established society in Virginia.

Although the English came first to Virginia, the most famous religious experiment in the New World began at Plymouth, Massachusetts, in 1620. While they are best described as English Puritans of Separatist sentiments, the world will forever remember them as the Pilgrims; and their saga is an inseparable part of American lore.

They came from England by way of Leyden in the Netherlands, escaping there to avoid persecution leveled against Puritans under the rule of James I. Receiving a charter for land in "Northern Virginia," the group of 101 passengers sailed from the English town of Plymouth on September 16,

1620 and crowded onto the *Mayflower* after another vessel, the *Speedwell,* proved unseaworthy. By mistake they landed on Cape Cod, first near Provincetown and then at Plymouth, and their fears regarding the legality of their venture led them to produce the famous "Mayflower Compact."

Like Jamestown, the colony experienced continued hardships and did not grow as rapidly or as successfully as other New England settlements. Nonetheless, Plymouth was settled by a truly outstanding group of individuals who dealt justly with the Indians, struggled valiantly for survival, and remained undaunted in their faith.

The real power and influence in New England developed in those settlements begun in the 1620s on the Massachusetts Bay. The colonists were nonseparating Puritans, loyal to the Church of England but seeking to purify it in a more thoroughly Protestant direction. Under the leadership of Governor John Winthrop, these Calvinists sought to build a "visible church" based on individual profession of faith and exemplary moral behavior. Their holy commonwealth was to be "a city set upon a hill" for all the world to behold.

Other colonies followed with beginnings perhaps less well known but no less unique than those of Virginia and Massachusetts. Providence, Rhode Island, founded in 1636 by the perennial dissenter, Roger Williams, was a seedbed of religious radicalism. Exiled from Massachusetts due to radical opinions regarding freedom of religion and Indian ownership of American land, Williams formed a colony where religious liberty was a primary concern. By 1639 other dissenters had founded settlements in Rhode Island, among them Newport, established by Dr. John Clarke, a physician of Baptist sentiments. Rhode Island quickly became a sanctuary for such religious radicals as Quakers, Baptists, Separatists, and other freethinking individuals.

Founded in 1634 by Cecil Calvert, Lord Baltimore, Maryland extended religious toleration but not complete freedom of worship. Calvert was a Catholic, and Maryland became an early center for the English Roman Catholic minority during the colonial era. In order to attract a larger number of settlers, the leaders of Maryland offered religious toleration to all who could profess belief in Jesus Christ. Those denying the doctrine of the Trinity were to be given the death penalty.[1] These more "open" policies drew Anglicans, Presbyterians, Baptists, Quakers, and others to the colony. With time, however, Anglican religion became the established church in Maryland.

Religious liberty was also inherent in the organization of Pennsylvania by Quaker William Penn in 1681. It represents the first colony to be governed by the pacifist Quakers who continually encountered conflicts between their theological ideals and the realities of secular society. By the 1750s the political control of Penn's "Holy Experiment" had passed to non-Quaker hands.

Another colony founded with a distinctive theological and ethnic heritage was New Amsterdam, permanently organized in 1625 by the Dutch West India Company. The religion and language was that of the Dutch Reformed Church; but Quakers, Puritans, and others contributed to the pluralism of the area. By 1664 the English had gained military and political control, New Amsterdam became New York, and the Anglican Church had become the established religion in the colony. The Dutch Reformed Church continued to exercise strong influence on the area.

In the South, the area known as the Carolinas was established in 1663 under a charter providing religious toleration. North Carolina was settled by numerous religious groups including Presbyterians, Quakers, and Anglicans. Anglicanism was early established in South Carolina, and this brought frequent conflict with the Huguenots (French Protestants), Baptists, and other minority groups who located there.

Georgia, chartered in 1732, was founded as both a buffer against the Spanish Catholic influence further south and as a humanitarian experiment. Founders such as James Oglethorpe hoped that debtors might be given a second chance and be permitted to work off their debts in the new colony rather than to languish in deplorable English prisons. In spite of this noble ideal, Georgia was a long time in prospering.

The colony developed an Anglican Establishment to which both John and Charles Wesley came as missionaries in the 1730s. George Whitefield founded his famous orphanage in Savannah as part of his early missionary endeavors. Georgia was also a center of Moravian colonization, and their tradition of German Pietism no doubt had a lasting effect on the region's appreciation for "heart religion."

As these and other colonies began, the newcomers confronted numerous problems that affected religious life. The sources selected for this section illustrate the hardships faced by the colonial "Pilgrims," the search for church order in the midst of the American wilderness, and the controversies that arose therein.

The first document, an excerpt from William Bradford's *History of Plimouth Plantation,* describes some of the struggles of the most famous American Pilgrims. It also contains the classic "Mayflower Compact," by which the settlers formed a covenant for government in the New World. The Compact was the basis of political union at Plymouth until 1691.

Each of the colonies experienced a time of difficulty. Plymouth lost half of the original colonists after the first winter, and their "thanksgiving" with Indian guests was less a source of gratitude for material bounty than somber and grateful confession that some had merely managed to survive.

This portion of Bradford's *History* describes some of the difficulties encountered by the Separatists in both the Old World and the New. Leaving Holland under persecution, fearing that their children would be corrupted by the worldliness of Dutch youth, and desiring to establish a base for further propagation of the faith, they found that dissent and worldliness were not completely left behind. After suffering the rigors of the first winter, the settlers found that one "Mr. Morton," a licentious settler at the colony in Wollaston, had fostered immorality and corruption in the new world through "frisking" with the Indians, dancing, and even erecting a Maypole which the irate Puritans soon cut down. Miles Standish himself was sent to arrest Morton, who was shipped back to England as quickly as possible.

Bradford likewise mentions the problems caused by Roger Williams, whom the Separatists admired but whose uncompromising stand on various political and theological issues led to his exile from the colony. Bradford laments, "I hope he belongs to the Lord, and that he will shew him mercie . . . ." The *History of Plimouth Plantation* is a dramatic account of life in the early years of the holy commonwealth of New England.

As they survived and gained strength, the churches sought to establish some type of order appropriate to the needs of the new environment. The early Diocesan Canons of Virginia illustrate issues growing out of certain unique colonial problems and practices. The relation of the church to the state and the work of the clergy and their payment (in tobacco, corn, and so forth) is described. Problems arising from large parishes and a shortage of clergy are evident in the appointment of deacons to carry out certain ministerial functions and the increased influence of lay vestries in church administration.

The final treatise in this section reveals but one of many controversies which confronted the early colonists. Roger Williams, a brilliant but uncompromising teacher in churches in Salem and Plymouth, was brought to trial and exiled in 1636 for his unorthodox political and religious views. After securing a charter for Rhode Island, Williams worked to give the colony secure legal foundation. In 1644, while in England seeking legal sanctions for his colony, he wrote a dramatic statement for religious liberty, *The Bloudy Tenent of Persecution for the Cause of Conscience Discussed.*

In this work Williams attacked the idea that force may be used against those who refuse to conform due to principles of conscience. Instead of harassment, reason and reconciliation are to be used. The real weapons to be used against heresy were spiritual, not temporal or physical. The history of persecution in matters of conscience, Williams believed, was so deplorable that it might be labeled a bloody tenent, or principle, and a terrible contradiction of the life and spirit of Jesus, the Prince of Peace.

In this treatise Williams proposes an ideal regarding religious freedom which was to have far-reaching effects for later American democracy. Williams insists that the state is not to persecute those who hold dissenting religious beliefs or no beliefs at all. The heretic and even the unbeliever were not to be punished by the state for their views. They were to answer ultimately to God. He was the true judge of the conscience of every man and woman.

These views precipitated a Tractarian debate with the notable Puritan divine, John Cotton, who defended an established church in a work entitled *The Bloudy Tenent Washed White in the Bloud of the Lamb*. Williams countered with a further attack called *The Bloudy Tenent Made More Bloudy*. His opposition to establishment religion in the colonies was but one of the many controversies contributing to the diversity of American religious views in an increasingly pluralistic ecclesiastical arena.

The American colonies began with physical hardships, religious idealism, and the search for order in the midst of great diversity. The controversies and practices which developed in these formative years served to shape the direction of American religion for generations.

1

WILLIAM BRADFORD

Of Plimoth Plantation

AND first of ye occasion and indũsments ther unto; the which that I may truly unfould, I must begine at ye very roote & rise of ye same. The which I shall endevor to manefest in a plaine stile, with singuler regard unto ye simple trueth in all things, at least as near as my slender judgmente can attaine the same . . . .

When as by the travell & diligence of some godly & zealous preachers, & Gods blessing on their labours, as in other places of ye land, so in ye North parts, many became inlightened by ye word of God, and had their ignorance & sins discovered unto them, and begane by his grace to reforme their lives, and make conscience of their wayes, the worke of God was no sooner manifest in them, but presently they were both scoffed and scorned by ye prophane multitude, and ye ministers urged with ye yoak of subscription, or els must be silenced; and ye poore people were so vexed with apparators, & pursuants, & ye comis-sarie courts, as truly their affliction was not smale; which, notwithstanding, they bore sundrie years with much patience, till they were occasioned (by ye continuance & encrease of these troubls, and other means which ye Lord raised up in those days) to see further into things by the light of ye word of God. How not only these base and beggerly ceremonies were unlawfull, but also that ye lordly & tiranous power of ye prelats ought not to be submitted unto; which thus, contrary to the freedome of the gospell, would load & burden mens consciences, and by their compulsive power make a prophane mixture of persons & things in ye worship of God. And that their offices & calings, courts & cannons, &c. were unlawfull and antichristian; being such as have no warrante in ye word of God; but the same y^t were used in poperie, & still retained . . . .

[6] So many therfore of these proffessors as saw ye evill of these things, in thes parts, and whose harts ye Lord had touched wth heavenly zeale for his trueth, they shooke of this yoake of antichristian bondage, and as ye Lords free people, joyned them selves (by a covenant of the Lord) into a church estate, in ye felowship of ye gospell, to walke in all his wayes, made known, or to be made known unto them, according to their best en-deavours, whatsoever it should cost them, the Lord assisting them. And that it cost them something this ensewing historie will declare . . . .

But after these things they could not long continue in any peaceable condition, but were hunted & persecuted on every side, so as their former afflictions were but as flea-bitings in comparison of these which now came upon them. For some were taken & clapt up in prison, others had their houses besett & watcht night and day, & hardly escaped their hands; and ye most were faine to flie & leave their howses & habitations, and the means of their livelehood. Yet these & many other sharper things which affterward befell them, were no other then they looked for, and therfore were ye better prepared to bear them by ye assistance of Gods grace & spirite. Yet seeing them selves thus molested, [7] and that ther was no hope of their con-tinuance ther, by a joynte consente they resolved to goe into ye Low-Countries, wher they heard was freedome of Religion for all men . . . .

An°. 1608.

BEING thus constrained to leave their native soyle and countrie, their lands & livings, and all their freinds & famillier acquaintance, it was much, and thought marvelous by many. But to goe into a countrie they knew not (but by hearsay), wher they must learne a new language, and get their livings they knew not how, it being a dear place, & subjecte to ye misseries of warr, it was by many thought an adventure almost desperate, a case intolerable, & a misserie worse then death. Espetially seeing they were not aquainted with trads nor traffique, (by which yt countrie doth subsiste,) but had only been used to a plaine countrie life, & ye inocente trade of husbandrey. But these things did not dismay them (though they did some times trouble them) for their desires were sett on ye ways of God, & to injoye his ordinances; but they rested on his providence, & knew whom they had beleeved. Yet [8] this was not all, for though they could not stay, yet were ye not suffered to goe, but ye ports & havens were shut against them, so as they were faine to seeke secrete means of conveance, & to bribe & fee ye mariners, & give exterordinarie rates for their passages. And yet were they often times betrayed (many of them), and both they & their goods intercepted & surprised, and therby put to great trouble & charge . . . .

They removed to Leyden, a fair & bewtifull citie, and of a sweete situation, but made more famous by ye universitie wherwith it is adorned, in which of late had been so many learned men. But wanting that traffike by sea which Amsterdam injoyes, it was not so beneficiall for their outward means of living & estats. But being now hear pitchet they fell to such trads & imployments as they best could; valewing peace & their spirituall comforte above any other riches whatsoever. And at length they came to raise a competente & comforteable living, but with hard and continuall labor.

Being thus setled (after many difficulties) they continued

many years in a comfortable condition, injoying much sweete & delightefull societie & spirituall comforte togeather in ye wayes of God, under ye able ministrie, and prudente governmente of M^r. John Robinson, & M^r. William Brewster . . . .

AFTER they had lived in this citie about some 11. or 12. years, (which is ye more observable being ye whole time of y^t famose truce between that state & ye Spaniards,) and sundrie of them were taken away by death, & many others begane to be well striken in years, the grave mistris Experience haveing taught them many things, [16] those prudent governours with sundrie of ye sagest members begane both deeply to apprehend their present dangers, & wisely to foresee ye future, & thinke of timly remedy. In ye agitation of their thoughts, and much discours of things hear aboute, at length they began to incline to this conclusion, of remoovall to some other place. Not out of any newfanglednes, or other such like giddie humor, by which men are oftentimes transported to their great hurt & danger, but for sundrie weightie & solid reasons; some of ye cheefe of which I will hear breefly touch. And first, they saw & found by experience the hardnes of ye place & countrie to be such, as few in comparison would come to them, and fewer that would bide it out, and continew with them. For many y^t came to them, and many more y^t desired to be with them, could not endure y^t great labor and hard fare, with other inconveniences which they underwent & were contented with. But though they loved their persons, approved their cause, and honoured their sufferings, yet they left them as it weer weeping, as Orpah did her mother in law Naomie, or as those Romans did Cato in Utica, who desired to be excused & borne with, though they could not all be Catoes. For many, though they desired to injoye ye ordinances of God in their puritie, and ye libertie of the gospell with them, yet, alass, they admitted of bondage, with danger of conscience, rather then to indure these hardships; yea, some preferred & chose ye prisons in England, rather then this libertie in

Holland, with these afflictions. But it was thought that if a better and easier place of living could be had, it would draw many, & take away these discouragments. Yea, their pastor would often say, that many of those w° both wrate & preached now against them, if they were in a place wher they might have libertie and live comfortably, they would then practise as they did.

2ˡʸ. They saw that though yᵉ people generally bore all these difficulties very cherfully, & with a resolute courage, being in yᵉ best & strength of their years, yet old age began to steale on many of them, (and their great & continuall labours, with other crosses and sorrows, hastened it before yᵉ time,) so as it was not only probably thought, but apparently seen, that within a few years more they would be in danger to scatter, by necessities pressing them, or sinke under their burdens, or both. And therfore according to yᵉ devine proverb, yᵗ a wise man seeth yᵉ plague when it cometh, & hideth him selfe, Pro. 22. 3., so they like skillfull & beaten souldiers were fearfull either to be intrapped or surrounded by their enimies, so as they should neither be able to fight nor flie; and therfor thought it better to dislodge betimes to some place of better advantage & less danger, if any such could be found. [16] Thirdly; as necessitie was a taskmaster over them, so they were forced to be such, not only to their servants, but in a sorte, to their dearest chilldren; the which as it did not a litle wound yᵉ tender harts of many a loving father & mother, so it produced likwise sundrie sad & sorowful effects. For many of their children, that were of best dispositions and gracious inclinations, haveing lernde to bear yᵉ yoake in their youth, and willing to bear parte of their parents burden, were, often times, so oppressed with their hevie labours, that though their minds were free and willing, yet their bodies bowed under yᵉ weight of yᵉ same, and became decreped in their early youth; the vigor of nature being consumed in yᵉ very budd as it were. But that which was more lamentable, and of all sorowes most heavie to be borne, was that many of their children, by these occasions, and ye great licentiousnes of youth in y^t countrie, and ye manifold temptations of the place, were drawne away by evill examples into extravagante & dangerous courses, getting ye raines off their neks, & departing from their parents. Some became souldiers, others tooke upon them farr viages by sea, and other some worse courses, tending to dissolutnes & the danger of their soules, to ye great greefe of their parents and dishonour of God. So that they saw their posteritie would be in danger to degenerate & be corrupted.

Lastly, (and which was not least,) a great hope & inward zeall they had of laying some good foundation, or at least to make some way therunto, for ye propagating & advancing ye gospell of ye kingdom of Christ in those remote parts of ye world; yea, though they should be but even as stepping-stones unto others for ye performing of so great a work.

These, & some other like reasons, moved them to undertake this resolution of their removall; the which they afterward prosecuted with so great difficulties, as by the sequell will appeare.

The place they had thoughts on was some of those vast & unpeopled countries of America, which are frutfull & fitt for habitation, being devoyd of all civill inhabitants, wher ther are only salvage & brutish men, which range up and downe, litle otherwise then ye wild beasts of the same. This proposition being made publike and coming to ye scaning of all, it raised many variable opinions amongst men, and caused many fears & doubts amongst them selves . . . .

It was answered, that all great & honourable actions are accompanied with great difficulties, and must be both enterprised and overcome with answerable courages. It was granted ye dangers were great, but not desperate; the difficulties were many, but not invincible. For though their were many of them likly, yet they were not cartaine; it might be sundrie of ye things feared might never befale; others by providente care & ye use of good means, might in a great measure be prevented; and all of them, through yᵉ help of God, by fortitude and patience, might either be borne, or overcome. True it was, that such atempts were not to be made and undertaken without good ground & reason; not rashly or lightly as many have done for curiositie or hope of gaine, &c. But their condition was not ordinarie; their ends were good & honourable; their calling lawfull, & urgente; and therfore they might expecte yᵉ blessing of God in their proceding. Yea, though they should loose their lives in this action, yet might they have comforte in the same, and their endeavors would be honourable. They lived hear but as men in exile, & in a poore condition; and as great miseries might possibly befale them in this place, for yᵉ 12. years of truce were now out, & ther was nothing but beating of drumes, and preparing for warr, the events wherof are allway uncertaine. Yᵉ Spaniard might prove as cruell as [18] the salvages of America, and yᵉ famine and pestelence as sore hear as ther, & their libertie less to looke out for remedie. After many other perticuler things answered & aledged on both sids, it was fully concluded by yᵉ major parte, to put this designe in execution, and to prosecute it by the best means they could . . . .

AND first after thir humble praiers unto God for his direction & assistance, & a generall conferrence held hear aboute, they consulted what perticuler place to pitch upon, & prepare for. Some (& none of yᵉ meanest) had thoughts & were ernest for Guiana, or some of those fertill places in those hott climats; others were for some parts of Virginia, wher yᵉ English had all ready made enterance, & begining . . . .

AT length, after much travell and these debats, all things were got ready and provided. A smale ship was bought, & fitted in Holand, which was intended as to serve to help to transport them, so to stay in yᵉ cuntrie and atend upon fishing and shuch other affairs as might be for yᵉ good & benefite of yᵉ colonie when they came ther. Another was hired at London, of burden about 9. score; and all other things gott in readines. So being ready to departe, they had a day of solleme humiliation, their pastor taking his texte from Ezra 8. 21. *And ther at ye river, by Ahava, I proclaimed a fast, that we might humble ourselves before our God, and seeke of him a right way for us, and for our children, and for all our substance.* Upon which he spente a good parte of ye day very profitably, and suitable to their presente occasion. The rest of the time was spente in powering out prairs to ye Lord with great fervencie, mixed with abundance of tears. And ye time being come that they must departe, they were accompanied with most of their brethren out of ye citie, unto a towne sundrie miles of called Delfes-Haven, wher the ship lay ready to receive them. So they lefte y^t goodly & pleasante citie, which had been ther resting place near 12. years; but they knew they were pilgrimes, & looked not much on those things, but lift up their eyes to ye heavens, their dearest cuntrie, and quieted their spirits. When they [37] came to ye place they found ye ship and all things ready; and shuch of their freinds as could not come with them followed after them, and sundrie also came from Amsterdame to see them shipte and to take their leave of them. That night was spent with litle sleepe by ye most, but with freindly entertainmente & christian discourse and other reall expressions of true christian love. The next day, the wind being faire, they wente aborde, and their freinds with them, where truly dolfull was ye sight of that sade and mournfull parting; to see what sighs and sobbs and praires did sound amongst them, what tears did gush from every eye, & pithy speeches peirst each harte; that sundry of ye Dutch strangers y^t stood on ye key as spectators, could not refraine from tears. Yet comfortable & sweete it was to see shuch lively and true expressions of dear & unfained love. But ye tide (which stays for no man) caling them away y^t were thus loath to departe, their Reve^d: pastor falling downe on his knees, (and they all with him,) with watrie cheeks comended them with most fervente praiers to the Lord and his blessing. And then with mutuall imbrases and many tears, they tooke their leaves one of an other; which promed to be ye last leave to many of them.

Thus hoysing saile, with a prosperus winde they came in
short time to Southhamton, wher they found the bigger ship
come from London, lying ready, wth all the rest of their company. After a joyfull wellcome, and mutuall congratulations,
with othe^r frendly entertainements, they fell to parley aboute
their bussines, how to dispatch with ye best expedition . . . .

SEPT^R: 6.

They put to sea againe with a prosperus winde, which continued diverce days togeather, which was some incouragmente
unto them; yet according to ye usuall maner many were afflicted
with sea-sicknes. And I may not omite hear a spetiall worke of
Gods providence. Ther was a proud & very profane yonge man,
one of ye sea-men, of a lustie, able body, which made him the
more hauty; he would allway be contemning ye poore people in
their sicknes, & cursing them dayly with greeous execrations,
and did not let to tell them, that he hoped to help to cast halfe of
them over board before they came to their jurneys end, and to
make mery with what they had; and if he were by any gently
reproved, he would curse and swear most bitterly. But it plased
God before they came halfe seas over, to smite this yong man
with a greeveous disease, of which he dyed in a desperate
maner, and so was him selfe ye first y^t was throwne overbord.
Thus his curses light on his owne head; and it was an as-
tonishmente to all his fellows, for they noted it to be ye just hand
of God upon him.

After they had injoyed faire winds and weather for a season,
they were incountred many times with crosse winds, and mette
with many feirce stormes, with which ye shipe was shroudly
shaken, and her upper works made very leakie; and one of the
maine beames in ye midd ships was bowed & craked, which put
them in some fear that ye shipe could not be able to performe y^e
vioage . . . .

But to omite other things, (that I may be breefe,) after longe
beating at sea they fell with that land which is called Cape Cod;

the which being made & certainly knowne to be it, they were not a litle joyfull. After some deliberation had amongst them selves & with ye m^r. of ye ship, they tacked aboute and resolved to stande for ye southward (ye wind & weather being faire) to finde some place aboute Hudsons river for their habitation. But after they had sailed y^t course aboute halfe ye day, they fell amongst deangerous shoulds and roring breakers, and they were so farr intangled ther with as they conceived them selves in great danger; & ye wind shrinking upon them withall, they resolved to bear up againe for the Cape, and thought them selves hapy to gett out of those dangers before night overtooke them, as by Gods providence they did. And ye next day they gott into ye Cape-harbor wher they ridd in saftie. A word or too by ye way of this cape; it was thus first named by Capten Gosnole & his company, An^o: 1602, and after by Capten Smith was caled Cape James; but it retains ye former name amongst seamen. Also y^t pointe which first shewed those dangerous shoulds unto them, they called Pointe Care, & Tuckers Terrour; but ye French & Dutch to this day call it Malabarr, by reason of those perilous shoulds, and ye losses they have suffered their.

Being thus arived in a good harbor and brought safe to land, they fell upon their knees & blessed ye God of heaven, who had brought them over ye vast & furious ocean, and delivered them from all ye periles & miseries therof, againe to set their feete on ye firme and stable earth, their proper elemente. And no marvell if they were thus joyefull, seeing wise Seneca was so affected with sailing a few miles on ye coast of his owne Italy; as he affirmed, that he had rather remaine twentie years on his way by land, then pass by sea to any place in a short time; so tedious & dreadfull was ye same unto him.

But hear I cannot but stay and make a pause, and stand half amased at this poore peoples presente condition; and so I thinke will the reader too, when he well considers [47] ye same. Being thus passed ye vast ocean, and a sea of troubles before in their preparation (as may be remembred by y^t which wente before), they had now no freinds to wellcome them, nor inns to entertaine or refresh their weatherbeaten bodys, no houses or much less townes to repaire too, to seeke for succoure. It is recorded in scripture as a mercie to yᵉ apostle & his shipwraked company, yᵗ the barbarians shewed them no smale kindnes in refreshing them, but these savage barbarians, when they mette with them (as after will appeare) were readier to fill their sids full of arrows then otherwise. And for yᵉ season it was winter, and they that know yᵉ winters of yᵗ cuntrie know them to be sharp & violent, & subjecte to cruell & feirce stormes, deangerous to travill to known places, much more to serch an unknown coast. Besids, what could they see but a hidious & desolate wildernes, full of wild beasts & willd men? and what multituds ther might be of them they knew not. Nether could they, as it were, goe up to yᵉ tope of Pisgah, to vew from this willdernes a more goodly cuntrie to feed their hops; for which way soever they turnd their eys (save upward to yᵉ heavens) they could have litle solace or content in respecte of any outward objects. For sumer being done, all things stand upon them with a wetherbeaten face; and yᵉ whole countrie, full of woods & thickets, represented a wild & savage heiw. If they looked behind them, ther was yᵉ mighty ocean which they had passed, and was now as a maine barr & goulfe to seperate them from all yᵉ civill parts of yᵉ world . . . .

It is true, indeed, yᵉ affections & love of their brethren at Leyden was cordiall & entire towards them, but they had litle power to help them, or them selves; and how yᵉ case stode betweene them & yᵉ marchants at their coming away, hath allready been declared. What could now sustaine them but yᵉ spirite of God & his grace? May not & ought not the children of these fathers rightly say: *Our faithers were Englishmen which came over this great ocean, and were ready to perish in this willdernes; but they cried unto yᵉ Lord, and he heard their voyce, and looked on their adversitie, &c. Let them therfore praise yᵉ Lord, because he is good, & his mercies endure for ever. Yea, let them which have been redeemed of yᵉ Lord, shew how he hath delivered them from ye hand of ye oppressour. When they wandered in ye deserte willdernes out of ye way, and found no citie to dwell in, both hungrie, & thirstie, their sowle was overwhelmed in them. Let them confess before ye Lord his loving kindnes, and his wonderfull works before ye sons of men . . . .*

[48] BEING thus arrived at Cap-Cod ye 11. of November, and necessitie calling them to looke out a place for habitation, (as well as the maisters & mariners importunitie,) they having brought a large shalop with them out of England, stowed in quarters in ye ship, they now gott her out & sett their carpenters to worke to trime her up; but being much brused & shatered in ye shipe wth foule weather, they saw she would be longe in mending. Wherupon a few of them tendered them selves to goe by land and discovere those nearest places, whilst ye shallop was in mending; and ye rather because as they wente into y^t harbor ther seemed to be an opening some 2. or 3 leagues of, which ye maister judged to be a river. It was conceived ther might be some danger in ye attempte, yet seeing them resolute, they were permited to goe, being 16. of them well armed, under ye conduct of Captain Standish, having shuch instructions given them as was thought meete. They sett forth ye 15. of Nove^br: and when they had marched aboute ye space of a mile by ye sea side, they espied 5. or 6. persons with a dogg coming towards them, who were salvages; but they fled from them, & rāne up into ye woods, and ye English followed them, partly to see if they could speake with them, and partly to discover if ther might not be more of them lying in ambush. But ye Indeans seeing them selves thus followed, they againe forsooke the woods, & rane away on ye sands as hard as they could, so as they could not come near them, but followed them by ye tracte of their feet sundrie miles, and saw that they had come the same way . . . .

The remainder of An⁰: 1620.

I SHALL a litle returne backe and begine with a combination made by them before they came ashore, being yᵉ first foundation of their governmente in this place; occasioned partly by yᵉ discontented & mutinous speeches that some of the strangers amongst them had let fall from them in yᵉ ship—That when they came a shore they would use their owne libertie; for none had power to comͫand them, the patente they had being for Virginia, and not for New-england, which belonged to an other Goverment, with which yᵉ Virginia Company had nothing to doe. And partly that shuch an [54] acte by them done (this their condition considered) might be as firme as any patent, and in some respects more sure.

The forme was as followeth.

> In yᵉ name of God, Amen. We whose names are underwriten, the loyall subjects of our dread soveraigne Lord, King James, by yᵉ grace of God, of Great Britaine, Franc, & Ireland king, defender of yᵉ faith, &c., haveing undertaken, for yᵉ glorie of God, and advancemente of yᵉ Christian faith, and honour of our king & countrie, a voyage to plant yᵉ first colonie in yᵉ Northerne parts of Virginia, doe by these presents solemnly & mutualy in yᵉ presence of God, and one of another, covenant & combine our selves togeather into a civill body politick, for our better ordering & preservation & furtherance of yᵉ ends aforesaid; and by vertue hearof to enacte, constitute, and frame such just & equall lawes, ordinances, acts, constitutions, & offices, from time to time, as shall be thought most meete & convenient for yᵉ generall good of yᵉ Colonie, unto which we promise all due submission and obedience. In witnes wherof we have hereunder subscribed our names at Cap-Codd yᵉ 11. of November, in yᵉ year of yᵉ raigne of our soveraigne lord, King James, of England, France, & Ireland yᵉ eighteenth, and of Scotland yᵉ fiftie fourth. An⁰: Dom. 1620.

After this they chose, or rather confirmed, Mʳ. John Carver (a man godly & well approved amongst them) their Governour for that year. And after they had provided a place for their goods, or comone store, (which were long in unlading for want of boats, foulnes of winter weather, and sicknes of diverce,) and begune some small cottages for their habitation, as time would admitte, they mette and consulted of lawes & orders, both for their civill & military Govermente, as ye necessitie of their condition did require, still adding therunto as urgent occasion in severall times, and as cases did require . . . .

[61] Anno. 1621.

THEY now begane to dispatch ye ship away which brought them over, which lay tille aboute this time, or ye begining of Aprill. The reason on their parts why she stayed so long, was ye necessitie and danger that lay upon them, for it was well towards ye ende of Desember before she could land any thing hear, or they able to receive any thing ashore. Afterwards, ye 14. of Jan: the house which they had made for a generall randevoze by casulty fell afire, and some were faine to retire abord for shilter. Then the sickness begane to fall sore amongst them, and ye weather so bad as they could not make much sooner any dispatch. Againe, the Govr & cheefe of them, seeing so many dye, and fall downe sick dayly, thought it no wisdom to send away the ship, their condition considered, and ye danger they stood in from ye Indeans, till they could procure some shelter; and therfore thought it better to draw some more charge upon them selves & freinds, then hazard all. The m^r. and sea-men likewise, though before they hasted ye passengers a shore to be goone, now many of their men being dead, & of ye ablest of them, (as is before noted,) and of ye rest many lay sick & weake, ye m^r. durst not put to sea, till he saw his men begine to recover, and ye hart of winter over.

Afterwards they (as many as were able) began to plant ther corne, in which servise Squanto stood them in great stead, showing them both ye maner how to set it, and after how to dress & tend it. Also he tould them excepte they gott fish & set with it (in these old grounds) it would come to nothing, and he showed them y^t in ye midle of Aprill they should have store enough come up ye brooke, by which they begane to build, and taught them how to take it, and wher to get other provissions necessary for them; all which they found true by triall & experience. Some English seed they sew, as wheat & pease, but it came not to good, eather by ye badnes of ye seed, or latenes of ye season, or both, or some other defecte.

[62] In this month of *Aprill* whilst they were bussie about their seed, their Govr (M^r. John Carver) came out of ye feild very sick, it being a hott day; he complained greatly of his head, and lay downe, and within a few howers his sences failed, so as he never spake more till he dyed, which was within a few days after. Whoss death was much lamented, and caused great heavines amongst them, as ther was cause. He was buried in ye best maner they could, with some vollies of shott by all that bore armes; and his wife, being a weak woman, dyed within 5. or 6. weeks after him.

Shortly after William Bradford was chosen Gove^r in his stead, and being not yet recoverd of his ilnes, in which he had been near ye point of death, Isaak Allerton was chosen to be an Asistante unto him, who, by renewed election every year, continued sundry years together, which I hear note once for all.

May 12. was ye first mariage in this place, which, according to ye laudable custome of ye Low-Cuntries, in which they had lived, was thought most requisite to be performed by the magistrate, as being a civill thing, upon which many questions aboute inheritances doe depende, with other things most proper to their cognizans, and most consonante to ye scripturs, Ruth 4. and no wher found in ye gospell to be layed on ye ministers as a part of their office . . . .

After this, ye 18. of Sepemb^r: they sente out ther shalop to the Massachusets, with 10. men, and Squanto for their guid and [65] interpreter, to discover and veiw that bay, and trade with ye natives; the which they performed, and found kind entertainement. The people were much affraid of ye Tarentins, a people to ye eastward which used to come in harvest time and take away their corne, & many times kill their persons. They returned in saftie, and brought home a good quanty of beaver, and made reporte of ye place, wishing they had been ther seated; (but it seems ye Lord, who assignes to all men ye bounds of their habitations, had apoynted it for an other use). And thus they found ye Lord to be with them in all their ways, and to blesse their outgoings & incomings, for which let his holy name have ye praise for ever, to all posteritie.

They begane now to gather in ye small harvest they had, and to fitte up their houses and dwellings against winter, being all well recovered in health & strenght, and had all things in good plenty; for as some were thus imployed in affairs abroad, others were excersised in fishing, aboute codd, & bass, & other fish, of which y^ey tooke good store, of which every family had their portion. All ye somer ther was no wante. And now begane to come in store of foule, as winter aproached, of which this place did abound when they came first (but afterward decreased by degrees). And besids water foule, ther was great store of wild Turkies, of which they tooke many, besids venison, &c. Besids they had aboute a peck a meale a weeke to a person, or now since harvest, Indean corne to y^t proportion. Which made many afterwards write so largly of their plenty hear to their freinds in England, which were not fained, but true reports . . . .

[1628] Aboute some 3. or 4. years before this time, ther came over one Captaine Wolastone, (a man of pretie parts,) and with him 3. or 4. more of some eminencie, who brought with them a great many servants, with provissions & other implments for to begine a plantation; and pitched them selves in a place within the Massachusets, which they called, after their Captains name, Mount-Wollaston. Amongst whom was one M^r. Morton, who, it should seeme, had some small adventure (of his owne or other mens) amongst them; but had litle respecte [159] amongst them, and was sleghted by ye meanest servants. Haveing continued ther some time, and not finding things to answer their expectations, nor profite to arise as they looked for, Captaine Wollaston takes a great part of ye sarvants, and transports them to Virginia, wher he puts them of at good rates, selling their time to other men; and writs back to one M^r. Rassdall, one of his cheefe partners, and accounted their marchant, to bring another parte of them to Verginia likewise, intending to put them of ther as he had done ye rest. And he, wth ye consente of ye said Rasdall, appoynted one Fitcher to be his Livetenante, and governe ye remaines of ye plantation, till he or Rasdall returned to take further order theraboute. But this Morton abovesaid, haveing more craft then honestie, (who had been a kind of petiefogger, of Furnefells Inne,) in ye others absence, watches an oppertunitie, (commons being but hard amongst them,) and gott some strong drinck & other junkats, & made them a feast; and after they were merie, he begane to tell them, he would give them good counsell. You see (saith he) that many of your fellows are carried to Virginia; and if you stay till this Rasdall returne, you will also be carried away and sould for slaves with ye rest. Therfore I would advise you to thruste out this Levetenant Fitcher; and I, having a parte in the plantation, will receive you as my partners and consociats; so may you be free from service, and we will converse, trad, plante, & live togeather as equalls, & supporte & protecte one another, or to like effecte. This counsell was easily received; so they tooke oppertunitie, and thrust Levetenante Fitcher out a dores, and would suffer him to come no more amongst them, but forct him to seeke bread to eate, and other releefe from his neigbours, till he could gett passages for England. After this they fell to great licenciousnes, and led a dissolute life, powering out them selves into all profanenes. And Morton became lord of misrule, and maintained (as it were) a schoole of Athisme. And after they had gott some good into their hands, and gott much by trading with ye Indeans, they spent it as vainly, in quaffing & drinking both wine & strong waters in great exsess, and, as some reported, 10th. worth in a morning. They allso set up a May-pole, drinking and dancing aboute it many days togeather, inviting the Indean women, for their consorts, dancing and frisking togither, (like so many fairies, or furies rather,) and worse practises. As if they had anew revived & celebrated the feasts of ye Roman Goddes Flora, or ye beasly practieses of ye madd Bacchinalians. Morton likwise (to shew his poetrie) composed sundry rimes & verses, some tending to lasciviousnes, and others to ye detraction & scandall of some persons, which he affixed to this idle or idoll May-polle. They chainged allso the name of their place, and in stead of calling it Mounte Wollaston, they call it Meriemounte, [160] as if this joylity would have lasted ever. But this continued not long, for after Morton was sent for England, (as follows to be declared,) shortly after came over that worthy gentlman, M^r. John Indecott, who brought over a patent under ye broad seall, for ye governmente of ye Massachusets, who visiting those parts caused y^t May-polle to be cutt downe, and rebuked them for their profannes, and admonished them to looke ther should be better walking; so they now, or others, changed ye name of their place againe, and called it Mounte-Dagon.

Now to maintaine this riotous prodigallitie and profuse excess, Morton, thinking him selfe lawless, and hearing what gaine ye French & fisher-men made by trading of peeces, powder, & shotte to ye Indeans, he, as ye head of this consortship, begane ye practise of ye same in these parts; and first he taught them how to use them, to charge, & discharg, and what proportion of powder to give ye peece, according to ye sise or bignes of ye same; and what shotte to use for foule, and what for deare. And having thus instructed them, he imployed some of them to hunte & fowle for him, so as they became farr more active in that imploymente then any of ye English, by reason of ther swiftnes of foote, & nimblnes of body, being also quick-sighted, and by continuall exercise well knowing ye hants of all sorts of game. So as when they saw ye execution that a peece would doe, and ye benefite that might come by ye same, they became madd, as it were, after them, and would not stick to give any prise they could attaine too for them; accounting their bowes & arrowes but bables in comparison of them.

And here I may take occasion to bewaile ye mischefe that this wicked man began in these parts, and which since base covetousnes prevailing in men that should know better, has now at length gott ye upper hand, and made this thing comōne, notwithstanding any laws to ye contrary; so as ye Indeans are full of peeces all over, both fouling peeces, muskets, pistols, &c. They have also their moulds to make shotte, of all sorts, as muskett bulletts, pistoll bullets, swane & gose shote, & of smaler sorts; yea, some have seen them have their scruplats to make scrupins them selves, when they wante them, with sundery other implements, wherwith they are ordinarily better fited & furnished then ye English them selves. Yea, it is well knowne that they will have powder & shot, when the English want it, nor cannot gett it; and y^t in a time of warr or danger, as experience hath manifested, that when lead hath been scarce, and men for their owne defence would gladly have given a groat a li., which is dear enoughe, yet hath it bene bought up & sent to other places, and sould to shuch as trade it with y^e Indeans, at 12. pence y^e li.; and it is like they give 3. or 4.$^{s.}$ y^e pound, for they will have it at any rate. And these things have been done in y^e same times, when some of their neigbours & freinds are daly killed by y^e Indeans, or are in deanger therof, and live but at y^e Indeans mercie. [161] Yea, some (as they have acquainted them with all other things) have tould them how gunpowder is made, and all ye materialls in it, and that they are to be had in their owne land; and I am confidente, could they attaine to make saltpeter, they would teach them to make powder. O the horiblnes of this vilanie! how many both Dutch & English have been latly slaine by those Indeans, thus furnished; and no remedie provided, nay, ye evill more increased, and ye blood of their brethren sould for gaine, as is to be feared; and in what danger all these colonies are in is too well known. Oh! that princes & parlements would take some timly order to prevente this mischeefe, and at length to suppress it, by some exemplerie punishmente upon some of these gaine thirstie murderers, (for they deserve no better title,) before their collonies in these parts be over throwne by these barbarous savages, thus armed with their owne weapons, by these evill instruments, and traytors to their neighbors and cuntrie. But I have forgott my selfe, and have been to longe in this digression; but now to returne. This Morton having thus taught them ye use of peeces, he sould them all he could spare; and he and his consorts detirmined to send for many out of England, and had by some of ye ships sente for above a score. The which being knowne, and his neigbours meeting ye Indeans in ye woods armed with guns in this sorte, it was a terrour unto them, who lived straglingly, and were of no strenght in any place. And other places (though more remote) saw this mischeefe would quictly spread over all, if not pre-vented. Besides, they saw they should keep no servants, for Morton would entertaine any, how vile soever, and all ye scume of ye countrie, or any discontents, would flock to him from all places, if this nest was not broken; and they should stand in more fear of their lives & goods (in short time) from this wicked & deboste crue, then from ye salvages them selves.

So sundrie of ye cheefe of ye stragling plantations, meeting togither, agreed by mutuall consente to sollissite those of Plimoth (who were then of more strength then them all) to joyne with them, to prevente ye further grouth of this mischeefe, and suppress Morton & his consortes before y^{ey} grewe to further head and strength . . . . Those that joyned in this acction (and after contributed to ye charge of sending him for England) were from Pascataway, Namkeake, Winisimett, Weesagascusett, Natasco, and other places wher any English were seated. Those of Plimoth being thus sought too by their messengers & letters, and waying both their reasons, and the comone danger, were willing to afford them their help; though them selves had least cause of fear or hurte. So, to be short, they first resolved joyntly to write to him, and in a freindly & neigborly way to admonish

him to forbear these courses, & sent a messenger with their
letters to bring his answer. But he was so highe as he scorned all
advise, and asked who had to doe with him; he had and would
trade peeces with ye Indeans in dispite of all, with many other
scurillous termes full of disdaine. They sente to him a second
time, and bad him be better advised, and more temperate in his
termes, for ye countrie could not beare ye injure he did; it was
against their comone saftie, and against ye king's proclamation.
He answerd in high terms as before, and that ye kings proc-
laimation was no law; demanding what penaltie was upon it. It
was answered, more then he could [162] bear, his majesties
displeasure. But insolently he persisted, and said ye king was
dead and his displeasure with him, & many ye like things; and
threatened withall that if any came to molest him, let them looke
to them selves, for he would prepare for them. Upon which they
saw ther was no way but to take him by force; and having so farr
proceeded, now to give over would make him farr more hautie
& insolente. So they mutually resolved to proceed, and obtained of ye Govr of Plimoth to send Captaine Standish, & some
other aide with him, to take Morton by force. The which accordingly was done; but they found him to stand stifly in his defence,
having made fast his dors, armed his consorts, set diverse
dishes of powder & bullets ready on ye table; and if they had not
been over armed with drinke, more hurt might have been done.
They somaned him to yeeld, but he kept his house, and they
could gett nothing but scofes & scorns from him; but at length,
fearing they would doe some violence to ye house, he and some
of his crue came out, but not to yeeld, but to shoote; but they
were so steeld with drinke as their peeces were to heavie for
them; him selfe with a carbine (over charged & allmost halfe fild
with powder & shote, as was after found) had thought to have
shot Captaine Standish; but he stept to him, & put by his peece,
& tooke him. Neither was ther any hurte done to any of either
side, save y^t one was so drunke y^t he rane his owne nose upon y^e
pointe of a sword y^t one held before him as he entred ye house;

but he lost but a litle of his hott blood. Morton they brought away to Plimoth, wher he was kepte, till a ship went from ye Ile of Shols for England, with which he was sente to ye Counsell of New-England; and letters writen to give them information of his course & cariage; and also one was sent at their comone charge to informe their Ho^{rs} more perticulerly, & to prosecute against him. But he foold of ye messenger, after he was gone from hence, and though he wente for England, yet nothing was done to him, not so much as rebukte, for ought was heard; but returned ye nexte year. Some of ye worst of ye company were disperst, and some of ye more modest kepte ye house till he should be heard from. But I have been too long aboute so unworthy a person, and bad a cause . . . .

M^r. Roger Williams (a man godly & zealous, having many precious parts, but very unsettled in judgmente) came over first to ye Massachusets, but upon some discontente left y^t place, and came hither, (wher he was friedly entertained, according to their poore abilitie,) and exercised his gifts amongst them, & after some time was admitted a member of ye church; and his teaching well approoved, for ye benefite wherof I still blese God, and am thankfull to him, even for his sharpest admonitions & reproufs, so farr as they agreed with truth. He this year begane to fall into some strang oppiions, and from opinion to practise; which caused some controversie between ye church & him, and in ye end some discontente on his parte, by occasion wherof he left them some thing abruptly. Yet after wards sued for his dismission to ye church of Salem, which was granted, with some caution to them concerning him, and what care they ought to have of him. But he soone fell into more things ther, both to their and ye goverments troble and [196] disturbance. I shall not need to name perticulers, they are too well knowen now to all, though for a time ye church here wente under some hard censure by his occasion, from some that afterwards smarted them selves. But he is to be pitied, and prayed for, and so I shall leave ye matter, and desire ye Lord to shew him his errors, and reduse him into ye way of truth, and give him a setled judgment and constancie in ye same; for I hope he belongs to ye Lord, and y^t he will shew him mercie.

2

ROGER WILLIAMS

The Bloudy Tenent of Persecution

WHILE I plead the cause of truth and innocency against the bloody doctrine of persecution for cause of conscience, I judge it not unfit to give alarm to myself, and to [all] men, to prepare to be persecuted or hunted for cause of conscience.

Whether thou standest charged with ten or but two talents, if thou huntest any for cause of conscience, how canst thou say thou followest the Lamb of God, who so abhorred that practice?

If Paul, if Jesus Christ, were present here at London, and the question were proposed, what religion would they approve of—the papists, prelatists, Presbyterians, Independents, &c., would each say, Of mine, Of mine?

But put the second question: if one of the several sorts should by major vote attain the sword of steel, what weapons doth Christ Jesus authorize them to fight with in his cause? Do not all men hate the persecutor, and every conscience, true or false, complain of cruelty, tyranny, &c.?

Two mountains of crying guilt lie heavy upon the backs of all men that name the name of Christ, in the eyes of Jews, Turks, and Pagans.

First. The blasphemies of their idolatrous inventions, superstitions, and most unchristian conversations.

Secondly. The bloody, irreligious, and inhuman oppressions

and destructions under the mask or veil of the name of Christ, &c.

Oh! how likely is the jealous Jehovah, thè consuming fire, to end these present slaughters of the holy witnesses in a greater slaughter! *Rev.* v.

Six years preaching of so much truth of Christ as that time afforded in K. Edward's days, kindles the flames of Q. Mary's bloody persecutions.

Who can now but expect that after so many scores of years preaching and professing of more truth, and amongst so many great contentions amongst the very best of protestants, a fiery furnace should be heat, and who sees not now the fires kindling?

I confess I have little hopes, till those flames are over, that this discourse against the doctrine of persecution for cause of conscience should pass current, I say not amongst the wolves and lions, but even amongst the sheep of Christ themselves. Yet, *liberavi animam meam,* I have not hid within my breast my soul's belief. And, although sleeping on the bed either of the pleasures or profits of sin, thinkest thou thy conscience bound to smite at him that dares to waken thee? Yet in the midst of all these civil and spiritual wars, I hope we shall agree in these particulars,

First. However the proud (upon the advantage of a higher earth or ground) overlook the poor, and cry out schismatics, heretics, &c., shall blasphemers and seducers escape unpunished? Yet there is a sorer punishment in the gospel for despising of Christ than Moses, even when the despiser of Moses was put to death without mercy, Heb. x. 28, 29. *He that believeth shall not be damned,* Mark xvi. 16.

Secondly. Whatever worship, ministry, ministration, the best and purest, are practised without faith and true persuasion that they are the true institutions of God, they are sin, sinful worships, ministries, &c. And however in civil things we may be servants unto men, yet in divine and spiritual things the poorest peasant must disdain the service of the highest prince.

Be ye not the servants of men, 1 Cor. vii. [23].

Thirdly. Without search and trial no man attains this faith and right persuasion. 1 Thes. v. [21], *Try all things.*

In vain have English parliaments permitted English bibles in the poorest English houses, and the simplest man or woman to search the scriptures, if yet against their souls persuasion from the scripture, they should be forced, as if they lived in Spain or Rome itself without the sight of a bible, to believe as the church believes.

Fourthly. Having tried, we must hold fast, 1 Thes. v. [21], upon the loss of a crown, Rev. iii. [11]; we must not let go for all the fleabitings of the present afflictions, &c. Having bought truth dear, we must not sell it cheap, not the least grain of it for the whole world; no, not for the saving of souls, though our own most precious; least of all for the bitter sweetening of a little vanishing pleasure:—For a little puff of credit and reputation from the changeable breath of uncertain sons of men: for the broken bags of riches on eagles' wings: for a dream of these— any or all of these, which on our death-bed vanish and leave tormenting stings behind them. Oh! how much better is it from the love of truth, from the love of the Father of lights from whence it comes, from the love of the Son of God, who is the way and the truth, to say as he, John xviii. 37: *For this end was I born, and for this end came I into the world, that I might bear witness to the truth.*

The Answer of Mr. John Cotton

The question which you put is, whether persecution for cause of conscience be not against the doctrine of Jesus Christ, the King of kings?

Now, by persecution for cause of conscience, I conceive you mean, either for professing some point of doctrine which you believe in conscience to be the truth, or for practising some work which in conscience you believe to be a religious duty.

Now in points of doctrine some are fundamental, without right belief whereof a man cannot be saved; others are circumstantial, or less principal, wherein men may differ in judgment without prejudice of salvation on either part.

In like sort, in points of practice, some concern the weightier duties of the law, as, what God we worship, and with what kind of worship; whether such as, if it be right, fellowship with God is held; if corrupt, fellowship with him is lost.

Again, in points of doctrine and worship less principal, either they are held forth in a meek and peaceable way, though the things be erroneous or unlawful: or they are held forth with such arrogance and impetuousness, as tendeth and reacheth (even of itself) to the disturbance of civil peace.

Finally, let me add this one distinction more: when we are persecuted for conscience' sake, it is either for conscience rightly informed, or for erroneous and blind conscience.

These things premised, I would lay down mine answer to the question in certain conclusions.

First, it is not lawful to persecute any for conscience' sake rightly informed; for in persecuting such, Christ himself is persecuted in them, Acts ix. 4.

Secondly, for an erroneous and blind conscience, (even in fundamental and weighty points) it is not lawful to persecute any, till after admonition once or twice; and so the apostle directeth, Tit. iii. 10, and giveth the reason, that in fundamental and principal points of doctrine or worship, the word of God in such things is so clear, that he cannot but be convinced in conscience of the dangerous error of his way after once or twice admonition, wisely and faithfully dispensed. And then, if any one persist, it is not out of conscience, but against his conscience, as the apostle saith, ver. 11, He *is subverted, and sinneth, being condemned of himself;* that is, of his own conscience. So that if such a man, after such admonition, shall still persist in the error of his way, and be therefore punished, he is not persecuted for cause of conscience, but for sinning against his own conscience.

Thirdly. In things of lesser moment, whether points of doctrine or worship, if a man hold them forth in a spirit of Christian meekness and love, though with zeal and constancy, he is not to be persecuted, but tolerated, till God may be pleased to manifest his truth to him, Phil. iii. 17; Rom. xiv. 1—4.

3

Virginia's Mother Church

ACT I.

First, It is ordered, That there be a uniformitie throughout this colony both in substance and circumstance to the cannons and constitutions of the church of England as neere as may bee and that every person yeild readie obedience unto them uppon penaltie of the paynes and forfeitures in that case appointed.

ACT II.

And it is thought fitt, That the statutes for cominge to church every Sonday and Holidayes be dulie executed what is to say that the churchwardens doe levy one shillinge for every tyme of any persons absence from the church havinge no lawfull or reasonable excuse to bee absent. And for due execution hereof the governor and counsell togeather with the Burgisses of this Grand Assembly doe in Gods name earnestlie require and charge all commanders, captaynes and church-wardens that they shall endeavour themselves to the uttermost of theire knowledge that the due and true execution hereof may be done and had through this colony as they will answer before God for such evills and paynes wherewith Almightie God may justlie punish his people for neglectinge this good and wholesome lawe.

ACT III.

It is ordered, That as many of the mynisters as convenientlie may, and one of the churchwardens at the least of everie parish be present yearlie at midsomer quarter cortes holden at James Citty, on the first day of June and there to make theire presentments uppon oath together with a register of all Burialls, christenings and marriages as likewise theire accounts of all levyes, collections or disbursements as have beene or fallen out in their tymes concerning the church affayers. And further that they choose church-wardens at the feast of Easter yearelie.

ACT IV.

Noe man shall disparage a mynister whereby the mynds of his parishioners may bee alienated from him and his mynistrie prove lesse effectuall uppon payne of severe censure of the Governor and Counsell.

ACT V.

Noe mynister shall celebrat matrymony betweene any persons without a facultie or lycense graunted by the Governor except the banes of matrymony have beene first published three severall Sondays or holidayes in the tyme of divine service in the parish churches where the sayd persons dwell accordinge to the booke of common prayer, neither shall any mynister under any pretense whatsoever, joyne any persons so lycensed in marriage at any unseasonable tymes but onlie betweene the howres of eight and twelve in the forenoon, nor when banes are thrice asked, and no lycense in that respect necessary, before the parents or governors of the parties to be maryed yf they be under the age of twenty one yeares, shall either personally or by sufficient testimony, signifie to him theire consents given to the sayd marriage.

ACT VI.

Every mynister in this colony havinge cure of soules shall preach one sermon every Sonday in the yeare, having no lawfull impediment, and yf the mynister shall neglect their chardge by unnecessarie absence or otherwise, the church-wardens are to present it. But because in this colony the places of theire cure are in many parts farr distant; It is thought fitt, that the mynisters doe soe devide theire turnes as by the joynt agreement of the parishioners shall be desired.

ACT VII.

It is thought fitt, That uppon every Sonday the mynisters shall halfe an hower or more before eveninge prayer examine, catechise, and instruct the youth and ignorant persons of his parish in the ten commandments, the articles of the beliefe and the Lords prayer. And shall diligentlie heere, instruct and teach them the catichisme, sett forth in the booke of common prayer, and all fathers, mothers, maysters and mistresses shall cause theire children, servants, and apprentizes which have not learned the catechisme to come to the church at the tyme appointed obedientlie to heere and to be ordered by the mynister until they have learned the same. And yf any of the said ffathers, mothers, maysters, or mistresses, children, servants, or apprentizes shall neglect theire duties as the one sort in not causinge them to come, and in the other in refusinge to learne as aforesayd, they shall be censured by the corts in those places holden.

ACT VIII.

And it is further ordered and thought expedient, according to a former order made by the Governor and Counsell, that all church-wardens shall take this oath and that it be administered before those that are of the commission for the monthlie corts, vizt:

"You shall sweare that you shall make true presentments of all such persons as shall lead a prophane or ungodly life, or such as shall be common swearers, drunkards or blasphemers, that shall ordinarilie prophane the saboth dayes or contemne Gods holy word, or sacraments; you shall also present all adulterers or fornicators, such as shall abuse their neighbours by slanderings, tale carryinge or backbiting, or that shall not behave themselves orderlie and soberlie in the church during devine service.

Likewise you shall present such masters and mistresses as shall be delinquent in catechizing of the youth and ignorant persons, soe help you God."

ACT IX.

When any person is dangerously sicke in any parish the mynister havinge knowledge thereof shall resort unto him or her to instruct and comfort them in theire distress.

ACT X.

In every parish church within this colony shall be kept, by the mynister a booke, wherein shall be written, the day and yeare of every christeninge, weddinge and burriall.

ACT XI.

Mynisters shall not give themselves to excesse in drinking, or ryott, spending theire tyme idelie by day or by night playing at dice, cards, or any other unlawfull game, but at all tymes convenient they shall heare or reade somewhat of the holy scriptures, or shall occupie themselves with some other honest studies, or exercise, always doinge the things which shall apperteyne to honestie and endeavour to profitt the church of God, havinge always in mynd that they ought to excell all others in puritie of life, & should be examples to the people, to live well and christianlie.

ACT XII.

In every parish church within this colony the holy communion shall be administered by the mynister thrice in the yeare whereof the feast of Easter to be one.

ACT XIII.

And all preachinge, administeringe of the communion baptizinge of children and marriages, shall be done in the church except in cases of necessitie.

ACT XIV.

The Governor and Counsell, togeather with the Burgisses of this Grand Assembly uppon the petition of the mynisters within this colony, have taken into theire considerations by what way theire might be a sufficient means allowed unto the sayd mynisters, for theire mynistry, and thereuppon have ordeyned and enacted, That theire shall be payd unto the said mynisters, the former allowance of 10 lb. of tobacco and a bushell of corne, in such manner as formerlie hath been due. And because of the low rates of tobacco at present, it is further graunted and ordered that theire shall be likewise due to the mynisters, from the first day of March last past, for and during the term of one whole yeare next ensueing, the twentyeth calfe, and twentyeth kidd of goates and the twentyieth pigge throughout all the plantations in this colony: and where the nomber of the calves, kidds, or pigges arise to twenty, then the owner is to choose five out of the sayd nomber of twenty, and the mynister to make choyse in the sixt place, but yf it soe fall out that the nomber bee lesse than twenty, then the mynister shall sett the price, and the owner either to take the sayd calves, kidds or piggs then fallen and to pay the mynister the twentyeth part or else the mynister to take the same and allow unto the owner so much as shall be due unto him. And it is thought fitt, That the owner shall keep the sayd calves, kids, or piggs, untill the tyme that they be weanable, that is to say, for calves the owner to keepe them seaven weekes, and the kidds likewise seaven weeks and piggs one month. And the parishioners are to give notice unto theire mynisters when they are to fetch theire calves, kidds and piggs that be due unto them.

ACT XV.

It is likewise ordered, That the mynisters shall have these petty duties followinge, vizt:

ffor marriage 2s–0
ffor churchinge .... 1 –0
ffor burrying .... 1 –0

ACT XVI.

It is ordered, That uppon the 25th of October, yf it bee not Sonday, & then the day followinge the church wardens shall give notice to the parishioners, that they bringe in the dutie of 10 lbs. of tobacco for the mynisters unto a place to be appoynted, within that plantation by the church wardens, and that the mynisters be warned to be there, or appoynt some other to receive the same. And it is likewise ordered, That the dutie of a bushell of corne, be brought in uppon the 19th day of December to the place appoynted within that plantation, by the mynister. And no planter or parishioners may neglect the bringinge of the tobacco, or corne as aforesayd, uppon the penaltie that yf any make default, they shall forfeite double the quantitie of tobacco and corne, to be levyed by distresse, by the authoritie of the commanders. And likewise all arrerages of tobacco and corne which have been due to the mynisters as duties shall and may be recovered by distresse, by virtue of this act of this Assembly, and yf the church wardens shall fayle in the execution of theire office, hereby enjoyned, then the commander shall take order, that what shall remayne unpayd, and owinge to the mynisters shall be levyed by distress out of the church wardens goods and chattels.

ACT XVII.

It is ordeyned and enacted, That in all such places where any churches are wantinge or decayed, the inhabitants shall be tyed to contribute towards the buildinge of a church, or repayringe any decayed church. The commissioners together with the mynisters, church wardens and cheife of the parish, shall appoynt both the most convenient place for all parts to assemble togeather and also to hire and procure any workemen and order such necessarie businesses as are requisite to be done in such workes. This they are to effect before the feast of the nativitie of our Saviour Christ, or else the sayd commissioners yf they be deficient in theire duties to forfeite £50 in money. And it is ordered in like manner, That there be a certain portion of ground appoynted out, impaled or fenced in to be for the buriall of the dead upon the penaltie of 20 marks.

Extract from ACT XXIII.

And it is therefore further ordered, That the present commander of the fort at Poynt Comfort, uppon the arrival of any shipp or shipps or other vessell out of the sea shall immediately make his repayre aboard and there require the commander, captayne, and master of the sayd shipp or shipps or other vessell to deliver unto him a true list of all such persons as were inbarqued in theire shipp at theire cominge out of England, togeather with theire ages, countreyes and townes where they were borne; and to keepe record of the same, and he the sayd commander of the fort shall administer unto them the oaths of supremacy and allegiance, which yf any shall refuse to take that he committ him to them to imprisonment . . .

Comment: The purpose of this law was to keep out of Virginia all Roman Catholics and all Protestants who were disloyal to the king. No Roman Catholic could honestly take the oath of the king's supremacy, because that oath included an explicit denial of spiritual allegiance or obedience to the Pope or to the papal hierarchy. It must be noted that no one was required to take an oath of conformity to the Church of England. Other laws in the code made provision that only ministers who conformed to the doctrine, discipline and worship of the Church of England should hold parishes in Virginia, but there was nothing in the code which prevented any dissenter from settling in the colony provided he was loyal to the king and the royal government. It must be remembered that the difficulties between king and Parliament began in England in that year 1632, and the colony was determined to show its loyalty. For that reason, all persons who refused to take oaths of supremacy and allegiance upon their arrival at Point Comfort were to be imprisoned and held for questioning and, if necessary, deported from the colony.

ACT LX.

It is ordered, That the 22nd day of March be yearlie kept Holy day in commemoration of our deliverance from the Indians at that bloudie massacre which happened upon the 22d of March, 1621.

Note

1. Sydney Ahlstrom, *A Religious History of the American People* (New Haven: Yale University Press, 1972), p. 334.

II

DENOMINATIONS DEVELOP

The denomination became a major vehicle for organizing both the practical and theological dimensions of American religious life. Practically, denominations provided a means for structuring church life in a society where religious liberty and pluralism prevailed over state churches. It enabled religious bodies large and small to develop a framework for evangelism, missions, finances, and other programs. Theologically, the denomination was a "neutral" term used by those who insisted that no single ecclesiastical organization could be identified exclusively with the true church.

John Wesley clarified this view: "I . . . refuse to be distinguished from other men by any but the common principles of Christianity . . . I renounce and detest all marks of distinction. But from real Christians, of *whatever denomination*, I earnestly desire not to be distinguished at all . . . Dost thou love and fear God? It is enough! I give thee the right hand of fellowship."[1]

The denominational concept developed around distinctive doctrines formed for the most part in Europe but modified by the American experience. This chapter contains materials that illustrate varying aspects of American denominational life in the period surrounding and following the Revolutionary War.

The Presbyterians, Congregationalists, and Episcopalians represent the "big three" American denominations prior to the Revolution. The Anglican Church had come to America as the established religion of the mother country. It was the religion of the gentry, numbering George Washington, Patrick Henry, and James Madison among its colonial adherents. Anglicanism was the official religion of Virginia from the founding of the colony but also gained establishment in Maryland, New York, Georgia, and the Carolinas.

In spite of their prominence, the Anglicans confronted

major problems. The shortage of clergymen led to the growth of lay influence through trusteeships in the churches. This frequently led to conflict between the clergy and the laity. The absence of an American bishop and the efforts to secure one created numerous difficulties for the church. The identification of the Anglican Church with the Tory cause in the Revolution greatly weakened the church in America after the war.

Presbyterians and Congregationalists, however, benefited from independence. Most of their members had strongly supported the Revolutionary endeavor. Presbyterians came to America largely through the Scotch-Irish immigration. The first presbytery in America was founded in 1706 under the leadership of Frances Makemie, a major force among early Presbyterians. Churches spread throughout the colonies but were particularly strong in New Jersey and Pennsylvania. By the period of the Revolution, Presbyterians were an influential force in the colonies.

The Congregationalists were secure in their New England sanctuary. Here such renowned preachers as John Cotton, Increase and Cotton Mather, and Jonathan Edwards became a vital part of the American religious heritage. The Congregationalists founded Harvard in 1636 and Yale in 1701 in order to provide proper ministerial training for their young people. By the end of the Revolution, they had the prestige, the numbers, and the influence which made them the major American denomination. Schism and controversy would weaken the body significantly by the mid-nineteenth century.

Anglicans, Presbyterians, and Congregationalists represent the "mainline" American denominations in the colonial epoch. Other bodies were growing in America and would, with time and circumstance, rival the more established groups in terms of numbers, influence, or impact on the culture.

The Quakers were the center of controversy from the time of their arrival in America. Founded in England in the 1650s through the work and teachings of George Fox, Quakers zealously preached a doctrine of social and spiritual equality based on the concept of the "Inner Light" within all persons. They rejected the outward trappings of religion in favor of a laity-centered church gathering for silent worship and were committed to pacifism and other social reforms. During the 1600s Quakers were intense in their missionary fervor, often exhibiting a strong martyr complex. Their unorthodox methods and doctrines resulted in extensive persecution in England and America. In fact, the earliest executions of religious dissenters in America were carried out against the Quakers. In 1660 Mary Dyer, the first Quaker woman executed in America, was hanged in Boston for her radical behavior. In spite of persecution Quakers thrived in Rhode Island, Pennsylvania, and throughout the colonies. George Fox himself visited America in 1672.

It was in John Woolman, however, that the Quaker concepts of mystical religion and social reform were best exemplified in colonial America. Woolman, 1720-1772, was a mystic given to ecstatic experiences with the divine and concerned that each individual discover "that of Christ within." His belief in the worth of every individual under God led him to champion the cause of the poor, the disenfranchised, and the slave. Almost single-handedly, Woolman traveled throughout the South urging Quakers to free their slaves. He insisted on paying slaves for their services and refused to stay in the homes of slaveholders. Through his efforts Quakers in America opposed slavery earlier than any other major religious body.

Woolman's great concern for the impoverished is evident in the treatise "A Word of Remembrance and Caution to the Rich," also known as "A Plea for the Poor." In it he revealed some principles for sharing labor and wealth. First, Woolman sought to establish the idea that the rich had a basic duty to confront the needs of the poor. The wealthy were "fathers of the poor" and thus must seek to understand and respond to their plight. He then urged certain practical programs for expanding the labor force.

Woolman then provided a prophetic response by urging that the wealthy must learn to have fewer material benefits in order that others might merely have something of the necessities of life. He warned of the tension between riches and Christian spirituality, fearful that the obsession with material gain would lead to warfare and suffering. Wealth was linked to power, power to oppression, and oppression to war. The solution, Woolman believed, was found in the exercise of divine love among all persons.

In this treatise Woolman illustrates the strengths and insights of Quaker social concern. In spite of their minority status as an American denomination, the Quakers have made an outstanding contribution to the nation's religious and social conscience.

The Methodists began not as a separate denomination but as a "society" within the Church of England. The Wesleys, John and Charles, were loyal Anglican clergymen whose preaching and organizational skills led them to organize small groups gathered by common evangelical experience for Bible study, confession, and spiritual encouragement.

Methodist lay preachers came to this country as early as 1766, and their heartwarming message was enthusiastically received. A few circuits were established, and the movement showed positive signs in the pre-Revolutionary era. Like their Anglican mentors, the Methodists were frequently associated with the Tory cause during the Revolution. After the war, the difficulty of association with the Anglican church forced John Wesley himself to appoint and ordain clergymen for America. Thomas Vasey and Richard Whatcoat were ordained in 1784, and Dr. Thomas Coke and Francis Asbury were named "Superintendents" (later called bishops) for Methodists in America. At the "Christmas Conference" held in Baltimore in December 1784, the Methodist Episcopal Church was born.

Francis Asbury, 1745-1816, more than any other, may be called the "Father of American Methodism." His boundless energy as organizer, preacher, and circuit rider set the pattern for the itinerant Methodist ministry, the genius of the movement. The portion of his *Journal* provided here contains Asbury's observations on the meeting in Baltimore as well as providing an indication of the work of a man who each year traveled some five thousand miles on horseback, bringing word, sacrament, and order to the young churches. Through the ministry of the circuit riders, the organization of laity-led small groups, and a theology of free grace and personal experience, the Methodists became the largest denomination in America by the mid-nineteenth century.

The Catholics were no strangers to the American continent. They made significant contributions to what is now the southwestern United States, Mexico, Canada, and South America. English Catholics during the colonial period were a tiny minority, located primarily in portions of Maryland, Pennsylvania, and New York.

America during this era was dominated by Protestants who mistrusted the Catholics both theologically and politically. The Reformation was seen as a repudiation of the Catholic corruption of Christian faith, a rediscovery of the true New Testament teaching, and a rejection of the Roman papacy that many equated with the Antichrist. Politically, the Catholics were often viewed as having an allegiance to a foreign monarch, the Pope, and his allies the French and Spanish. The imperialistic activities of these Catholic powers greatly disturbed the English colonials.

During the Revolutionary War, however, public opinion regarding Roman Catholics was modified significantly. Most Catholics were loyal to the patriot cause. Many served in the army; and Charles Carroll, a prominent Catholic churchman, was a signer of the Declaration of Independence. The participation of the Catholic French on the side of American liberty also moderated public sentiments. For many Americans of the Revolutionary War era, the Antichrist was no longer the Pope, but the King of England!

With American independence, actions were taken in Rome which provided for the official organization of the Roman Catholic Church in America. John Carroll, 1735-1815, a member of a distinguished Maryland family, was appointed the superior of the Catholic mission in the United States in 1784. In 1790 he was consecrated bishop of

Baltimore, and the American Catholic episcopacy was born.

The documents provided give evidence of Carroll's desire to identify Catholics with the cause of the United States and to respond to the challenges which confronted the church in a democratic society. Very early the Catholic laity in America had exercised a greater degree of control in churches due to a shortage of clergymen and the influence of American democracy. This democratic spirit created frequent problems for a church founded on hierarchal, clergy-centered polity. Missions and expansion were also concerns of American Catholics and additional (suffragan) bishoprics were established by 1808 at Boston, New York, Philadelphia, and Bardstown, Kentucky (a center of Catholicism on the frontier).

Catholics in America would remain a rather mistrusted minority until the mid-nineteenth century, when emigration of European Catholics created new challenges for Catholics and Protestants alike. With increasing numerical strengths, American Catholics had become a major religious force by the mid-1800s.

If ever a denomination served to illustrate the pluralism of American religion, it is the people called Baptists. Perhaps no other body demonstrated so many divisions promoting such diverse theological and practical views under the same denominational name. In 1977 studies revealed some fifty-three different groups in America, each claiming the name Baptist. Theological positions varied from Free Will (Arminian) Baptists to Two-Seed-in-the-Spirit Predestinarian Baptists to the modified Calvinism of the huge Southern Baptist Convention. Beginning in England in the 1600s, Baptists came to America with two basic theological orientations: Particular Baptists, advocating a Calvinistic theology, and General Baptists, holding to Arminian views.

The first Baptist church in America was probably founded at Providence, Rhode Island, by Roger Williams in 1639. Soon other congregations were formed at Newport by

1644 and at Boston in 1665. In the middle colonies Baptists organized churches first at Pennepack in Pennsylvania in 1686 and Philadelphia in 1698. Indeed, the first associational organization of Baptist churches occurred with the Philadelphia Association, founded in 1707. This group also approved the first Confession of Faith to be used by Baptists in America. Known as the Philadelphia Confession of 1742, it is a thoroughly Calvinistic document drawn primarily from the earlier London Confession of Particular Baptists written in 1689.

Regardless of these developments, the real growth among Baptists occurred from the effects of religious awakenings that swept the colonies in the 1700s and the frontier in the 1800s. Revivalistic "Separate" Baptists traveled from New England into the Carolinas under the leadership of Shubal Stearns and Daniel Marshall. They preached a conversionist gospel within a context of local church autonomy and congregational church government.

This type of church structure and evangelical technique was particularly important to Baptist expansion on the American frontier during the early 1800s. Local autonomy meant that a Baptist congregation could be organized by a group of like-minded persons in a community without the sanction of any other church group or leader. These congregations appeared across the frontier areas of Ohio, Indiana, Kentucky, and Tennessee, and were served by the so-called "farmer-preachers." Such men lived in the community, worked their fields during the week, and functioned as minister and preacher to their neighbors. Many of the men were laymen, some licensed, some ordained under a democratic polity in which any church member could administer ordinances of baptism and the Lord's Supper with congregational consent.

The document from frontier Baptists provided in this volume indicates the personal dimension of Baptist faith as it relates to the ministry. Conversion and call under divine inspiration were the basic criteria for all ordinations among Baptists. Education was less important and sometimes feared as a detriment to "heart religion." The Baptists grew on the frontier. By the 1860s they were second only to the Methodists as the largest American denomination.

The revival spirit on the frontier was also a prominent factor in the development of indigenous denominations, among them the controversial "Disciples of Christ." Thomas Campbell and his son Alexander began their ministries as Presbyterians, became Baptists, and by 1827 had renounced denominations in favor of a restoration of the true New Testament church of "Christians" or "Disciples" only. Their doctrine stressed the importance of the New Covenant over the Old, sharing of the Lord's Supper each Sunday, and baptism "for the remission of sins." Practices such as the use of musical instruments in worship and the use of the term "reverend" for ministers were abolished as having no New Testament basis. Faith was based less on personal experience or sensations than mental assent to the truth of the gospel.

The followers of Campbell were formidable controversialists, and their restorationist views won numerous new converts as well as drawing adherents from other established denominations. Their early doctrinal compatibility with another restorationist group, the Christian Church, led by revivalist Barton W. Stone, produced a union of groups in this Christian tradition.

Other indigenous denominations appeared on the American scene in the nineteenth century. Unitarians divided Congregationalists in New England, and Adventists evolved from the millennial fervor of the 1840s. In America, individual denominations rose and declined; but denominationalism remained the basic form for organization of the pluralistic American religion.

1

The Quakers

JOHN WOOLMAN

A Word of Remembrance
and Caution
to the Rich

SECTION I.

WEALTH desired for its own sake obstructs the increase of virtue, and large possessions in the hands of selfish men have a bad tendency, for by their means too small a number of people are employed in useful things, and some of them are necessitated to labor too hard, while others would want business to earn their bread, were not employments invented which, having no real usefulness, serve only to please the vain mind.

Rents on lands are often so high that persons of but small substance are straitened in taking farms, and while tenants are healthy and prosperous in business, they often find occasion to labor harder than was intended by our gracious Creator. Oxen and horses are often seen at work when, through heat and too much labor, their eyes and the motions of their bodies manifest that they are oppressed. Their loads in wagons are frequently so heavy that when weary with hauling them far, their drivers find occasion in going up hills, or through mire, to get them forward by whipping. Many poor people are so thronged in their business that it is difficult for them to provide shelter for their cattle against the storms. These things are common when in health, but through sickness and inability to labor, through loss of cattle, and miscarriage in business, many are so straitened that much of their increase goes to pay rent, and they have not wherewith to buy what they require.

Hence one poor woman, in providing for her family and attending the sick, does as much business as would for the time be suitable employment for two or three; and honest persons are often straitened to give their children suitable learning. The money which the wealthy receive from the poor, who do more than a proper share of business in raising it, is frequently paid to other poor people for doing business which is foreign to the true use of things. Men who have large estates and live in the spirit of charity; who carefully inspect the circumstances of those who occupy their estates, and, regardless of the customs of the times, regulate their demands agreeably to universal love, being righteous on principle, do good to the poor without placing it to an act of bounty. Their example in avoiding superfluities tends to excite moderation in others; their uprightness in not exacting what the laws and customs would support them in tends to open the channel to moderate labor in useful affairs, and to discourage those branches of business which have not their foundation in true wisdom.

To be busied in that which is but vanity and serves only to please the insatiable mind, tends to an alliance with those who promote that vanity, and is a snare in which many poor tradesmen are entangled. To be employed in things connected with virtue is most agreeable with the character and inclinations of an honest man. While industrious, frugal people are borne down with poverty, and oppressed with too much labor in useful things, the way to apply money without promoting pride and vanity remains open to such as truly sympathize with them in their various difficulties.

SECTION II.

The Creator of the earth is the owner of it. He gave us being thereon, and our nature requires nourishment from the produce of it. He is kind and merciful to his creatures; and while they live answerably to the design of their creation, they are so far entitled to convenient subsistence that we may not justly deprive them of it. By the agreements and contracts of our predecessors, and by our own doings, some enjoy a much greater share of this world than others; and while those possessions are faithfully improved for the good of the whole, it agrees with equity; but he who, with a view to self-exaltation, causeth some to labor immoderately, and with the profits arising therefrom employs others in the luxuries of life, acts contrary to the gracious designs of Him who is the owner of the earth; nor can any possessions, either acquired or derived from ancestors, justify such conduct. Goodness remains to be goodness, and the direction of pure wisdom is obligatory on all reasonable creatures.

Though the poor occupy our estates by a bargain, to which they in their poor circumstances agree, and we may ask even less than a punctual fulfilling of their agreement, yet if our views are to lay up riches, or to live in conformity to customs which have not their foundation in the truth, and our demands are such as require from them greater toil or application to business than is consistent with pure love, we invade their rights as inhabitants of a world of which a good and gracious God is the proprietor, and under whom we are tenants.

Were all superfluities and the desire of outward greatness laid aside, and the right use of things universally attended to, such a number of people might be employed in things useful as that moderate labor with the blessing of Heaven would answer all good purposes, and a sufficient number would have time to attend to the proper affairs of civil society.

SECTION III.

While our spirits are lively, we go cheerfully through business; either too much or too little action is tiresome, but a right portion is healthful to the body and agreeable to an honest mind.

Men who have great estates stand in a place of trust; and to have it in their power to live without difficulty in that manner which occasions much labor, and at the same time to confine themselves to that use of things prescribed by our Redeemer, and confirmed by his example and the examples of many who lived in the early age of the Christian church, that they may more extensively relieve objects of charity, requires close attention to Divine love.

Our gracious Creator cares and provides for all his creatures. His tender mercies are over all his works, and so far as true love influences our minds, so far we become interested in his workmanship and feel a desire to make use of every opportunity to lessen the distresses of the afflicted and to increase the happiness of the creation. Here we have a prospect of one common interest from which our own is inseparable, *so that to turn all we possess into the channel of universal love becomes the business of our lives.*

Men of large estates, whose hearts are thus enlarged, are like fathers to the poor; and in looking over their brethren in distressed circumstances, and considering their own more easy condition, they find a field for humble meditation, and feel the strength of the obligations they are under to be kind and tender-hearted towards them. Poor men, eased of their burdens and released from too close an application to business, are enabled to hire assistance, to provide well for their cattle, and to find time to perform those duties among their neighbors which belong to a well-guided social life. When the latter reflect on the opportunity such had to oppress them, and consider the goodness of their conduct, they behold it lovely and consistent with brotherhood; and as the man whose mind is conformed to universal love hath his trust settled in God and finds a firm foundation in any changes or revolutions that happen among men, so also the goodness of his conduct tends to spread a kind, benevolent disposition in the world.

SECTION IV.

Our blessed Redeemer, in directing us how to conduct ourselves one towards another, appeals to our own feelings: "Whatsoever ye would that men should do to you, do ye even so to them." Now, when some who have never experienced hard labor themselves live in fulness on the labor of others, there is often a danger of their not having a right feeling of the laborers' condition, and of being thereby disqualified to judge candidly in their case, not knowing what they themselves would desire, were they to labor hard from one year to another to raise the necessaries of life, and pay high rent besides. It is good for those who live in fulness to cultivate tenderness of heart, and to improve every opportunity of being acquainted with the hardships and fatigues of those who labor for their living; and thus to think seriously with themselves, Am I influenced by true charity in fixing all my demands? Have I no desire to support myself in expensive customs, because my acquaintances live in such customs?

If a wealthy man, on serious reflection, finds a witness in his own conscience that he indulges himself in some expensive customs which might be omitted consistently with the true design of living, and which, were he to change places with those who occupy his estate, he would desire to be discontinued by them; whoever is thus awakened will necessarily find the injunction binding: "Do ye even so to them." Divine love imposeth no rigorous or unreasonable commands, but graciously points out the spirit of brotherhood and the way to happiness, in attaining which it is necessary that we relinquish all that is selfish.

Section V.

To enforce the duty of tenderness to the poor, the inspired law-giver referred the children of Israel to their own experience: "Ye know the heart of a stranger, seeing ye were strangers in the land of Egypt." He who hath been a stranger among unkind people, or under the government of those who were hard-hearted, has experienced this feeling; but a person who hath never felt the weight of misapplied power comes not to this knowledge but by an inward tenderness, in which the heart is prepared to sympathize with others.

Let us reflect on the condition of a poor innocent man, on whom the rich man, from a desire after wealth and luxuries, lays heavy burdens; when this laborer looks over the cause of his heavy toil and considers that it is laid on him to support that which hath no foundation in pure wisdom, we may well suppose that an uneasiness ariseth in his mind towards one who might without any inconvenience deal more favorably with him. When he considers that by his industry his fellow-creature is benefited and sees that this wealthy man is not satisfied with being supported in a plain way, but to gratify a desire of conforming to wrong customs increaseth to an extreme the labors of those who occupy his estate, *we may reasonably judge that he will think himself unkindly used.* When he considers that the proceedings of the wealthy are agreeable to the customs of the times, and sees no means of redress in this world, how will the sighings of this innocent person ascend to the throne of that great and good Being who created all, and who hath a constant care over his creatures! He who toils year after year to furnish others with wealth and superfluities, until by overmuch labor he is wearied and oppressed, understands the meaning of that language, "Ye know the heart of a stranger, seeing ye were strangers in the land of Egypt."

Many at this day who know not the heart of a stranger indulge themselves in ways of life which occasion more labor than Infinite Goodness intends for man, and yet compassionate the distresses of such as come directly under their observation; were these to change circumstances awhile with their laborers, were they to pass regularly through the means of knowing the heart of a stranger and come to a feeling knowledge of the straits and hardships which many poor innocent people pass through in obscure life; were these who now fare sumptuously every day to act the other part of the scene until seven times had passed over them and return again to their former states,—I believe many of them would embrace a less expensive life, and would lighten the heavy burdens of some who now labor out of their sight, and who pass through straits with which they are but little acquainted. To see their fellow-creatures under difficulties to which they are in no degree accessory tends to awaken tenderness in the minds of all reasonable people; but if we consider the condition of those who are depressed in answering our demands, who labor for us out of our sight while we pass our time in fulness, and consider also that much less than we demand would supply us with things really useful, what heart will not relent, or what reasonable man can refrain from mitigating that grief of which he himself is the cause, when he may do so without inconvenience?

Section VI.

If more men were usefully employed, and fewer ate bread as a reward for doing that which is not useful, food and raiment would on a reasonable estimate be more in proportion to labor than they are at present; for if four men working eight hours per day can do a portion of labor in a certain number of days, then five men equally capable may do the same business in the same time by working only six hours and twenty-four minutes per day. In proceeding agreeably to sound wisdom, a small portion of daily labor might suffice to keep a proper stream gently circulating through all the channels of society; and this portion of labor might be so divided and taken in the most advantageous parts of the day that people would not have that plea for the use of strong liquors which they have at present. The quantity of spirituous liquors imported and made in our country is great; nor can so many thousand hogsheads of it be drunk every year without having a powerful effect on our habits and morals.

People spent with much labor often take strong liquor to revive them. The portion of the necessaries of life is such that those who support their families by day labor find occasion to labor hard, and many of them think strong drink a necessary part of their entertainment.

When people are spent with action and take these liquors not only as a refreshment from past labors, but also to enable them to go on without giving sufficient time to recruit by resting, it gradually turns them from that calmness of thought which attends those who apply their hearts to true wisdom. That the spirits being scattered by too much bodily motion and again revived by strong drink makes a person unfit for Divine meditation, I suppose will not be denied; and as multitudes of people are in this practice who do not take so much as to hinder them from managing their affairs, this custom is strongly supported; but as through Divine goodness I have found that there is a more quiet, calm, and happy way intended for us to walk in, I am engaged to express what I feel in my heart concerning it. As cherishing the spirit of love and meekness belongs to the family of Jesus Christ, so to avoid those things which are known to work against it is an indispensable duty. Every degree of luxury of what kind soever, and every demand for money inconsistent with Divine order, hath some connection with unnecessary labor. By too much labor the spirits are exhausted, and nature craves help from strong drink; and the frequent use of strong drink works in opposition to the celestial influence on the mind. There is in the nature of people some degree of likeness with that food and air to which they have been accustomed from their youth; this frequently appears in those who, by a separation from their native air and usual diet, grow weak and unhealthy for want of them; nor is it reasonable to suppose that so many thousand hogsheads of fiery liquor can be drunk every year and the practice continued from age to age without altering in some degree the natures of men and rendering their minds less apt to receive the pure truth in the love of it.

As many who manifest some regard to piety in degree conform to those ways of living and of collecting wealth which increase labor beyond the bounds fixed by Divine wisdom, my desire is that they may so consider the connection of things as to take heed lest by exacting of poor men more than is consistent with universal righteousness they promote that by their conduct which in word they speak against. To treasure up wealth for another generation by means of the immoderate labor of those who in some measure depend upon us is doing evil at present without knowing that wealth thus gathered may not be applied to evil purposes when we are gone. To labor hard or cause others to do so that we may live conformably to customs which Christ our Redeemer discountenanced by his example in the days of his flesh, and which are contrary to Divine order, is to manure a soil for propagating an evil seed in the earth. They who enter deeply into these considerations and live under the weight of them will feel these things so heavy and their ill effects so extensive that the necessity of attending singly to Divine wisdom will be evident; and will thereby be directed in the right use of things in opposition to the customs of the times; and will be supported to bear patiently the reproaches attending singularity. To conform a little strengthens the hands of those who carry wrong customs to their utmost extent; and the more a person appears to be virtuous and heavenly-minded, the more powerfully does his conformity operate in favor of evil-doers. Lay aside the profession of a pious life, and people expect little or no instruction from the example; but while we profess in all cases to live in constant opposition to that which is contrary to universal righteousness, what expressions are equal to the subject, or what language is sufficient to set forth the strength of the obligations we are under to beware lest by our example we lead others astray!

Section VII.

If by our wealth we make our children great, without a full persuasion that we could not bestow it better, and thus give them power to deal hardly with others more virtuous than they, it can after death give us no more satisfaction than if by this treasure we had raised others above our own, and had given them power to oppress them.

Did a man possess as much land as would suffice for twenty industrious frugal people, and supposing that, being the lawful heir to it, he intended to give this great estate to his children; yet if he found on research into the title that one half of this estate was the undoubted right of a number of poor orphans, who as to virtue and understanding appeared to him as hopeful as his own children, the discovery would give him an opportunity to consider whether he was attached to any interest distinct from the interest of those orphans.

Some of us have estates sufficient for our children, and as many more to live upon, if they all employed their time in useful business, and lived in that plainness which becomes the true disciples of Christ; and we have no reason to believe that our children will be more likely to apply them to benevolent purposes than would some poor children with whom we are acquainted; and yet did we believe that after our decease our estates would go equally among our children and the children of the poor, it would be likely to give us uneasiness. This may show to a thoughtful person that to be redeemed from all the remains of selfishness, to have a universal regard to our fellow-creatures, and to love them as our Heavenly Father loves them, we must constantly attend to the influence of his spirit.

When our hearts are enlarged to contemplate the nature of Divine love, we behold it harmonious; but if we attentively consider that moving of selfishness which makes us uneasy at the apprehension of that which is in itself reasonable, and which, when separated from all previous conceptions and expectations, appears so, we see an inconsistency in it, for the subject of such uneasiness is future, and will not affect our children until we are removed into that state of being in which there is no possibility of our taking delight in anything contrary to the pure principle of universal love.

As that natural desire of superiority in us, when given way to, extends to such of our favorites as we expect will succeed us; and as the grasping after wealth and power for them adds greatly to the burdens of the poor, and increaseth the evil of covetousness in this age,—I have often desired that in looking towards posterity we may remember the purity of that rest which is prepared for the Lord's people; the impossibility of our taking pleasure in anything distinguishable from universal righteousness; and how vain and weak it is to give wealth and power to those who appear unlikely to apply it to the general good when we are gone.

As Christians, all we possess is the gift of God, and in the distribution of it we act as his stewards; it becomes us therefore to act agreeably to that Divine wisdom which he graciously gives to his servants. If the steward of a great family takes that with which he is intrusted, and bestows it lavishly on some to the injury of others and to the damage of his employer, he degrades himself and becomes unworthy of his office.

The true felicity of man in this life and in that which is to come, is in being inwardly united to the Fountain of universal love and bliss. When we provide for posterity, and make settlements which will not take effect until after we are centred in another state of being, if we therein knowingly act contrary to universal love and righteousness, such conduct must arise from a false, selfish pleasure; and if, after such settlements, our wills continue to stand in opposition to the Fountain of universal light and love, will there not be an impassable gulf between the soul and true felicity? But if after such settlement, and when too late for an alteration, we attain to that purified state which our Redeemer prayed his Father that his people might attain to, of being united to the Father and to the Son, must not a sincere repentance for all things done in a will separate from universal love, precede this inward sanctification? And though in such depth of repentance and reconciliation all sins may be forgiven, can we reasonably suppose that our partial determinations in favor of those whom we selfishly loved will then afford us pleasure?

SECTION VIII.

To labor for an establishment in Divine love, in which the mind is disentangled from the power of darkness, is the great business of man's life; the collecting of riches, covering the body with fine wrought, costly apparel, and having magnificent furniture, operate against universal love and tend to feed self, so that it belongs not to the children of the light to desire these things. He who sent ravens to feed Elijah in the wilderness, and increased the poor woman's small remains of meal and oil, is now as attentive as ever to the necessities of his people. When he saith unto his people, "Ye are my sons and daughters," no greater happiness can be desired by them, who know how gracious a Father he is.

The greater part of the necessaries of life are so far perishable that each generation hath occasion to labor for them; and when we look towards a succeeding age with a mind influenced by universal love, instead of endeavoring to exempt some from those cares which necessarily relate to this life, and to give them power to oppress others, we desire that they may all be the Lord's children and live in that humility and order becoming his family. Our hearts, being thus opened and enlarged, will feel content with a state of things as foreign to luxury and grandeur as that which our Redeemer laid down as a pattern.

By desiring wealth for the power and distinction it gives, and gathering it on this motive, a person may become rich; but his mind being moved by a draught distinguishable from the drawings of the Father, he cannot be united to the heavenly society, where God is the strength of our life. "It is easier," saith our Saviour, "for a camel to go through the eye of a needle than for a rich man to enter the kingdom of God." Here our Lord uses an instructive similitude, for as a camel while in that form cannot pass through the eye of a needle, so a man who trusteth in riches and holds them for the sake of the power and distinction attending them, cannot in that spirit enter into the kingdom. Now every part of a camel may be so reduced as to pass through a hole as small as the eye of a needle; yet such is the bulk of the creature and the hardness of its bones and teeth, that it could not be so reduced without much labor; so must man cease from that spirit which craves riches, and be brought into another disposition before he inherits the kingdom, as effectually as a camel must be changed from the form of a camel in passing through the eye of a needle.

When our Saviour said to the rich youth, "Go, sell what thou hast, and give to the poor," though undoubtedly it was his duty to have done so, yet to enjoin the selling of all as a duty on every true Christian would be to limit the Holy One. Obedient children, who are intrusted with much outward substance, wait for wisdom to dispose of it agreeably to His will, "in whom the fatherless find mercy." It may not be the duty of every one to commit at once their substance to other hands, but rather from time to time to look round among the numerous branches of the great family as the stewards of Him who provides for the widows and fatherless; but as disciples of Christ, although intrusted with much goods, they may not conform to sumptuous or luxurious living; for, as he lived in perfect plainness and simplicity, the greatest in his family cannot by virtue of his station claim a right to live in worldly grandeur without contradicting him who said, "It is enough for the disciple to be as his Master."

When our eyes are so single as to discern the selfish spirit clearly, we behold it the greatest of all tyrants. Many thousand innocent people under some of the Roman emperors, being confirmed in the truth of Christ's religion by the powerful effects of his Holy Spirit upon them, and scrupling to conform to heathenish rites, were put to death by various kinds of cruel and lingering torments, as is largely set forth by Eusebius.

Now, if we single out Domitian, Nero, or any other of the persecuting emperors, the man, though terrible in his time, will appear as a tyrant of small consequence compared with this selfish spirit; for, though his bounds were large, yet a great part of the world was out of his reach; and though he grievously afflicted the bodies of innocent people, yet the minds of many were divinely supported in their greatest agonies, and being faithful unto death they were delivered from his tyranny. His reign, though cruel for a time, was soon over; and he in his greatest pomp appears to have been a slave to a selfish spirit.

Thus tyranny as applied to a man riseth up and soon has an end; but if we consider the numerous oppressions in many states, and the calamities occasioned by contending nations in various countries and ages of the world, and remember that selfishness hath been the original cause of them all; if we consider that those who are unredeemed from this selfish spirit not only afflict others but are afflicted themselves, and have no real quietness in this life nor in futurity, but, according to the sayings of Christ, have their portion "where the worm dieth not and the fire is not quenched"; if we consider the havoc that is made in this age, and how numbers of people are hurried on, striving to collect treasure to please that mind which wanders from perfect resignedness, and in that wisdom which is foolishness with God are perverting the true use of things, laboring as in the fire, contending with one another even unto blood, and exerting their power to support ways of living foreign to the life of one wholly crucified to the world; if we consider what great numbers of people are employed in preparing implements of war, and the labor and toil of armies set apart for protecting their respective territories from invasion, and the extensive miseries which attend their engagements; while they who till the land and are employed in other useful things in supporting not only themselves but those employed in military affairs, and also those who own the soil, have great hardships to encounter through too much labor; while others, in several kingdoms, are busied in fetching men to help to labor from distant parts of the world, to spend the remainder of their lives in the uncomfortable condition of slaves, and that self is the bottom of these proceedings;—amidst all this confusion, and these scenes of sorrow and distress, can we remember that we are the disciples of the Prince of Peace, and the example of humility and plainness which he set for us, without feeling an earnest desire to be disentangled from everything connected with selfish customs in food, in raiment, in houses and in all things else? That being of Christ's family, and walking as he walked, we may stand in that uprightness wherein man was first made, and have no fellowship with those inventions which men in their fallen wisdom have sought out.

SECTION IX.

The way of carrying on wars common in the world is so far distinguishable from the purity of Christ's religion that many scruple to join in them. Those who are so redeemed from the love of the world as to possess nothing in a selfish spirit have their "life hid with Christ in God," and he preserves them in resignedness, even in times of commotion.

As they possess nothing but what pertains to his family, anxious thoughts about wealth or dominion have little or nothing in them on which to work; and they learn contentment in being disposed of according to His will who, being omnipotent and always mindful of his children, causeth all things to work for their good; but when that spirit works which loves riches, and in its working gathers wealth and cleaves to customs which have their root in self-pleasing, whatever name it hath it still desires to defend the treasures thus gotten. This is like a chain in which the end of one link encloseth the end of another. The rising up of a desire to obtain wealth is the beginning; this desire being cherished, moves to action; and riches thus gotten please self; and while self has a life in them it desires to have them defended. Wealth is attended with power, by which bargains and proceedings contrary to universal righteousness are supported; and hence oppression, carried on with worldly policy and order, clothes itself with the name of justice and becomes like a seed of discord in the soul. And as a spirit which wanders from the pure habitation prevails, so the seeds of war swell and sprout and grow and become strong until much fruit is ripened. Then cometh the harvest spoken of by the prophet, which "is a heap in the day of grief and desperate sorrows." O that we who declare against wars, and acknowledge our trust to be in God only, may walk in the light, and therein examine our foundation and motives in holding great estates! May we look upon our treasures, the furniture of our houses, and our garments, and try whether the seeds of war have nourishment in these our possessions. Holding treasures in the self-pleasing spirit is a strong plant, the fruit whereof ripens fast. A day of outward distress is coming, and Divine love calls to prepare against it.

Section X.

"The heaven, even the heavens, are the Lord's; but the earth hath he given to the children of men." As servants of God our land or estates we hold under him as his gifts; and in applying the profits it is our duty to act consistently with the designs of our Benefactor. Imperfect men may give from motives of misguided affection, but perfect wisdom and goodness gives agreeably to his own nature; nor is this gift absolute, but conditional, for us to occupy as dutiful children and not otherwise; for He alone is the true proprietor. "The world," saith He, "is mine, and the fulness thereof." The inspired lawgiver directed that such of the Israelites as sold their inheritance should sell it for a term only, and that they or their children should again enjoy it in the year of jubilee, settled on every fiftieth year. "The land shall not be sold forever, for the land is mine, saith the Lord, for ye are strangers and sojourners with me." This was designed to prevent the rich from oppressing the poor by too much engrossing the land; and our blessed Redeemer said, "Till heaven and earth pass, one jot or one tittle shall in no wise pass from the law, till all be fulfilled."

When Divine love takes place in the hearts of any people, and they steadily act in a principle of universal righteousness, then the true intent of the law is fulfilled, though their outward modes of proceeding may be various; but when men are possessed by that spirit hinted at by the prophet, and, looking over their wealth, say in their hearts, "Have we not taken to us horns by our own strength?" they deviate from the Divine law, and do not count their possessions so strictly God's, nor the weak and poor entitled to so much of the increase thereof, but that they may indulge their desires in conforming to worldly pomp. Thus when house is joined to house and field laid to field, until there is no place, and the poor are thereby straitened, though this is done by bargain and purchase, yet so far as it stands distinguished from universal love, so far that woe predicted by the prophet will accompany their proceedings. As He who first founded the earth was then the true proprietor of it, so he still remains, and though he hath given it to the children of men, so that multitudes of people have had their sustenance from it while they continued here, yet he hath never alienated it, but his right is as good as at first; nor can any apply the increase of their possessions contrary to universal love, nor dispose of lands in a way which they know tends to exalt some by oppressing others without being justly chargeable with usurpation.

Section XI.

If we count back one hundred and fifty years and compare the inhabitants of Great Britain with the nations of North America on the like compass of ground, the latter, I suppose, would bear a small proportion to the former. On the discovery of this fertile continent many of those thickly settled inhabitants coming over, the natives at first generally treated them with kindness; and as they brought iron tools and a variety of things for man's use, they gladly embraced the opportunity of traffic and encouraged these foreigners to settle; I speak only of improvements made peaceably.

Thus our Gracious Father, who beholds the situation of all his creatures, hath opened a way for a thickly settled land; now if we consider the turning of God's hand in thus far giving us some room in this continent, and that the offspring of those ancient possessors of the country, in whose eyes we appear as new-comers, are yet owners and inhabitants of the land adjoining us, and that their way of life, requiring much room, hath been transmitted to them from their predecessors and probably settled by the custom of a great many ages, we may see the necessity of cultivating the lands already obtained of them and applying the increase consistently with true wisdom so as to accommodate the greatest number of people, before we have any right to plead, as members of the one great family, the equity of their assigning to us more of their possessions and living in a way requiring less room.

Did we all walk as became the followers of our blessed Saviour, were all the fruits of the country retained in it which are sent abroad in return for strong drink, costly array, and other luxuries, and the labor and expense of importing and exporting applied to husbandry and useful trades, a much greater number of people than now reside here might, with the Divine blessing, live comfortably on the lands already granted us by those ancient possessors of the country. If we faithfully serve God, who has given us such room in this land, I believe he will make some of us useful among the natives, both in publishing the doctrines of his Son, our Saviour, and in pointing out to them the advantages of cultivating the earth; while people are so much more thickly settled in some parts than others, a trade in some serviceable articles may be to mutual advantage and may be carried on with much more regularity and satisfaction to a sincere Christian than trade now generally is.

One person continuing to live contrary to true wisdom commonly draws others into connection with him, and when these embrace the way the first hath chosen, their proceedings are like a wild vine which springing from a single seed and growing strong, its branches extend, and their little tendrils twist round all herbs and boughs of trees within their reach, and are so braced and locked in that without much labor and great strength they are not disentangled. Thus these customs, small in their beginning, as they increase promote business and traffic, and many depend on them for a living; but it is evident that all business which hath not its foundation in true wisdom is not becoming a faithful follower of Christ, who loves God not only with all his heart, but with all his strength and ability. And as the Lord is able and will support those whose hearts are perfect towards him in a way agreeably to his unerring wisdom, it becomes us to meditate on the privileges of his children, to remember that "where the spirit of the Lord is, there is liberty," and that in joining to customs which we know are wrong there is a departing from his government and a certain degree of alienation from him. Some well-inclined people are entangled in such business, and at times may have a desire of being freed from it; our ceasing from these things may therefore be made helpful to them; and though for a time their business may fail, yet if they humbly ask wisdom of God and are truly resigned to him, he will not fail them nor forsake them. He who created the earth and hath provided sustenance for millions of people in past ages is as attentive to the necessities of his children as ever. To press forward to perfection is our duty; and if herein we lessen a business by which some poor people earn their bread, the Lord who calls to cease from those things will take care of those whose business fails by it, if they sincerely seek him. If the connection we have with the inhabitants of these provinces, and our interest considered as distinct from others, engage us to promote plain living in order to enrich our country, though a plain life is in itself best, yet by living plain in a selfish spirit we advance not in true religion.

Divine love which enlarges the heart towards mankind universally is that alone which stops every corrupt stream and opens those channels of business and commerce in which nothing runs that is not pure, and so establishes our goings that when in our labors we meditate on the universal love of God and the harmony of holy angels, the serenity of our minds may never be clouded by remembering that some part of our employments tends to support customs which have their foundation in the self-seeking spirit.

SECTION XII.

While our minds are prepossessed in favor of customs distinguishable from perfect purity, we are in danger of not attending with singleness to that light which opens to our view the nature of universal righteousness.

In the affairs of a thickly settled country are variety of useful employments besides tilling the earth; so that for some men to have more land than is necessary to build upon and to answer the occasions of their families may consist with brotherhood; and from the various gifts which God hath bestowed on those employed in husbandry, for some to possess and occupy much more than others may likewise so consist; but when any, on the strength of their possessions, demand such rent or interest as necessitates their tenants to a closer application to business than our merciful Father designed for us, it puts the wheels of perfect brotherhood out of order and leads to employments the promoting of which belongs not to the family of Christ, whose example in all points being a pattern of wisdom, the plainness and simplicity of his outward appearance may well make us ashamed to adorn our bodies with costly array or treasure up wealth by the least oppression.

Though by claims grounded on prior possession great inequality appears among men; yet the instructions of the Great Proprietor of the earth are necessary to be attended to in all our proceedings as possessors or claimers of the soil. "The steps of a good man are ordered of the Lord," and those who are thus guided and whose hearts are enlarged in his love give directions concerning their possessions agreeably thereto; and that claim which stands on universal righteousness is a good right; but the continuance of that right depends on properly applying the profits thereof. The word "right" commonly relates to our possessions. We say, a right of propriety to such a division of a province, or a clear, indisputable right to the land within certain bounds. Thus this word is continued as a remembrancer of the original intent of dividing the land by boundaries, and implies that it was equitably or rightly divided, that is, divided according to righteousness. In this—that is, in equity and righteousness—consists the strength of our claim. If we trace an unrighteous claim and find gifts or grants proved by sufficient seals and witnesses, it gives not the claimant a right; for that which is opposite to righteousness is wrong, and the nature of it must be changed before it can be right.

Suppose twenty free men, professed followers of Christ, discovered an island, and that they with their wives, independent of all others, took possession of it and, dividing it equally, made improvements and multiplied; suppose these first possessors, being generally influenced by true love, did with paternal regard look over the increasing condition of the inhabitants, and, near the end of their lives, gave such directions concerning their respective possessions as best suited the convenience of the whole and tended to preserve love and harmony; and that their successors in the continued increase of people generally fol-

lowed their pious example and pursued means the most effectual to keep oppression out of their island; but that one of these
first settlers, from a fond attachment to one of his numerous
sons, no more deserving than the rest, gives the chief of his
lands to him, and by an instrument sufficiently witnessed
strongly expressed his mind and will;—suppose this son, being
landlord to his brethren and nephews, demands such a portion
of the fruits of the earth as may supply himself, his family, and
some others, and that these others thus supplied out of his store
are employed in adorning his building with curious engravings
and paintings, preparing carriages to ride in, vessels for his
house, delicious meats, fine wrought apparel and furniture, all
suiting that distinction lately arisen between him and other
inhabitants; and that, having the absolute disposal of these
numerous improvements, his power so increaseth that in all
conferences relative to the public affairs of the island these
plain, honest men, who are zealous for equitable establishments, find great difficulty in proceeding agreeably to their
righteous inclinations;—suppose this son, from a fondness to
one of his children, joined with a desire to continue this grandeur under his own name, confirms the chief of his possessions
to him, and thus for many ages there is one great landlord over
near a twentieth part of this island, and the rest are poor oppressed people, to some of whom, from the manner of their
education, joined with a notion of the greatness of their predecessors, labor is disagreeable; who therefore, by artful applications to the weakness, unguardedness, and corruptions of
others in striving to get a living out of them, increase the
difficulties among them, while the inhabitants of other parts,
who guard against oppression and with one consent train up
their children in frugality and useful labor, live more harmoni-
ously;—if we trace the claims of the ninth or tenth of these great
landlords down to the first possessor and find the claim supported throughout by instruments strongly drawn and witnessed, after all we could not admit a belief into our hearts that

he had a right to so great a portion of land after such a numerous increase of inhabitants.

The first possessor of that twentieth part held no more, we suppose, than an equitable portion; but when the Lord, who first gave these twenty men possession of this island unknown to all others, gave being to numerous people who inhabited the twentieth part, whose natures required the fruits thereof for their sustenance, this great claimer of the soil could not have a right to the whole to dispose of it in gratifying his irregular desires; but they, as creatures of the Most High God, Possessor of heaven and earth, had a right to part of what this great claimer held, though they had no instruments to confirm their right. Thus oppression in the extreme appears terrible; but oppression in more refined appearances remains to be oppression, and when the smallest degree of it is cherished it grows stronger and more extensive.

To labor for a perfect redemption from this spirit of oppression is the great business of the whole family of Christ Jesus in this world.

2

The Methodists

FRANCIS ASBURY[2]

Journal

DELAWARE.—*Saturday, October* 2. I preached in our new chapel at Dover, in the state of Delaware, on faith, hope, charity. At Barrats's I believe I was alarming, on Isaiah iii, 10, 11. I was moved in the evening towards the boys to school at C——: I spoke till they wept aloud. O my God! their parents fear thee—bring them home, with them, to thyself.

MARYLAND.—*Thursday,* 7. I rode in the afternoon to Queen Annes, visited and prayed with B. Ellis in affliction, and was persuaded God would spare him. Poor F. is overtaken by the adversary; and R. is gone astray. Alas, how are the mighty fallen!

Friday, 8. Came to Angiers. Here they had the flux; but I did not feel free to leave the house, until I had delivered my message: my testimony was low, but serious and weighty.

Wednesday, 13. At Hopper's, the congregation was large indeed. I was greatly at liberty; and I hope the seed was not all lost. Here I met with brother Garrettson—all love and peace.

Thursday, 14. I rode twenty miles to visit Kent Island for the first time. Here we had an unusual collection of people, and surely all was not in vain. We had a good time at Newcomb's: the word of God has greatly triumphed over the prejudices of rich and poor. We went on to Cambridge. Here George, a poor negro in our society, we found under sentence of death for theft committed before he became a Methodist; he appeared to be much given up to God: he was reprieved under the gallows: a merchant, who cursed the negro for praying, died in horror. I pity the poor slaves. O that God would look down in mercy, and take their cause in hand!

Wednesday, 20. I was distressed by the levity of some spirits. We had a long ride to Taylor's Island; we had a profitable season there: and next day going twenty-four miles to Todd's, I found a warm people indeed. I injured myself by speaking too loud.

Saturday, 23. Rode thirty miles to Mr. Airy's, preaching by the way. We had a great time—multitudes attended. Dorset is now in peace, and the furies are still.

Sunday, 24. This day has been so much taken up, that I had no time to spare. My mind is with the Lord, and every day is a Sabbath with me. Here B. T., who was a great Churchman, after hearing F. G. a second time, was seized with conviction on his way home, and fell down in the road, and spent great part of the night crying to God for mercy. It was suggested to him that his house was on fire; his answer was, "It is better for me to lose my house than my soul."

VIRGINIA.—*Sunday*, 31. We rose early, and rode twenty miles to Downing's. I lectured at Burton's in the evening.

Monday, November 1. After riding twenty miles to Col. Paramore's, I preached with liberty. The family is kind; the father, mother, son, and niece have tender impressions. The people hereabout are gay, blind in spiritual matters, wellfeatured, and hospitable, and good livers.

Tuesday, 2. After preaching at Garrettson chapel, I rode to Col. Burton's, and was kindly received.

Friday, 5. I came back to Col. Burton's. Since I went from this house, I have ridden about one hundred miles, spent five hours in delivering five public discourses, and ten hours in family and public prayer, and read two hundred pages in Young's Works. I have enjoyed great peace, and hope to see a great and glorious work.

The Presbyterians came down here about thirty years ago; many were moved, and some advances were made towards a reformation. A house was built for public worship. About six years past the Baptists visited these parts, and there was some stir among the people. I think the Methodists are most likely to have permanent success, because the inhabitants are generally Episcopalians. We preached some time before any regular circuit was formed, or any people had joined us; now brother Willis is stationed here, and there are one hundred in society.

The land here is low and level, and is refreshed with fine breezes from the sea; there is an abundance in the productions of the earth and of the waters; the people are generous, social, and polished in their manners.

Saturday, 6. Came to Downing's, and had a large congregation for the time and place. I see a difficulty in saying anything of any denomination of people—it is so much like evil speaking to mention their faults behind their backs: I will avoid it, and endeavour to prevent others doing it in my presence.

MARYLAND.—*Sunday*, 7. I rode twelve miles to Snow-Hill. Here the judge himself opened the court-house, and a large congregation of people of different denominations attended: the subject was the certainty, universality, and justice of God's proceeding at the day of judgment.

Sunday, 14. I came to Barratt's chapel: here, to my great joy, I met these dear men of God, Dr. Coke, and Richard Whatcoat; we were greatly comforted together. The Doctor preached on "Christ our wisdom, righteousness, sanctification, and redemption." Having had no opportunity of conversing with them before public worship, I was greatly surprised to see brother Whatcoat assist by taking the cup in the administration of the sacrament. I was shocked when first informed of the intention of these my brethren in coming to this country: it may be of

God. My answer then was, if the preachers unanimously choose me, I shall not act in the capacity I have hitherto done by Mr. Wesley's appointment. The design of organizing the Methodists into an Independent Episcopal Church, was opened to the preachers present, and it was agreed to call a general conference, to meet at Baltimore the ensuing Christmas; as also that brother Garrettson go off to Virginia to give notice thereof to our brethren in the south.

DELAWARE.—I was very desirous the Doctor should go upon the track I had just been over, which he accordingly did. I came to Dover, and preached on Eph. v, 6; was close, and, I hope, profitable.

MARYLAND.—*Tuesday*, 16. Rode to Bohemia, where I met with Thomas Vasey, who came over with the Doctor and R. Whatcoat. My soul is deeply engaged with God to know his will in this new business.

Wednesday, 17. Rode to quarterly meeting at Deer-Creek; thence, by Mr. Gough's, to Baltimore. I preached in the evening to a solemn people, on, "O wicked man, thou shalt surely die:" about the ending of the sermon the floor of the house gave way, but no injury followed.

Tuesday, 23. We rode twenty miles to Frederick quarterly meeting, where brother Vasey preached on, "The Lord is my Shepherd; I shall not want." Our love-feast was attended with the power and presence of God. Leaving Frederick, I went to Calvert quarterly meeting. Brother Poythress and myself had much talk about the new plan. At our quarterly meeting we had a good time; the love-feast was in great life and power. I admire the work of God among the coloured people in these parts.

Friday, 26. I observed this day as a day of fasting and prayer, that I might know the will of God in the matter that is shortly to come before our conference; the preachers and people seem to be much pleased with the projected plan; I myself am led to think it is of the Lord. I am not tickled with the honour to be gained—I see danger in the way. My soul waits upon God. O that he may lead us in the way we should go! Part of my time is, and must necessarily be, taken up with preparing for the conference.

Tuesday, 30. I preached with enlargement to rich and poor, on, "That we may have boldness in the day of judgment." The Lord has done great things for these people. The Rev. M. W——s and myself had an interesting conversation on the subject of the Episcopal mode of Church-government. I spent the evening with D. Weems, and spoke to the black people.

Saturday, December 4. Rode to Baltimore, and preached on Mark xiv, 29, 30, with freedom. I spent some time in town, and was greatly grieved at the barrenness of the people; they appear to be swallowed up with the cares of the world.

Sunday, 12. At the Point my heart was made to feel for the people, while I enlarged on, "Blessed are the pure in heart," &c. I was close and fervent in town at four o'clock. A young man pushed the door open while we were meeting the society; he was carried before a justice of the peace, and committed to jail, but he was bailed out.

Tuesday, 14. I met Dr. Coke at Abingdon, Mr. Richard Dallam kindly taking him there in his coach; he preached on, "He that hath the Son hath life." We talked of our concerns in great love.

Wednesday, 15. My soul was much blest at the communion, where I believe all were more or less engaged with God. I feel it necessary daily to give up my own will. The Dr. preached a great sermon on, "He that loveth father or mother more than me," &c.

Saturday, 18. Spent the day at Perry-Hall, partly in preparing for conference. My intervals of time I passed in reading the third volume of the British Arminian Magazine. Continued at Perry-Hall until *Friday*, the twenty-fourth. We then rode to Baltimore, where we met a few preachers: it was agreed to form ourselves into an Episcopal Church, and to have superintendents, elders, and deacons. When the conference was seated, Dr. Coke and myself were unanimously elected to the superintendency of the Church, and my ordination followed, after being previously ordained deacon and elder, as by the following certificate may be seen.

Know all men by these presents, That I, Thomas Coke, Doctor of Civil Law; late of Jesus College, in the University of Oxford, Presbyter of the Church of England, and Superintendent of the Methodist Episcopal Church in America; under the protection of Almighty God, and with a single eye to his glory; by the imposition of my hands, and prayer, (being assisted by two ordained elders,) did on the twenty-fifth day of this month, December, set apart Francis Asbury for the office of a deacon in the aforesaid Methodist Episcopal Church. And also on the twenty-sixth day of the said month, did by the imposition of my hands, and prayer, (being assisted by the said elders,) set apart the said Francis Asbury for the office of elder in the said Methodist Episcopal Church. And on this twenty-seventh day of the said month, being the day of the date hereof, have, by the imposition of my hands, and prayer, (being assisted by the said elders,) set apart the said Francis Asbury for the office of a superintendent in the said Methodist Episcopal Church, a man whom I judge to be well qualified for that great work. And I do hereby recommend him to all whom it may concern, as a fit person to preside over the flock of Christ. In testimony whereof I have here-unto set my hand and seal this twenty-seventh day of December, in the year of our Lord 1784.   THOMAS COKE.

3

The Catholics

JOHN CARROLL

Addresses

THE ESTABLISHMENT OF THE CATHOLIC RELIGION IN THE UNITED STATES [1790]

Towards the end of the reign of James I. king of England, who died in 1625, the Catholics, oppressed by the penal laws of that kingdom, sought afar an asylum from the persecution which they suffered at home. Lord Baltimore, a Catholic, obtained from the king a grant of all those lands which now form the State of Maryland. This grant was confirmed to him by a charter issued in form immediately after the accession of Charles I. to the throne of his father. By this same charter, the king granted to all who should emigrate to the new Province, the liberty of exercising their religion, and the rights of citizens. A great number of Catholics, and especially the descendants of ancient families, quitted England, and settled in America, towards the year 1630, under the conduct of Lord Baltimore. With them came Father Peter White, an English Jesuit. This band of emigrants chose for their residence a district of country near the junction of the Potomac and St. Mary's river: the latter afterwards gave its name to the first town that was built there, and which continued to be in the capital of the country, during seventy or eighty years.

Father White, finding himself unequal to the duties which pressed upon him, returned to Europe, in order to procure missionaries: and, from the very imperfect memoirs before me, it appears, that he brought over with him Fathers Copley, Harkey and Perret. Their principal residence was a place which they called St. *Inigo*, a Spanish word which signifies Ignatius. They acquired there a considerable tract of land, a part of which is still in the possession of the Jesuits.

All historians, Protestant as well as Catholic, speak, in favourable terms, of the first Catholic emigrants, who faithfully observed the laws of justice, and by their humane deportment, gained the confidence of the Indians. Not an inch of land did they take by violence from the aboriginal inhabitants: but they purchased a large district, and honourably confined themselves within the limits traced out in the charter, insomuch that neither fraud nor bloodshed disgraced the birth of this rising colony.

In proportion as it increased, (and its progress was rapid,) the heads of the establishment advanced into the country, accompanied by some clergymen; who, for their subsistence, and that of their successors, made several acquisitions of lands.

Towards the year 1640, a design was formed to carry the Gospel to the Indians of the neighbouring parts. In the MS. which was lent me, I find, that the Provincial of the Jesuits wrote, this year, to the young men at Liege, exhorting them to consecrate their services to this difficult and perilous enterprise. In consequence of this invitation, more than twenty requested, in urgent language, to be associated in the new mission: but, from what I can learn from contemporary monuments, it does not appear that they ever crossed the ocean: prevented, in all probability, by the influence of the Protestants who inhabited the district of Virginia; and who saw, with a jealous eye, the incomparably better understanding that existed between the Catholics and the Indians, than between themselves and the tribes around them. Add to this the troubles which arose, the same year, (1640,) in England, and ended in the deposition and decapitation of Charles I. in 1649. The incredible hatred which the dominant party of that kingdom entertained against the Catholics, and the umbrage which was taken by the factious, at any enterprise that could further the promotion of the Catholic Religion, rendered it necessary for the emigrants to break off all communication with the Indians.

As long as Cromwell was in power, the Catholics of Maryland were cruelly harassed: Lord Baltimore was removed from the government, the Catholics were excluded from all offices of trust which they had held before, and the clergy were reduced to the necessity of exercising their functions in secret, and with great circumspection.

From this epoch, I cannot discover any steps taken to diffuse the knowledge of the Gospel among the Indians. Before the death of Cromwell, it is probable that they removed into the interior to a very great distance, and in Maryland, there were hardly clergymen enough to discharge the duties towards the Catholics. The power and influence of the Protestants, supported by the English government, and favoured by the colonies that surrounded them, had greatly increased: and the jealousy, formerly occasioned on the part of the Catholics by their correspondence with the Indians, was still alive.

After the restoration of Charles the Second, Maryland again flourished under the genial government of Lord Baltimore, and his representatives. Pious establishments were formed, and the clergymen were scattered through the different sections of the province. They subsisted not on the contributions of the faithful, but on the products of the lands which they had obtained.

But after the revolution which followed in England, the Catholics were again deprived of public offices, and of the exercise of their religion, contrary to the privileges granted in their charter.

In consequence of this intolerance, Lord Baltimore would again have been stript of his authority, had he not unfortunately yielded to the times, and conformed to the Protestant religion. From this era, a tax was levied on all the colonists without distinction, for the support of the ministers of the Anglican Church. Many attempts were made to enforce the penal laws; and if they were not generally carried into execution, but only in certain places, and that, too, at intervals, it was, according to all appearances, less through a spirit of toleration, than through policy. The most distinguished families, impatient of the restrictions, and induced, perhaps, by the example of Lord Baltimore, forsook the Catholic Church. By this means, the Protestant party became strengthened: the seat of government was transferred from St. Mary's to Annapolis, where the Protestants were more numerous: and the Catholics, oppressed and persecuted, were reduced to poverty and contempt.

Notwithstanding these misfortunes, several congregations existed in the province, with resident priests; and others, which were occasionally visited by the missionaries. But they were so removed and dispersed, that a great number of families could not assist at mass, and receive instructions, but once in the month: and though pains were taken by the pious heads of families to instruct their children, it must have been done but imperfectly. Among the poor, many could not read, and those who could, were without books, to procure which it was necessary to send to England: and the laws against printers and sellers of Catholic books were extremely rigorous. It is surprising that, notwithstanding all these difficulties, there were still so many Catholics in Maryland who were regular in their habits, and at peace with all their neighbours. The propriety of their conduct was a subject of edification to all, and continued to be so, until the new emigrants from foreign parts introduced a licentiousness of manners, which exposed the Catholic Religion to the reproach of its enemies.

Near the residences of the clergy, and on the lands belonging to them, small chapels were built, but few elsewhere: so that it was necessary to say mass in private houses. The people contributed nothing towards the expenses of the clergy, who, poor as they were, had to provide for their own support, for the decoration, &c. of the altars, and for their travels from place to place. They demanded nothing, as long as the produce of their lands could suffice for their maintainance.

Towards the year 1730, Father Grayton, a Jesuit, (all the clergymen, it should be remarked, who laboured in the colonies, were Jesuits), went from Maryland to Philadelphia, and laid the foundation of the Catholic religion in that city. He resided there until the year 1750. Long before his death, he built the chapel near the presbytery (St. Joseph's) and formed a numerous congregation, which has continued to increase to the present day. "I remember," said Archbishop Carroll, whose language I here use, "to have seen, in 1748, that venerable man, at the head of his flock."

He was succeeded by Father [Robert] Harding, whose memory is still in benediction in that city: and under whose auspices, and the untiring energies of whose zeal, the beautiful Church of St. Mary's was erected.

In the year 1741, two German Jesuits were sent to Pennsylvania, for the purpose of instructing the German Emigrants who has settled in that province. These were Father [Theodore] Schneider, a Bavarian, and Father [William] Wap[p]eler, a Hollander, men full of zeal and prudence. The former was particularly gifted with a talent for business, and possessed, says the MS. before me, "consummate prudence and intrepid courage." The latter, after having laboured eight years in America, during which he converted many, was, in consequence of his bad health, constrained to return to Europe. He was the founder of the establishment now called *Conewago*. Father Schneider formed several congregations in Pennsylvania, built the Church at *Cosenhopen*, and propagated the Catholic religion around that country. Every month, he visited the Germans who lived in Philadelphia, until the time when he judged it expedient to establish a resident German Priest in that city. The gentleman chosen to fill that post, was the Reverend Father Farmer, a distinguished and highly respected personage, who, some years before, had arrived in America, and been stationed at Lancaster, where his life was truly apostolical. It was about the year 1760, that he took possession of his new appointment. "No one can be ignorant," remarks my MS. "of the labours which were undergone by this servant of God." His memory is in veneration among all who knew him, or have heard of his merit. He continued to be a model for all succeeding Pastors, until his death, which occurred in 1786.

In 1776, the American Independence was declared, and a revolution effected, not only in political affairs, but also in those relating to Religion. For while the thirteen provinces of North America rejected the yoke of England, they proclaimed, at the same time, freedom of conscience, and the right of worshipping the Almighty, according to the spirit of the religion to which each one should belong. Before this great event, the Catholic faith had penetrated into two provinces only, viz. Maryland and Pennsylvania. In all the others the laws against the Catholics were in force. Any Priest coming from foreign parts, was subject to the penalty of death; all who professed the Catholic faith, were not merely excluded from offices of government, but could hardly be tolerated in a private capacity. While this state of things continued, it is not surprising that but very few of them settled in those provinces: and they, for the most part, forsook their religion. Even in Maryland and Pennsylvania, as was before mentioned, the Catholics were oppressed: the missionaries were insufficient for the wants of those two provinces, and it was next to impossible to disseminate the faith beyond their boundaries.

By the declaration of independence, every difficulty was removed: the Catholics were placed on a level with their fellow-christians, and every political disqualification was done away.

Several reasons are assigned in the MS. for the immediate adoption of the article, extending to all the members of the States, an unqualified freedom of conscience.

I. The leading characters of the first assembly, or Congress, were, through principle, opposed to every thing like vexation on the score of Religion: and, as they were perfectly acquainted with the maxims of the Catholics, they saw the injustice of persecuting them for adhering to their doctrines.

II. The Catholics evinced a desire, not less ardent than that of the Protestants, to render the provinces independent of the mother country: and, it was manifest, that, if they joined the common cause, and exposed themselves to the common danger, they should be entitled to a participation in the common blessings which crowned their efforts.

III. France was negotiating an alliance with the United Provinces: and nothing could have retarded the progress of that alliance more effectually, than the demonstration of any ill-will against the religion which France professed.

IV. The aid, or at least the neutrality of Canada was judged necessary for the success of the enterprise of the Provinces: and by placing the Catholics on a level with all other christians, the Canadians, it was believed, could not but be favourably disposed towards the revolution.

It was not till after the war, that the good effects of freedom of conscience began to develop themselves. The Priests were few in number, and, almost all superannuated. There was but little communication between the Catholics of America, and their Bishop, the Vicar apostolic of the district of London, on whose spiritual jurisdiction they were dependent. But, whether he did not wish to have any relation to a people whom he regarded in the light of rebels; or whether it was owing, says my old MS., to the natural apathy of his disposition, it is certain, that he had hardly any communication either with the Priests, or the laity, on this side of the Atlantic. Anteriourly to the declaration of Independence, he had appointed the Rev. Mr. Lewis, his vicar; and it was this gentleman who governed the mission of America, during the time that the Bishop remained inactive.

Shortly after the war, the Clergy of Maryland and of Pennsylvania, convinced of the necessity of having a superior on the spot, and knowing, too, that the United States were opposed to any jurisdiction in England, applied to the Holy See, to grant them the privilege of choosing a superior from their own body. The request was acceded to: and their unanimous suffrages centred in the Rev. John Carroll, whose election was approved by the Holy See, and on whom ample power, even that of administering Confirmation, was immediately conferred.

The number of Catholics, at this period, in Maryland, amounted to about sixteen thousand: the greater part of whom were dispersed through the country, and employed in agriculture. In Pennsylvania, there were about seven thousand, and in the other States, as far as it was possible to ascertain, there were about fifteen hundred. In this number, however, were not comprised the Canadians, or French, or their descendants, who inhabited the country to the west of the Ohio, and the banks of the Mississippi.

In Maryland the Priests were nineteen in number: in Pennsylvania but five. Of these, five were worn out with infirmities and age, and the rest were advanced in years. None, except those in Baltimore and Philadelphia, subsisted on the contributions of their flocks.

AN ADDRESS FROM THE ROMAN CATHOLICS OF AMERICA
TO GEORGE WASHINGTON, ESQ. PRESIDENT OF THE UNITED STATES

London: M,DCC,XC.

[Preface] THE following Address from the Roman Catholics, which was copied from the American News papers,—whilst it breathes fidelity to the States which protect them, asserts, with decency, the common rights of mankind; and the answer of the President truly merits that esteem, which his liberal sentiments, mild administration, and prudent justice have obtained him.—Under his sanction an Academy is founded and funded.—The wisdom and policy of the measure is resplendent.—At home may be obtained that which our Nation obliges us to seek in foreign climes at a vast expence.—It is governed by a Roman Catholic Bishop, (Dr. John Carroll) a Protestant Divine, and a Dissenting Minister;—they live in harmony;—the discipline, with calm moderation, yet exactness, is duly kept up;—and the students succeed.—A profusion of polite knowledge—Law—Physic, &c. is the prospect of this infant undertaking.—There are to be Schools for Divinity.— Presidents and Professors through the range of Nations are sought;—they must excel, or they will not have the appointment.—Whilst others exclude the Monastic—the Religious life,—America invites to, and throws open her asylum.—The Dominicans and the Capuchins have commenced on that Mission.—And so late as April, 1790, a Colony of Tersian Nuns, under the Abbess of Hoogstreat,—an English Lady superiorly distinguished for accomplishments and piety, has left that Cloister, with permission, and the promise of subjects ready to join her, with protection from the State, and the prospect of establishing another in Philadelphia; where beside the religious observance of her Rule she has been solicited to adopt the tuition of their daughters,—Two Priests, the one was Confessor to the English Dames at Brussels, the other at Antwerp, have accompanied our courageous country women in their perilous voyage and laborious undertaking.

Is this not a lesson?—Britons remain intolerant and inexorable to the claims of sound policy and of nature. Ties of kindred and friends,—whose sacred aspiration—Alas! To NOMINAL LIBERTY, suffers the fettering sanguinary edicts still to blacken her golden aeras,—exile some of her most valuable subjects, and divide their interests, or force their religious compliance to disguise and debase principles, which, if suffered to practise, would constitute and confirm the most lasting affection to their Prince and the country which give them birth.—Is it true policy, that the Roman Catholics should become voluntary exiles for the free practise of their faith—to educate their children,—to study for their ministry,—or retire to their sacred Cloister?—and this only to serve God in their own way,—not a different God, but adored equally by all! Whilst it is an acknowledged fact, there are laws sufficient to make men, good citizens and good subjects,—where is the boasted liberty which suffers not a disposall of ourselves, but aims so effectually to shackle and annihilate the sould from God.—Britons, view and blush!

THE ADDRESS OF THE ROMAN CATHOLICS
TO GEORGE WASHINGTON, ESQ.
PRESIDENT OF THE UNITED STATES. SIR,

WE have been long impatient to testify our joy, and un-
bounded confidence on your being called, by an Unanimous
Vote, to the first station of a country, in which that unanimity
could not have been obtained, without the previous merit of
unexampled services, of eminent wisdom, and unblemished
virtue. Our congratulations have not reached you sooner, because our scattered situation prevented our communication,
and the collecting of those sentiments, which warmed every
breast. But the delay has furnished us with the opportunity, not
merely of presaging the happiness to be expected under your
Administration, but of bearing testimony to that which we
experience already. It is your peculiar talent, in war and in
peace, to afford security to those who commit their protection
into your hands. In war you shield them from the ravages of
armed hostility; in peace, you establish public tranquility, by
the justice and moderation, not less than by the vigour, of your
government. By example, as well as by vigilance, you extend
the influence of laws on the manners of our fellow-citizens. You
encourage respect for religion; and inculcate, by words and
actions, that principle, on which the welfare of nations so much
depends, that a superintending providence governs the events
of the world, and watches over the conduct of men. Your exalted
maxims, and unwearied attention to the moral and physical
improvement of our country, have produced already the happiest effects. Under your administration, America is animated
with zeal for the attainment and encouragement of useful literature. She improves her agriculture; extends her commerce; and

acquires with foreign nations a dignity unknown to her before. From these happy events, in which none can feel a warmer interest than ourselves, we derive additional pleasure, by recollecting that you, Sir, have been the principal instrument to effect so rapid a change in our political situation. This prospect of national prosperity is peculiarly pleasing to us, on another account; because, whilst our country preserves her freedom and independence, we shall have a well founded title to claim from her justice, the equal rights of citizenship, as the price of our blood spilt under your eyes, and of our common exertions for her defence, under your auspicious conduct—rights rendered more dear to us by the remembrance of former hardships. When we pray for the preservation of them, where they have been granted—and expect the full extension of them from the justice of those States, which still restrict them;—when we solicit the protection of Heaven over our common country, we neither omit, nor can omit recommending your preservation to the singular care of Divine Providence; because we conceive that no human means are so available to promote the welfare of the United States, as the prolongation of your health and life, in which are included the energy of your example, the wisdom of your counsels, and the persuasive eloquence of your virtues. John Carroll, In behalf of the Roman Catholic Clergy. Charles Carroll, of Carrollton, Daniel Carroll, Dominick Lynch, Thomas Fitzsimmons. In behalf of the Roman Catholic Laity.

4

The Frontier Baptists

The "Religious Experience"
of a Candidate for the Ministry
as Related Before the Church

I was the subject of religious impressions when quite young. I recollect that while attending a Sabbath School the Summer after I was 8 years old, my mind was considerably exercised on the subject, particularly while reading the Darymans Daughter, a tract which I received at S. S. I thought that I too was a sinner, & could not expect to die the happy death which this little girl did, except I become a Christian. From these impressions I made some resolutions, that I would try to become a Christian, at least, before I was very old. I would frequently try to pray before I went to sleep at night; but rarely tried to pray in the morning. Thus it is evident that it was not from any love to prayer that I prayed; but from a consciousness of guilt & a fear of being punished. But these serious impressions lasted but a short time: I soon left off trying to pray entirely. Thus early did my Heavenly Father begin to call after, & admonish his disobedient, & refractory child; and thus early did the native enmity of my heart to God, begin to be manifest. But thro' abounding mercy other means were employed to remind me of my duty to God. My dear Mother would frequently talk to me on the subject of religion & sometimes pray with me—at those seasons my conscience was tender—and not unfrequently after hearing a sermon or being at a prayer-meeting, was my mind considerably impressed. If I recollect the spring after I was 13 years old there was an extensive revival of Religion in (the) (Town) Lowville the Town where I then resided. I recollect on one Sabbath, my Parents having both gone to Meeting, being alone I employed myself in reading the Bp. Magazine, which my Father then took, I read in that, a Sermon or Newyears address written by the editor, from these words 'This year thou shalt die;' My mind was arrested.—I gave it a second reading. I saw that I was exposed to Death every moment—that I was unprepared to die. I believed that except I became a Christian I must be lost forever. My mind was now more deeply impressed than at any time previous. I made new resolutions—resumed the habit of trying to pray, hoping that I should yet become a Christian. I was the subject of similar exercises for several months 'till at length I lost nearly all of them, & became almost thoughtless on the subject of my soul's Salvation; except when some alarming Providence awoke in me a little sense of my danger for a few moments.

But O the loveing kindness & forbearance of God towards this chief of sinners! The rejected, grieved, Spirit did not take its everlasting flight! In the Spring after I was 18, in the year 1831 I became again the subject of its strivings. My mind was not at rest—My Mother & others exorted me to repent & prayed for me. This seemed to probe the wound which I felt, deeper. There was about to be a protracted Meeting in the Bp. Ch. near where I lived. I secretly hoped that I might become a Christian before the Meeting terminated, and at the same time resolve to keep it to myself—that no one should know any thing of my exercises. Such were my selfish, incorrect, views of the Religion of Christ at that time.

When mingling with my associates I affected an entire indifference on the subject; but when alone the faithful admonitions of conscience gave me no rest. It seemed to me that every day my heart was growing harder wickeder instead of better. I began to be alarmed for fear that God would justly give me up to hardness of heart & reprobate mind. The anticipated Meeting commenced—An aged Minister conversed with me, on the subject of my soul's Salvation, very affectionately but pointedly. I felt the truth of what he said. And faithfully exorted me to repenance; and says he, 'if you live to get home, on your knees before God read the 1st Chap. of Prov and the 3^d of John. I did. I was now more deeply convicted of my self as a sinner against God. My feelings were pungent, yet I strove to conceal them from my friends. For some days my feelings were various—I saw that I was indeed a great sinner, but I was too proud to become a disciple of Christ. Sometimes I sought relief in trying to banish the whole from my mind; and then trembled for fear of being left to perish and would pray for conviction in my sins. At other times my mind was filled with Infidel principles—one evening at Meeting, I requested the prayers of Christians by saying, *if* there is a reality in religion, I wish Christians to pray for me. No sooner had I sat down, than a sense of this awful sin of unbelief seemed to roll in upon my soul with a mountains weight. I began to think that I was too great a sinner to receive pardon—it seemed that *my* sins were the most agrivating—I had sinned against light—had long been resisting the strivings of God's Holy Spirit—and was now questioning the reality of the holy religion of Jesus Christ. The next eve' (Sabbath eve) I arose in public & *begged* prayers of Christians expressing, as well as I could, my feelings. Several christians united in fervent prayer in my behalf & I tried to pray for myself. Nothing but the Blood of Christ seemed to be between me & (Death) hell.—This evening the meeting closed—I arose early in the morning with this fixed resolution—to make the Salvation of my Soul, the chief business of my life—that if I perished I would perish at the feet of Jesus,—praying for mercy, & Salvation for His sake. It seemed to me perfectly reasonable that I should love & serve

God with all my heart; and If I did love and serve Him, all my life I should do no more than was my duty to do.—Arrangements had been made that I should spend a few months with Mr. A. Waters a member of the Bp. Ch. (and now a successful Minister of Christ's Gospel). My younger Brother went with me. On my way I told him what my resolutions were; and exhorted him not to put off the Salvation of his Soul, till he become so great a sinner as I was. During the day Mr. Waters conversed with me on the subject of religion. I told him what my feelings were and begged his prayers in my behalf. My mind remained about the same till Wednesday, when I was on the borders of despair—every sin that I had committed, seemed agravating enough to sink me to hell—O how I had treated the Lord Jesus!—I was ploughing—I stoped my team,—and resolved to try again to cast my soul, my wicked heart, my all, just as I was, upon the Mercy of Christ whom I had so much abused—I tried to pray—and it was Lord save or I perish!—with strong cryings and tears. But to my astonishment I soon forgot the urgency of *my* case, and was praying for the Spread of the Redeemers kingdom, and for the Salvation of others. In my urgency in prayer I had unconsciously lost those feelings which were near dispare. This alarmed me. I feared that God had left me—I tried to pray for conviction, but could not realise those painful feelings which I had felt. My sins looked very sinful; but I could not be distressed about them as I had been. The life of the Christian looked reasonable, and delightful. And I felt determined to love & serve God to the extent of my ability. I dare not indulge the least hope that I was a christian, lest I should be deceived. The State of my mind remained much the same during the rest of the week. On the following Sabbath, when a convenient opportunity was offered, I publicly related the state of my mind, and solicited the prayers of the Saints for me. And I trust they did pray for me: for soon my soul was happy in God; and I rejoiced in God my Saviour. I then began to cherish a little hope that I had passed from death unto life;—This was in April 1831. Suffice it to say that in June I related my experience to the Bp.

Ch. in Lowville & Venmark, and was rec'd by Baptism.

Some of my exercises with regard to *preaching the Gospel of my Redeemer*. I have often thought that the very pious and devoted family of Bro Waters, was rendered a great blessing to me. As Br. W. was gone from home much of the time, the duty, of leading in family worship, morning & evening, devolved upon me. This perhaps served to make me more watchful & prayerful, than I otherwise should have been: I also enjoyed their christian instruction. It was good for me to bear the yoke in my youth. Soon after I became a member of the Ch. of Christ, my soul was particularly drawn out in prayer for those who have not the Blessed gospel preached unto them—and that they might speedily hear its joyful sound. I had an opportunity of reading the N. Y. Bp. Regr. which contained much Missionary intelligence. With this, I was, in particular, highly interested, I would look out the Missionary intelligence, first, when I took the paper to read. Often when alone reading the precious Bible, I would exclaim—O what a *Treasure!*—O that those poor heathen enjoyed what I now do!

During the autumn & winter of 1831 I read the life Rev. Samuel Pierce. Memoirs Mrs. Judson with what other Missionary intelligence I could get. Perhaps this served to awake in me this important inquiry:—Lord what wilt thou have me to do? I had become convinced, that every christian, however limited his ability or opportunity, may be useful in his appropriate sphere; and that (the) our Divine Master has an appropriate work in His vineyard, for every one of his disciples to do. I thought that it was realy the desire of my soul to be useful to the utmost extent of my ability. And I began seriously to enquire in what way I could most glorify God; and be most useful in building up the Redeemers kingdom. This was my special prayer—Lord what wilt thou have me to do?—Sometimes I wished that I was competent to instruct the poor heathen Idolitors in the way of Life and Salvation, from the Word of God. I had not long thus enquired what the Lord would have me do; when my mind was arrested with this impression;—

prepare to preach the Gospel—The more I thought and prayed about it the stronger the impression was that I must some time try to preach the Blessed Gospel; and that it was my duty to prepare to preach it. Tho' I had for some time considered the work of Preaching Christ's holy gospel, as a blessed and desirable work, to the man who is called of God to preach it yet, it seemed to me that I could raise a 1000 objections against myself trying to preach it. Tried evade it by excuses—I was, it seemed to me, every way unqualified for it—had no gift for public speaking,—my education was extremely limited—was wholly destitute of means to defray the expense of an education—and above all I lacked a natural ability.—I thought that I could select hundreds of young men that were far better qualified every way than I was. Why is it not their duty to preach the Gospel? At such seasons I was often much distressed and could find peace of mind only by yeilding the point—casting myself wholly upon the Grace of Christ, with the determination, to do what seemed to be present duty to the extent my ability leaving the result with God. In the meantime I commenced going to a district School for the winter. But my mind was not at rest (with regard) in refference to the duty of preaching the Gospel. The work seemed the most delightful one, that I could possibly engage in; were I qualified;—and were I sure that I was called of God to the Work.

I had been careful to keep all my trials, on this subject, to myself. For was fearful that they were the temptations of the Adversary.—On the 12th of Feb. I think, Eld. T. A. Warner, who was pastor of the Ch. asked me, if I had not some exercises of mind, relative to the duty of Preaching the Gospel. I acknowledged to him that I had, and related to him, the trials of my mind on the subject, as well as I could. I recollect, that, in the eve', I was much ashamed to think that I had told him so many of my exercises.

Missionary intelligence was increasingly interesting—my mind dwelt much on the situation of those without the Gospel and the great call for labourers among them. One night in my sleep I thought I was with two Bros. in a cottage with a company of swarthy heathen teaching them now to read, & preaching the gospel of Christ unto them.—It was a heaven to my soul—I awoke—I thought they were the happiest moments of my life. This made some impression on my mind; and I tried to search my heart to see if I was willing to devote my life to such a work. I thought I would joyfully if I could most glorify God in so doing. Soon after this I think I enjoyed more of the sensible presence of God in my soul than ever before; and my mind was more deeply exercised relative to the duty of Preaching Christ. Sometimes when thinking of the destitute portions of the Earth—of the millions who are perishing for the lack of knowledge—I would exclaim weeping, "Lord here am I send me." And at other times a sense of my inability seemed to forbid it entirely.

In April, Br. Calvin Horr related his exercises relative to preaching the Gospel to the Ch. and rec'd. a license.

At this time I was much affected but was not willing to have my exercises known to the Ch.—Soon after I had further conversation with Eld. Warner—asked council of him—he advised me to cherish the impression, & make it a special subject of prayer. I also had an interview with Eld. J. Blodget—an aged Minister in whom I had the most implicit confidence, & to whom I had been to School when quite young; I told him my trials & solicited his advice & prayers. This man of God gave them as freely & affectionately as a Father. He advised me make known my feelings to the Ch.—he thought perhaps it would be a relief to my mind. Eld. Warner concured with him—soon an opportunity was given me to relate to the Ch. my exercises. I did; that I might have their advice & prayers.

I did not feel it my duty to engage immediately in trying to Preach; but that this duty was before me, & that I ought to use every means in my power to qualify me for it. My Brethren advised me to cherish this impression of duty prayerfully, and to be free in exercising my gift in exortation whenever I felt it my duty. Eld. W. advised me to try go to School as soon as I could. My mind was now greatly revived. I resolved to try to do what seemed to be present duty, to the extent of my ability; and to leave the result with God.

I had a great desire to go to school, but my Father needing my labour it was not practicable for me to go.

In the following Spring 1833. My impression of duty was about the same, and my resolutions the same.

My Father told me, that, as I had a desire to acquire an education; he would try to do without my labour, but that he could not give me any encouragement of assistance from him; for he was not able.

(I was 20. Decr 16, 1832) By labouring for one of my neighbours, about 2 months, with the kindness of some brethren & friends; I was enabled to attend a select School 13 weeks.

5

The Disciples of Christ

ALEXANDER CAMPBELL

The Destiny of Our Country

GENTLEMEN:—

No one can really understand any thing, who does not know
something of every thing. Circles, cycles and centres compose
the machinery of the universe. Suns, moons and stars have their
respective centres, their orbits and their cycles. But there is one
centre that regulates and that governs all other centres; for every
centre is both attractive and radiating. It communicates and it
receives. It supports and is supported. There must, then, be one
self-sustaining centre, and that centre must be forever at rest. It
is both the centre of gravity and the centre of motion. And that
centre is not God himself, for he is everywhere. He is himself a
circle, whose centre is everywhere, and whose circumference is
nowhere.

There is a reason for every thing, if there be any reason in any
thing. Of what use light, if there be not an eye? And of what use
an eye, if there be not light? Creator and creature are correlates.
The one implies the other. There is, therefore, in the human

mind, a necessity for the being and perfections of God. His existence is essential to ours; but our existence is not essential to his. We *are*, because he *was*. Had he not been, we never could have been. We are not self-existent. He must, then, be self-existent; consequently, infinite, eternal and immutable.

But there is in God something passive, as well as something active. A human muscle is passive without a nerve of motion. A nerve of motion is passive without a will; and, therefore, *will*, and will only, is the *primum mobile*—the first cause and the last end of this universe. For God's pleasure, or will, we are and were created.

How much philosophy find we, then, in that beautiful word UNIVERSE! It is a *versus in unum. It is every thing in motion around one thing, which is immovably fixed.* The true centre of gravity is, then, the true centre of motion. But there is not much gravity in a volition. Volitions are very etheral entities. Oh for Ithuriel's spear, to dissect one of them! Oh that we could place ourselves yonder, "where fields of light and liquid ether flow"!

But here we must place ourselves upon an assumption. We do not like that word *assumption*. We shall, therefore, call it a *postulatum*. But its very assertion is its proof. It is this: THE UNIVERSE IS FOUNDED UPON A MORAL IDEA. God did not create the universe because he had wisdom to *design* it. He did not create the universe because he had *power* to create it. For both wisdom and power are passive instruments. Goodness alone is necessarily, eternally, immutably active. It is essentially and perpetually communicative. It is communicative when it radiates and when it attracts. It is the cause of all motion. But for it, nothing would ever have been. The universe is, therefore, a necessary existence. *It must be, because God was.* It must be, because Jehovah was God—the absolute Good One. It is but a temple, in which goodness lives, moves and has its being—its local habitation and its home. For its glory all things are and were created. This, and this only, is physical, intellectual, moral and religious orthodoxy. It is orthodoxy in essence, in form, in substance. It is the philosophy of philosophy, and the religion of religion. It is the immovable centre of all the centres of the universe. And here we place our foot upon the Rock of Ages. Our only postulatum is the *"Rock of Ages."*

Man having been created in the image of God, and cradled in a universe in perpetual motion, his mind is necessarily active. As soon as man begins to think, he begins to construct circles of thought around some perception or idea; and these, according to their specific nature, are formed into what are properly called *systems,* or sciences. He has an ideal *ontology* and a *deontology,* before he knows the meaning of a single word. His primordial conceptions are, first, *being,* then *relation,* then *dependence,* then *duty,* then *pleasure,* then *pain.* These are all arranged before he understands a word or a thing. These are the centres of his thoughts, his volitions and his actions. But he is surrounded by bad teachers, and has a fallen and, consequently, a shattered constitution. He is passive, and easily led astray. His mind is perverted by bad teachers and bad associations. He soon finds himself in error, and sets about correcting it. He again finds an error in his mode of correcting it; and so the conflict between truth and error, good and evil, begins long before he knows any one thing. This is an inherent calamity, consequent upon an ancestral catastrophe.

He is necessarily obliged to classify perceptions, reflections, volitions, actions and their consequences. He is born with a pope in his stomach, and that is a very indigestible substance. Hence the dogmatism of children, simpletons and charlatans. Of these *big children* we have yet a sample in every family of science. I say *family of science,* for these families have grown and multiplied, and replenished the whole earth. Our great-great-grandfathers had but *seven* sciences—the number of perfection. But we have seventy sciences; and yet we want another. With the great Hooker, we will say, that "no science doth make known the first principles on which it buildeth." But in this age of progress, any art, or species of knowledge, is called a *science.* Any one *specific* idea may become the centre of a science. Indeed, we have, without knowing it, been moving forward to a new nomenclature on the grand subject of sciences, sects and schisms, in all the knowledges of earth, of time, of the universe. The time may come, if it be not already come, when every generic and specific idea shall become the foundation of a science, a sect, a party and a school. Take the following words—*Papist, Protestant, Episcopalian, Presbyterian, Congregationalist, Methodist, Baptist, Monarchist, Aristocrat, Democrat,* &c. Does not each one of these terms indicate one specific idea? And is not that one idea, to all within its circle, a centre of attraction, and to all beyond it, a centre of repulsion?

General assemblies, synods, diets, councils, conventions, &c. are constituted, held and perpetuated upon the sub-basis of one idea, which is the one only essential and differential attribute or idea of the school or party. These ought to be styled the centripetal and centrifugal ideas of all bodies. They are the souls of all ecclesiastical and political corporations. Not one of these bodies has two souls, nor any of these souls two bodies. And just at this corner, this *punctum saliens,* I place my Jacob's staff on every survey I make of the ecclesiastical and political plantations in our beloved country.

The body of a democrat differs but in a few accidents from the body of an aristocrat. The essential difference is in their souls. This idea is the living, moving, acting, essential idea which gives them animation, name, action and reaction.

There is but a paper wall, say some in Scotland, and some in England, and but one idea inscribed upon it, between prelatic and papal episcopacy. And they retort with equal zeal and evidence, that there is but one idea between episcopacy and the moderator of a general assembly. And the Congregationalist says there is but one idea between Old England and New England Congregationalism and Scotch and English Presbyterianism. And all the umpires on the walls of Zion say Amen! But that one idea—that dear, divine and glorious idea, is as centripetal and centrifugal as the law that guides and compacts the spheres of the natural universe. We place it upon our armorial—it is inscribed upon our flag. Its associations are as dear as life and stronger than death. But further on this subject deponent saith not. My charity hopeth all things, and your charity, my respected auditors, endureth all things. And now for the *destiny* of our divinely favored and beloved country.

Every word I have yet spoken has been spoken with a single reference to our country, our beloved country, and its destiny. Individuals constitute families, families make tribes, tribes constitute nations, nations empires, and empires a world. Nations and empires stand to each other as members of an individual family stand to one another.

A well-developed family is a miniature world. The duties we owe our superiors, inferiors and equals, and the privileges we derive from them in the family circle, contain in them all the elements that enter into all the relations, duties, obligations, rights, privileges, honors and rewards of the most enlarged communities and corporations, civil or ecclesiastic. And as the individual members of a family have each an individual destiny involved in that of the whole family, each individual has also a mission into that family, upon the perfect or imperfect accomplishment of which his own destiny, for good or for evil, for weal or for woe, must inevitably depend. This is a law of reason, a law of experience; and, above all, it is a law of God.

When the God of Israel sold Israel, or sent them into captivity under an Assyrian yoke, he enjoined them by his prophet "to seek the good of the country into which he had caused them to be delivered into captivity," and added, as a reason or motive, "for in the peace thereof you shall enjoy peace." Their condition, at that time, was a very special and peculiar providence; ours is equally so now. That nation had one great idea committed to it for the benefit of the world. It was the unity, spirituality and ubiquity of God. It was his inflexible justice, his immaculate purity and his inviolate truthfulness, as specially the God of the Jews, and generally the God of the whole family of man.

All Christendom has its special condition, and its special commission into the world. In this designation we comprehend the Greek, the Roman and the Protestant States of Europe, in whatever country or of whatever language. Their mission is very different from that of God's ancient people, the Jews. Polytheism was the damning sin of Pagandom. Gods many, created by the human imagination, against one only living and true God, was their apostasy and their ruin. Polytheism never winked at, and polygamy merely tolerated in certain cases, became the fountains of iniquity, injustice and inhumanity, during the patriarchal and Jewish epocha of the world. Christianity, the consummation of Divine wisdom and benevolence, at a proper period of human experience, at the manhood of the world, was introduced, and gradually and gloriously developed and confirmed. It was not a mere *family* religion, like the Patriarchal, nor was it a mere *national* religion, as the Jewish. It was *œcumenical,* or universal. It recognized neither Jew nor Greek, neither Barbarian nor Scythian, neither bond nor free, neither male nor female; but made the same gracious tender of remission, justification, reconciliation, adoption and glorification, on the principle of sovereign favor, through the absolute merit of the sacrifice of the great Redeemer, and through the sanctification of the Holy Spirit, who, on the formation of the Church of Christ, became its *Holy Guest.*

As the admission of many gods constituted the damning sin of the Patriarchal and Jewish ages of the world, so the introduction of many mediators, many altars, priests and sacrifices, constitutes the damning sin under the benignant reign of grace, usually styled the Remedial Dispensation. And thus we approach the destiny of our country. But there is yet another step.

The Popedom, in its long, dark despotism over Europe and Asia, took away the key of knowledge from the Christian Church, read prayers in an unknown tongue, substituted for Christian ordinances unmeaning and idle ceremonies, consecrated relics, erected holy crosses, hallowed forbidden altars, mitred their priests, girdled a representative of Peter with the keys of paradise, handed to the priests alone the golden chalice of their spiritually medicated wine, established an empty ceremonial, paganized Christian doctrine through an empty and deceitful philosophy, and with unblushing effrontery prated against the dangers of thinking for one's self, of liberty of speech and freedom of action. Thus was consummated the long, dark night of Papal supremacy, during which the immortal Luther was born.

Protestantism was the legitimate consummation of Lutheranism. Yet had it not been for the threatening attitude of the Turks, Charles the Fifth would not have called a diet at Speyer, A.D. 1529, to ask help from the German princes; and had not Ferdinand, Archduke of Austria, and other Popish princes in this diet, decreed that in the countries in which Luther's views had been received, they should be merely tolerated till a general council could meet, and that during the interval no Roman Catholic should be allowed to turn Lutheran, in other words, to think differently from Archduke Ferdinand, and that during the interval the Reformers should not attack the pure and unadulterated doctrine of Popery, Protestantism might never have been born.

Six Lutheran princes and thirteen deputies of imperial towns, solemnly *protested* against this gag law,—this Papal ordinance against thinking or speaking contrary to the dicta of one man and his ecclesiastic advisers. Thus Protestantism was born, and although Lutherans were the first occasion of the decree, Calvinists and all other dissenters—that is, *thinkers* and *talkers* against his infallible excellency—became heirs in common of all the rights, titles, honors and emoluments of the name and style of *Protestants*.

Having given an historical definition of the word *Protestant*, we must form a clear conception of its import. It is neither a Lutheran nor a Calvinist, as such; neither an Arminian nor a Methodist; neither a high church man nor a low church man; neither an Episcopalian nor a Presbyterian, a whig nor a tory, a monarchist nor a republican. It is a mere *generic* term. These are all specific terms. A true and well-defined Protestant might enter his protest against any one and all of these, and be a better Protestant than any one or all of them. A reverend gentleman educated, I think, within these walls, once said to his congregation, "Brethren, there is a *blue*, and a better *blue;* but, brethren, we are the true blue." So there are three degrees of comparison amongst Protestants.

But there are two species of Protestantism. There is ecclesiastic Protestantism, and there is political Protestantism. These, indeed, have more than a chemical affinity.

There are, indeed, three species of Protestantism. There is political, ecclesiastic and spiritual Protestantism. These are the positive, comparative and superlative degrees of an abstract, anomalous noun substantive. At its commencement church and state were so mixed and confounded that there was not a metaphysician in Rome or out of it, that could tell where the state ended and the church began. They had the same geographical and astronomical metes and boundaries. Lands intersected by a narrow frith, or river, hated each other for God's sake and man's sake; for their State polity and their church polity were lodged in the same crazy vessels. In the purest casks of ancient Protestantism, there was a considerable sediment of worldly prudence and temporal policy. But the fierce ordeal and fiery trial of the sixteenth and seventeenth centuries, separated much of the worldly of the times of Luther, and Puritanism began to have a local habitation and a name. The Mayflower ferried over the Atlantic the seeds gathered from the early harvests, the choicest first-fruits of European Protestantism. Brought directly from Old England, they were planted in New England. The soil and climate, however rugged for the germs of earth, were most fertile and happy for the new seeds, and, consequently, rich harvests rewarded the labors of the puritanic husbandmen. God sent them to a new world, that they might institute, under the most favorable circumstances, new political and ecclesiastic institutions. Such, most assuredly, was their Divine mission. Their influence was direct and reflex. It gave life, and vigor, and enterprise to the mother land and those they left behind them, and planted deep and sowed broadcast the seeds of a great, and populous, and mighty empire. England lost at home, but, by her commerce and her missionaries abroad, she planted in the East, the far East, a population and principles homogeneous, more or less, with her American colonies. She became still more Protestant at home and more Protestant abroad. Her canvas whitened every sea, and wherever British power was felt, it might be said, mankind felt her mercies, too. From the days of Luther until now, her throne, her navies and her armed bands, have directly, or indirectly, been the bulwarks of Protestantism. With all her faults, and they are not few nor small, we love her still; because God has been her shield and buckler, her stay and strength. We are her children, and, according to the fifth commandment, we must honor our parents; though, as duteous sons, we may wish that our fathers had been more wise.

But Britain and America are of one paternity, of one religion, of one language and of one destiny. They stood by Luther, by the first Protestants, in the times that tried men's souls; and however occasionally perverted in judgment upon and around the throne, the heart of England has ever sympathized with young America, and with all the Protestant States of Europe. From untold myriads of family altars, morning and evening prayers and praises for young America and her infant institutions, and for infant Protestantism, have ascended into the ears of the Lord of Hosts. Councils of States against England and Protestantism, alliances abroad, armies on the continent, armadas on the seas, and treasons at home, have been thwarted, confounded and annihilated, in answer to her prayers.

To the Saxons in Europe, to the Anglo-Saxons in Britain, to the American Anglo-Saxons on this continent, God has given the sceptre of Judah, the harp of David, the strength of Judah's Lion, and the wealth of the world. He has given to them the oceans of earth, the golden regions of the far West, and the golden regions of the far, far East. California and Australia pour their treasures into their coffers, and Anglo-American arts, and sciences, and language, pervade the earth, and permeate the populations of the civilized world. To Britain and America God has granted the possession of the new world; and because the sun never sets upon our religion, our language and our arts, he has vouchsafed to us, through these sciences and arts, the power that annihilates time and annuls the inconveniences of space. Doubtless these are but preparations for a work which God has in store for us,—a great, a mighty, a stupendous work, that will bring into requisition the arts, the sciences and the resources with which he has so richly, so simultaneously and so marvellously endowed England and America.

There are means to ends, great and small, wisely and irrevocably established in all the cosmical and terrestrial operations, which are perpetually in progress. He gave to the mammoth and the mastodon bones, muscles, nerves, tools, and a covering adapted to their localities and to their work, in their day and generation. He does so still to all the existing species that people earth, or sea, or air. The eagle mounts above the clouds, and Leviathan ploughs the mighty deep, with as much ease as the gossamer constructs her filmy balloon or as the spider weaves his slender web. The beaver builds his dam, and the honeybee constructs his waxen honey-cells, with as much science and art as man displays in his stately palaces or in his golden temples.

Divine providence and moral government equally attest the same power, wisdom and goodness. These, associated with other moral excellencies in the government of the world, as in its creation, to the cultivated mind, with equal assurance, attest his condescending care and providence, in anticipation of all the changing scenes of man's earthly destiny. Coming events cast their shadows before them, while those that have passed away fling their shadows behind them. Hence the value of prophecy and history.

Men of reflection are wont to conceive of their mission into the world from an attentive survey of their own capacities, circumstances and opportunities. It was doubtless intended that it should be so. Hence, individual accountability will depend much on the use every one makes of those endowments, circumstances and opportunities, which the Governor of the world has vouchsafed to him in reference to the country, population and age in which God has located him.

The *kairon gnoothi* of Pittacus, is only second to the *gnoothi seauton* of Solon. To *"know an opportunity,"* is only second in importance to *"know thyself."* He is both a wise and a prudent man, that can combine in his own life and action these two. But should he add to these the oracle of Periander, *meletee to pan*—"nothing is impossible to industry"—he must, if the elements of greatness be in him, become a great man. These, to my taste, the wisest of the wise sayings of the Grecian sages, have, in modern times at least, been more eminently displayed in Britain and in the United States than amongst any other people on earth. And this I ascribe, not so much to soil or climate, or national superiority, or blood, as I do to the fact that these are the lands of Bibles and of Protestantism.

There is a nobility, a moral grandeur of soul, in saying, *I protest against* such a law or statute. To protest innocence, is sometimes just and necessary. To protest *against* political tyranny, is often expedient; but to protest against religious usurpation and ecclesiastic despotism, caps the climax of human nobility and grandeur. And none but Heaven's own noblemen can, *ex animo*, make such a sublime protestation. Hence temporizers, sycophants, aspirants after worldly honor and influence, could not, in the days of Luther, have protested against a Roman pontiff, when all Roman power and grandeur were leagued in favor of Papal aggrandizement and monopoly.

From all my premises, I am compelled to think that there is much of moral grandeur in the very name *Protestant*. There is a moral heroism in non-conformity to unjust laws and unholy requirements for the sake of five barley-loaves and two small fishes. These seven principles and the men who adopt them, will be condemned, now, henceforth and forever, before the bar of enlightened reason, of a generous philanthropy and of a just judgment. It was, in the esteem of Philosopher Locke, a fatal act of uniformity to the English hierarchy, which, on St. Bartholomew's day, ejected two thousand non-conformist ministers, alias uncompromising Protestants, from the national pulpits. Hence, it may be logically inferred that there may be occasionally a hypocrite even among Protestants.

But, in speaking of Protestantism we speak not of a pretended Protestantism, but of a true, real and unsophisticated Protestantism. And what is *Protestantism*, but a solemn negation of all human dictation and usurpation over man's understanding, conscience and affections; over his personal liberty of thought, of speech and of action, in reference to each and every thing pertaining to himself, his fellows, his God and his Redeemer?

Education, religion, morals and politics are, therefore, the fields and realms over which Protestantism, *de jure divino*, presides.

Man's whole destiny in this world is comprehended in these four words, education, religion, morals, and politics. I own the ambiguous use of these four cardinal points of human destiny. Volumes without number have been written, and our shelves are burdened with ponderous folios, quartos, octavos and duodecimos, on each and every one of these great centres of thought. And still they come. Yes, they come, and not in single file, but in platoons, extended wings and hollow squares, terrible as an army with banners. But, under a good intellectual and moral power-press, how meagre their solid contents! If even gold, as Newton affirmed, has more pores than particles, and water forty times more pores than solid parts, how beautifully gaseous must these volumes be!

Education is the development of a man's physical, intellectual and moral constitution; religion, his moral and spiritual obligations to God; morals, his duties and obligations to man; and politics, his duties and obligations to the state, or social compact, in which he lives and moves and has his being. In each and all of these Protestantism affirms he must think, will and act of and from himself, according to the free and unbiassed dictates of his own best thoughts and understanding.

Popery says of this grand principle of human responsibility, of free and voluntary action, of self-government, of merit and demerit, that it is, in essence, impiety, insubordination—a Pandora's box of ills and evils, intolerable and accursed. To Protestants, and in Protestant communities, they exclaim, How gross and infamous this calumny! See how resolutely, boldly and cheerfully *Saint* Carrol, of Maryland, and other distinguished Romanists, took active part in the Revolutionary War; "how they bared their breasts, and shed their generous blood," in support of the cause of American independence! Yes; but was this the real motive? Did they love England less, or Rome more, than American independence? Did they not, in other words, hate England ineffably more than they loved either church or state independence?

On landing in Philadelphia, a day after the commencement of the Revolutionary War, an honest son of the Emerald Isle, on hearing the news, taking his companion by the hand, exclaimed, "By Saint Patrick, Jack, I'll 'list and fight for nothing, for nothing, sir, against old Johnny Bull." He was an unsophisticated exponent of the part taken in the war of the Revolution by Romanists for American independence. It is not possible, or, in other words, it is not in human nature, to love liberty, freedom of thought, of speech and of action, in the state, and to hate it in the church; or to love it in the church and to hate it in the state. The love of liberty is a law or principle as uniform and immutable as the law of gravity. I mean liberty—rational, moral, social liberty; not licentiousness, recklessness, lawlessness. I mean not lust nor passion, the love of plunder and robbery. It is a moral principle, founded upon the perception and approbation of justice and humanity. If a Protestant becomes a tyrant, he is a hypocrite or a freebooter. And if a Romanist becomes a true republican, the *man* has triumphed over his religion, and cares not for it.

Do you think of the French Revolution? Do you say, France was then Catholic, and did she not array her power against tyranny and oppression? If you think so, you are not enlightened, and have never read with discrimination the history of the French Revolution.

Roman Catholicism had converted France into a nation of infidels, seared the national conscience, and inspired the masses with the spirit of murder and rapine. It was vengeance and freebooting, not benevolence and freedom, that erected bastilles and guillotines during the Reign of Terror. France, as a nation, was then infidel. She is so now, and has been so during the whole reign of Napoleon. Spain, Portugal, Italy and Austria, too, in the main, are infidel, much more than Roman Catholic. The whole heart of Popedom is gangrenous. Italy and Rome are but the centre of European infidelity and atheism. Nothing but French cannon and French bayonets has kept Pio Nono in St. Peter's worm-eaten chair. She took the sword, and Messiah's word is pledged that she shall perish by the sword. Be the day near or remote, Rome, eternal Rome, the Rome of the Caesars, the Rome of the Pontiffs, shall be baptized in blood and drenched with the gore of human sacrifice. There are still some names in Sardis that have not received the mark of the beast, and so we humbly hope a remnant may be saved.

But if any one desires to know Roman Catholicism, we advise him to go to Rome or to Paris. View it at home. Did I wish an inhabitant of the mountains of Wales or of Scotland to see our Indian corn in all its mid-summer or autumnal grandeur, should I invite him to the Valley of the Penobscot or to the Valley of the Mississippi, to view it in its glory? As impolitic in any American to judge of Romanism as it appears in New York, in Baltimore, in Cincinnati, in New Orleans, or in Mexico. Let him go to the meridian of St. Peter's, on the banks of the Tiber, and see it at home in all its glory. We ask no more.

That Protestantism is essential to political liberty, is the best-substantiated fact in the annals of European nations.

To Protestant America and Protestant England, young gentlemen, the world must look for its emancipation from the most heartless spiritual despotism that ever disfranchised, enslaved and degraded human kind. This is our special mission into the world as a nation and a people; and for this purpose the Ruler of nations has raised us up and made us the wonder and the admiration of the world.

A nation—a nation great and mighty and prosperous—has been born in a day. Compared with other nations, we have had no childhood. We were born and nurtured and developed in a day, some seventy-five years ago. And now I stand in the midst of the first literary society ever instituted in the immense Valley of the Mississippi. And this, strange to tell, is its fifty-fourth anniversary, and the first semi-centennial anniversary of Jefferson College, under whose generous maternal auspices it has been nurtured and matured.

And what an imposing scene presents itself here to the philosopher and the philanthropist! Here, on the environs of the Monongahela, on whose waters, just eighty years ago, the first white man's cabin was reared and the first Christian hymn was sung amidst the solemn stillness of the deep, dense forests in which, till then, had only echoed the warwhoop and the Indian's yell. The white man, moccasined with his deer-skin boots, wrapped in his hunting-shirt, with a tomahawk suspended from his girdle on his right side, and a scalping-knife, sheathed in a deer-skin scabbard, dangling on his left, with rifle on his shoulder, his faithful dog by his side, sallies forth from his cabin or his fort, at early dawn, and, with cautious step and listening ear, surveys his environs. If neither savage man nor savage beast greets his watchful eye, he grounds his rifle, seizes his axe, and begins to girdle the forest-tree, or, with mattock in hand, engages in grubbing the virgin earth in quest of his daily bread. Gathering courage as he proceeds, day after day the forests bow beneath his sturdy strokes, and an opening is made through which the sun penetrates the newly-opened soil and quickens into life the precious seeds which, with so much parsimony, he had hopefully deposited in the bosom of his mother earth. Thus began, twice forty years ago, the settlements around us. And what a change!

On every side around us, far as the eye can reach, a thousand hills and valleys, waving in rich harvests or covered with green pastures, overspread with bleating flocks of sheep or lowing herds of cattle, interspersed with beautiful villas and romantic hamlets, shaded with venerable oaks, the remains of ancient forests, or enclosed with evergreens of other climes, that vie with each other in lending enchantment to the scenes that environ the homesteads of the rugged pioneers of the great and mighty West, present themselves to our enraptured vision. They are alike the trophies of bold adventure, of successful enterprise, and the imposing evidence of industry, morality and good taste.

And what shall we say of the sons and daughters of those brave and magnanimous pioneers? We are unable to do them justice. The beautiful towns and cities spread all over the new western world, "with glistening spires and pinnacles adorned," pyramidal trophies of industrial art, monuments of generous liberality, piety and good sense, in solemn and majestic silence, speak their praise. Thrones of justice, solemn temples, stately residences, colleges, male and female seminaries, everywhere attest their good taste, their liberality, patriotism and genuine philanthropy.

The Americans very generally seem to have made a new and valuable discovery. They strongly affirm that good mothers make good sons, and that good fathers make good daughters. Hence the prudence and policy of educating both sexes with equal generosity.

Solomon long since discovered that a *man's* wisdom made his face to shine, but went no farther. The Yankees, however—a very shrewd people—with equal clearness discovered that a woman's learning made *her* face to shine with superior lustre. They went to work on this sound theory, and what has been the result? We look around us here and everywhere, on all public occasions, on crowds of ladies whose faces shine with such beauty that it is always dangerous for them to travel abroad unveiled. It is not the lily and the rose that vie with each other for precedence on their fair faces, but it is the sparkling, intellectual eye, the philosophic smile and the graceful assenting nod. So imposing are their charms and their influence, the fascinations of their imagination and the poetry of their manners, that no heart of man is proof against their charms. They have a decided and controlling influence upon all our seminaries of learning for young men. Students in our colleges grow pale over the midnight lamp, and are distilling the nectar of poetry and philosophy from Greek and Roman springs, to render themselves acceptable, in prose and verse, to the refined sensibilities, the chaste imaginations, the good sense and mellifluent eloquence of American ladies in general, and of Western American ladies in particular.

But, gentlemen, I know that you are not insensible to their charms. You are not such stoics or book-worms as not to lay down Plato or Socrates, Newton or Euclid, even Milton or Shakespeare, to hang in profound attention upon their soul-subduing disquisitions, their profound dissertations upon the higher magnetism and centripetal tendencies of the sublimer sentimentalities of their philosophy, which pauses not in the outer court of humanity, but reposes only in the penetralia of the human heart.

We have, young gentlemen, been involuntarily borne away from the plumb and square of a strictly logical address. But even the stars in their courses cannot move in perfect circles. The orbits of all planets are elliptical; and we are all but planets—not wandering stars, I hope, nor meteors of the night.

Your society lacks but twenty days of being fifty-four years old. Your regular members are fourteen hundred and eight, and your honorary members two hundred and twenty-nine; amongst which you have been pleased to place my humble name. In looking over your proper membership, we notice many eminent men, now filling high and important stations in both church and state. Amongst your honorary members we see a constellation of the most dignified and honored names in the annals of our country; men known all over Christendom, pre-eminent in the national executive department, on the bench, in the Cabinet, in the Senate, in the legislative halls and on the field of war. In this great valley, your college will continue to hold in the future, as it has done in the past, a pre-eminent place. Its destiny is not only onward, but upward. Its career will be still more brilliant in the future than it has been in the past. You will not only leave behind you, but you will carry with you in all the walks of life, an influence favorable to its usefulness and its honor.

The cause of education—of rational, moral, philosophical, religious education—is the most transcendent cause in any and every community. On it depend the prosperity, the influence, the honor and the happiness of every state and of every people. It has, therefore, intrinsically, the strongest claims upon the liberality, the fostering care, the aids, the smiles, the prayers and the patronage of both church and state. It is a law of God and it is a law of society, paramount and insuperable, that educated mind shall govern the world. It has done it, it now does it, and it will continue to do it till the last pulse of time, despite the clamors of ignorance and the thunders of the Vatican. How necessary, then, that it be conducted according to the genius of true religion and true humanity! How important that it be founded on the Bible—that great library of heaven, the combined product of four thousand years, the result of the labors of a constellation of forty divinely-inspired men, embracing a period of sixteen centuries, and holding positions the most dignified and honorable amongst men!

Of the one hundred and twenty-one colleges in the United States, ninety have been chartered since Jefferson College. But some thirty colleges are older than it. Of this aggregate, twelve are Roman Catholic. All the others are Protestant, or, what is the same thing, State institutions. Besides these, we have, in the American Union, forty-two theological schools, all Protestant. Romanists have no theological schools. Their colleges being wholly under the influence of their theology and church, they are, upon the whole, more theological than literary, and, more than either, scientific. Protestants, therefore, have the literature, the science and the arts of the country, we may say, exclusively under their direction. The whole literary and theological force of Romanists is, therefore, concentrated in twelve colleges. Indeed, Romanism is their body, soul and spirit. They are sold to the Pope and absolutism. With them, the church and state are one idea. Proportional to their number and their population, they are stronger, richer and more centralized than the Protestant institutions. They are conducted, too, with more secrecy than ours. They are pure crystallizations of self-ishness, and, like all secret societies, more to be feared than to be loved.

Their influence is the only portentous cloud in our horizon. It is seen charged with an electricity ominous to our destiny, because ominous of mischief to liberty of thought, of speech and of action on all the vital interests of such a community as ours. In a community based on universal suffrage, unless that community be enlightened, moral and religious, there is no guaranty of a prosperous and glorious career. A Protestant conscience is essential to political and religious liberty, and as necessarily tends that way as all the rivers of earth ultimately disembogue themselves into the ocean. And a Protestant conscience is the legitimate consequence of Bible literature and Bible institutions.

The star of our destiny is that star which attracted the attention of the Persian Magi, and directed their steps and their offerings to "the new-born King of the Jews," now the King of kings and Lord of lords, "by whom all the kings of the earth do reign, and all the princes thereof do decree justice." Philo-literary institutions, under Protestant colleges, under Protestant auspices, and Bible literature and morals, are the solid sub-basis of a free and an enlightened government, in the church and in the state—the real Jachin and Boaz—the antitypes of the right and left brazen pillars which Solomon reared in the porch of the Temple, to emblazon its solemn and august entrance.

As through our verdant valleys flow the limpid rivulets that make our creeks, our rivers and our seas, on whose bosom float the gallant navies which, under the Stripes and Stars, the symbolic ensign of our nation's destiny, command the respect, the homage and the admiration of all the nations of the earth, so from your literary institutions, and from all similar ones in our colleges, flow those healing streams which swell the rivers that fill the ocean of literature that shall bless the world.

In our country's destiny is involved the destiny of Protestantism, and in its destiny that of all the nations of the world. God has given, in awful charge, to Protestant England and Protestant America—the Anglo-Saxon race—the fortunes, not of Christendom only, but of all the world. For this purpose he has given to them all the great discoveries and improvements in the arts and sciences that have made the wilderness and the solitary places glad, and that have caused the deserts to rejoice and blossom as the rose. He has vouchsafed to them "the splendor of Lebanon," and added "the excellency of Carmel and Sharon," and "has caused them to see the glory of the Land and the excellency of our God."

To us, especially, he has given the new world and all its hidden treasures, with all the arts and sciences of the old. Europe, Asia and Africa look to Protestant America as the wonder of the age, and as exerting a preponderating influence on the destinies of the world. We have, then, a fearful and a glorious responsibility. Let us cherish in our individual bosoms this feeling of personal as well as national responsibility; and not only enter upon, but *prosecute*, the duties which we owe to ourselves, our country and the human race. Thus, and thus only, will our career be glorious, our end victorious, and our destiny, and that of our country, "fair as the moon, clear as the sun," and to our enemies "terrible as an army with banners."

But there is yet one position which, because of its importance—its transcendent importance—I would make stand out before you in bold relief, and leave it with you in solemn charge, as the paramount duty of every American citizen, and especially of the educated and talented youth of our country, who, from a benevolent and insuperable law of the Great Philanthropist, must ever hold in their hands the casting vote on each and every great question in every grand crisis that may involve its future weal or woe. The position which I have in my eye is founded on one strongly affirmed, viz. *that educated mind must govern the world.* It is the grand corollary of my address, first in intention, though last in execution. It is more than a corollary. It is the *corolla* itself. It is the flower that contains the seed that yields the fruit of the political tree of life to every community on earth, and more especially in a community to which God has given in solemn charge the key that opens the chest that holds the covenant of future peace and happiness to man, as a social and immortal being.

Not to prolong, nor to increase your suspense, I must reiterate an aphorism early announced on this occasion—that God created the universe, not because of his wisdom or power to do it, but to find a vent for his goodness. Now, the object and aim of goodness is happiness—prolonged, not momentary happiness; increasing, not stationary happiness; multiform, not uniform happiness. Hence it is that the perpetuity and prosperity of a people, or nation, are wholly dependent upon their goodness, their humanity, their philanthropy. And what is either individual or social goodness or humanity, but the proper combination of three ingredients—justice, truth and piety? No nation ever survived the death of these three principles, and no nation ever can die, or will die, till these principles become, with them, a dead letter. A Roman once said, *Fiat justitia, ruat cælum;* we say, *Fiant justitia, veritas, et benevolentia, et non ruet. cælum in sæcula sæculorum.* Let our nation, then, be just, true and benevolent to all nations and to herself, and it will stand while time endures. These are bright stars—a glorious constellation—and they will be the unwaning and unsetting stars of her destiny, and that of every other nation and people. The Jews, the monumental nation—God's ancient elect kingdom—would have remained till the final trumpet, the paragon of nations, had they continued true to these principles.

The Saviour once said that Sodom and Gomorrah, on certain principles, might have remained till his coming. Righteousness exalteth a nation, but sin is a reproach and a desolation to any people. It must be so, because the laws of nature and the laws of God were all fashioned and established under the dynasty or supremacy of the moral sentiments. The pulse of time and of human life is not merely indicative of, but absolutely dependent upon, the action of the heart. The universe was conceived and born in the bosom of absolute, eternal and immutable benevolence. Benevolence has for its sisters righteousness and truth. This being the moral character of the divine being, is immutable and eternal. On these principles our country stands; and on these principles alone she can stand, and rise, and flourish, to meet not only her own wishes and her own happiness, but the expectations and the prayers of all the great and wise and good of mankind.

Let it, then, be so established and published to the world, that we are the stern, uncompromising advocates of human rights; that America is not only "the home of the brave," but "the land of the free;" that we supremely love equal rights, and bow to no sovereignty but to that of God and the moral sentiments; that with open arms and warm hearts we welcome to our shores the oppressed and down-trodden of all nations and languages; and that while the old world is pouring into our harbors and into our homes her ignorant, superstitious and down-trodden serfs and masses, we will, by common schools and common ministrations of benevolence, dispossess them of the demons of priestcraft and kingcraft, and show them our religion by pointing to our common schools, our common churches, our common colleges, and our common respect for the Bible, the Christian religion and its divine and glorious Founder—the Supreme Philanthropist. But you may ask me what special bearing have these views and sentiments on you, gentlemen, as members of the Philo-Literary Institute. Think for a moment of the moral, as well as of the literal, import of your name.

The founders of your society, gentlemen, were peculiarly happy in the selection and adoption of its name—a name so apropos to the condition of this great locality, when first they met *sub tegmine fagi,* and resolved to call it the *Philo-Literary Society* of Jefferson College. The name of Jefferson, had it no other association than the reputation of the memorable and justly celebrated Declaration of the Independence of the American colonies, will descend to the latest generations in that halo of glory which encircled the sun of our destiny on the first morn of its rising. But that, gentlemen, is not the point, nor the association of ideas on which I would congratulate you, nor from which I would argue with you. It is the special name of your own society, the *Philo-Literary Society.* And here, for a moment, let us pause and formally propound the question, What is *literature?* "The knowledge of letters," you promptly respond. But this is a definition too etymological for my taste, or for my use on the present occasion. Literature, in its rhetorical use, denotes not mere letters. It is, indeed, learning. But in its usual and well-defined distinctive sense, while it excludes the *positive* sciences, it embraces languages, history, grammar, rhetoric, logic, criticism, belles-lettres and poetry. Be it so, then, according to our most approved lexicography. In literature we have, therefore, all the machinery of positive science, without which we could, in fact, have no real science of any sort whatever.

In my youthful days I sometimes wondered why, in the Scotch universities, this form of literature, or the study of these dead tongues, was called humanity, or, rather, humanities. I ultimately discovered the philosophy of this portion of their nomenclature. The Scotch, you know, are a nation of long heads, while the English, at least of the Puritan stamp, were called round heads, probably more from the cut of the hair without, than from the form of the brains within. Be this as it may, the Scotch early discovered that the gift of tongues, or of languages, was located in the forehead. They imagined that, language being the symbol of ideas, a man of much language had many ideas. Amongst that people, the arts of acquiring and communicating knowledge were highly appreciated and cultivated. Of them they said—

"These polish'd arts have humanized mankind,
 Soften'd the rude, and calm'd the boisterous mind."

Consequently, they had professors of the humanities called grammar, logic, rhetoric, poetry.

Literature is, indeed, in its proper import, a lever of prodigious arm. It wants but the Δοζ Που Στο of Archimedes, to lift a world from earth to heaven. But this affirmation might overstimulate some weak and nervous heads, and therefore it ought to be diluted according to the ratios of our modern panaceas, in the ratio of one grain of sense, two of reason and four of faith.

Religion and morals come to us *objectively*, through literature. Yet literature is no more religion or morals, than lead is water because the water passes through it. Still it happens, if you have not the leaden pipe, you can have no water in the cup. Now, as religion comes to us through the Bible, or through literature, if you have not some Divine literature in your heads or ears, you will never have Divine love in your hearts. Literature is not paper or parchment. It is that which is inscribed upon it. The envelope of a letter, any more than the paper on which it is written, is not the letter. The letter is the written word. And yet the written word is itself but an envelope. The power that smites the conscience, that melts the heart, that cheers the broken spirit, is not the paper, the ink, the written symbol, but something that underlies the whole. It is the mind, the idea, the spirit, the conception, clothed, embodied, uttered, perceived, received, accredited, that agonizes or consoles, that softens and subdues, that purifies and ennobles the heart, that transforms the man, and adorns him with the beauty of purity, the true graces of religion and morality.

We have not yet, gentlemen, capped the climax of the honors due and actually vouchsafed to literature. The Eternal Spirit employed literature in creating light, heaven's own symbol of knowledge, purity and love. How passing strange, beautiful and sublime, the commendation given to language in the first paragraph of the oldest book in the world! God not only *said*, "Let there be light," but he created all things by language or by words; and what are words, but the utterances of ideas, emotions, volitions? All literature is but the pictured symbols of vocables. Language, rudimentally, is literature, fashioned by the tongue, guided by the ear. Hence the deaf can manufacture no language, can articulate no ideas. Language is fashioned by the ear, addressed to the ear, enters into the brain, and thence enters into the understanding, the conscience and the heart. From the heart again it responds by the tongue and the lips, and enters into the ear, the understanding, the conscience and the heart. Language is, therefore, the spiritual or intellectual and moral currency between man and man, between nation and nation, between ancestors and their descendants; by which, though dead, they commune with us and we with them. This is the whole circuit of language that decorates, enriches and beautifies the halls of literature, science and religion.

As all the learning, science and religion in the world, are thus embodied in language, those who are initiated into these sciences, as the graduates of our colleges are presumed to be, go out into the world like a regular army, panoplied *cap-à-pie*, for a grand and solemn mission; for a sacred warfare against ignorance and error in all their forms. They are, by their education, to become the captains and leaders of the people, especially the uneducated masses, which in all countries, even in our own, constitute the great and fearful majority. Associated with moral excellence and moral character, they are prepared to be the great benefactors of their country and of their contemporaries. When we consider what one well-educated mind has achieved in any one of the departments of literature, of science, or of art, for his country and the world, we are not prepared to estimate or anticipate what may be accomplished, for weal or for woe, by the mighty hosts that are annually pouring forth from all our halls of science, literature and religion, in the great fields of humanity which spread out before us.

Approve or disapprove it who may, it is a law of reason, a law of God, that the educated portion of every community must direct and form public opinion. In theology, in law, in politics, in physics and metaphysics; in all the errors and diseases of the head, the conscience, the heart, as well as in the body natural, the body ecclesiastic, the body politic, they must exercise an immense power. Approve or disapprove it who may, it is as immutable and uncontrollable as the law that governs the spheres and regulates the seasons of the year.

Have not a few distinguished individuals, well educated in almost all the fields of literature, science, politics and religion, indelibly stamped their image upon a nation, an age, an empire, a world? These are facts so obvious, so uncontrollable, that to controvert them would be only to stultify one's self, or to falsify the annals of nations and the history of the world. When, then, we speak of the destiny, the special destiny of our beloved country, we cannot but contemplate it through the medium of our schools of learning, of science, politics and religion. Our schools, then, one and all, should command and occupy the profound, the patriotic, the religious deliberation, consideration and supervision of the combined wisdom, talent and learning of the age. Every patriot, every philanthropist, and every Christian, will say from his heart, Amen. Seeing it is a law of God, a principle incorporated in the very constitution of society, it must be wisely, cheerfully and gratefully acquiesced in and submitted to. It must also be regulated and managed with a care, a wisdom, a diligent supervision, commensurate with the immense and eternal interests involved in it.

Patriotism, it is conceded, has no special place in the Christian religion. Its founder never pronounced a single sentence in commendation of it. The reason is, I presume to say, that the world was his field, and as patriotism is only an extension of the principle of selfishness, he deigned it no regard; because selfishness is now the great and damning sin of mankind. Still, the very test of morality is self-love. We are commanded to love our neighbor as we love ourselves, neither more nor less. And in his enlarged mind and heart, our neighbor is every man in the world. Charity, it is said, begins at home, but at home it does not stay. It goes abroad, and radiates its blessings according to its strength, to the utmost domicile of man. But few men can extend their charity, in its special currency, beyond their village, their parish, or their church. Still, when the frozen Icelander or the sunburned Moor comes within our sphere of doing good, we will, as we ought, pour into his wounds and bruises the soothing and mollifying ointment of Christian benevolence. Our country, then, for the most part, engages our attention, and exhausts all our means of doing good. But in promoting its moral excellence, its wealth, its honor, its character, we increase its power and extend its means of communicating blessings which, without it, no Christian man could bestow upon his species.

The United States of America, as they grow in learning, in the arts and sciences, and in all the elements of human wealth and power, can extend blessings to many nations; indeed, to the four quarters of the world. In promoting her health, her wealth and greatness, especially that natural characteristic of a paramount regard for the freedom, amelioration, civilization, as well as the evangelization of foreign lands, we lay for her prosperity, for our own, for that of our children, for that of the human race, the most solid, substantial and enduring basis, pregnant, too, with the civilization and advancement of the great family of man. In this way, too, we secure for ourselves and for our posterity the richest inheritance which mortals can secure in heaven or on earth. Philanthropy, like honesty, is the best national, as it is the best individual, policy. It acts and reacts; it blesses and is blessed; it glorifies and is glorified. If, then, as a nation and a people we stand out upon the canvas of time as the most generous, magnanimous and benevolent nation, we will, as certainly as the sun radiates and attracts, bless the nations and be blessed by them, and grow in every element and characteristic of a great, a mighty, a prosperous and a happy people.

Now, my young friends, in forming your beau ideal of your individual duty, honor and happiness, should you concur with these views and principles, you will carry with you, in all the private or public walks of life, an influence most benignant and beatific. You will guide the less favored of mankind, because they cannot but look up to you. You will thus form their views, guide their aims and elicit their suffrage, on every question you advocate for the public interest, honor and happiness. And that you may do so—be blessed in blessing, be elevated in elevating, be honored in honoring—is not only the wish of your humble orator, but, doubtless, that of every one who takes any real interest in your true and real happiness, in that of your country and of the human race.

Notes

1. Winthrop Hudson, "Denominationalism as a Basis for Ecumenicity: a 17th Century Conception" in *Denominationalism*, ed. Russell E. Richey (Nashville: Abingdon Press, 1977), pp. 21-22. For other theories of denominational development, refer to this collection.

2. From *The Journal of Francis Asbury*, 1784.

III

AMERICAN REVIVALISM

If denominations provided an organizational structure for American religion, revivals provided a means for securing members and revitalizing declining churches. In fact, revivalism has been one of the most colorful and influential aspects of American religious life. Whether in the meeting houses of Puritan New England, the brush arbors of the frontier camp meetings, or the sawdust trails of the tent evangelists, thousands of Americans have "gotten religion" through the exuberance of revivalistic experience.

This chapter contains documents that illustrate leaders and issues from three important strains of American revivalism. The work of Jonathan Edwards is set in the context of the First Great Awakening of the 1730s and 40s. The selections from Peter Cartwright's autobiography provide an account of certain activities evident during the Second Great Awakening on the American frontier, 1790-1830. The final work, written by the famed evangelist Charles G. Finney, provides an introduction to principles used in "modern" revivalism.

The term revival may be used to describe a period of awakening or fervor more intense than that of the normal religious life of the churches. Revivalism may also reflect the institutionalization of various techniques and procedures utilized in revival meetings.

The movement known as the First Great Awakening brought an outpouring of personal, "experimental" religion into the staid colonial churches, particularly among the Presbyterians and the Congregationalists. Some believe that it began as early as 1726 among the Dutch Reformed churches of New Jersey under the preaching of Theodore Frelinghuysen. Frelinghuysen's sermons attacked the formalism and "corpse cold orthodoxy" of the churches. He suggested that true religion began with personal conversion and demanded that his parishioners have such an experience of divine grace. His influence was localized and limited.

The Presbyterians in Pennsylvania experienced an awakening largely through the work of William Tennent and his family. A preacher of conversionist faith, Tennent founded a school called Log College near his home in Bucks County, Pennsylvania. It served as a training ground for Tennent's four sons and other young men concerned for revivals.

In New England, perhaps the most famous revivalist was Jonathan Edwards, pastor of the church at Northampton, Massachusetts. Edwards, descended from a line of Congregational preachers, succeeded his maternal grandfather, Solomon Stoddard, at the Northampton church. Stoddard had served there over sixty years and adapted covenant theology in ways with which Edwards disagreed. Stoddard's willingness to admit baptized but unconverted persons to communion was a practice rejected by Edwards.

In 1734, concerned about the state of religion in the church and community, Edwards began a series of sermons on justification by faith alone. He attacked the doctrines of "Arminianism" and "works" as offering a false security regarding personal salvation. Humanity, Edwards believed, was totally depraved; and only the ineffable grace of a sovereign God could keep a sinner from falling deservedly into a fiery hell.

Numerous conversions followed, and soon the town was aflame with spiritual enthusiasm. The movement spread, and before long other New England churches were experiencing awakening as preachers warned of the dangers of hell and exalted the glories of God's grace while parishioners wept, screamed for mercy, and bemoaned their sins.

By 1737, however, the revival spirit had begun to subside. This was certain evidence, Edwards insisted, that only God could instigate and sustain a true revival. In response to this miraculous experience Edwards wrote *A Faithful Narrative of the Surprising Work of God* in 1737. In it he described the state of religion in Northampton prior to the revival, the events of the revival as they occurred in the church, and the evidences of true piety in the lives of the participants. One of these persons, Abigail Hutchinson, experienced conversion on her deathbed, while another, Phebe Bartlet, was converted at the age of four.

In each case Edwards traced the process of salvation. Though specific circumstances might vary, the procedure normally involved an extreme sense of sinfulness and separation from God, agony over one's spiritual condition and the prospect of eternal judgment, contrition before the sovereign God, and sorrow for sin. Then, sometimes calmly, sometimes dramatically, came the dawning of God's light along with a spirit of rejoicing and gratitude for the overwhelming grace of God. Conversion was seldom an immediate experience but a process that might continue for days or weeks. Edwards made it clear, however, that each experience was unique. He proclaimed that "the work of God has been glorious in its variety."

For Jonathan Edwards, a revival was a divine miracle, beginning and ending by the determination of God's sovereign will. The *Faithful Narrative* and other of Edwards' works were used by later generations in interpreting and organizing other religious awakenings. Edwards himself was one of the great American theologians whose thought has had a significant impact on various aspects of American religious ideology.

The localized revivals such as the one at Northampton were united into a Great (widespread) Awakening largely through the preaching of that "Grand Itinerant," George Whitefield. An Anglican priest with Calvinist theology and a lifelong friendship with the Wesleys, Whitefield's unorthodox methods and outstanding pulpit skills drew huge crowds throughout the colonies. His "ecumenical" spirit gave unity to the revival movements as members of dissenting and established churches joined in a common evangelical task. Whitefield's travels throughout the colonies in 1740 represent the height of the Awakening as thousands of Americans from Georgia to New England were converted to personal Christian faith.

Success also brought controversy as many came to reject

the emotional excesses and other outward manifestations of revivalistic zeal as detrimental to the order and dignity essential to true worship. Critics attacked revivalists as simplistic, unorthodox, and prone to sensationalism.

Charles Chauncy, pastor of First Church, Boston, became one of the major opponents of the revivalistic fervor. In Chauncy's view, the confusion and emotional outbursts created by the Awakening could not be of God since God was not "the author of confusion." In a treatise called *Seasonable Thoughts on the State of Religion in New England,* published in 1743, Chauncy urged that churches use the Word of God more thoroughly in evaluating the revival. Real Christian conversion should produce humility and Christlike behavior, not the passionate and slanderous response of the fanatical revivalists. Not all who had emotional experiences were truly converted, Chauncy insisted.

Edwards himself responded in a *Treatise Concerning Religious Affections* by agreeing that emotional expressions were not always indicative of true conversion. Yet all "religious affections" were not to be dismissed due to the excesses of a few. Grace, Edwards suggested, affects the whole person—mind, soul, and emotions. The need was to monitor religious behavior following conversion as to its validity and impact on the individual life.

Chauncy's remarks may well have been provoked by such extremists as John Davenport, whose erratic behavior led to numerous excesses in revivalistic zeal. Davenport, a man of mental instability, traveled throughout America provoking such strong emotional outbursts and fanatical extremes that even many supporters of the revivals opposed him. He later repented and confessed that he had acted inappropriately in his religious zeal.

Several denominations experienced actual divisions as Congregationalists divided between prorevival forces, called New Lights, and their opponents, the Old Lights. Presbyterians split into Old Side and New Side camps, while Baptists divided into "Separates" who favored the revival and "Regular" Baptists who hesitated to give the awakening their complete support.

By the mid-1740s the Awakening was in decline. Its impact produced numerous new converts for the churches and influenced the founding of several new institutions of higher learning, among them Princeton, Brown, and Dartmouth. It represents one of the earliest movements of unity and purpose evident in the fragmented young colonies. The awakening likewise revealed the importance of millennial theories during the period. Many prominent preachers, including Jonathan Edwards, believed that the revivals were a prelude to a golden age of the church prior to the establishment of the millennial kingdom. These optimistic views indicate the influence of early postmillennial concepts in American life.

By the end of the eighteenth century the colonial preachers were becoming increasingly concerned with the state of religion in America. The Revolutionary War left churches weakened and membership declining; and "infidelity," the rationalistic philosophy of European intellectuals, was a common target of pulpit polemicists. Worse yet, Americans were moving by the droves to the new lands of the frontier, west of the Alleghenies. There, the preachers believed, the harsh demands of the wilderness, the lack of civilization, and the absence of churches created problems of barbarism and godlessness. The time was ripe for a new outpouring of the Divine Spirit to meet the needs of the East and the frontier.

The movement known as the Second Great Awakening began in the churches and colleges of New England and the East Coast. One center of the early enthusiasm developed at Yale College through the preaching of Timothy Dwight. The grandson of Jonathan Edwards, Dwight became president of Yale in 1795. In response to the skepticism of the student body, he began a series of sermons against "infidel philosophy." The campus was swept by a revival spirit in which great numbers of students were converted. These conversions were basically quiet and sober experiences with little of the emotionalism of earlier eras.

As the revival spread to other colleges and churches, young revivalists moved west, taking their experimental faith onto the rough and volatile frontier. One of these young men, a Presbyterian named James McGready, became pastor of three Kentucky churches on the Red, Muddy, and Gasper Rivers. His revivalistic sentiments led him to propose a "sacramental meeting" for four days in June 1800, at the Red River Church. Joined by ministers of other denominations, McGready and company preached to unexpectedly large crowds. A great spirit of repentance and conversion was evident as some of the most reprobate individuals were converted. Other such gatherings were held throughout Kentucky with similar results, and soon the camp meeting became a primary method of frontier revivalism.

Perhaps the most infamous of these meetings was held in August 1801 at Cane Ridge in Bourbon County, Kentucky. Barton W. Stone, pastor of the Presbyterian congregation at Cane Ridge, called the meeting; but it was truly a nondenominational affair often with numerous preachers simultaneously demanding repentance from pulpits throughout the grounds. Converts frequently encountered erratic outbursts of religious response—jerking uncontrollably, laughing uproariously, running until exhausted, and falling as if struck down.

In the lonely anonymity of the frontier, the camp meeting was a social as well as a religious event. Men and women courted at such gatherings. Rowdies lurked on the outskirts of the camps where "likkor" flowed freely. Antagonists frequently made forays into the meetings to mock preachers and the repentant.

The camp meeting was thus a valuable contribution to frontier life. As denominations became less cooperative, the Methodists became the chief heirs of the camp meeting phenomenon. They, more than any other group, used camp meetings for evangelical outreach. Baptists soon moved from camp meetings to "protracted meetings" held in local churches for extended periods.

Peter Cartwright, 1785–1872, was one of the best known of the early Methodist camp meeting preachers. He was often as rough as the frontier folk to whom he preached.

Flamboyant and outspoken, he traveled circuits in Illinois and Indiana but frequented camp meetings in Kentucky and other wilderness areas. Cartwright's autobiography reveals aspects of his early life, conversion, and camp meeting experiences. The work reveals something of the competition among denominations on the frontier as Cartwright confronted Universalists, Baptists, Presbyterians, and sectarians with his own staunch Methodist sentiments. It is one of the most colorful documents that describes the Second Awakening.

As in the First Awakening, these revivals produced divisions within the churches. The Presbyterians were perhaps the hardest hit. In 1802 a group of revivalistic Presbyterians were brought under the discipline of the church in Kentucky due to their tendency to lower requirements for ordination. They ordained men without proper educational qualifications because of the need for ministers in the churches swelled by new converts. As a result of the disciplinary action, the revivalists formed their own body, the Cumberland Presbyterians. Barton W. Stone moved from a Presbyterian affiliation to found the nonsectarian "Christian Church" at Cane Ridge in 1804.

The Second Awakening also had numerous positive effects. The revival movement helped to bring civilization to the frontier. It produced some important responses to such social problems as alcohol and family abuse. There was likewise extensive interest in missionary outreach both at home and abroad. The Awakening also introduced practices into the churches which soon became rather standardized, accepted means for conducting and producing revivals.

Much of this latter emphasis was due to the work of the famed evangelist Charles G. Finney, 1792–1875. Converted in 1821 during the latter days of the Second Awakening, Finney became one of the most prominent evangelists in American religious history. His "new measures" introduced into revival practice contributed to his being labeled the father of modern revivalism.

Finney's primary concern was for the rapidly developing

urban frontiers in the East where wickedness seemed rampant. His campaigns were concentrated on the population centers of New York, Boston, and Philadelphia during the 1820s and 30s. In Finney's view it was a hard and sinful era, requiring new methods for attracting the attention of the ungodly.

Finney thus resorted to direct methods—naming sinners from the pulpit, praying for the salvation of specific individuals. In each service he utilized the "anxious bench" where those in need of salvation might come for prayer and counsel. Visitors went door to door seeking converts and inviting folk to the meetings. Women were given new opportunities to exercise religious gifts in public by testifying and praying in public gatherings.

Finney also inspired numerous individuals who, after conversion, turned their evangelical zeal to the alleviation of social problems, particularly slavery. A strong segment of the abolitionist movement in America was influenced by Finney's concern for both personal and social religion. His decision to become professor of theology and later president of the newly formed Oberlin College in 1837 was due to his concern to aid the young revivalists who formed the school out of evangelical zeal and abolitionist protest.

A postmillennialist, Finney believed that the converted could bring about valuable social reforms in preparation for the return of Christ. The conversion of sinners and the Christian response to social problems were intricately related.

The excerpt from Finney's *Lectures on Revivals of Religion* provides insight into his revivalistic philosophy. Like Edwards' *Faithful Narrative*, it became an important source book for later revivalists. It introduced the idea of revival not as miracle but as "the right use of the constituted means." This principle was a major impetus for developing new techniques in American revivalism. One did not sit idly by, waiting for God to act. Such inaction was sin, Finney believed, and was a philosophy that had doomed thousands of unconverted souls. Rather, the church was to develop methods of prayer, preaching, and organization that the Spirit could use in drawing men and women to Christ. Finney's methods thus set a standard for "praying down a revival" used by churches and evangelists throughout the nineteenth and twentieth centuries. His principles have been utilized by saints and charlatans to become both blessing and curse to later generations of revival preachers in America.

Revivalism had a tremendous impact on American religion. It provided a means for securing great numbers of converts while bringing a renewed zeal to the churches. American revivalism produced a style of worship incorporated into the worship of churches in numerous denominations. Hymnody, preaching, prayer, and congregational response frequently took on a distinctively revivalistic style. Evangelism, missions, and specific forms of social endeavors were also interpreted by many American churches in light of revivalistic influence. For many Americans in the nineteenth and twentieth centuries, the "old time religion" was not that of Augustine, Luther, or Calvin, but of Edwards, Cartwright, and Finney.

JONATHAN EDWARDS

A Faithful Narrative
of the Surprising Work
of God

IN A LETTER TO THE REV. DR. COLMAN, OF BOSTON, &C.

Rev. and Honoured Sir,

HAVING seen your Letter to my honoured uncle Williams, of Hatfield, of July 20, wherein you inform him of the notice that has been taken of the late wonderful work of God, in this, and some other towns in this county; by the Rev. *Dr. Watts* and *Dr. Guyse* of London, and the congregation to which the last of these preached on a monthly day of solemn prayer; as also of your desire to be more perfectly acquainted with it, by some of us on the spot: and having been since informed by my uncle Williams, that you desire me to undertake it; I would now do it, in as just and faithful a manner as in me lies.

The people of the county, in general, I suppose, are as sober, and orderly, and good sort of people, as in any part of New England; and I believe they have been preserved the freest by far, of any part of the country, from error, and variety of sects and opinions. Our being so far within the land, at a distance from sea-ports, and in a corner of the country, has doubtless been one reason why we have not been so much corrupted with vice, as most other parts. But without question, the religion and good order of the county, and their purity in doctrine, has, under God, been very much owing to the great abilities, and eminent piety of my venerable and honoured grandfather Stoddard. I suppose we have been the freest of any part of the land from unhappy divisions, and quarrels in our ecclesiastical and religious affairs, till the late lamentable Springfield Contention.

We being much separated from other parts of the province, and having comparatively but little intercourse with them, have from the beginning, till now, always managed our ecclesiastical affairs within ourselves: it is the way in which the country from its infancy, has gone on, by the practical agreement of all, and the way in which our peace and good order has hitherto been maintained.

The town of Northampton is of about 82 years standing, and has now about 200 families; which mostly dwell more compactly together than any town of such a bigness in these parts of the country; which probably has been an occasion that both our corruptions and reformations have been, from time to time, the more swiftly propagated, from one to another, through the town. Take the town in general, and so far as I can judge, they are as rational and understanding a people as most I have been acquainted with. Many of them have been noted for religion, and particularly, have been remarkable for their distinct knowledge in things that relate to heart religion, and christian experience, and their great regards thereto.

I am the third minister that has been settled in the town: the Rev. Mr. Eleazar Mather, who was the first, was ordained in July, 1669. He was one whose heart was much in his work, abundant in labours for the good of precious souls; he had the high esteem and great love of his people, and was blessed with no small success. The Rev. Mr. Stoddard, who succeeded him, came first to the town the November after his death, but was not ordained till September 11, 1672, and died February 11, 1728-9. So that he continued in the work of the ministry here, from his first coming to town, near 60 years. And as he was eminent and renowned for his gifts and grace; so he was blessed, from the beginning, with extraordinary success in his ministry, in the conversion of many souls. He had five harvests, as he called them: the first was about 57 years ago: the second about 53 years; the third about 40; the fourth about 24; the fifth and last about 18 years ago. Some of these times were much more remarkable than others, and the ingathering of souls more plentiful. Those that were about 53, and 40, and 24 years ago, were much greater than either the first or the last: but in each of them, I have heard my grandfather say, the bigger part of the young people in the town, seemed to be mainly concerned for their eternal salvation.

After the last of these, came a far more degenerate time, (at least among the young people) I suppose, than ever before. Mr. Stoddard, indeed, had the comfort before he died, of seeing a time when there were no small appearances of a divine work amongst some, and a considerable ingathering of souls, even after I was settled with him in the ministry, which was about two years before his death; and I have reason to bless God for the great advantage I had by it. In these two years there were near twenty that Mr. Stoddard hoped to be savingly converted; but there was nothing of any general awakening. The greater part seemed to be at that time very insensible of the things of religion, and engaged in other cares and pursuits. Just after my grandfather's death, it seemed to be a time of extraordinary dulness in religion: licentiousness for some years greatly prevailed among the youth of the town; they were many of them very much addicted to night-walking, and frequenting the tavern, and lewd practices, wherein some, by their example, exceedingly corrupted others. It was their manner very frequently to get together, in conventions of both sexes, for mirth and jollity, which they called frolicks; and they would often spend the greater part of the night in them, without regard to any order in the families they belonged to: and indeed family-government did too much fail in the town. It was become very customary with many of our young people, to be indecent in their carriage at Meeting, which doubtless would not have prevailed to such a degree, had it not been that my grandfather through his great age, (though he retained his powers surprisingly to the last) was not so able to observe them. There had also long prevailed in the town, a spirit of contention between two parties, into which they had for many years been divided, by which was maintained a jealousy one of the other, and they were prepared to oppose one another in all public affairs.

But in two or three years after Mr. Stoddard's death, there began to be a sensible amendment of these evils; the young people shewed more of a disposition to hearken to counsel, and by degrees left off their frolicking, and grew observably more decent in their attendance on the public worship, and there were more that manifested a religious concern than there used to be.

At the latter end of the year 1733, there appeared a very unusual flexibleness, and yielding to advice, in our young people. It had been too long their manner to make the evening after the sabbath, and after our public lecture, to be especially the times of their mirth and company-keeping. But a sermon was now preached on the sabbath before the lecture, to shew the evil tendency of the practice, and to persuade them to reform it; and it was urged on heads of families, that it should be a thing agreed upon among them, to govern their families, and keep their children at home, at these times; and withal it was more privately moved, that they should meet together, the next day, in their several neighbourhoods, to know each other's minds: which was accordingly done, and the motion complied with throughout the town. But parents found little or no occasion for the exercise of government in the case: the young people declared themselves convinced by what they had heard from the pulpit, and were willing of themselves to comply with the counsel that had been given: and it was immediately, and, I suppose, almost universally complied with: and there was a thorough reformation of these disorders thenceforward, which has continued ever since.

Presently after this, there began to appear a remarkable religious concern at a little village belonging to the congregation, called Pascommuck, where a few families were settled, at about three miles distance from the main body of the town. At this place, a number of persons seemed to be savingly wrought upon. In the April following, *Anno* 1734, there happened a very sudden and awful death of a young man, in the bloom of his youth; who being violently seized with a pleurisy, and taken immediately very delirious, died in about two days; which (together with what was preached publicly on that occasion) much affected many young people. This was followed with another death of a young married woman, who had been considerably exercised in mind, about the salvation of her soul, before she was ill, and was in great distress, in the beginning of her illness; but seemed to have satisfying evidences of God's saving mercy to her, before her death; so that she died very full of comfort, in a most earnest and moving manner warning, and counselling others. This seemed much to contribute to the solemnizing of the spirits of many young persons; and there began evidently to appear more of a religious concern on peoples' minds.

In the fall of the year, I proposed it to the young people, that they should agree among themselves to spend the evenings after lectures in social religion, and to that end divide themselves into several companies to meet in various parts of the town; which was accordingly done, and those meetings have been since continued, and the example imitated by elder people. This was followed by the death of an elderly person, which was attended with many unusual circumstances, by which many were much moved and affected.

About this time, began the great noise that was in this part of the country, about Arminianism, which seemed to appear with a very threatening aspect upon the interest of religion here. The friends of vital piety trembled for fear of the issue; but it seemed, contrary to their fear, strongly to be overruled for the promoting of religion. Many who looked on themselves as in a Christless condition, seemed to be awakened by it, with fear that God was about to withdraw from the land, and that we should be given up to heterodoxy, and corrupt principles; and that then their opportunity for obtaining salvation would be past; and many who were brought a little to doubt about the truth of the doctrines they had hitherto been taught, seemed to have a kind of a trembling fear with their doubts, lest they should be led into by-paths, to their eternal undoing: and they seemed with much concern and engagedness of mind, to enquire what was indeed the way in which they must come to be accepted with God. There were then some things said publicly on that occasion, concerning justification by faith alone.

Although great fault was found with meddling with the controversy in the pulpit, by such a person, and at that time, and though it was ridiculed by many elsewhere; yet it proved a word spoken in season here; and was most evidently attended with a very remarkable blessing of heaven to the souls of the people in this town. They received thence a general satisfaction, with respect to the main thing in question, which they had been in trembling doubts and concern about; and their minds were engaged the more earnestly to seek that they might come to be accepted of God, and saved in the way of the gospel, which had been made evident to them to be the true and only way. And then it was, in the latter part of December, that the Spirit of God began extraordinarily to set in, and wonderfully to work amongst us; and there were, very suddenly, one after another, five or six persons, who were to all appearances savingly converted, and some of them wrought upon in a very remarkable manner.

Particularly, I was surprised with the relation of a young

woman, who had been one of the greatest company-keepers in the whole town: when she came to me, I had never heard that she was become in any wise serious, but by the conversation I then had with her, it appeared to me, that what she gave an account of, was a glorious work of God's infinite power and sovereign grace; and that God had given her a new heart, truly broken and sanctified. I could not then doubt of it, and have seen much in my acquaintance with her since to confirm it.

Though the work was glorious, yet I was filled with concern about the effect it might have upon others: I was ready to conclude (though too rashly) that some would be hardened by it, in carelessness and looseness of life: and would take occasion from it to open their mouths, in reproaches of religion. But the event was the reverse, to a wonderful degree; God made it, I suppose, the greatest occasion of awakening to others, of any thing that ever came to pass in the town. I have had abundant opportunity to know the effect it had, by my private conversation with many. The news of it seemed to be almost like a flash of lightning, upon the hearts of young people, all over the town, and upon many others. Those persons amongst us, who used to be farthest from seriousness, and that I most feared would make an ill improvement of it, seemed greatly to be awakened with it; many went to talk with her, concerning what she had met with; and what appeared in her seemed to be to the satisfaction of all that did so.

Presently upon this, a great and earnest concern about the great things of religion, and the eternal world, became universal in all parts of the town, and among persons of all degrees, and all ages; the noise amongst the dry bones waxed louder and louder: all other talk but about spiritual and eternal things, was soon thrown by; all the conversation in all companies, and upon all occasions, was upon these things only, unless so much as was necessary for people carrying on their ordinary secular business. Other discourse than of the things of religion, would scarcely be tolerated in any company. The minds of people were wonderfully taken off from the world, it was treated amongst us as a thing of very little consequence: they seemed to follow their worldly business, more as a part of their duty, than from any disposition they had to it; the temptation now seemed to lie on that hand, to neglect worldly affairs too much, and to spend too much time in the immediate exercise of religion: which thing was exceedingly misrepresented by reports that were spread in distant parts of the land, as though the people here had wholly thrown by all worldly business, and betook themselves entirely to reading, and praying, and such like religious exercises.

But although people did not ordinarily neglect their worldly business; yet there then was the reverse of what commonly is: religion was with all sorts the great concern, and the world was a thing only by the bye. The only thing in their view was to get the kingdom of heaven, and every one appeared pressing into it: the engagedness of their hearts in this great concern could not be hid, it appeared in their very countenances. It then was a dreadful thing amongst us to lie out of Christ, in danger every day of dropping into hell; and what person's minds were intent upon was to escape for their lives, and to 'fly from the wrath to come.' All would eagerly lay hold of opportunities for their souls; and were wont very often to meet together in private houses, for religious purposes: and such meetings when appointed were wont greatly to be thronged.

There was scarcely a single person in the town, either old or young, that was left unconcerned about the great things of the eternal world. Those that were wont to be the vainest, and loosest, and those that had been most disposed to think, and speak slightly of vital and experimental religion, were now generally subject to great awakenings. And the work of conversion was carried on in a most astonishing manner, and increased more and more; souls did as it were come by flocks to Jesus Christ. From day to day, for many months together, might be seen evident instances of sinners brought out of darkness into marvellous light,' and delivered 'out of an horrible pit, and from the miry clay, and set upon a rock,' with a 'new song of praise to God in their mouths.'

This work of God, as it was carried on, and the number of true saints multiplied, soon made a glorious alteration in the town; so that in the spring and summer following, *Anno* 1735, the town seemed to be full of the presence of God: it never was so full of love nor joy, and yet so full of distress, as it was then. There were remarkable tokens of God's presence in almost every house. It was a time of joy in families on the account of salvation's being brought unto them; parents rejoiced over their children as new born, and husbands over their wives, and wives over their husbands. The goings of God were then seen in his sanctuary, God's day was a delight, and his tabernacles were amiable. Our public assemblies were then beautiful; the congregation was alive in God's service, every one earnestly intent on the public worship, every hearer eager to drink in the words of the minister as they came from his mouth; the assembly in general were, from time to time, in tears while the word was preached; some weeping with sorrow and distress, others with joy and love, others with pity and concern for the souls of their neighbours.

Our public praises were then greatly enlivened; God was then served in our psalmody, in some measure, in the beauty of holiness. It has been observable, that there has been scarce any part of divine worship, wherein good men amongst us have had grace so drawn forth, and their hearts so lifted up in the ways of God, as in singing his praises: our congregation excelled all that ever I knew in the external part of the duty before, the men generally carrying regularly, and well, three parts of music, and the women a part by themselves: but now they were evidently wont to sing with unusual elevation of heart and voice, which made the duty pleasant indeed.

In all companies, on other days, on whatever occasions persons met together, Christ was to be heard of, and seen in the midst of them. Our young people, when they met, were wont to spend the time in talking of the excellency and dying love of Jesus Christ, the gloriousness of the way of salvation, the wonderful, free, and sovereign grace of God, his glorious work in the conversion of a soul, the truth and certainty of the great things of God's word, the sweetness of the views of his perfections, &c. And even at weddings, which formerly were mere occasions of mirth and jollity, there was now no discourse of any thing but the things of religion, and no appearance of any but spiritual mirth.

Those amongst us that had been formerly converted, were greatly enlivened and renewed with fresh and extraordinary incomes of the spirit of God; though some much more than others, according to the measure of the gift of Christ; many that before had laboured under difficulties about their own state, had now their doubts removed by more satisfying experience, and more clear discoveries of God's love.

When this work of God first appeared, and was so extraordinarily carried on amongst us in the winter, others round about us, seemed not to know what to make of it; and there were many who scoffed at and ridiculed it; and some compared what we called conversion, to certain distempers. But it was very observable of many, that occasionally came amongst us from abroad, with disregardful hearts, that what they saw here cured them of such a temper of mind: Strangers were generally surprised to find things so much beyond what they had heard, and were wont to tell others that the state of the town could not be conceived of by those that had not seen it. The notice that was taken of it by the people that came to town on occasion of the court, that sat here in the beginning of March, was very observeable. And those that came from the neighbourhood to our public lectures, were for the most part remarkably affected. Many that came to town, on one occasion, or other, had their consciences smitten, and awakened, and went home with wounded hearts, and with those impressions that never wore off till they had hopefully a saving issue; and those that before had serious thoughts, had their awakenings and convictions greatly increased. And there were many instances of persons that came from abroad on visits, or on business, that had not been long here before to all appearance they were savingly wrought upon, and partook of that shower of divine blessings that God rained down here, and went home rejoicing; till at length the same work began evidently to appear and prevail in several other towns in the county.

In the month of March, the people in South-Hadley began to be seized with deep concern about the things of religion; which very soon became universal: and the work of God has been very wonderful there; not much, if any thing, short of what it has been here, in proportion to the bigness of the place. About the same time, it began to break forth in the west part of Suffield, (where it also has been very great) and it soon spread into all parts of the town. It next appeared in Sunderland, and soon overspread the town; and I believe was, for a season, not less remarkable than it was here. About the same time it began to appear in a part of Deerfield, called Green River, and afterwards filled the town, and there has been a glorious work there: it began also to be manifest, in the south part of Hatfield, in a place called the Hill, and after that the whole town, in the second week in April, seemed to be seized, as it were at once, with concern about the things of religion; and the work of God has been great there. There has been also a very general awakening at West-Springfield, and Long-Meadow; and in Enfield, there was for a time a pretty general concern amongst some that before had been very loose persons. About the same time that this appeared at Enfield, the Rev. Mr. Bull of Westfield informed me, that there had been a great alteration there, and that more had been done in one week there than in seven years before. Something of this work likewise appeared in the first precinct in Springfield, principally in the north and south extremes of the parish. And in Hadley old town, there gradually appeared so much of a work of God on souls, as at another time would have been thought worthy of much notice. For a short time there was also a very great and general concern, of the like nature, at Northfield. And wherever this concern appeared, it seemed not to be in vain: but in every place God brought saving blessings with him, and his word attended with his spirit (as we have all reason to think) returned not void. It might well be said at that time in all parts of the county, 'who are these that fly as a cloud, and as doves to their windows?'

As what other towns heard of and found in this, was a great means of awakening them; so our hearing of such a swift, and extraordinary propagation, and extent of this work, did doubtless for a time serve to uphold the work amongst us. The continual news kept alive the talk of religion, and did greatly quicken and rejoice the hearts of God's people, and much awakened those that looked on themselves as still left behind, and made them the more earnest that they also might share in the great blessings that others had obtained.

This remarkable pouring out of the Spirit of God, which thus extended from one end to the other of this county, was not confined to it, but many places in Connecticut have partook in the same mercy: as for instance, the first parish in Windsor, under the pastoral care of the Rev. Mr. Marsh, was thus blest about the same time as we in Northampton, while we had no knowledge of each other's circumstances: there has been a very great ingathering of souls to Christ in that place, and something considerable of the same work began afterwards, in East Windsor, my honoured father's parish, which has in times past, been a place favoured with mercies of this nature, above any on this western side of New England, excepting Northampton; there having been four, or five seasons of the pouring out of the spirit to the general awakening of the people there, since my Father's settlement amongst them.

There was also the last spring and summer a wonderful work

of God carried on at Coventry, under the ministry of the Rev. Mr. Meacham: I had opportunity to converse with some Coventry people, who gave me a very remarkable account of the surprising change that appeared in the most rude and vicious persons there. The like was also very great at the same time in a part of Lebanon, called the Crank, where the Rev. Mr. Wheelock, a young gentleman, is lately settled: and there has been much of the same at Durham, under the ministry of the Rev. Mr. Chauncey; and to appearance no small ingathering of souls there. And likewise amongst many of the young people in the first precinct in Stratford, under the ministry of the Rev. Mr. Gould; where the work was much promoted by the remarkable conversion of a young woman that had been a great company-keeper, as it was here.

Something of this work appeared in several other towns in those parts, as I was informed when I was there, the last fall. And we have since been acquainted with something very remarkable of this nature at another parish in Stratford called Ripton, under the pastoral care of the Rev. Mr. Mills. And there was a considerable revival of religion last summer at Newhaven old town, as I was once and again informed by the Rev. Mr. Noyes the minister there, and by others: and by a letter which I very lately received from Mr. Noyes, and also by information we have had otherwise. This flourishing of religion still continues, and has lately much increased: Mr. Noyes writes, that many this summer have been added to the church, and particularly mentions several young persons that belong to the principal families of that town.

There has been a degree of the same work at a part of Guildford; and very considerable at Mansfield, under the ministry of the Rev. Mr. Eleazar Williams; and an unusual religious concern at Tolland; and something of it at Hebron, and Bolton. There was also no small effusion of the spirit of God in the north parish in Preston, in the eastern part of Connecticut, which I was informed of, and saw something of it, when I was the last Autumn, at the house, and in the congregation of the Rev. Mr. Lord, the minister there; who, with the Rev. Mr. Owen of Groton, came up hither in May, the last year, on purpose to see the work of God here; and having heard various and contradictory accounts of it, were careful when they were here to inform, and satisfy themselves; and to that end particularly conversed with many of our people; which they declared to be entirely to their satisfaction; and that 'the one half had not been told them,' nor could be told them. Mr. Lord told me that, when he got home, he informed his congregation of what he had seen, and that they were greatly affected with it, and that it proved the beginning of the same work amongst them, which prevailed till there was a general awakening, and many instances of persons, who seemed to be remarkably converted. I also have lately heard that there has been something of the same work at Woodbury.

But this shower of divine blessing has been yet more extensive: there was no small degree of it in some parts of the Jerseys; as I was informed when I was at New York, (in a long journey I took at that time of the year for my health) by some people of the Jerseys, whom I saw; especially the Rev. Mr. William Tennent, a minister, who seemed to have such things much at heart, told me of a very great awakening of many in a place called the Mountains, under the ministry of one Mr. Cross; and of a very considerable revival of religion in another place under the ministry of his brother the Rev. Mr. Gilbert Tennent; and also at another place, under the ministry of a very pious young gentleman, a Dutch minister, whose name as I remember was Freelinghousa.

This seems to have been a very extraordinary dispensation of providence; God has in many respects gone out of, and much beyond his usual, and ordinary way. The work in this town, and some others about us, has been extraordinary on account of the universality of it, affecting all sorts, sober and vicious, high and low, rich and poor, wise and unwise; it reached the most considerable families and persons, to all appearance, as much as others. In former stirrings of this nature, the bulk of the young people have been greatly affected; but old men, and little children have been so now. Many of the last have, of their own accord formed themselves into religious societies, in different parts of the town; a loose careless person could scarcely find a person in the whole neighbourhood; and if there was any one that seemed to remain senseless or unconcerned, it would be spoken of as a strange thing.

This dispensation has also appeared very extraordinary in the numbers of those, on whom we have reason to hope it has had a saving effect: we have about six hundred and twenty communicants, which include almost all our adult persons. The church was very large before; but persons never thronged into it, as they did in the late extraordinary time:—our sacraments are eight weeks asunder, and I received into our communion about a hundred, before one sacrament, and fourscore of them at one time, whose appearance, when they presented themselves together to make an open explicit profession of christianity, was very affecting to the congregation:—I took in near sixty before the next sacrament day: and I had very sufficient evidence of the conversion of their souls, through divine grace, though it is not the custom here, as it is in many other churches in this country, to make a credible relation of their inward experiences the ground of admission to the Lord's Supper.

I am far from pretending to be able to determine how many have lately been the subjects of such mercy; but if I may be allowed to declare any thing that appears to me probable in a thing of this nature, I hope that more than 300 souls were savingly brought home to Christ, in this town in the space of half a year, (how many more I do not guess) and about the same number of males as females; which, by what I have heard Mr. Stoddard say, was far from what has been usual in years past, for he observed that in his time, many more women were converted than men. Those of our young people, that are on other accounts most likely and considerable, are mostly, as I hope, truly pious, and leading persons in the ways of religion. Those that were formerly looser young persons, are generally, to all appearance, become true lovers of God and Christ, and spiritual in their dispositions. And I hope that by far the greater part of persons in this town, above 16 years of age, are such as have the saving knowledge of Jesus Christ; and so by what I heard I suppose it is in some other places, particularly at Sunderland and South Hadley.

This has also appeared to be a very extraordinary dispensation, in that the spirit of God has so much extended not only his awakening, but regenerating influences, both to elderly persons, and also those that are very young. It has been a thing heretofore rarely to be heard of, that any were converted past middle age; but now we have the same ground to think, that many such have in this time been savingly changed, as that others have been so in more early years. I suppose there were upwards of fifty persons in this town above forty years of age; and more than twenty of them above fifty, and about ten of them above sixty, and two of them above seventy years of age.

It has heretofore been looked on as a strange thing, when any have seemed to be savingly wrought upon, and remarkably changed in their childhood; but now, I suppose, near thirty were to appearance so wrought upon between ten and fourteen years of age, and two between nine and ten, and one of about four years of age; and because I suppose this last will be most difficultly believed, I will hereafter give a particular account of it. The influences of God's spirit have also been very remarkable on children in some other places, particularly at Sunderland and South Hadley, and the west part of Suffield. There are several families in this town that are all hopefully pious; yea, there are several numerous families, in which, I think, we have reason to hope that all the children are truly godly, and most of them lately become so: and there are very few houses in the whole town, into which salvation has not lately come, in one or more instances. There are several negroes, that from what was seen in them then, and what is discernable in them since, appear to have been truly born again in the late remarkable season.

God has also seemed to have gone out of his usual way, in the quickness of his work, and the swift progress his spirit has made in his operations on the hearts of many: it is wonderful that persons should be so suddenly, and yet so greatly changed: many have been taken from a loose and careless way of living, and seized with strong convictions of their guilt and misery, and in a very little time old things have passed away, and all things have become new with them.

God's work has also appeared very extraordinary, in the degrees of the influences of his spirit, both in the degree of awakening and conviction, and also in the degree of saving light, and love and joy, that many have experienced. It has also been very extraordinary in the extent of it, and its being so swiftly propagated from town to town. In former times of the pouring out of the spirit of God on this town, though in some of them it was very remarkable, yet it reached no further than this town, the neighbouring towns all around continued unmoved.

The work of God's spirit seemed to be at its greatest height in this town, in the former part of the spring, in March and April; at which time God's work in the conversion of souls was carried on amongst us in so wonderful a manner, that so far as I, by looking back, can judge from the particular acquaintance I have had with souls in this work, it appears to me probable, to have been at the rate, at least, of four persons in a day, or near thirty in a week, take one with another, for five or six weeks together: when God in so remarkable a manner took the work into his own hands, there was as much done in a day or two, as at ordinary times, with all endeavours that men can use, and with such a blessing as we commonly have, is done in a year.

I am very sensible how apt many would be, if they should see the account I have here given, presently to think with themselves that I am very fond of making a great many converts, and of magnifying and aggrandizing the matter; and to think that, for want of judgment, I take every religious pang, and enthusiastic conceit, for saving conversion; and I don't much wonder if they should be apt to think so: and for this reason I have forborne to publish an account of this great work of God, though I have often been put upon it; but having now as I thought a special call to give an account of it, upon mature consideration I thought it might not be beside my duty to declare this amazing work, as it appeared to me, to be indeed divine, and to conceal no part of the glory of it, leaving it with God to take care of the credit of his own work, and running the venture of any censorious thoughts, which might be entertained of me to my disadvantage: but that distant persons may be under as great advantage as may be, to judge for themselves of this matter, I would be a little more large and particular.

I therefore proceed to give an account of the manner of persons being wrought upon; and here there is a vast variety, perhaps as manifold as the subjects of the operation; but yet in many things there is a great analogy in all.

Persons are first awakened with a sense of their miserable condition by nature, the danger they are in of perishing eternally, and that it is of great importance to them that they speedily escape and get into a better state. Those that before were secure and senseless, are made sensible how much they were in the way to ruin in their former courses. Some are more suddenly seized with convictions; it may be, by the news of others conversion, or something they hear in public, or in private conference, their consciences are suddenly smitten, as if their hearts were pierced, through with a dart: others have awakenings that come upon them more gradually, they begin at first to be something more thoughtful and considerate, so as to come to a conclusion in their minds, that it is their best and wisest way to delay no longer, but to improve the present opportunity; and have accordingly set themselves seriously to meditate on those things that have the most awakening tendency, on purpose to obtain convictions; and so their awakenings have increased, till a sense of their misery, by God's spirit setting in therewith, has had fast hold of them. Others that, before this wonderful time, had been something religious and concerned, for their salvation, have been awakened in a new manner, and made sensible that their slack and dull way of seeking was never like to obtain their purpose, and so have been roused up to a greater violence for the kingdom of heaven.

These awakenings when they have first seized on persons have had two effects: one was, that they have brought them immediately to quit their sinful practices, and the looser sort have been brought to forsake and dread their former vices and extravagancies. When once the spirit of God began to be so wonderfully poured out in a general way through the town, people had soon done with their old quarrels, backbitings, and intermeddling with other men's matters; the tavern was soon left empty, and persons kept very much at home; none went abroad unless on necessary business, or on some religious account, and every day seemed in many respects like a Sabbath-day. And the other effect was, that it put them on earnest application to the means of salvation, reading, prayer, meditation, the ordinances of God's house, and private conference: their cry was, 'What shall we do to be saved?' The place of resort was now altered, it was no longer the tavern, but the minister's house; that was thronged far more than ever the tavern had been wont to be.

There is a very great variety, as to the degree of fear and trouble that persons are exercised with, before they attain any comfortable evidences of pardon and acceptance with God: some are from the beginning carried on with abundantly more encouragement and hope than others: some have had ten times less trouble of mind than others, in whom yet the issue seems to be the same. Some have had such a sense of the displeasure of God, and the great danger they were in of damnation, that they could not sleep at nights; and many have said that when they have laid down, the thoughts of sleeping in such a condition have been frightful to them, and they have scarcely been free from terror while they have been asleep, and they have awaked with fear, heaviness, and distress still abiding on their spirits. It has been very common, that the deep and fixed concern that has been on persons' minds, has had a painful influence on their bodies, and given disturbance to animal nature.

The awful apprehensions persons have had of their misery, have for the most part been increasing, the nearer they have approached to deliverance; though they often pass through many changes and alterations in the frame and circumstances of their minds: sometimes they think themselves wholly sense-less, and fear that the spirit of God has left them, and that they are given up to judicial hardness; yet they appear very deeply exercised about that fear, and are in great earnest to obtain convictions again.

Together with those fears, and that exercise of mind which is rational, and which they have just ground for, they have often suffered many needless distresses of thought, in which Satan probably has a great hand, to entangle them, and block up their way; and sometimes the distemper of melancholy has been evidently mixed; of which when it happens, the tempter seems to make great advantage, and puts an unhappy bar in the way of any good effect: one knows not how to deal with such persons, they turn every thing that is said to them the wrong way, and most to their own disadvantage: and there is nothing that the devil seems to make so great a handle of, as a melancholy humour, unless it be the real corruption of the heart.

But it has been very remarkable, that there has been far less of this mixture, in this time of extraordinary blessing, than there was wont to be in persons under awakenings at other times; for it is evident that many that before had been exceedingly in-volved in such difficulties, seemed now strangely to be set at liberty: some persons that had before, for a long time, been exceedingly entangled with peculiar temptations, of one sort or other, and unprofitable and hurtful distresses, were soon helped over former stumbling blocks, that hindered any progress towards saving good; and convictions have wrought more kindly, and they have been successfully carried on in the way to life. And thus Satan seemed to be restrained, till towards the latter end of this wonderful time, when God's spirit was about to withdraw.

Many times persons under great awakenings were concerned, because they thought they were not awakened, but miserable, hard-hearted, senseless, sottish creatures still, and sleeping upon the brink of hell: the sense of the need they have to be awakened, and of their comparative hardness, grows upon them with their awakenings; so that they seem to themselves to be very senseless, when indeed most sensible. There have been some instances of persons that have had as great a sense of their danger and misery, as their natures could well subsist under, so that a little more would probably have destroyed them; and yet they have exprest themselves much amazed at their own insensibility and sottishness, in such an extraordinary time as it then was.

Persons are sometimes brought to the borders of despair, and it looks as black as midnight to them a little before the day dawns in their souls; some few instances there have been of persons, who have had such a sense of God's wrath for sin, that they have been overborn, and made to cry out under an astonishing sense of their guilt, wondering that God suffers such guilty wretches to live upon earth, and that he doth not immediately send them to hell; and sometimes their guilt doth so glare them in the face, that they are in exceeding terror for fear that God will instantly do it; but more commonly their distresses under legal awakenings have not been to such a degree. In some these terrors do not seem to be so sharp, when near comfort, as before; their convictions have not seemed to work so much that way, but they seem to be led further down into their own hearts, to a further sense of their own universal depravity and deadness in sin.

The corruption of the heart has discovered itself in various exercises, in the time of legal convictions; sometimes it appears in a great struggle, like something roused by an enemy, and Satan the old inhabitant seems to exert himself, like a serpent disturbed and enraged. Many in such circumstances, have felt a great spirit of envy, towards the godly, especially towards those that are thought to have been lately converted, and most of all towards acquaintance and companions, when they are thought to be converted: indeed, some have felt many heart-risings against God, and murmurings at his ways of dealing with mankind, and his dealings with themselves in particular. It has been much insisted on, both in public and private, that persons should have the utmost dread of such envious thoughts, which if allowed, tend exceedingly to quench the spirit of God, if not to provoke him finally to forsake them. And when such a spirit has much prevailed, and persons have not so earnestly strove against it as they ought to have done, it has seemed to be exceedingly to the hindrance of the good of their souls: but in some other instances where persons have been much terrified at the sight of such wickedness in their hearts, God has brought good to them out of evil; and made it a means of convincing them of their own desperate sinfulness, and bringing them off from all self-confidence.

The drift of the spirit of God in his legal strivings with persons, has seemed most evidently to be, to make way for, and to bring to, a conviction of their absolute dependance on his sovereign power and grace, and universal necessity of a mediator, by leading them more and more to a sense of their exceeding wickedness and guiltiness in his sight; the pollution and insufficiency of their own righteousness, that they can in no wise help themselves, and that God would be wholly just and righteous in rejecting them, and all that they do, and in casting them off for ever: though there be a vast variety, as to the manner, and distinctness of persons' convictions of these things.

As they are gradually more and more convinced of the corruption and wickedness of their hearts, they seem to themselves to grow worse and worse, harder and blinder, and more desperately wicked, instead of growing better: they are ready to be discouraged by it, and oftentimes never think themselves so far off from good, as when they are nearest. Under the sense which the spirit of God gives them of their sinfulness, they often think that they differ from all others; their hearts are ready to sink with the thought, that they are the worst of all, and that none ever obtained mercy that were so wicked as they.

When awakenings first begin, their consciences are commonly most exercised about their outward vicious course, or other acts of sin; but afterwards, are much more burdened with a sense of heart-sins, the dreadful corruption of their nature, their enmity against God, the pride of their hearts, their unbelief, their rejection of Christ, the stubbornness and obstinacy of their wills; and the like. In many, God makes much use of their own experience, in the course of their awakenings and endeavours after saving good, to convince them of their own vile emptiness and universal depravity.

Very often under first awakenings, when they are brought to reflect on the sin of their past lives, and have something of a terrifying sense of God's anger, they set themselves to walk more strictly, and confess their sins, and perform many religious duties, with a secret hope of appeasing God's anger and making up for the sins they have committed: and oftentimes, at first setting out, their affections are moved, and they are full of tears, in their confessions and prayers, which they are ready to make very much of, as though they were some atonement, and had power to move correspondent affections in God too: and hence they are for awhile big with expectation of what God will do for them; and conceive that they grow better apace, and shall soon be thoroughly converted. But these affections are but short-lived, they quickly find that they fail, and then they think themselves to be grown worse again; they do not find such a prospect of being soon converted, as they thought: instead of being nearer, they seem to be farther off; their hearts they think are grown harder, and by this means their fears of perishing greatly increase. But though they are disappointed, they renew their attempts again and again; and still as their attempts are multiplied so are their disappointments; all fails, they see no token of having inclined God's heart to them, they do not see that he hears their prayers at all, as they expected he would; and sometimes there have been great temptations arising hence to leave off seeking, and to yield up the case. But as they are still more terrified with fears of perishing, and their former hopes of prevailing on God to be merciful to them in a great measure fail; sometimes their religious affections have turned into heart-risings against God, because that he will not pity them, and seems to have little regard to their distress, and piteous cries, and to all the pains that they take: they think of the mercy that God has shown to others, how soon, and how easily others have obtained comfort, and those too that were worse than they, and have not laboured so much as they have done, and sometimes they have had even dreadful blasphemous thoughts, in these circumstances.

But when they reflect on these wicked workings of heart against God, if their convictions are continued, and the spirit of God is not provoked utterly to forsake them, they have more distressing apprehensions of the anger of God towards those whose hearts work after such a sinful manner about him; and it may be, have great fears that they have committed the unpardonable sin, or that God will surely never shew mercy to them that are such vipers; and are often tempted to leave off in despair. But then perhaps by something they read or hear of the infinite mercy of God, and all-sufficiency of Christ for the chief of sinners; they have some encouragement and hope renewed; but think that as yet they are not fit to come to Christ; they are so wicked that Christ will never accept of them: and then it may be they set themselves upon a new course of fruitless endeavours in their own strength to make themselves better, and still meet with new disappointments: they are earnest to enquire what they shall do? They do not know but there is something else to be done, in order to their obtaining converting grace, that they have never done yet. It may be they hope that they are something better than they were; but then the pleasing dream all vanishes again. If they are told, that they trust too much to their own strength and righteousness, they cannot unlearn this practice all at once, and find not yet the appearance of any good, but all looks as dark as midnight to them. Thus they wander about from mountain to hill, seeking rest, and finding none: when they are beat out of one refuge they fly to another, till they are as it were debilitated, broken, and subdued with legal humblings; in which God gives them a conviction of their own utter helplessness and insufficiency, and discovers the true remedy in a clearer knowledge of Christ and his Gospel.

When they begin to seek salvation, they are commonly profoundedly ignorant of themselves; they are not sensible how blind they are, and how little they can do towards bringing themselves to see spiritual things aright, and towards putting forth gracious exercises in their own souls: they are not sensible how remote they are from love to God, and other holy dispositions, and how dead they are in sin. When they see unexpected pollution in their own hearts, they go about to wash away their own defilements and make themselves clean; and they weary themselves in vain, till God shows them that it is in vain, and that their help is not where they have sought it, but elsewhere.

But some persons continue wandering in such a kind of labyrinth, ten times as long as others, before their own experience will convince them of their insufficiency; and so it appears not to be their own experience only, but the convincing influence of God's spirit with their experience, that attains the effect: and God has of late abundantly shown, that he does not need to wait to have men convinced by long and often repeated fruitless trials; for in multitudes of instances he has made a shorter work of it: he has so awakened and convinced persons' consciences, and made them so sensible of their exceeding great vileness, and given them such a sense of his wrath against sin, as has quickly overcome all their vain self-confidence, and borne them down into the dust before a holy and righteous God.

There have been some who have not had great terrors, but have had a very quick work. Some of those that have not had so deep a conviction of these things before their conversion, have, it may be, much more of it afterwards. God has appeared far from limiting himself to any certain method in his proceedings with sinners under legal convictions. In some instances it seems easy for our reasoning powers to discern the methods of divine wisdom, in his dealings with the soul under awakenings: in others his footsteps cannot be traced, and his ways are past finding out: and some that are less distinctly wrought upon, in what is preparatory to grace, appear no less eminent in gracious experiences afterwards.

There is in nothing a greater difference, in different persons, than with respect to the time of their being under trouble; some but a few days, and others for months or years. There were many in this town, that had been, before this effusion of God's spirit upon us, for years, and some for many years, concerned about their salvation; though probably they were not thoroughly awakened, yet they were concerned to such a degree as to be very uneasy, so as to live an uncomfortable disquieted life, and so as to continue in a way of taking considerable pains about their salvation, but had never obtained any comfortable evidence of a good estate, who now in this extraordinary time have received light; but many of them were some of the last: they first saw multitudes of others rejoicing, and with songs of deliverance in their mouths, who seemed wholly careless and at ease, and in pursuit of vanity, while they had been bowed down with solicitude about their souls; yea, some had lived licentiously, and so continued till a little before they were converted, and grew up to a holy rejoicing in the infinite blessings God had bestowed upon them.

And whatever minister has a like occasion to deal with souls, in a flock under such circumstances, as this was in the last year, I cannot but think he will soon find himself under a necessity, greatly to insist upon it with them, that God is under no manner of obligation to shew any mercy to any natural man, whose heart is not turned to God: and that a man can challenge nothing either in absolute justice, or by free promise, from any thing he does before he has believed on Jesus Christ, or has true repentance begun in him. It appears to me, that if I had taught those that came to me under trouble, any other doctrine, I should have taken a most direct course utterly to have undone them; I should have directly crossed what was plainly the drift of the spirit of God in his influences upon them; for if they had believed what I said, it would either have promoted self-flattery and carelessness, and so put an end to their awakenings; or cherished and established their contention and strife with God, concerning his dealings with them and others, and blocked up their way to that humiliation before the Sovereign Disposer of life and death, whereby God is wont to prepare them for his consolations. And yet those that have been under awakenings, have oftentimes plainly stood in need of being encouraged, by being told of the infinite and all-sufficient mercy of God in Christ; and that it is God's manner to succeed diligence, and to bless his own means, that so awakenings and encouragements, fear and hope may be duly mixed, and proportioned to preserve their minds in a just medium between the two extremes of self-flattery and despondence, both which tend to slackness and negligence, and in the end to security. I think I have found that no discourses have been more remarkably blessed, than those in which the doctrine of God's absolute sovereignty with regard to the salvation of sinners, and his just liberty, with regard to answering the prayers, or succeeding the pains of natural men, continuing such, have been insisted on. I never found so much immediate saving fruit, in any measure, of any discourses I have offered to my congregation, as some from these words, Rom. iii. 19. 'That every mouth may be stopped;' endeavouring to shew from thence, that it would be just with God for ever to reject and cast off mere natural men.

In those in whom awakenings seem to have a saving issue, commonly the first thing that appears after their legal troubles, is a conviction of the justice of God in their condemnation, in a sense of their own exceeding sinfulness, and the vileness of all their performances: in giving an account of this, they express themselves very variously; some, that they saw that God was sovereign, and might receive others and reject them: some, that they were convinced, that God might justly bestow mercy on every person in the town, and on every person in the world, and damn themselves to all eternity; some, that they see that God might justly have no regard to all the pains they have taken, and all the prayers they have made; some, that they see that if they should seek, and take the utmost pains all their lives, God might justly cast them into hell at least, because all their labours, prayers, and tears cannot make an atonement for the least sin, nor merit any blessing at the hands of God; some have declared themselves to be in the hands of God, that he can, and may, dispose of them just as he pleases; some, that God may glorify himself in their damnation, and they wonder that God has suffered them to live so long, and has not cast them into hell long ago.

Some are brought to this conviction by a great sense of their sinfulness, in general, that they are such vile wicked creatures in heart and life: others have the sins of their lives in an extraordinary manner set before them, multitudes of them coming just then fresh to their memory, and being set before them with their aggravations; some have their minds especially fixed, on some particular wicked practice they have indulged; some are especially convinced by a sight of the corruption and wickedness of their hearts: some, from a view they have of the horridness of some particular exercises of corruption, which they have had in the time of their awakening, whereby the enmity of the heart against God has been manifested; some are convinced especially by a sense of the sin of unbelief, the opposition of their hearts to the way of salvation by Christ, and their obstinacy in rejecting him and his grace.

There is a great deal of difference as to persons distinctness here; some, that have not so clear a sight of God's justice in their condemnation, yet mention things that plainly imply it. They find a disposition to acknowledge God to be just and righteous in his threatenings, and that they are deserving of nothing: and many times, though they had not so particular a sight of it at the beginning, they have very clear discoveries of it soon afterwards, with great humblings in the dust before God.

Commonly persons minds immediately before this discovery of God's justice are exceeding restless, and in a kind of struggle and tumult, and sometimes in mere anguish; but generally, as soon as they have this conviction, it immediately brings their minds to a calm, and a before-unexpected quietness and composure; and most frequently, though not always, then the pressing weight upon their spirits is taken away, and a general hope arises, that some time or other God will be gracious, even before any distinct and particular discoveries of mercy; and often they then come to a conclusion within themselves, that they will lie at God's feet, and wait his time; and they rest in that, not being sensible that the spirit of God has now brought them to a frame whereby they are prepared for mercy: for it is remarkable that persons when they first have this sense of the justice of God, rarely, in the time of it, think any thing of its being that humiliation that they have often heard insisted on, and that others experience.

In many persons, the first conviction of the justice of God in their condemnation, which they take particular notice of, and probably the first distinct conviction of it that they have, is of such a nature, as seems to be above any thing merely legal: though it be after legal humblings, and much of a sense of their own helplessness and of the insufficiency of their own duties; yet it does not appear to be forced by mere legal terrors and convictions; but rather from a high exercise of grace, in saving repentance, and evangelical humiliation; for there is in it a sort of complacency of soul, in the attribute of God's justice, as displayed in his threatenings of eternal damnation to sinners. Sometimes at the discovery of it, they can scarcely forbear crying out, IT IS JUST! IT IS JUST! Some express themselves, that they see the glory of God would shine bright in their own condemnation; and they are ready to think that if they are damned, they could take part with God against themselves, and would glorify his justice therein. And when it is thus, they commonly have some evident sense of free and all-sufficient grace, though they give no distinct account of it, but it is manifest, by that great degree of hope and encouragement that they then conceive, though they were never so sensible of their own vileness and ill-deservings as they are at that time.

Some, when in such circumstances, have felt that sense of the excellency of God's justice, appearing in the vindicative exercises of it, against such sinfulness as theirs was, and have had such a submission of mind in their idea of this attribute, and of those exercises of it, together with an exceeding loathing of their own unworthiness, and a kind of indignation against themselves, that they have sometimes almost called it a willingness to be damned; though it must be owned they had not clear and distinct ideas of damnation, nor does any word in the Bible require such self-denial as this. But the truth is, as some have more clearly expressed it, that salvation has appeared too good for them, that they were worthy of nothing but condemnation, and they could not tell how to think of salvation's being bestowed upon them, fearing it was inconsistent with the glory of God's majesty, that they had so much contemned and affronted.

That calm of spirit that some persons have found after their legal distresses, continues some time before any special and delightful manifestation is made to the soul of the grace of God, as revealed in the gospel; but very often some comfortable and sweet view of a merciful God, of a sufficient Redeemer, or of some great and joyful things of the gospel, immediately follows, or in a very little time: and in some, the first sight of their just desert of hell, and God's sovereignty with respect to their salvation, and a discovery of all-sufficient grace, are so near, that they seem to go as it were together.

These gracious discoveries that are given, whence the first special comforts are derived, are in many respects very various; more frequently Christ is distinctly made the object of the mind, in his all-sufficiency and willingness to save sinners: but some have their thoughts more especially fixed on God, in some of his sweet and glorious attributes manifested in the gospel, and shining forth in the face of Christ: some view the all-sufficiency of the mercy and grace of God; some chiefly the infinite power of God, and his ability to save them, and to do all things for them; and some look most at the truth and faithfulness of God: in some, the truth and certainty of the gospel in general is the first joyful discovery they have; in others, the certain truth of some particular promises; in some, the grace and sincerity of God in his invitations, very commonly in some particular invitation in the mind, and it now appears real to them that God does indeed invite them. Some are struck with the glory and wonderfulness of the dying love of Christ; and some with the sufficiency and preciousness of his blood, as offered to make an atonement for sin; and others with the value and glory of his obedience and righteousness. In some the excellency and loveliness of Christ, chiefly engages their thoughts; in some his divinity, that he is indeed the Son of the living God; and in others, the excellency of the way of salvation by Christ, and the suitableness of it to their necessities.

Some have an apprehension of these things so given, that it seems more natural to them to express it by sight or discovery;

others think what they experience better expressed by the realizing conviction, or a lively or feeling sense of heart; meaning, as I suppose, no other difference but what is merely circumstantial or gradual.

There is, often, in the mind, some particular text of scripture, holding forth some evangelical ground of consolation; sometimes a multitude of texts, gracious invitations and promises flowing in one after another, filling the soul more and more, with comfort and satisfaction: and comfort is first given to some, while reading some portion of scripture; but in some it is attended with no particular scripture at all, either in reading or meditation. In some, many divine things seem to be discovered to the soul as it were at once; others have their minds especially fixing on some one thing at first, and afterwards a sense is given of others; in some with a swifter, and others a slower succession, and sometimes with interruptions of much darkness.

The way that grace seems sometimes first to appear after legal humiliation, is in earnest longings of soul after God and Christ, to know God, to love him, to be humbled before him, to have communion with Christ in his benefits; which longings, as they express them, seem evidently to be of such a nature as can arise from nothing but a sense of the superlative excellency of divine things, with a spiritual taste and relish of them, and an esteem of them as their highest happiness and best portion. Such longings as I speak of, are commonly attended with firm resolutions to pursue this good for ever, together with a hoping, waiting disposition. When persons have begun in such frames, commonly other experiences and discoveries have soon followed, which have yet more clearly manifested a change of heart.

It must needs be confessed that Christ is not always distinctly and explicitly thought of in the first sensible act of grace, (though most commonly he is?) but sometimes he is the object of the mind only implicitly. Thus sometimes when persons have seemed evidently to be stripped of all their own righteousness, and to have stood self-condemned as guilty of death, they have been comforted with a joyful and satisfying view, that the mercy and grace of God is sufficient for them; that their sins, though never so great, shall be no hindrance to their being accepted; that there is mercy enough in God for the whole world, and the like, when they give no account of any particular or distinct thought of Christ? but yet when the account they give is duly weighed, and they are a little interrogated about it, it appears that the revelation of the mercy of God in the gospel, is the ground of this their encouragement and hope; and that it is indeed the mercy of God through Christ that is discovered to them, and that it is depended on in him, and not in any wise moved by any thing in them.

So sometimes disconsolate souls amongst us, have been revived and brought to rest in God, by a sweet sense given of his grace and faithfulness, in some special invitation or promise, in which is no particular mention of Christ, nor is it accompanied with any distinct thought of him in their minds; but yet it is not received as out of Christ, but as one of the invitations or promises made of God to poor sinners through his Son Jesus, as it is indeed: and such persons have afterwards had clear and distinct discoveries of Christ, accompanied with lively and special actings of faith and love towards him.

It has more frequently been so amongst us, that when persons have first had the gospel-ground of relief for lost sinners discovered to them, and have been entertaining their minds with the sweet prospect, they have thought nothing at that time of their being converted: to see that there is such an all-sufficiency in God, and such plentiful provision made in Christ, after they have been borne down, and sunk with a sense of their guilt and fears of wrath, exceedingly refreshes them; the view is joyful to them, as it is in its own nature glorious, and gives them quite new, and more delightful ideas of God and Christ, and greatly encourages them to seek conversion, and begets in them a strong resolution to give up themselves, and devote their whole lives to God and his Son, and patiently to wait till God shall see fit to make all effectual; and very often they entertain a strong persuasion, that he will in his own time do it for them.

There is wrought in them a holy repose of soul in God through Christ, and a secret disposition to fear and love him, and to hope for blessings from him in this way: and yet they have no imagination that they are now converted, it does not so much as come into their minds: and very often the reason is, that they do not see that they do accept of this sufficiency of salvation, that they behold in Christ, having entertained a wrong notion of acceptance; not being sensible that the obedient and joyful entertainment which their hearts give to this discovery of grace, is a real acceptance of it: they know not that the sweet complacency they feel in the mercy and complete salvation of God, as it includes pardon and sanctification, and is held forth to them only through Christ, is a true receiving of this mercy, or a plain evidence of their receiving it. They expected I know not what kind of act of soul, and perhaps they had no distinct idea of it themselves.

And indeed it appears very plainly in some of them, that before their own conversion they had very imperfect ideas what conversion was: it is all new and strange, and what there was no clear conception of before. It is most evident as they themselves acknowledge, that the expressions that were used to describe conversion, and the graces of God's spirit, such as a spiritual sight of Christ, faith in Christ, poverty of spirit, trust in God, resignedness to God, &c. were expressions that did not convey those special and distinct ideas to their minds which they were intended to signify: perhaps to some of them it was but little more than the names of colours are to convey the ideas to one that is blind from his birth.

This town is a place where there has always been a great deal of talk of conversion and spiritual experiences; and therefore people in general had before formed a notion in their own minds what these things were; but when they come to be the subjects of them themselves, they find themselves much confounded in their notions, and overthrown in many of their former conceits. And it has been very observable, that persons of the greatest understanding, and that had studied most about things of this nature, have been more confounded than others. Some such persons that have lately been converted, declare that all their former wisdom is brought to nought, and that they appear to have been mere babes, who knew nothing. It has appeared that none have stood more in need of enlightening and instruction, even of their fellow Christians, concerning their own circumstances and difficulties than they: and it has seemed to have been with delight, that they have seen themselves, thus brought down and become nothing, that free grace, and divine power may be exalted in them.

It was very wonderful to see after what manner persons' affections were sometimes moved and wrought upon, when God did as it were, suddenly open their eyes and let into their minds, a sense of the greatness of his grace, and fulness of Christ, and his readiness to save, who before were broken with apprehensions of divine wrath, and sunk into an abyss under a sense of guilt, which they were ready to think was beyond the mercy of God: their joyful surprise has caused their hearts as it were to leap, so that they have been ready to break forth into laughter, tears often at the same time issuing like a flood, and intermingling a loud weeping: and sometimes they have not been able to forbear crying out with a loud voice, expressing their great admiration. In some even the view of the glory of God's sovereignty in the exercises of his grace has surprised the soul with such sweetness, as to produce the same effects. I remember an instance of one, who, reading something concerning God's sovereign way of saving sinners, as being self-moved, and having no regard to men's own righteousness as the motive of his grace, but as magnifying himself and abasing man, or to that purpose, felt such a sudden rapture of joy and delight in the consideration of it: and yet then suspected himself to be in a Christless condition, and had been long in great distress for fear that God would not have mercy on him.

Many continue a long time in a course of gracious exercises and experiences, and do not think themselves to be converted, but conclude themselves to be otherwise; and none knows how long they would continue so, were they not helped by particular instruction. There are undoubted instances of some that have lived in this way for many years together; and a continuing in these circumstances of being converted and not believing it, has had various consequences, with various persons, and with the same persons, at various times; some continue in great encouragement and hope, that they shall obtain mercy, in a stedfast resolution to persevere in seeking it, and in an humble waiting for it at God's foot; but very often when the lively sense of the sufficiency of Christ, and the riches of divine grace begins to vanish, upon a withdraw of the influences of the spirit of God, they return to greater distress than ever; for they have now a far greater sense of the misery of a natural condition than before, being in a new manner sensible of the reality of eternal things, and the greatness of God, and his excellency, and how dreadful it is to be separated from him, and to be subject to his wrath; so that they are sometimes swallowed up with darkness and amazement. Satan has a vast advantage in such cases to ply them with various temptations, which he is not wont to neglect. In such a case persons do very much need a guide to lead them to an understanding of what we are taught in the word of God of the nature of grace, and to help them to apply it to themselves.

I have been much blamed and censured by many, that I should make it my practice, when I have been satisfied concerning persons good estate, to signify it to them: which thing has been greatly misrepresented abroad, as innumerable other things concerning us, to prejudice the country against the whole affair. But let it be noted, that what I have undertaken to judge of, has rather been qualifications, and declared experiences, than persons: not but that I have thought it my duty as a pastor to assist and instruct persons in applying scripture-rules and characters to their own case, (in doing of which, I think many greatly need a guide;) and have, where I thought the case plain, used freedom in signifying my hope of them, to others: but have been far from doing this concerning all that I have had some hopes of; and I believe have used much more caution than many have supposed. Yet I should account it a great calamity to be deprived of the comfort of rejoicing with those of my flock, that have been in great distress, whose circumstances I have been acquainted with, when there seems to be good evidence that those that were dead are alive, and those that were lost are found. I am sensible the practice would have been safer in the hands of one of a riper judgment and greater experience; but yet there has seemed to be an absolute necessity of it on the forementioned accounts; and it has been found to be that which God has most remarkably owned and blessed amongst us, both to the persons themselves, and others.

Grace in many persons, through this ignorance of their state, and their looking on themselves still as the objects of God's displeasure, has been like the trees in winter, or like seed in the spring suppressed under a hard clod of earth; and many in such cases have laboured to their utmost to divert their minds from the pleasing and joyful views they have had, and to suppress those consolations and gracious affections that arose thereupon. And when it has once come into their minds to enquire whether or no this was not true grace, they have been much afraid lest they should be deceived with common illuminations and flashes of affection, and eternally undone with a false hope. But when they have been better instructed, and so brought to allow of hope, this has awakened the gracious disposition of their hearts into life and vigour, as the warm beams of the sun in the spring, have quickened the seeds and productions of the earth: grace being now at liberty, and cherished with hope, has soon flowed out to their abundant satisfaction and increase.

There is no one thing that I know of that God has made such a means of promoting his work amongst us, as the news of others conversion; in the awakening sinners, and engaging them earnestly to seek the same blessing, and in the quickening of saints. Though I have thought that a minister's declaring his judgment about particular persons experiences might from these things be justified, yet I am often signifying to my people how unable man is to know another's heart, and how unsafe it is depending merely on the judgment of ministers, or others, and have abundantly insisted on it with them, that a manifestation of sincerity in fruits brought forth, is better than any manifestation they can make of it in words alone, can be; and that without this, all pretences to spiritual experiences are vain; as all my congregation can witness. And the people in general, in this late extraordinary time, have manifested an extraordinary dread of being deceived, being exceeding fearful lest they should build wrong, and some of them backward to receive hope, even to a great extreme, which has occasioned me to dwell longer on this part of the narrative.

Conversion is a great and glorious work of God's power, at once changing the heart, and infusing life into the dead soul; though that grace that is then implanted does more gradually display itself in some than in others. But as to fixing on the precise time when they put forth the very first act of grace, there is a great deal of difference in different persons; in some it seems to be very discernible when the very time of this was; but others are more at a loss. In this respect, there are very many that do not know the time, (as has been already observed) that when they have the first exercises of grace, do not know that it is the grace of conversion, and sometimes do not think it to be so till a long time after: and many, even when they come to entertain great hope that they are converted, if they remember what they experienced in the first exercises of grace, they are at a loss whether it was any more than a common illumination; or whether some other more clear and remarkable experience, that they had afterwards, was not the first that was of a saving nature. And the manner of God's work on the soul is (sometimes especially) very mysterious, and it is with the kingdom of God as to its manifestation in the heart of a convert, as is said, Mark iv. 26, 27, 28. 'So is the kingdom of God, as if a man should cast seed into the ground, and should sleep, and rise night and day, and the seed should spring, and grow up, he knoweth not how; for the earth bringeth forth of herself, first the blade, then the ear, then the full corn in the ear.'

In some, converting light is like a glorious brightness suddenly shining in upon a person, and all around him: they are in a remarkable manner brought 'out of darkness into marvellous light.' In many others it has been like the dawning of the day, when at first but a little light appears, and it may be is presently hid with a cloud; and then it appears again, and shines a little brighter, and gradually increases, with intervening darkness, till at length, perhaps, it breaks forth more clearly from behind the clouds. And many are, doubtless, ready to date their conversion wrong, throwing by those lesser degrees of light that appeared at first dawning, and calling some more remarkable experience, that they had afterwards, their conversions; which often in great measure arises from a wrong understanding of what they have always been taught, that conversion is a great change, wherein 'old things are done away, and all things become new,' or at least from a false arguing from that doctrine.

Persons commonly at first conversion, and afterwards; have had many texts of scripture brought to their minds, that are exceeding suitable to their circumstances, which often come with great power, and as the word of God or Christ indeed; and many have a multitude of sweet invitations, promises, and doxologies flowing in one after another, bringing great light and comfort with them, filling the soul brimful, enlarging the heart, and opening the mouth in religion. And it seems to me necessary to suppose, that there is an immediate influence of the spirit of God, oftentimes in bringing texts of scripture to the mind: not that I suppose it is done in a way of immediate revelation, without any manner of use of the memory; but yet there seems plainly to be an immediate and extraordinary influence, in leading their thoughts to such and such passages of scripture, and exciting them in the memory. Indeed in some God seems to bring texts of scripture to their minds no otherwise than by leading them into such frames and meditations, as harmonize with those scriptures; but in many persons there seems to be something more than this.

Those that, while under legal convictions, have had the greatest terrors, have not always obtained the greatest light and comfort; nor have they always light most suddenly communicated; but yet, I think, the time of conversion has generally been most sensible in such persons. Oftentimes, the first sensible change after the extremity of terrors, is a calmness, and then the light gradually comes in; small glimpses at first, after their midnight darkness, and a word or two of comfort, as it were softly spoken to them; they have a little taste of the sweetness of divine grace, and the love of a Saviour, when terror and distress of conscience begins to be turned into an humble, meek sense of their own unworthiness before God; and there is felt inwardly, perhaps, some disposition to praise God; and after a little while the light comes in more clearly and powerfully. But yet, I think, more frequently, great terrors have been followed with more sudden and great light, and comfort; when the sinner seems to be as it were subdued and brought to a calm, from a kind of tumult of mind, then God lets in an extraordinary sense of his great mercy through a Redeemer.

The converting influences of God's spirit very commonly bring an extraordinary conviction of the reality and certainty of the great things of religion; (though in some this is much greater, some time after conversion, than at first:) they have that sight and taste of the divinity, or divine excellency, that there is in the things of the gospel, that is more to convince them, than reading many volumes of arguments without it. It seems to me, that in many instances amongst us, when the divine excellency and glory of the things of Christianity have been set before persons, and they have at the same time as it were seen, and tasted, and felt the divinity of them, they have been as far from doubting of the truth of them, as they are from doubting whether there be a sun, when their eyes are open in the midst of a clear hemisphere, and the strong blaze of his light overcomes all objections against his being. And yet many of them, if we should ask them why they believed those things to be true, would not be able well to express, or communicate a sufficient reason to satisfy the enquirer, and perhaps would make no other answer but that they see them to be true: but a person might soon be satisfied, by a particular conversation with them, that what they mean by such an answer is, that they have intuitively beheld, and immediately felt, most illustrious works, and powerful evidence of divinity in them.

Some are thus convinced of the truth of the gospel in general, and that the scriptures are the word of God: others have their minds more especially fixed on some particular great doctrine of the gospel, some particular truths that they are meditating on; or are in a special manner convinced of the divinity of the things they are reading of, in some portion of scripture. Some have such convictions in a much more remarkable manner than others: and there are some that never had such a special sense of the certainty of divine things, impressed upon them with such inward evidence and strength, have yet very clear exercises of grace; *i.e.* of love to God, repentance and holiness. And if they may be more particularly examined, they appear plainly to have an inward firm persuasion of the reality of divine things, such as they do not use to have before their conversion. And those that have the most clear discoveries of divine truth, in the manner that has been spoken of, cannot have this always in view. When the sense and relish of the divine excellency of these things fades, on a withdrawal of the spirit of God, they have not the medium of the conviction of their truth at command: in a dull frame they cannot recall the idea, and inward sense they had, perfectly to mind; things appear very dim to what they did before, and though there still remains an habitual strong persuasion; yet not so as to exclude temptations to unbelief, and all possibility of doubting, as before: but then at particular times, by God's help, the same sense of things revives again, like fire that lay hid in ashes.

I suppose the grounds of such a conviction of the truth of divine things to be just and rational, but yet in some God makes use of their own reason much more sensibly than in others. Oftentimes persons have (so far as could be judged) received the first saving conviction from reasoning, which they have heard from the pulpit; and often in the course of reasoning, which they are led into in their own meditations.

The arguments are the same that they have heard hundreds of times; but the force of the arguments, and their conviction by them, is altogether new; they come with a new and before unexperienced power: before they heard it was so, and they allowed it to be so; but now they see it to be so indeed. Things now look exceeding plain to them, and they wonder they did not see them before.

They are so greatly taken with their new discovery, and things appear so plain and so rational to them, that they are often at first ready to think they can convince others; and are apt to engage in talk with every one they meet with, almost to this end; and when they are disappointed, are ready to wonder that their reasonings seem to make no more impression.

Many fall under such a mistake as to be ready to doubt of their good estate, because there was so much use made of their own reason in the convictions they have received; they are afraid that they have no illumination above the natural force of their own faculties: and many make that an objection against the spirituality of their convictions, that it is so easy to see things as they now see them. They have often heard that conversion is a work of mighty power, manifesting to the soul what no man nor angel can give such a conviction of; but it seems to them that the things that they see are so plain, and easy, and rational, that any body can see them: and if they are enquired of, why they never saw so before; they say it seems to them it was because they never thought of it. But very often these difficulties are soon removed by those of another nature; for when God withdraws, they find themselves as it were blind again, they for the present lose their realizing sense of those things that looked so plain to them, and by all that they can do they cannot recover it till God renews the influences of his spirit.

Persons after their conversion often speak of things of religion as seeming new to them; that preaching is a new thing; that it seems to them they never heard preaching before; that the Bible is a new book: they find there new chapters, new psalms, new histories, because they see them in a new light. Here was a remarkable instance of an aged woman, of above 70 years, that had spent most of her days under Mr. Stoddard's powerful ministry; who reading in the New Testament concerning Christ's sufferings for sinners, seemed to be surprised and astonished at what she read, as at a thing that was real and very wonderful, but quite new to her; insomuch that at first, before she had time to turn her thoughts, she wondered within herself that she had never heard of it before; but then immediately recollected herself, and thought she had often heard of it, and read it, but never till now saw it as a thing real; and then cast in her mind, how wonderful this was, that the Son of God should undergo such things for sinners, and how she had spent her time in ungratefully sinning against so good a God, and such a Saviour; though she was a person, as to what was visible, of a very blameless and inoffensive life. And she was so overcome by those considerations, that her nature was ready to fail under them: those that were about her, and knew not what was the matter, were surprised, and thought she was a dying.

Many have spoken much of their hearts being drawn out in love to God and Christ; and their minds being wrapt up in delightful contemplation of the glory, and wonderful grace of God, and the excellency, and dying love of Jesus Christ; and of their souls going forth in longing desires after God and Christ. Several of our young children have expressed much of this; and have manifested a willingness to leave father and mother and all things in the world, to go to be with Christ. Some persons have had longing desires after Christ, which have risen to that degree, as to take away their natural strength. Some have been so overcome with a sense of the dying love of Christ, to such poor, wretched, and unworthy creatures, as to weaken the body. Several persons have had so great a sense of the glory of God, and excellency of Christ, that nature and life has seemed almost to sink under it; and in all probability, if God had showed them a little more of himself, it would have dissolved their frame. I have seen some, and been in conversation with them in such frames, who have certainly been perfectly sober, and very remote from any thing like enthusiastic wildness? And have talked, when able to speak, of the glory of God's perfections, and the wonderfulness of his grace in Christ, and their own unworthiness, in such a manner that cannot be perfectly expressed after them. Their sense of their exceeding littleness and vileness, and their disposition to abase themselves before God, has appeared to be great in proportion to their light and joy.

Such persons amongst us as have been thus distinguished with the most extraordinary discoveries with God, have commonly in nowise appeared with the assuming, and self-conceited, and self-sufficient airs, of enthusiasts; but exceedingly the contrary; and are eminent for a spirit of meekness, modesty, self-diffidence, and low opinion of themselves: no persons seem to be so sensible of their need of instruction, and so eagar to receive it, as some of them; nor so ready to think others better than themselves. Those that have been thought to be converted amongst us have generally manifested longing to lie low, and in the dust before God; withal complaining of their not being able to lie low enough.

They very often speak much of their sense of the excellency of the way of salvation, by free and sovereign grace, through the righteousness of Christ alone; and how it is with delight that they renounce their own righteousness, and rejoice in having no account made of it. Many have expressed themselves to this purpose, that it would lessen the satisfaction they hope for in heaven to have it by their own righteousness, or in any other way than as bestowed by free Grace, and for Christ's sake alone. They speak much of the inexpressibleness of what they experience, how their words fail, so that they can in nowise declare it: and particularly speak with exceeding admiration of the superlative excellency of that pleasure and delight of soul, which they sometimes enjoy; how a little of it is sufficient to pay them for all the pains and trouble they have gone through in seeking salvation; and how far it exceeds all earthly pleasures: and some express much of the sense which these spiritual views give them of the vanity of earthly enjoyments, how mean and worthless all these things appear to them.

Many, while their minds have been filled with spiritual delights, have as it were forgot their food; their bodily appetite has failed, while their minds have been entertained with 'meat to eat that' others 'knew not of.' The light and comfort which some of them enjoy, gives a new relish to their common blessings, and causes all things about them to appear as it were beautiful, sweet and pleasant to them: all things abroad, the sun, moon and stars, the clouds and sky, the heavens and earth, appear as it were with a cast of divine glory and sweetness upon them. The sweetest joy that these good people amongst us express, though it include in it a delightful sense of the safety of their own state, and that now they are out of danger of hell; yet frequently, in times of their highest spiritual entertainment, this seems not to be the chief object of their fixed thought and meditation. The supreme attention of their minds is to the glorious excellencies of God and Christ, which they have in view; not but that there is very often a ravishing sense of God's love accompanying a sense of his excellency, and they rejoice in a sense of the faithfulness of God's promises, as they respect the future eternal enjoyment of God.

The joy that many of them speak of is that to which none is to be parralleled, is that which they find when they are lowest in the dust, emptied most of themselves, and as it were annihilating themselves before God, when they are nothing, and God is all, are seeing their own unworthiness, depending not at all on themselves, but alone on Christ, and ascribing all glory to God: then their souls are most in the enjoyment of satisfying rest; excepting that, at such times they apprehend themselves to be not sufficiently self-abased; for then above all times do they long to be lower. Some speak much of the exquisite sweetness, and rest of soul, that is to be found in the exercises of a spirit of resignation to God, and humble submission to his will. Many express earnest longings of soul to praise God; but at the same time complain that they cannot praise him as they would do, and they want to have others help them in praising him: they want to have every one praise God, and are ready to call upon every thing to praise him. They express a longing desire to live to God's glory, and to do something to his honour; but at the same time cry out of their insufficiency and barrenness, that they are poor impotent creatures, can do nothing of themselves, and are utterly insufficient to glorify their Creator and Redeemer.

While God was so remarkably present amongst us by his spirit, there was no book so delighted in as the Bible; especially the Book of Psalms, the Prophecy of Isaiah, and the New Testament. Some, by reason of their esteem and love to God's word, have, at some times, been greatly and wonderfully delighted and affected at the sight of a bible; and then, also, there was no time so prized as the Lord's-day, and no place, in this world, so desired as God's house. Our converts then remarkably appeared united in dear affection to one another, and many have expressed much of that spirit of love which they felt toward all mankind; and particularly to those that have been least friendly to them. Never, I believe, was so much done in confessing injuries, and making up differences, as the last year. Persons, after their own conversion, have commonly expressed an exceeding desire for the conversion of others: some have thought that they should be willing to die for the conversion of any soul, though of one of the meanest of their fellow-creatures, or of their worst enemies; and many have, indeed, been in great distress with desires and longings for it. This work of God had also a good effect to unite the people's affections much to their minister.

There are some persons that I have been acquainted with, but more especially two, that belong to other towns, that have been swallowed up exceedingly with a sense of the awful greatness and majesty of God; and both of them told me to this purpose, that if they, in the time of it, had had the least fear that they were not at peace with this so great a God, they should instantly have died.

It is worthy to be remarked, that some persons, by their conversion, seem to be greatly helped as to their doctrinal notions of religion; it was particularly remarkable in one, who having been taken captive in his childhood, was trained up in Canada, in the Popish religion; and some years since returned to this his native place, and was in a measure brought off from popery; but seemed very awkward and dull of receiving any true and clear notion of the Protestant scheme, till he was converted; and then he was remarkably altered in this respect.

There is a vast difference, as has been observed, in the degree, and also in the particular manner of persons' experiences, both at, and after conversion; some have grace working more sensibly in one way, others in another. Some speak more fully of a conviction of the justice of God in their condemnation; others more of their consenting to the way of salvation by Christ; some more of the actings of love to God and Christ: some more of acts of affiance, in a sweet and assured conviction of the truth and faithfulness of God in his promises; others more of their choosing and resting in God as their whole and everlasting portion, and of their ardent and longing desires after God, to have communion with him; others, more of their abhorrence of themselves for their past sins, and earnest longings to live to God's glory for the time to come: some have their minds fixed more on God; others on Christ, as I have observed before, and am afraid of too much repetition; but it seems evidently to be the same work, the same thing done, the same habitual change wrought in the heart; it all tends the same way, and to the same end; and it is plainly the same spirit that breathes and acts in various persons. There is an endless variety in the particular manner and circumstances in which persons are wrought on, and an opportunity of seeing so much of such a work of God, will shew that God is further from confining himself to certain steps, and a particular method, in his work on souls, than it may be some do imagine. I believe it has occasioned some good people amongst us, that were before too ready to make their own experience a rule to others, to be less censorious and more extended in their charity, and this is an excellent advantage indeed. The work of God has been glorious in its variety, it has the more displayed the manifoldness and unsearchableness of the wisdom of God, and wrought more charity among his people.

There is a great difference among those that are converted, as to the degree of hope and satisfaction that they have concerning their own state. Some have a high degree of satisfaction in this matter almost constantly: and yet it is rare that any do enjoy so full an assurance of their interest in Christ, that self-examination should seem needless to them; unless it be at particular seasons, while in the actual enjoyment of some great discovery, that God gives of his glory, and rich grace in Christ, to the drawing forth of extraordinary acts of grace. But the greater part, as they sometimes fall into dead frames of spirit, are frequently exercised with scruples and fears concerning their condition.

They generally have an awful apprehension of the dreadfulness and undoing nature of a false hope; and there has been observeable in most a great caution, lest in giving an account of their experiences, they should say too much, and use too strong terms: and many after they have related their experiences, have been greatly afflicted with fears, lest they have played the hypocrite, and used stronger terms than their case would fairly allow of; and yet could not find how they could correct themselves.

I think that the main ground of the doubts and fears, that persons, after their conversion, have been exercised with about their own state, has been, that they have found so much corruption remaining in their hearts. At first, their souls seem to be all alive, their hearts are fixed, and their affections flowing; they seem to live quite above the world, and meet with but little difficulty in religious exercises; and they are ready to think it will always be so: though they are truly abased under a sense of their vileness, by reason of former acts of sin, yet they are not then sufficiently sensible what corruption still remains in their hearts; and, therefore, are surprised when they find that they begin to be in dull and dead frames, to be troubled with wandering thoughts in the time of public and private worship, and to be utterly unable to keep themselves from them; also, when they find themselves unaffected at seasons in which, they think, there is the greatest occasion to be affected; and when they feel wordly dispositions working in them, and it may be pride, and envy, and stirrings of revenge, or some ill spirit towards some person that has injured them, as well as other workings of indwelling sin: their hearts are almost sunk with the disappointment; and they are ready presently to think that all this they have met with is nothing, and that they are mere hypocrites.

They are ready to argue, that if God had, indeed, done such great things for them, as they hoped, such ingratitude would be inconsistent with it: they cry out of the hardness and wicked-ness of their hearts; and say there is so much corruption, that it seems to them impossible that there should be any goodness there: and many of them seem to be much more sensible how corrupt their hearts are, than ever they were before they were converted; and some have been too ready to be impressed with fear, that instead of becoming better, they are grown much worse, and make it an argument against the goodness of their state. But in truth, the case seems plainly to be, that now they feel the pain of their own wound; they have a watchful eye upon their hearts, that they did not use to have: they take more notice what sin is there, and sin is now more burdensome to them, they strive more against it, and feel more of the strength of it.

They are somewhat surprised that they should in this respect, find themselves so different from the idea that they generally had entertained of godly persons; for though grace be indeed of a far more excellent nature than they imagined: yet those that are godly have much less of it, and much more remaining corruption, than they thought. They never realized it, that persons were wont to meet with such difficulties, after they were once converted. When they are thus exercised with doubts about their state, through the deadness of their frames of spirit, as long as these frames last, they are commonly unable to satisfy themselves of the truth of their grace, by all their self-examination. When they hear of the signs of grace laid down for them to try themselves by, they are often so clouded, that they do not know how to apply them: they hardly know whether they have such and such things in them or no, and whether they have experienced them or not: that which was sweetest, and best, and most distinguished in their experiences, they cannot recover a sense or idea of. But on a return of the influences of the Spirit of God, to revive the lively actings of grace, and light breaks through the cloud, and doubting and darkness soon vanish away.

Persons are often revived out of their dead and dark frames, by religious conversation: while they are talking of divine things, or ever they are aware, their souls are carried away into holy exercises with abundant pleasure. And oftentimes, while they are relating their past experiences to their Christian brethren, they have a fresh sense of them revived, and the same experiences in a degree again renewed. Sometimes while persons are exercised in mind with several objections against the goodness of their state, they have scriptures, one after another, coming to their minds, to answer their scruples, and unravel their difficulties, exceeding apposite and proper to their circumstances; by which means their darkness is scattered; and often before the bestowment of any new remarkable comforts, especially after long continued deadness and ill frames, there are renewed humblings, in a great sense of their own exceeding vileness and unworthiness, as before their first comforts were bestowed.

Many in the country have entertained a mean thought of this great work that there has been amongst us, from what they have heard of impressions that have been made on persons' imaginations. But there have been exceeding great misrepresentations, and innumerable false reports, concerning that matter. It is not, that I know of, the profession or opinion of any one person in the town, that any weight is to be laid on any thing seen with the bodily eyes: I know the contrary to be a received and established principle amongst us. I cannot say that there have been no instances of persons that have been ready to give too much heed to vain and useless imaginations; but they have been easily corrected, and I conclude it will not be wondered at, that a congregation should need a guide in such cases, to assist them in distinguishing wheat from chaff. But such impressions, on the imagination as have been more usual, seem to me, to be plainly no other than what is to be expected in human nature in such circumstances, and what is the natural result of the strong exercise of the mind, and impressions on the heart.

I do not suppose that they themselves imagined that they saw any thing with their bodily eyes; but only have had within them ideas strongly impressed, and as it were, lively pictures in their minds: as for instance, some when in great terrors, through fear of hell, have had lively ideas of a dreadful furnace. Some, when their hearts have been strongly impressed, and their affections greatly moved with a sense of the beauty and excellency of Christ, it has wrought on their imaginations so, that together with a sense of his glorious spiritual perfections, there has arisen in the mind an idea of one of glorious majesty, and of a sweet and a gracious aspect: so some, when they have been greatly affected with Christ's death, have at the same time a lively idea of Christ hanging upon the cross, and of his blood running from his wounds; which things will not be wondered at by them that have observed how strong affections about temporal matters will excite lively ideas and pictures of different things in the mind.

But yet the vigorous exercise of the mind, does doubtless more strongly impress it with imaginary ideas, in some than others, which probably may arise from the difference of constitution, and seems evidently in some, partly to arise from their peculiar circumstances: when persons have been exercised with extreme terrors, and there is a sudden change to light and joy, the imagination seems more susceptive of strong ideas, and the inferior powers, and even the frame of the body, is much more affected and wrought upon, than when the same persons have as great spiritual light and joy afterwards; of which it might, perhaps, be easy to give a reason. The forementioned Reverend Messrs. Lord and Owen, who, I believe, are esteemed persons of learning and discretion where they are best known, declared that they found these impressions on persons' imaginations quite different things from what fame had before represented to them, and that they were what none need to wonder at, or be stumbled by, or to that purpose.

There have indeed been some few instances of impressions on persons' imaginations, that have been something mysterious to me, and I have been at a loss about them; for though it has been exceeding evident to me by many things that appeared in them, both then (when they related them) and afterwards, that they indeed had a greater sense of the spiritual excellency of divine things accompanying them; yet I have not been able well to satisfy myself, whether their imaginary ideas have been more than could naturally arise from their spiritual sense of things. However, I have used the utmost caution in such cases; great care has been taken both in public and in private to teach persons the difference between what is spiritual and what is merely imaginary. I have often warned persons not to lay the stress of their hope on any ideas of any outward glory, or any external thing whatsoever, and have met with no opposition in such instructions. But it is not strange if some weaker persons, in giving an account of their experiences, have not so prudently distinguished between the spiritual and imaginary part; which some that have not been well affected to religion might take advantage of.

There has been much talk in many parts of the country, as though the people have symbolized with the Quakers, and the Quakers themselves have been moved with such reports; and came here, once and again, hoping to find good waters to fish in; but without the least success, and seem to be discouraged, and have left off coming. There have also been reports spread about the country, as though the first occasion of so remarkable a concern on peoples' minds here, was an apprehension that the world was near to an end, which was altogether a false report: indeed after this stirring and concern became so general and extraordinary, as has been related, the minds of some were filled with speculation, what so great a dispensation of divine providence might forebode; and some reports were heard from abroad, as though certain Divines and others thought the conflagration was nigh; but such reports were never generally looked upon worthy of notice.

The work that has now been wrought on souls is evidently the same that was wrought in my venerable predecessor's days; as I have had abundant opportunity to know, having been in the ministry here two years with him, and so conversed with a considerable number that my grandfather thought to be savingly converted in that time: and having been particularly acquainted with the experiences of many that were converted under his ministry before. And I know no one of them, that in the least doubts of its being the same spirit, and the same work. Persons have now no otherwise been subject to impressions on their imaginations than formerly: the work is of the same nature, and has not been attended with any extraordinary circumstances, excepting such as are analogous to the extraordinary degree of it before described. And God's people, there were formerly converted, have now partook of the same shower of divine blessing, in the renewing, strengthening, edifying influences of the Spirit of God, that others have, in his converting influences; and the work here has also been plainly the same with that which has been wrought in those of other places, that have been mentioned, as partaking of the same blessing. I have particularly conversed with persons about their experiences that belong to all parts of the country, and in various parts of Connecticut, where a religious concern has lately appeared; and have been informed of the experiences of many others by their own pastors.

It is easily perceived by the foregoing account that it is very much the practice of the people here, to converse freely one with another of their spiritual experiences; which is a thing that many have been disgusted at. But however our people may have, in some respects, gone to extremes in it, yet it is doubtless, a practice that the circumstances of this town, and neighbouring towns, have naturally led them into. Whatsoever people are in such circumstances, where all have their minds engaged to such a degree, in the same affair, that it is ever uppermost in their thoughts; they will naturally make it the subject of conversation one with another when they get together, in which they will grow more and more free: restraints will soon vanish; and they will not conceal from one another what they meet with. And it has been a practice which, in the general, has been attended with many good effects, and what God has greatly blessed amongst us: but it must be confessed, there may have been some ill consequences of it: which yet are rather to be laid to the indiscreet management of it than to the practice itself; and none can wonder, if among such a multitude some fail of exercising so much prudence in choosing the time, manner, and occasion of such discourse, as is desirable.

But to give a clearer idea of the nature and manner of the operation of God's Spirit, in this wonderful effusion of it, I would give an account of two particular instances. The first is an adult person, a young woman whose name was Abigail Hutchinson. I pitch upon her especially, because she is now dead, and so it may be more fit to speak freely of her than of living instances: though I am under far greater disadvantages, on other accounts, to give a full and clear narrative of her experiences, than I might of some others; nor can any account be given but what has been retained in the memories of her near friends, and some others, of what they have heard her express in her life-time.

She was of a rational understanding family: there could be nothing in her education that tended to enthusiasm, but rather to the contrary extreme. It is in no wise the temper of the family to be ostentatious of experiences, and it was far from being her temper. She was before her conversion, to the observation of her neighbours, of a sober and inoffensive conversation; and was a still, quiet, reserved person. She had long been infirm of body, but her infirmity had never been observed at all to incline her to be notional or fanciful, or to occasion any thing of religious melancholy. She was under awakenings scarcely a week, before there seemed to be plain evidence of her being savingly converted.

She was first awakened in the winter season, on Monday, by something she heard her brother say of the necessity of being in good earnest in seeking regenerating grace, together with the news of the conversion of the young woman before mentioned, whose conversion so generally affected most of the young people here. This news wrought much upon her, and stirred up a spirit of envy in her towards this young woman, whom she thought very unworthy of being distinguished from others by such a mercy; but withal it engaged her in a firm resolution to do her utmost to obtain the same blessing; and considering with herself what course she should take, she thought, that she had not a sufficient knowledge of the principles of religion, to render her capable of conversion; whereupon she resolved thoroughly to search the scriptures; and accordingly immediately began at the beginning of the Bible, intending to read it through. She continued thus till Thursday: and then there was a sudden alteration, by a great increase of her concern, in an extraordinary sense of her own sinfulness, particularly the sinfulness of her nature, and wickedness of her heart, which came upon her (as she expressed it) as a flash of lightning, and struck her into an exceeding terror. Upon which she left off reading the Bible, in course as she had begun, and turned to the New Testament, to see if she could not find some relief there for her distressed soul.

Her great terror, she said, was, that she had sinned against God: her distress grew more and more for three days; until (as she said) she saw nothing but blackness of darkness before her, and her very flesh trembled for fear of God's wrath: she wondered and was astonished at herself, that she had been so concerned for her body, and had applied so often to physicians to heal that, and had neglected her soul. Her sinfulness appeared with a very awful aspect of her, especially in three things: viz. her original sin, and her sin in murmuring at God's providence, in the weakness and afflictions she had been under, and in want of duty to parents, though others had looked upon her to excel in dutifulness. On Saturday she was so earnestly engaged in reading the Bible, and other books, that she continued on it, searching for something to relieve her, till her eyes were so dim, that she could not know the letters. While she was thus engaged in reading, prayer, and other religious exercises, she thought of those words of Christ, wherein he warns us not to be 'as the heathen,' that 'think they shall be heard for their much speaking;' which, she said, led her to see that she had trusted to her own prayers and religious performances, and now she was put to a nonplus, and knew not which way to turn herself, or where to seek relief.

While her mind was in this posture, her heart, she said, seemed to fly to the minister for refuge; hoping that he could give her some relief. She came the same day to her brother, with the countenance of a person in distress, expostulating with him, why he had not told her more of her sinfulness, and earnestly enquiring of him what she should do. She seemed that day to feel in herself an enmity against the Bible, which greatly affrighted her. Her sense of her own exceeding sinfulness continued increasing from Thursday till Monday; and she gave this account of it, that it had been an opinion, which till now she had entertained, that she was not guilty of Adam's sin, nor any way concerned in it, because she was not active in it; but that now she saw she was guilty of that sin, and all over defiled by it; and that the sin which she brought into the world with her, was alone sufficient to condemn her.

On the sabbath-day she was so ill that her friends thought it not best that she should go to public worship, of which she seemed very desirous; but when she went to bed on the sabbath-day night, she took up a resolution that she would the next morning go to the minister, hoping to find some relief there. As she awaked on Monday morning, a little before day, she wondered within herself at the easiness and calmness she felt in her mind, which was of that kind which she never felt before; as she thought of this, such words as these were in her mind: The words of the Lord are pure words, health to the soul, and marrow to the bones: and then these words came to her mind; 'the blood of Christ cleanses from all sin;' which were accompanied with a lively sense of the excellency of Christ, and his sufficiency to satisfy for the sins of the whole world. She then thought of that expression, It is a pleasant thing for the eyes to behold the sun; which words then seemed to her to be very applicable to Jesus Christ. By these things her mind was led into such contemplations and views of Christ, as filled her exceeding full of joy. She told her brother, in the morning, that she had seen (i. e. in realizing views by faith) Christ the last night, and that she had really thought that she had not knowledge enough to be converted; but, says she, God can make it quite easy! On Monday she felt all day a constant sweetness in her soul. She had a repetition of the same discoveries of Christ three mornings together, that she had on Monday morning, and much in the same manner, at each time, waking a little before day; but brighter and brighter every time.

At the last time, on Wednesday morning, while in the enjoyment of a spiritual view of Christ's glory and fulness, her soul was filled with distress for Christless persons, to consider what a miserable condition they were in: and she felt in herself a strong inclination immediately to go forth to warn sinners; and proposed it the next day to her brother to assist her in going from house to house; but her brother restrained her, by telling her of the unsuitableness of such a method. She told one of her sisters that day, that she loved all mankind, but especially the people of God. Her sister asked her why she loved all mankind? She replied, because God had made them. After this, there happened to come into the shop, where she was at work, three persons that were thought to have been lately converted; her seeing them as they stepped in one after another into the door, so affected her, and so drew forth her love to them, that it overcame her, and she almost fainted: and when they began to talk of the things of religion, it was more than she could bear; they were obliged to cease on that account. It was a very frequent thing with her to be overcome with a flow of affection to them that she thought godly, in conversation with them, and sometimes only at the sight of them.

She had many extraordinary discoveries of the glory of God and Christ; sometimes, in some particular attributes, and sometimes in many. She gave an account, that once, as those four words passed through her mind, WISDOM, JUSTICE, GOODNESS, and TRUTH, her soul was filled with a sense of the glory of each of these divine attributes, but especially the last. Truth, said she, sunk the deepest! And, therefore, as these words passed, this was repeated, TRUTH, TRUTH! Her mind was so swallowed up with the sense of the glory of God's truth and other perfections, that she said, it seemed as though her life was going, and that she saw that it was easy with God to take away her life by discoveries of himself. Soon after this she went to a private religious meeting, and her mind was full of a sense and view of the glory of God all the time; and when the exercise was ended, some asked her concerning what she had experienced: and she began to give them an account; but as she was relating it, it revived such a sense of the same things, that her strength failed; and they were obliged to take her and lay her upon the bed. Afterwards she was greatly affected, and rejoiced, with these words, 'Worthy is the Lamb that was slain!'

She had several days together a sweet sense of the excellency and loveliness of Christ in his meekness, which disposed her continually to be repeating over these words, which were sweet to her, MEEK AND LOWLY IN HEART, MEEK AND LOWLY IN HEART. She once expressed herself to one of her sisters to this purpose, that she had continued whole days and whole nights, in a constant ravishing view of the glory of God and Christ, having enjoyed as much as her life could bear. Once, as her brother was speaking of the dying love of Christ, she told him that she had such a sense of it, that the mere mentioning it was ready to overcome her.

Once, when she came to me, she told how that at such and

such a time she thought she saw as much of God, and had as much joy and pleasure as was possible in this life, and that yet afterwards God discovered himself yet far more abundantly, and she saw the same things that she had seen before, yet more clearly, and in another, and far more excellent and delightful manner, and was filled with a more exceeding sweetness; she likewise gave me such an account of the sense she once had, from day to day, of the glory of Christ, and of God, in his various attributes, that it seemed to me she dwelt for days together in a kind of beatific vision of God: and seemed to have, as I thought, as immediate an intercouse with him, as a child with a father: and at the same time, she appeared most remote from any high thought of herself, and of her own sufficiency; but was like a little child, and expressed a great desire to be instructed, telling me that she longed very often to come to me for instruction, and wanted to live at my house, that I might tell her her duty.

She often expressed a sense of the glory of God appearing in the trees, and growth of the fields, and other works of God's hands. She told her sister that lived near the heart of the town, that she once thought it a pleasant thing to live in the middle of the town, but now, says she, I think it much more pleasant to sit and see the wind blowing the trees, and to behold in the country what God has made. She had sometimes the powerful breathings of the spirit of God on her soul, while reading the scripture, and would express a sense that she had of the certain truth and divinity thereof. She sometimes would appear with a pleasant smile on her countenance; and once, when her sister took notice of it, and asked why she smiled, she replied, I am brim-full of a sweet feeling within! She often used to express how good and sweet it was to lie low before God, and the lower (says she) the better! and that it was pleasant to think of lying in the dust, all the days of her life, mourning for sin. She was wont to manifest a great sense of her own meanness and dependance. She often expressed an exceeding compassion, and pitiful love, which she found in her heart towards persons in a Christless condition; which was sometimes so strong, that as she was passing by such in the streets, or those that she feared were such, she would be overcome by the sight of them. She once said, that she longed to have the whole world saved, she wanted, as it were, to pull them all to her; she could not bear to have one lost.

She had great longings to die, that she might be with Christ: which increased until she thought she did not know how to be patient to wait till God's time should come. But once when she felt those longings, she thought with herself, if I long to die, why do I go to physicians? Whence she concluded that her longings for death were not well regulated. After this she often put it to herself, which she should choose, whether to live or to die, to be sick, or to be well; and she found she could not tell, till at last she found herself disposed to say these words; I am quite willing to live, and quite willing to die; quite willing to be sick, and quite willing to be well; and quite willing for any thing that God will bring upon me! And then, said she, I felt myself perfectly easy, in a full submission to the will of God. She then lamented much, that she had been so eager in her longings for death, as it argued want of such a resignation to God as ought to be. She seemed henceforward to continue in this resigned frame till death.

After this her illness increased upon her; and once after she had before spent the greater part of the night in extreme pain, she waked out of a little sleep with these words in her heart and mouth; I am willing to suffer for Christ's sake, I am willing to spend and be spent for Christ's sake, I am willing to spend life, even my very life, for Christ's sake! And though she had an extraordinary resignation, with respect to life or death, yet the thoughts of dying were exceeding sweet to her. At a time when her brother was reading in Job, concerning worms feeding on the dead body, she appeared with a pleasant smile; and being enquired of about it, she said, it was sweet to her to think of her being in such circumstances. At another time, when her brother mentioned to her the danger there seemed to be that the illness she then laboured under, might be an occasion of her death, it filled her with joy that almost overcame her. At another time, when she met a company following a corpse to the grave, she said, it was sweet to her to think, that they would in a little time follow her in like manner.

Her illness in the latter part of it was seated much in her throat; and swelling inward, filled up the pipe, so that she could swallow nothing but what was perfectly liquid, and but very little of that, and with great and long strugglings and stranglings, that which she took in, flying out at her nostrils, till she at last could swallow nothing at all: she had a raging appetite to food, so that she told her sister, when talking with her about her circumstances, that the worst bit that she threw to her swine, would be sweet to her: but yet when she saw that she could not swallow it, she seemed to be as perfectly contented without it, as if she had no appetite to it. Others were greatly moved to see what she underwent, and were filled with admiration at her unexampled patience. At a time when she was striving in vain to get down a little food, something liquid, and was very much spent with it; she looked up on her sister with a smile, saying, O sister, this is for my good! At another time, when her sister was speaking of what she underwent, she told her, that she lived an heaven upon earth for all that. She used sometimes to say to her sister, under her extreme sufferings, It is good to be so! Her sister once asked her, why she said so; why, says she, because God would have it so: it is best that things should be as God would have them: it looks best to me. After her confinement, as they were leading her from the bed to the door, she seemed overcome by the sight of things abroad, as shewing forth the glory of the Being that had made them. As she lay on her death-bed, she would often say these words, God is my friend! And once looking upon her sister, with a smile, and, O sister! How good it is! How sweet and comfortable it is to consider,

and think of heavenly things! and used this argument to persuade her sister to be much in such meditations.

She expressed on her death-bed, an exceeding longing, both
for persons in a natural state, that they might be converted, and
for the godly that they might see and know more of God. And
when those that looked on themselves, as in a Christless state
came to see her, she would be greatly moved with compassionate affection. One in particular that seemed to be in great distress about the state of her soul, and had come to see her from
time to time, she desired her sister to persuade not to come any
more, because the sight of her so wrought on her compassions
that it overcame her nature. The same week that she died, when
she was in distressing circumstances as to her body, some of the
neighbours that came to see her, asked if she was willing to die?
She replied, that she was quite willing either to live or die; she
was willing to be in pain; she was willing to be so always as she
was then, if that was the will of God. She willed what God
willed. They asked her whether she was willing to die that
night! She answered, Yes, if it be God's will. And seemed to
speak all with that perfect composure of spirit, and with such a
cheerful and pleasant countenance, that it filled them with
admiration.

She was very weak a considerable time before she died,
having pined away with famine and thirst, so that her flesh
seemed to be dried upon her bones; and therefore could say but
little, and manifested her mind very much by signs. She said
she had matter enough to fill up all her time with talk, if she had
but strength. A few days before her death, some asked her,
whether she held her integrity still? Whether she was not afraid
of death? she answered to this purpose, that she had not the
least degree of fear of death. They asked her why she would be
so confident? She answered, if I should say otherwise, I should
speak contrary to what I know: there is, says she, indeed, a dark
entry, that looks something dark, but on the other side there
appears such a bright shining light, that I cannot be afraid! She
said not long before she died, that she used to be afraid how she

should grapple with death; but, says she, God has shewed me that he can make it easy in great pain. Several days before she died, she could scarcely say any thing but just yes, and no, to questions that were asked her, for she seemed to be dying for three days together; but seemed to continue in an admirable sweet composure of soul, without any interruption, to the last, and died as a person that went to sleep, without any struggling, about noon, on Friday, June 27, 1735.

She had long been infirm, and often had been exercised with great pain; but she died chiefly of famine. It was, doubtless, partly owing to her bodily weakness, that her nature was so often overcome, and ready to sink with gracious affection; but yet the truth was, that she had more grace, and greater discoveries of God and Christ, than the present frail state did well consist with. She wanted to be where strong grace might have more liberty; and be without the clog of a weak body; there she longed to be, and there she doubtless now is. She was looked upon amongst us, as a very eminent instance of christian experience; but this is but a very broken and imperfect account I have given of her: her eminency would much more appear, if her experiences were fully related, as she was wont to express, and manifest them, while living. I once read this account to some of her pious neighbours, who were acquainted with her, who said, to this purpose, that the picture fell much short of the life; and particularly that it much failed of duly representing her humility, and that admirable lowliness of heart, that at all times appeared in her. But there are, (blessed be God!) many living instances, of much the like nature, and in some things no less extraordinary.

But I now proceed to the other instance that I would give an account of, which is of the little child fore-mentioned. Her name is Phebe Bartlet, daughter of William Bartlet. I shall give the account as I took it from the mouths of her parents, whose veracity none that know them doubt of.

She was born in March, in the year 1731. About the latter end of April, or beginning of May, 1735, she was greatly affected by the talk of her brother, who had been hopefully converted a little before, at about eleven years of age, and then seriously talked to her about the great things of religion. Her parents did not know of it at that time, and were not wont, in the counsels they gave to their children, particularly to direct themselves to her, by reason of her being so young, and as they supposed, not capable of understanding: but after her brother had talked to her, they observed her very earnestly listen to the advice they gave to the other children; and she was observed very constantly to retire, several times in a day, as was concluded, for secret prayer: and grew more and more engaged in religion, and was more frequent in her closet; till at last she was wont to visit it five or six times in a day: and was so engaged in it, that nothing would at any time divert her from her stated closet exercises. Her mother often observed and watched her, when such things occurred, as she thought most likely to divert her, either by putting it out of her thoughts, or otherwise engaging her inclinations; but never could observe her to fail. She mentioned some very remarkable instances.

She once of her own accord spake of her unsuccessfulness, in that she could not find God, or to that purpose. But on Thursday, the last day of July, about the middle of the day, the child being in the closet, where it used to retire, its mother heard it speaking aloud; which was unusual, and never had been observed before. And her voice seemed to be as of one exceeding importunate and engaged; but her mother could distinctly hear only these words, (spoken in a childish manner, but seemed to be spoken with extraordinary earnestness, and out of distress of soul,) PRAY BLESSED LORD give me salvation! I PRAY, BEG pardon all my sins! when the child had done prayer, she came out of the closet, and came and sat down by her mother, and cried out aloud. Her mother very earnestly asked her several times, what the matter was, before she would make any answer; but she continued exceedingly crying, and wreathing her body to and fro, like one in anguish of spirit. Her mother then asked her, whether she was afraid that God would not give her salvation. She then answered, yes, I am afraid I shall go to Hell! Her mother then endeavoured to quiet her, and told her she would not have her cry, she must be a good girl, and pray every day, and she hoped God would give her salvation. But this did not quiet her at all; but she continued thus earnestly crying, and talking on for some time, till at length she suddenly ceased crying, and began to smile, and presently said with a smiling countenance, Mother, the kingdom of Heaven is come to me! Her mother was surprized at the sudden alteration, and at the speech; and knew not what to make of it; but at first said nothing to her. The child presently spake again, and said, there is another come to me, and there is another, there is three; and being asked what she meant, she answered, one is, Thy will be done, and there is another, Enjoy him for ever; by which it seems, that when the child said, there is three come to me, she meant three passages of her catechism that came to her mind.

After the child had said this, she retired again into her closet: and her mother went over to her brother's, who was next neighbour; and when she came back, the child, being come out of the closet, meets her mother with this cheerful speech; I can find God now! referring to what she had before complained of, that she could not find God. Then the child spoke again, and said, I love God! her mother asked her how well she loved God, whether she loved God better than her father and mother, she said, yes. Then she asked her whether she loved God better than her little sister Rachel. She answered, yes, better than any thing! Then her elder sister, referring to her saying she could find God now, asked her where she could find God. She answered, in Heaven: Why, said she, have you been in Heaven? No, said the child. By this it seems not to have been any imagination of any thing seen with bodily eyes, that she called God, when she said, I can find God now. Her mother asked her, whether she was afraid of going to Hell, and if that had made her cry? She answered, yes, I was; but now I shan't. Her mother asked her, whether she thought that God had given her salvation: she answered, yes. Her mother asked her, when? She answered, to-day. She appeared all that afternoon exceeding cheerful and joyful. One of the neighbours asked her, how she felt herself? She answered, I feel better than I did. The neighbour asked her, what made her feel better. She answered, God makes me. That evening, as she lay a-bed, she called one of her little cousins to her that was present in the room, as having something to say to him; and when he came, she told him, that Heaven was better than earth. The next day being Friday, her mother asked her her catechism, asked her what God made her for. She answered, to serve him; and added, every body should serve God, and get an interest in Christ.

The same day the elder children, when they came home from school, seemed much affected with the extraordinary change that seemed to be made in Phebe: And her sister Abigail standing by, her mother took occasion to counsel her, how to improve her time, to prepare for another world. On which Phebe burst out in tears, and cried out, poor Nabby! Her mother told her, she would not have her cry, she hoped that God would give Nabby salvation; but that did not quiet her, but she continued earnestly crying for some time; and when she had in a measure ceased, her sister Eunice being by her, she burst out again, and cried, poor Eunice! and cried exceedingly; and when she had almost done, she went into another room, and there looked up on her sister Naomi: and burst out again crying poor Amy! Her mother was greatly affected at such a behaviour in the child, and knew not what to say to her. One of the neighbours coming in a little after, asked her what she had cried for. She seemed at first backward to tell the reason: her mother told her she might tell that person, for he had given her an apple: upon which she said, she cried because she was afraid they would go to Hell.

At night, a certain minister, that was occasionally in the town, was at the house, and talked considerably with her, of the things of religion; and, after he was gone, she sat leaning on the table, with tears running out of her eyes: and being asked what made her cry, she said, it was thinking about God. The next day, being Saturday, she seemed great part of the day to be in a very affectionate frame, had four turns of crying, and seemed to endeavour to curb herself, and hide her tears, and was very backward to talk of the occasion of it. On the sabbath-day she was asked, whether she believed in God; she answered, yes. And being told that Christ was the son of God, she made ready answer, and said, I know it.

From this time there appeared a very remarkable abiding change in this child: she has been very strict upon the sabbath; and seems to long for the sabbath-day before it comes, and will often in the week time be enquiring how long it is to the sabbath-day, and must have the days particularly counted over that are between, before she will be contented. And she seems to love God's house, is very eager to go thither. Her mother once asked her why she had such a mind to go? whether it was not to see fine folks? She said, No, it was to hear Mr. Edwards preach. When she is in the place of worship, she is very far from spending her time there as children at her age usually do, but appears with an attention that is very extraordinary for such a child. She also appears very desirous at all opportunities to go to private religious meetings; and is very still and attentive at home, in prayer-time, and has appeared affected in time of family-prayer. She seems to delight much in hearing religious conversation. When I once was there with some others that were strangers, and talked to her something of religion, she seemed more than ordinary attentive; and when we were gone, she looked out very wistly after us, and said, I wish they would come! Her mother asked her why? Says she, I love to hear 'em talk.

She seems to have very much of the fear of God before her eyes, and an extraordinary dread of sin against him; of which her mother mentioned the following remarkable instance.

Some time in August, the last year, she went with some bigger children, to get some plumbs in a neighbour's lot, knowing nothing of any harm in what she did; but when she brought some of the plumbs into the house, her mother mildly reproved her, and told her that she must not get plumbs without leave, because it was sin: God had commanded her not to steal. The child seemed greatly surprized, and burst out in tears, and cried out, I wont have these plumbs! and turning to her sister Eunice, very earnestly said to her, Why did you ask me to go to that plumbtree? I should not have gone, if you had not asked me. The other children did not seem to be much affected or concerned; but there was no pacifying Phebe. Her mother told her, she might go and ask leave, and then it would not be sin for her to eat them; and sent one of the children to that end; and, when she returned, her mother told her, that the owner had given leave, now she might eat them, and it would not be stealing. This stilled her a little while; but presently she broke out again into an exceeding fit of crying. Her mother asked her, what made her cry again? Why she cried now, since they had asked leave? What it was that troubled her now? And asked her several times very earnestly, before she made any answer; but at last said, it was because, BECAUSE IT WAS SIN. She continued a considerable time crying; and said, she would not go again if Eunice asked her an hundred times; and she retained her aversion to that fruit for a considerable time, under the remembrance of her former sin.

She at sometimes appears greatly affected, and delighted with texts of Scripture that come to her mind. Particularly about the beginning of November, that text came to her mind, Rev. iii. 20. 'Behold, I stand at the door, and knock: If any man hear my voice, and open the door, I will come in, and sup with him, and he with me.' She spoke of it to those of the family, with a great appearance of joy, a smiling countenance, and elevation of voice, and afterwards she went into another room, where her mother over-heard her talking very earnestly to the children about it, and particularly heard her say to them, three or four times over, with an air of exceeding joy and admiration, Why it is to SUP WITH GOD. At some time about the middle of winter, very late in the night, when all were a-bed, her mother perceived that she was awake, and heard her, as though she was weeping. She called to her, and asked her what was the matter. She answered with a low voice, so that her mother could not hear what she said; but thinking that it might be occasioned by some spiritual affection, said no more to her; but perceived her to lie awake, and to continue in the same frame, for a considerable time. The next morning, she asked her, whether she did not cry the last night. The child answered, Yes, I did cry a little, for I was thinking about God and Christ, and they loved me. Her mother asked her, whether to think of God and Christ's loving her, made her cry: she answered, Yes, it does sometimes.

She has often manifested a great concern for the good of others' souls: and has been wont many times affectionately to counsel the other children. Once about the latter end of September, the last year, when she and some other of the children were in a room by themselves, a husking Indian corn, the child, after a while, came out and sat by the fire. Her mother took notice that she appeared with a more than ordinary serious and pensive countenance; but at last she broke silence, and said, I have been talking to Nabby and Eunice. Her mother asked her, what she had said to them. Why, said she, I told them they must pray, and prepare to die; that they had but a little while to live in this world, and they must be always ready. When Nabby came out, her mother asked her, whether she had said that to them. Yes, said she, she said that, and a great deal more. At other times, the child took her opportunities to talk to the other children about the great concern of their souls, sometimes, so as much to affect them, and set them into tears. She was once exceeding importunate with her mother to go with her sister Naomi to pray: her mother endeavoured to put her off; but she pulled her by the sleeve, and seemed as if she would not be denied. At last her mother told her, thy Amy must go and pray by herself; says the child, she will not go; and persisted earnestly to beg of her mother to go with her.

She has discovered an uncommon degree of a spirit of charity, particularly on the following occasion. A poor man that lives in the woods, had lately lost a cow that the family much depended on; and being at the house, he was relating his misfortune, and telling of the straits and difficulties they were reduced to by it. She took much notice of it, and it wrought exceedingly on her compassions; and, after she had attentively heard him awhile, she went away to her father, who was in the shop, and intreated him to give that man a cow: and told him, that the poor man had no cow! that the hunters, or something else, had killed his cow! and entreated him to give him one of theirs. Her father told her, that they could not spare one. Then she entreated him to let him and his family come and live at his house: and had much more talk of the same nature, whereby she ministered bowels of compassion to the poor.

She has manifested great love to her minister: particularly when I returned from my long journey for my health, the last fall, when she heard of it, she appeared very joyful at the news, and told the children of it, with an elevated voice, as the most joyful tidings: repeated it over and over, Mr. Edwards is come home! Mr. Edwards is come home! She still continues very constant is secret prayer, so far as can be observed, (for she seems to have no desire that others should observe her when she retires, but seems to be a child of a reserved temper) and every night, before she goes to bed, will say her catechism, and will by no means miss of it: she never forgot it but once, and then, after she was a-bed, thought of it, and cried out in tears, I han't said my catechism! and would not be quieted till her mother asked her the catechism as she lay in bed. She sometimes appears to be in doubt about the condition of her soul; and when asked, whether she thinks that she is prepared for death, speaks something doubtfully about it. At other times seems to have no doubt, but when asked, replies, Yes, without hesitation.

In the former part of this great work of God amongst us, till it got to its height, we seemed to be wonderfully smiled upon and blessed in all respects. Satan (as has been already observed) seemed to be unusually restrained: persons that before had been involved in melancholy, seemed to be as it were waked up out of it; and those that had been entangled with extraordinary temptations, seemed wonderfully to be set at liberty; and not only so, but it was the most remarkable time of health that ever I knew since I have been in the town. We ordinarily have several bills put up, every sabbath, for persons that are sick; but now we had not so much as one for many sabbaths together. But after this it seemed to be otherwise, when this work of God appeared to be at its greatest height, a poor weak man that belongs to the town, being in great spiritual trouble, was hurried with violent temptations to cut his own throat, and made an attempt, but did not do it effectually. He, after this, continued a considerable time exceedingly overwhelmed with melancholy; but has now of a long time been very greatly delivered, by the light of God's countenance lifted up upon him, and has expressed a great sense of his sin in so far yielding to temptation; and there are in him all hopeful evidences of his having been made a subject of saving mercy.

In the latter part of May, it began to be very sensible that the spirit of God was gradually withdrawing from us, and after this time Satan seemed to be more let loose, and raged in a dreadful manner. The first instance wherein it appeared, was a person's putting an end to his own life by cutting his throat. He was a gentleman of more than common understanding, of strict morals, religious in his behaviour, and an useful and honourable person in the town; but was of a family that are exceeding prone to the disease of melancholy, and his mother was killed with it. He had, from the beginning of this extraordinary time, been exceedingly concerned about the state of his soul, and there were some things in his experience that appeared very hopefully; but he durst entertain no hope concerning his own good estate. Towards the latter part of his time, he grew much discouraged, and melancholy grew amain upon him, till he was wholly overpowered by it, and was in great measure past a capacity of receiving advice, or being reasoned with to any purpose: the Devil took the advantage, and drove him into despairing thoughts. He was kept awake a-nights, meditating terror, so that he had scarce any sleep at all for a long time together; and it was observed at last, that he was scarcely well capable of managing his ordinary business, and was judged delirious by the coroner's inquest. The news of this extraordinarily affected the minds of people here, and struck them as it were with astonishment. After this, multitudes in this and other towns seemd to have it strongly suggested to them, and pressed upon them, to do as this person had done; and many that seemed to be under no melancholy, some pious persons, that had no special darkness or doubts about the goodness of their state, nor were under any special trouble or concern of mind about any thing spiritual or temporal, yet had it urged upon them as if somebody had spoke to them, Cut your own throat, now is a good opportunity. Now! now! So that they were obliged to fight with all their might to resist it, and yet no reason suggested to them why they should do it.

About the same time, there were two remarkable instances of persons led away with strange enthusiastic delusions: one at Suffield, and another at South Hadley. That which has made the greatest noise in the country was of the man at South Hadley, whose delusion was, that he thought himself divinely instructed to direct a poor man in melancholy and despairing circumstances to say certain words in prayer to God, as recorded in Psal. cxvi. 4. for his own relief. The man is esteemed a pious man: I have seen this error of his, had a particular acquaintance with him; and I believe none would question his piety that had such an acquaintance. He gave me a particular account of the manner how he was deluded, which is too long to be here inserted; but, in short, he was exceedingly rejoiced and elevated with this extraordinary work, so carried on in this part of the country; and was possessed with an opinion, that it was the beginning of the glorious times of the church spoken of in scripture: and had read it as the opinion of some divines, that there would be many in these times that should be endued with extraordinary gifts of the Holy Ghost, and had embraced the notion, though he had at first no apprehensions that any besides ministers would have such gifts. But he since exceedingly laments the dishonour he has done to God, and the wound he has given religion in it, and has lain low before God and man for it.

After these things, the instances of conversion were rare here in comparison of what they had before been (though that remarkable instance of the little child was after this;) and the spirit of God not long after this time appeared to be sensibly withdrawing from all parts of the country (though we have heard of its going on in some places of Connecticut, and that it continues to be carried on even to this day.) But religion remained here, and I believe in some other places, the main subject of conversation for several months after this. And there were some turns, wherein God's work seemed something to revive, and we were ready to hope that all was going to be renewed again; yet, in the main, there was a gradual decline of that general, engaged, lively spirit in religion, which had been before. Several things have happened since, that have diverted people's minds, and turned their conversation more to other affairs, as particularly his excellency the Governor's coming up, and the Committee of General Court on the Treaty with the Indians; and afterwards the Spring-field Controversy; and since that, our people in this town have been engaged in the building of a new meeting-house; and some other occurrences might be mentioned, that have been thought to be converted among us, in this time, they generally seem to be persons that have had an abiding change wrought on them. I have had particular acquaintance with many of them since, and they generally appear to be persons that have a new sense of things, new apprehensions and views of God, of the divine attributes, and Jesus Christ, and the great things of the gospel: they have a new sense of the truth of them, and they affect them in a new manner, though it is very far from being always alike with them, neither can they revive a sense of things when they please. Their hearts are often touched, and sometimes filled, with new sweetnesses and delights; there seems to be an inward ardour and burning of heart that they express, the like to which they never experienced before; sometimes, perhaps, occasioned only by the mention of Christ's name, or some one of the divine perfections: there are new appetites, and a new kind of breathings and pantings of heart, and groanings that cannot be uttered. There is a new kind of inward labour and struggle of soul towards heaven and holiness.

Some that before were very rough in their temper and manners, seem to be remarkably softened and sweetened. And some have had their souls exceedingly filled, and overwhelmed with light, love, and comfort, long since the work of God has ceased to be so remarkably carried on in a general way; and some have had much greater experiences of this nature than they had before. And there is still a great deal of religious conversation continued in the town, amongst young and old; a religious disposition appears to be still maintained amongst our people, by their upholding frequent private religious meetings; and all sorts are generally worshipping God at such meetings, on sabbath-nights, and in the evening after our public lecture. Many children in the town do still keep up such meetings among themselves. I know of no one young person in the town that has returned to former ways of looseness and extravagancy in any respect; but we still remain a reformed people, and

God has evidently made us a new people.

I can't say that there has been no instance of any one person that has carried himself so, that others should justly be stumbled concerning his profession; nor am I so vain as to imagine that we have not been mistaken concerning any that we have entertained a good opinion of, or that there are none that pass amongst us for sheep, that are indeed wolves in sheep's clothing; who probably may, some time or other, discover themselves by their fruits. We are not so pure, but that we have great cause to be humbled and ashamed that we are so impure; nor so religious, but that those that watch for our halting, may see things in us, whence they may take occasion to reproach us and religion; but in the main, there has been a great and marvellous work of conversion and sanctification among the people here; and they have paid all due respect to those who have been blest of God to be the instruments of it. Both old and young have shewn a forwardness to hearken not only to my counsels, but even to my reproofs from the pulpit.

A great part of the country have not received the most favourable thoughts of this affair; and to this day many retain a jealousy concerning it, and prejudice against it: I have reason to think that the meanness and weakness of the instrument, that has been made use of in this town, has prejudiced many against it; it does not appear to me strange that it should be so: but yet the circumstance of this great work of God, is analogous to other circumstances of it: God has so ordered the manner of the work in many respects, as very signally and remarkably to shew it to be his own peculiar and immediate work, and to secure the glory of it wholly to his own almighty power, and sovereign grace. And whatever the circumstances and means have been, and though we are so unworthy, yet so hath it pleased God to work! And we are evidently a people blessed of the Lord! And here, in this corner of the world, God dwells, and manifests his glory.

Thus, Reverend Sir, I have given a large and particular ac-

count of this remarkable affair; and yet, considering how manifold God's works have been amongst us, that are worthy to be
written, it is but a very brief one. I should have sent it much
sooner, had I not been greatly hindered by illness in my family,
and also in myself. It is probably much larger than you expected, and it may be than you would have chosen. I thought
that the extraordinariness of the thing, and the innumerable
misrepresentations which have gone abroad of it, many of
which have, doubtless, reached your ears, made it necessary
that I should be particular. But I would leave it entirely with
your wisdom to make what use of it you think best, to send a
part of it to England, or all, or none, if you think it not worthy; or
otherwise to dispose of it as you may think most for God's glory,
and the interest of religion. If you are pleased to send any thing
to the Rev. Dr. Guyse, I should be glad to have it signified to
him as my humble desire, that since he, and the congregation to
which he preached, have been pleased to make so much notice
of us, as they have, that they would also think of us at the throne
of grace, and seek there for us, that God would not forsake us,
but enable us to bring forth fruit answerable to our profession,
and our mercies, and that our light may so shine before men,
that others seeing our good works, may glorify our Father
which is in heaven.

When I first heard of the notice the Rev. Dr. Watts and Dr.
Guyse took of God's mercies to us, I took occasion to inform our
congregation of it in a discourse from these words—'A city that
is set upon a hill cannot be hid.' And having since seen a
particular account of the notice of the Rev. Dr. Guyse, and the
congregation he preached to, took of it, in a letter you wrote to
my honoured Uncle Williams, I read that part of your letter to
the congregation, and laboured as much as in me lay to enforce
their duty from it. The congregation were very sensibly moved
and affected at both times.

I humbly request of you, Reverend Sir, your prayers for this
county, in its present melancholy circumstances, into which it

is brought by the Springfield Quarrel, which, doubtless, above all things that have happened, has tended to put a stop to the glorious work here, and to prejudice this country against it, and hinder the propagation of it. I also ask your prayers for this town, and would particularly beg an interest in them for him, who is,

Honoured Sir,

With humble respect,

Your obedient Son and Servant,

JONATHAN EDWARDS.

Northampton,
  Nov. 6, 1736.

2

PETER CARTWRIGHT

The Autobiography of
Peter Cartwright

PARENTAGE.

I WAS born September 1st, 1785, in Amherst County, on James River, in the State of Virginia. My parents were poor. My father was a soldier in the great struggle for liberty, in the Revolutionary war with Great Britain. He served over two years. My mother was an orphan. Shortly after the united colonies gained their independence, my parents moved to Kentucky, which was a new country. It was an almost unbroken wilderness from Virginia to Kentucky at that early day, and this wilderness was filled with thousands of hostile Indians, and many thousands of the emigrants to Kentucky lost their lives by these savages. There were no roads for carriages at that time, and although the emigrants moved by thousands, they had to move on pack horses. Many adventurous young men went to this new country. The fall my father moved, there were a great many families who joined together for mutual safety, and started for Kentucky: Besides the two hundred families thus united, there were one hundred young men, well armed, who agreed to guard these families through, and, as a compensation, they were to be supported for their services. After we struck the wilderness we rarely traveled a day but we passed some white persons, murdered and scalped by the Indians while going to or returning from Kentucky. We traveled on till Sunday, and, instead of resting that day, the voice of the company was to move on.

It was a dark, cloudy day, misty with rain. Many Indians were seen through the day skulking round by our guards. Late in the evening we came to what was called "Camp Defeat," where a number of emigrant families had been all murdered by the savages a short time before. Here the company called a halt to camp for the night. It was a solemn, gloomy time; every heart quaked with fear.

Soon the captain of our young men's company placed his men as sentinels all round the encampment. The stock and the women and children were placed in the center of the encampment. Most of the men that were heads of families, were placed around outside of the women and children. Those who were not placed in this position, were ordered to take their stand outside still, in the edge of the brush. It was a dark, dismal night, and all expected an attack from the Indians.

That night my father was placed as a sentinel, with a good rifle, in the edge of the brush. Shortly after he took his stand, and all was quiet in the camp, he though he heard something moving toward him, and grunting like a swine. He knew there was no swine with the moving company, but it was so dark he could not see what it was. Presently he perceived a dark object in the distance, but nearer him than at first, and believing it to be an Indian, aiming to spring upon him and murder him in the dark, he leveled his rifle, and aimed at the dark lump as well as he could, and fired. He soon found he had hit the object, for it flounced about at a terrible rate, and my father gathered himself up and ran into camp.

When his gun fired, there was an awful screaming throughout the encampment by the women and children. My father was soon inquired of as to what was the matter. He told them the circumstances of the case, but some said he was scared and wanted an excuse to come in; but he affirmed that there was no mistake, that there was something, and he had shot it; and if they would get a light and go with him, if he did not show them something, then they might call him a coward forever. They got a light and went to the place, and there they found an Indian, with a rifle in one hand and a tomahawk in the other, dead. My father's rifle-ball had struck the Indian nearly central in the head.

There was but little sleeping in the camp that night. However, the night passed away without any further alarms, and many glad hearts hailed the dawn of a new day. The next morning, as soon as the company could pack up, they started on their journey.

In a few days after this, we met a lone man, who said his name was Baker, with his mouth bleeding at a desperate rate, having been shot by an Indian. Several of his teeth and his jaw bone were broken by a ball from the Indian's gun. His account of a battle with the Indians was substantially as follows:

There were seven young white men returning to Virginia from Kentucky, all well armed; one of them, a Frenchman, had a considerable sum of money with him. All seven were mounted on fine horses, and they were waylaid by seven Indians.

When the white men approached near the ambush, they were fired on by the Indians, and three shot down; the other four dismounted and shot down three of the Indians. At the second fire of the Indians, two more of the white men fell, and at the second fire of the white men, two more of the Indians fell. Then there were two and two. At the third fire of the Indians, Baker's only remaining companion fell, and he received the wound in the mouth. Thinking his chance a bad one, he wheeled and ran, loading his gun as he went. Finding a large, hollow tree, he crept into it, feet foremost, holding his rifle ready cocked, expecting them to look in, when he intended to fire. He heard the Indians cross and recross the log twice, but they did not look in.

At this perilous moment, he heard the large cow bell that was on one of the drove of cattle of our company, and shortly after he crawled out of the log, and make his way to us, the happiest man I think I ever saw. Our company of young men rushed to the battle-ground, and found the dead white men and Indians, and dug two separate graves, and buried them where they fell. They got all the horses and clothes of the white men slain, and the Frenchman's money, for the surviving Indians had not time to scalp or strip them.

When we came within seven miles of the Crab Orchard, where there were a fort and the first white settlement, it was nearly night. We halted, and a vote was taken whether we should go on to the fort, or camp there for the night. Indians had been seen in our rear through the day. All wanted to go through except seven families, who refused to go any further that night. The main body went on, but they, the seven families, carelessly stripped off their clothes, laid down without any guards, and went to sleep.

Some time in the night, about twenty-five Indians rushed on them, and every one, men, women, and children, was slain, except one man, who sprang from his bed and ran into the fort, barefooted and in his night clothes. He brought the melancholy news of the slaughter.

The captain of the fort was an old, experienced ranger and Indian warrior. These murderous bands of savages lived north of the Ohio River, and would cross over into Kentucky, kill and steal, and then recross the Ohio into their own country. The old captain knew the country well, and the places of their crossing the river. Early next morning he called for volunteers, mounted men, and said he could get ahead of them. A goodly company turned out, and, sure enough, they got ahead of the Indians, and formed an ambush for them. Soon they saw the Indians coming, and, at a given signal, the whites fired on them. At the first shot all were killed but three; these were pursued, two of them killed, and but one made his escape to tell the sad news. All the plunder of the murdered families was retaken.

Thus you see what perilous times the first settlers had to reach that new and beautiful country of *"canes and turkeys."*

Kentucky was claimed by no particular tribe of Indians, but was regarded as a common hunting-ground by the various tribes, east, west, north, and south. It abounded in various valuable game, such as buffalo, elk, bear, deer, turkeys, and many other smaller game, and hence the Indians struggled hard to keep the white people from taking possession of it. Many hard and bloody battles were fought, and thousands killed on both sides; and rightly was it named the "land of blood." But finally the Indians were overpowered and driven off, and the white man obtained a peaceable and quiet possession.

It was chiefly settled by Virginians, as noble and brave a race of men and women as ever drew the breath of life. But Kentucky was far in the interior, and very distant from the Atlantic shores; and though a part of the great Mississippi Valley, the mouth of the Mississippi and thousands of miles up this "father of waters" belonged to foreign, and, in some sense, hostile nations, that were not very friendly to the new republic.

The Kentuckians labored under many, very many, disadvantages and privations; and had it not been for the fertility of the soil and the abundance of wild meat, they must have suffered beyond endurance. But the country soon filled up, and entered into the enjoyment of improved and civilized life.

EARLY LIFE.

AFTER my father reached Kentucky he rented a farm for two years in Lincoln County, on what was called the "Hanging fork of Dicks River," near Lancaster, the county seat.

My mother, being a member of the Methodist Episcopal Church, sought and obtained an acquaintance with two Methodist traveling preachers, namely, John Page and Benjamin Northcut, men of precious memory—men that are to be numbered as early pioneers in the West, who labored hard and suffered much to build up the infant Methodist Church in the wilderness; and those two men are to be numbered among the oldest Methodist preachers on this continent that are now living. (Northcut has since died.)

In the fall of 1793 my father determined to move to what was then called the Green River country, in the southern part of the State of Kentucky. He did so, and settled in Logan County, nine miles south of Russellville, the county seat, and within one mile of the state line of Tennessee.

Shortly after our removal from Lincoln to Logan County my father's family was visited by Jacob Lurton, a traveling preacher of the Methodist Episcopal Church. Though my father was not a professor of religion, yet he was not an opposer of it, and when Jacob Lurton asked the liberty of preaching in his cabin, he readily assented.

I was then in my ninth year, and was sent out to invite the neighbors to come and hear preaching. Accordingly they crowded out, and filled the cabin to overflowing. Jacob Lurton was a real son of thunder. He preached with tremendous power, and the congregation were almost all melted to tears; some cried aloud for mercy, and my mother shouted aloud for joy.

Jacob Lurton traveled several years, married, and located in Kentucky, from whence he removed to Illinois, and settled near Alton, where he died many years ago. His end was peaceful and happy.

Shortly after Jacob Lurton preached at my father's cabin, he or his successor organized a small class, about four miles from my father's, where my mother attached herself again to the Church. I think there were thirteen members, one local preacher, one exhorter, and a class-leader. Here my mother regularly walked every Sabbath to class-meeting, for a number of years, and seldom missed this means of grace. This little society ebbed and flowed for years, until about 1799, when a mighty revival of religion broke out, and scores joined the society. We built a little church, and called it *Ebenezer*. This was in what was then called Cumberland Circuit, and Kentucky District, in the Western Conference, the seventh conference in the United States.

Logan County, when my father moved to it, was called "Rogues' Harbor." Here many refugees, from almost all parts of the Union, fled to escape justice or punishment; for although there was law, yet it could not be executed, and it was a desperate state of society. Murderers, horse thieves, highway robbers, and counterfeiters fled here until they combined and actually formed a majority. The honest and civil part of the citizens would prosecute these wretched banditti, but they would swear each other clear; and they really put all law at defiance, and carried on such desperate violence and outrage that the honest part of the citizens seemed to be driven to the necessity of uniting and combining together, and taking the law into their own hands, under the name of Regulators. This was a very desperate state of things.

Shortly after the Regulators had formed themselves into a society, and established their code of by-laws, on a court day at Russellville, the two bands met in town. Soon a quarrel commenced, and a general battle ensued between the rogues and Regulators, and they fought with guns, pistols, dirks, knives, and clubs. Some were actually killed, many wounded, the rogues proved victors, kept the ground, and drove the Regulators out of town. The Regulators rallied again, hunted, killed, and lynched many of the rogues, until several of them fled, and left for parts unknown. Many lives were lost on both sides, to the great scandal of civilized people. This is but a partial view of frontier life.

When my father settled in Logan County, there was not a newspaper printed south of Green River, no mill short of forty miles, and no schools worth the name. Sunday was a day set apart for hunting, fishing, horse-racing, card-playing, balls, dances, and all kinds of jollity and mirth. We killed our meat out of the woods, wild; and beat our meal and hominy with a pestle and mortar. We stretched a deer skin over a hoop, burned holes in it with the prongs of a fork, sifted our meal, baked our bread, eat it, and it was first-rate eating too. We raised, or gathered out of the woods, our own tea. We had sage, bohea, cross-vine, spice, and sassafras teas, in abundance. As for coffee, I am not sure that I ever smelled it for ten years. We made our sugar out of the water of the maple-tree, and our molasses too. These were great luxuries in those days.

We raised our own cotton and flax. We water-rotted our flax, broke it by hand, scutched it; picked the seed out of the cotton with our fingers; our mothers and sisters carded, spun, and wove it into cloth, and they cut and made our garments and bed-clothes, &c. And when we got on a new suit thus manufactured, and sallied out into company, we thought ourselves "*so big as anybody.*"

There were two large caves on my father's farm, and another about half a mile off, where was a great quantity of material for making saltpeter. We soon learned the art of making it, and our class-leader was a great powder-maker.

Let it be remembered, these were days when we had no stores of dry goods or groceries; but the United States had a military post at Fort Messick, on the north bank of the Ohio River and south end of the State of Illinois. Here the government kept stores of these things. After we had made a great quantity of saltpeter, and had manufactured it into powder, really number one, strange to say, it came into the mind of our class-leader to go to Fort Messick on a trading expedition. Then the question arose, what sort of a vessel should be made ready for the voyage. This difficulty was soon solved; for he cut down a large poplar-tree, and dug out a large and neat canoe, and launched it into Red River, to go out into Cumberland River, and at the mouth of said river to ascend the Ohio River to the fort.

Then proclamation was made to the neighborhood to come in with their money or marketing, but powder was the staple of the trading voyage. They were also notified to bring in their bills, duly signed, stating the articles they wanted. Some sent for a quarter of a pound of coffee, some one yard of ribbon, some a butcher-knife, some for a tin cup, &c., &c. I really wish I had the bill; I would give it as a literary curiosity of early days.

Our leader went and returned, safe and sound, made a good exchange, to the satisfaction of nearly all concerned; and for weeks it was a great time of rejoicing, that we, even in Kentucky, had found out the glorious advantages of navigation.

I was naturally a wild, wicked boy, and delighted in horse-racing, card-playing, and dancing. My father restrained me but little, though my mother often talked to me, wept over me, and prayed for me, and often drew tears from my eyes; and though I often wept under preaching, and resolved to do better and seek religion, yet I broke my vows, went into young company, rode races, played cards, and danced.

At length my father gave me a young race-horse, which well-nigh proved my everlasting ruin; and he bought me a pack of cards, and I was a very successful young gambler; and though I was not initiated into the tricks of regular gamblers, yet I was very successful in winning money. This practice was very fascinating, and became a special besetting sin to me, so that, for a boy, I was very much captivated by it. My mother remonstrated almost daily with me, and I had to keep my cards hid from her; for if she could have found them, she would have burned them, or destroyed them in some way. O, the sad delusions of gambling! How fascinating, and how hard to reclaim a practiced gambler! Nothing but the power of Divine grace saved me from this wretched sin.

My father sent me to school, boarding me at Dr. Beverly Allen's; but my teacher was not well-qualified to teach correctly, and I made but small progress. I, however, learned to read, write, and cipher a little, but very imperfectly. Dr. Allen, with whom I boarded, had, in an early day, been a traveling preacher in the Methodist Episcopal Church. He was sent South to Georgia, as a very gentlemanly and popular preacher, and did much good. He married in that country a fine, pious woman, a member of the Church; but he, like David, in an evil hour, fell into sin, violated the laws of the country, and a writ was issued for his apprehension. He warned the sheriff not to enter his room, and assured him if he did he would kill him. The sheriff rushed upon him, and Allen shot him dead. He fled from that country to escape justice, and settled in Logan County, then called "Rogues' Harbor." His family followed him, and here he practiced medicine. To ease a troubled conscience he drank in the doctrine of Universalism; but he lived and died a great friend to the Methodist Church.

It fell to my lot, after I had been a preacher several years, to visit the doctor on his dying bed. I talked to, and prayed with him. Just before he died I asked him if he was willing to die and meet his final Judge with his Universalist sentiments. He frankly said he was not. He said he could make the mercy of God cover every case in his mind but his own, but he thought there was no mercy for him; and in this state of mind he left the world, bidding his family and friends an eternal farewell, warning them not to come to that place of torment to which he felt himself eternally doomed.

CANE RIDGE CAMP-MEETING.

TIME rolled on, population increased fast around us the country improved, horse-thieves and murderers were driven away, and civilization advanced considerably. Ministers of different denominations came in, and preached through the country; but the Methodist preachers were the pioneer messengers of salvation in these ends of the earth. Even in Rogues' Harbor there was a Baptist Church, a few miles west of my father's, and a Presbyterian congregation a few miles north, and the Methodist *Ebenezer*, a few miles south.

There were two Baptist ministers, one an old man of strong mind and *good*, very *good*, natural abilities, having been brought up a rigid Calvinist, and having been taught to preach the doctrine of particular election and reprobation. At length his good sense revolted at the *horrid idea,* and, having no correct books on theology, he plunged into the opposite extreme, namely, universal redemption. He lived in a very wicked settlement. He appointed a day to publish his recantation of his old Calvinism, and his views on universal and unconditional salvation to all mankind. The whole country, for many miles around, crowded to hear the *joyful news.* When he had finished his discourse, the vilest of the vile multitude raised the shout, expressing great joy that there was no hell or eternal punishment.

I will here state a circumstance that occurred to the old gentleman and myself. He was a great smoker, and as he passed my father's one day, to marry a couple, he came to the fence and called to me, and said, "Peter, if you will bring me a coal of fire to light my pipe, I will tell you how to get out of hell, if you ever get there." Although I was very wicked, the expression exceedingly shocked me, and neither the devil nor any of his preachers have ever been able, from that day to this, seriously to tempt me to believe the *blasphemous doctrine.*

The other Baptist minister soon took to open drunkenness, and with him his salvation by *water* expired; but if ever there was a jubilee in hell, it was then and there held, over these apostate and fallen ministers B. A. and Dr. Allen.

Somewhere between 1800 and 1801, in the upper part of Kentucky, at a memorable place called "Cane Ridge," there was appointed a sacramental meeting by some of the Presbyterian ministers, at which meeting, seemingly unexpected by ministers or people, the mighty power of God was displayed in a very extraordinary manner; many were moved to tears, and bitter and loud crying for mercy. The meeting was protracted for weeks. Ministers of almost all denominations flocked in from far and near. The meeting was kept up by night and day. Thousands heard of the mighty work, and came on foot, on horseback, in carriages and wagons. It was supposed that there were in attendance at times during the meeting from twelve to twenty-five thousand people. Hundreds fell prostrate under the mighty power of God, as men slain in battle. Stands were erected in the woods from which preachers of different Churches proclaimed repentance toward God and faith in our Lord Jesus Christ, and it was supposed, by eye and ear witnesses, that between one and two thousand souls were happily and powerfully converted to God during the meeting. It was not unusual for one, two, three,and four to seven preachers to be addressing the listening thousands at the same time from the different stands erected for the purpose. The heavenly fire spread in almost every direction. It was said, by truthful witnesses, that at times more than one thousand persons broke out into loud shouting all at once, and that the shouts could be heard for miles around.

From this camp-meeting, for so it ought to be called, the news spread through all the Churches, and through all the land, and it excited great wonder and surprise; but it kindled a religious flame that spread all over Kentucky and through many other states. And I may here be permitted to say, that this was the first camp-meeting ever held in the United States, and here our camp-meetings took their rise.

As Presbyterian, Methodist, and Baptist ministers all united in the blessed work at this meeting, when they returned home to their different congregations, and carried the news of this mighty work, the revival spread rapidly throughout the land; but many of the ministers and members of the synod of Kentucky thought it all disorder, and tried to stop the work. They called their preachers who were engaged in the revival to account, and censured and silenced them. These ministers then rose up and unitedly renounced the jurisdiction of the Presbyterian Church, organized a Church of their own, and dubbed it with the name of *Christian*. Here was the origin of what was called the *New Lights*. They renounced the Westminster Confession of Faith, and all Church discipline, and professed to take the New Testament for their Church discipline. They established no standard of doctrine; every one was to take the New Testament, read it, and abide his own construction of it. Marshall, M'Namar, Dunlevy, Stone, Huston, and others, were the chief leaders in this *trash trap*. Soon a diversity of opinion sprang up, and they got into a Babel confusion. Some preached Arian, some Socinian, and some Universalist doctrines; so that in a few years you could not tell what was *harped* or what was *danced*. They adopted the mode of immersion, the water-god of all exclusive errorists; and directly there was a mighty controversy about the way to heaven, whether it was by water or by dry land.

In the meantime a remnant of preachers that broke off from the Methodist Episcopal Church in 1792, headed by James O'Kelly, who had formed a party because he could not be a bishop in said Church, which party he called the Republican Methodist Church, came out to Kentucky, and formed a union with these New Lights. Then the Methodist Episcopal Church had war, and rumors of war, almost on every side. The dreadful diversity of opinion among these New Lights, their want of any standard of doctrines, or regular Church discipline, made them an easy prey to prowling wolves of any description.

Soon the Shaker priests came along, and off went M'Namar, Dunlevy, and Huston, into that foolish error. Marshall and others retraced their steps. B. W. Stone stuck to his New Lightism, and fought many bloodless battles, till he grew old and feeble, and the mighty Alexander Campbell, the *great*, arose and poured such floods of regenerating water about the old man's cranium, that he formed a union with this giant errorist, and finally died, not much lamented out of the circle of a few friends. And this is the way with all the New Lights, in the government, morals, and discipline of the Church.

This Christian, or New Light Church, is a feeble and scattered people, though there are some good Christians among them. I suppose since the day of Pentecost, there was hardly ever a greater revival of religion than at Cane Ridge; and if there had been steady, Christian ministers, settled in Gospel doctrine and Church discipline, thousands might have been saved to the Church that wandered off in the mazes of vain, speculative divinity, and finally made shipwreck of the faith, fell back, turned infidel, and lost their religion and their souls forever. But evidently a new impetus was given to the work of God, and many, very many, will have cause to bless God forever for this revival of religion throughout the length and breadth of our Zion.

CONVERSION.

IN 1801, when I was in my sixteenth year, my father, my eldest half brother, and myself, attended a wedding about five miles from home, where there was a great deal of drinking and dancing, which was very common at marriages in those days. I drank little or nothing; my delight was in dancing. After a late hour in the night, we mounted our horses and started for home. I was riding my race-horse.

A few minutes after we had put up the horses, and were sitting by the fire, I began to reflect on the manner in which I had spent the day and evening. I felt guilty and condemned. I rose and walked the floor. My mother was in bed. It seemed to me, all of a sudden, my blood rushed to my head, my heart palpitated, in a few minutes I turned blind; an awful impression rested on my mind that death had come and I was unprepared to die. I fell on my knees and began to ask God to have mercy on me.

My mother sprang from her bed, and was soon on her knees by my side, praying for me, and exhorting me to look to Christ for mercy, and then and there I promised the Lord that if he would spare me, I would seek and serve him; and I never fully broke that promise. My mother prayed for me a long time. At length we lay down, but there was little sleep for me. Next morning I rose, feeling wretched beyond expression. I tried to read in the Testament, and retired many times to secret prayer through the day, but found no relief. I gave up my race-horse to my father, and requested him to sell him. I went and brought my pack of cards, and gave them to mother, who threw them into the fire, and they were consumed. I fasted, watched, and prayed, and engaged in regular reading of the Testament. I was so distressed and miserable, that I was incapable of any regular business.

My father was greatly distressed on my account, thinking I must die, and he would lose his only son. He bade me retire altogether from business, and take care of myself.

Soon it was noised abroad that I was distracted, and many of my associates in wickedness came to see me, to try and divert my mind from those gloomy thoughts of my wretchedness; but all in vain. I exhorted them to desist from the course of wickedness which we had been guilty of together. The class-leader and local preacher were sent for. They tried to point me to the bleeding Lamb, they prayed for me most fervently. Still I found no comfort, and although I had never believed in the doctrine of unconditional election and reprobation, I was sorely tempted to believe I was a reprobate, and doomed, and lost eternally, without any chance of salvation.

At length one day I retired to the horse-lot, and was walking and wringing my hands in great anguish, trying to pray, on the borders of utter despair. It appeared to me that I heard a voice from heaven saying, "Peter, look at me." A feeling of relief flashed over me as quick as an electric shock. It gave me hopeful feelings, and some encouragement to seek mercy, but still my load of guilt remained. I repaired to the house, and told my mother what had happened to me in the horse-lot. Instantly she seemed to understand it, and told me the Lord had done this to encourage me to hope for mercy, and exhorted me to take encouragement, and seek on, and God would bless me with the pardon of my sins at another time.

Some days after this, I retired to a cave on my father's farm to pray in secret. My soul was in an agony; I wept, I prayed, and said, "Now, Lord, if there is mercy for me, let me find it," and it really seemed to me that I could amost lay hold of the Saviour, and realize a reconciled God. All of a sudden, such a fear of the devil fell upon me that it really appeared to me that he was surely personally there, to seize and drag me down to hell, soul and body, and such a horror fell on me that I sprang to my feet and ran to my mother at the house. My mother told me this was a device of Satan to prevent me from finding the blessing then. Three months rolled away, and still I did not find the blessing of the pardon of my sins.

This year, 1801, the Western Conference existed, and I think there was but one presiding elder's district in it, called the Kentucky District. William M'Kendree (afterward bishop) was appointed to the Kentucky District. Cumberland Circuit, which, perhaps, was six hundred miles round, and lying partly in Kentucky and partly in Tennessee, was one of the circuits of this district. John Page and Thomas Wilkerson were appointed to this circuit.

In the spring of this year, Mr. M'Grady, a minister of the Presbyterian Church, who had a congregation and meeting-house, as we then called them, about three miles north of my father's house, appointed a sacramental meeting in this congregation, and invited the Methodist preachers to attend with them, and especially John Page, who was a powerful Gospel minister, and was very popular among the Presbyterians. Accordingly he came, and preached with great power and success.

There were no camp-meetings in regular form at this time, but as there was a great waking up among the Churches, from the revival that had broken out at Cane Ridge, before mentioned, many flocked to those sacramental meetings. The church would not hold the tenth part of the congregation. Accordingly, the officers of the Church erected a stand in a contiguous shady grove, and prepared seats for a large congregation.

The people crowded to this meeting from far and near. They came in their large wagons, with victuals mostly prepared. The women slept in the wagons, and the men under them. Many stayed on the ground night and day for a number of nights and days together. Others were provided for among the neighbors around. The power of God was wonderfully displayed; scores of sinners fell under the preaching, like men slain in mighty battle; Christians shouted aloud for joy.

To this meeting I repaired, a guilty, wretched sinner. On the Saturday evening of said meeting, I went, with weeping multitudes, and bowed before the stand, and earnestly prayed for mercy. In the midst of a solemn struggle of soul, an impression was made on my mind, as though a voice said to me, "Thy sins are all forgiven thee." Divine light flashed all round me, unspeakable joy sprung up in my soul. I rose to my feet, opened my eyes, and it really seemed as if I was in heaven; the trees, the leaves on them, and everything seemed, and I really thought were, praising God. My mother raised the shout, my Christian friends crowded around me and joined me in praising God; and though I have been since then, in many instances, unfaithful, yet I have never, for one moment, doubted that the Lord did, then and there, forgive my sins and give me religion.

Our meeting lasted without intermission all night, and it was believed by those who had a very good right to know, that over eighty souls were converted to God during its continuance. I went on my way rejoicing for many days. This meeting was in the month of May. In June our preacher, John Page, attended at our little church, *Ebenezer*, and there in June, 1801, I joined the Methodist Episcopal Church, which I have never for one moment regretted.

To show the ignorance the early Methodist preachers had to contend with in the Western wilds I will relate an incident or two that occurred to Wilson Lee in Kentucky. He was one of the early pioneer Methodist preachers sent to the West. He was a very solemn and grave minister. At one of his appointments, at a private house on a certain day, they had a motherless pet lamb. The boys of the family had mischievously learned this lamb to butt. They would go near it, and make motions with their heads, and the lamb would back and then dart forward at them, and they would jump out of the way, so that the sheep would miss them.

A man came into the congregation who had been drinking and frolicking all the night before. He came in late, and took his seat on the end of a bench nearly in the door, and, having slept none the night before, presently he began to nod; and as he nodded and bent forward, the pet lamb came along by the door, and seeing this man nodding and bending forward, he took it as a banter, and straightway backed and then sprang forward, and gave the sleeper a severe jolt right on the head, and over he tilted him, to the no small amusement of the congregation, who all burst out into laughter; and grave as the preacher, Mr. Lee, was, it so excited his risibilities that he almost lost his balance. But recovering himself a little, he went on in a most solemn and impressive strain. His subject was the words of our Lord: "Except a man deny himself, and take up his cross, he cannot be my disciple." He urged on his congregation, with melting voice and tearful eyes, to take up the cross, no matter what it was, take it up.

There were in the congregation a very wicked Dutchman and his wife, both of whom were profoundly ignorant of the Scriptures and the plan of salvation. His wife was a notorious scold, and so much was she given to this practice, that she made her husband unhappy, and kept him almost always in a perfect fret, so that he led a most miserable and uncomfortable life. It pleased God that day to cause the preaching of Mr. Lee to reach their guilty souls and break up the great deep of their hearts. They wept aloud, seeing their lost condition, and they, then and there, resolved to do better, and from that time forward to take up the cross and bear it, be it what it might.

The congregation were generally deeply affected. Mr. Lee

exhorted them and prayed for them as long as he consistently could, and, having another appointment some distance off that evening, he dismissed the congregation, got a little refreshment, saddled his horse, mounted, and started for his evening appointment. After riding some distance, he saw, a little ahead of him, a man trudging along, carrying a woman on his back. This greatly surprised Mr. Lee. He very naturally supposed that the woman was a cripple, or had hurt herself in some way, so that she could not walk. The traveler was a small man, and the woman large and heavy.

Before he overtook them Mr. Lee began to cast about in his mind how he could render them assistance. When he came up to them, lo and behold, who should it be but the Dutchman and his wife that had been so affected under his sermon at meeting. Mr. Lee rode up and spoke to them, and inquired of the man what had happened, or what was the matter that he was carrying his wife.

The Dutchman turned to Mr. Lee and said, "Besure you did tell us in your sarmon dat we must take up de cross and follow de Saviour, or dat we could not be saved or go to heaven, and I does desire to go to heaven so much as any pody; and dish vife is so pad, she scold and scold all de time, and dish woman is de createst cross I have in de whole world, and I does take her up and pare her, for I must save my soul."

You may be sure that Mr. Lee was posed for once, but after a few moments' reflection he told the Dutchman to put his wife down, and he dismounted from his horse. He directed them to sit down on a log by the road side. He held the reins of his horse's bridle and sat down by them, took out his Bible, read to them several passages of Scripture, and explained and expounded to them the way of the Lord more perfectly. He opened to them the nature of the cross of Christ, what it is, how it is to be taken up, and how they were to bear that cross; and after teaching and advising them some time, he prayed for them by the road side, left them deeply affected, mounted his horse, and rode on to his evening appointment.

Long before Mr. Lee came around his circuit to his next appointment the Dutchman and his scolding wife were both powerfully converted to God, and when he came round he took them into the Church. The Dutchman's wife was cured of her scolding. Of course he got clear of this cross. They lived together long and happily, adorning their profession, and giving ample evidence that religion could cure a scolding wife, and that God could and did convert poor ignorant Dutch people.

This Dutchman often told his experience in love-feasts, with thrilling effect, and hardly ever failed to melt the whole congregation into a flood of tears; and on one particular occasion which is vividly printed on my recollection, I believe the whole congregation in the love-feast, which lasted beyond the time allotted for such meetings, broke out into a loud shout.

Thus Brother Lee was the honored instrument in the hand of God of planting Methodism, amid clouds of ignorance and opposition, among the early settlers of the far West. Brother Lee witnessed a good confession to the end. At an early period of his ministry he fell from the walls of Zion with the trump of God in his hand, and has gone to his reward in heaven. Peace to his memory.

THE GREAT REVIVAL.

FROM 1801 for years a blessed revival of religion spread through almost the entire inhabited parts of the West, Kentucky, Tennessee, the Carolinas, and many other parts, especially through the Cumberland country, which was so called from the Cumberland River, which headed and mouthed in Kentucky, but in its great bend circled south through Tennessee, near Nashville. The Presbyterians and Methodists in a great measure united in this work, met together, prayed together, and preached together.

In this revival originated our camp-meetings, and in both these denominations they were held every year, and, indeed, have been ever since, more or less. They would erect their camps with logs or frame them, and cover them with clapboards or shingles. They would also erect a shed, sufficiently large to protect five thousand people from wind and rain, and cover it with boards or shingles; build a large stand, seat the shed, and here they would collect together from forty to fifty miles around, sometimes further than that. Ten, twenty, and sometimes thirty ministers, of different denominations, would come together and preach night and day, four or five days together; and, indeed, I have known these camp-meetings to last three or four weeks, and great good resulted from them. I have seen more than a hundred sinners fall like dead men under one powerful sermon, and I have seen and heard more than five hundred Christians all shouting aloud the high praises of God at once; and I will venture to assert that many happy thousands were awakened and converted to God at these camp-meetings. Some sinners mocked, some of the old dry professors opposed, some of the old starched Presbyterian preachers preached against these exercises, but still the work went on and spread almost in every direction, gathering additional force, until our country seemed all coming home to God.

In this great revival the Methodists kept moderately balanced; for we had excellent preachers to steer the ship or guide the flock. But some of our members ran wild, and indulged in some extravagancies that were hard to control.

The Presbyterian preachers and members, not being accustomed to much noise or shouting, when they yielded to it went into great extremes and downright wildness, to the great injury of the cause of God. Their old preachers licensed a great many young men to preach, contrary to their Confession of Faith. That Confession of Faith required their ministers to believe in unconditional election and reprobation, and the unconditional and final perseverance of the saints. But in this revival they, almost to a man, gave up these points of high Calvinism, and preached a free salvation to all mankind. The Westminster Confession required every man, before he could be licensed to preach, to have a liberal education; but this qualification was dispensed with, and a great many fine men were licensed to preach without this literary qualification or subscribing to those high-toned doctrines of Calvinism.

This state of things produced great dissatisfaction in the Synod of Kentucky, and messenger after messenger was sent to wait on the Presbytery to get them to desist from their erratic course, but without success. Finally they were cited to trial before the constituted authorities of the Church. Some were censured, some were suspended, some retraced their steps, while others surrendered their credentials of ordination, and the rest were cut off from the Church.

While in this amputated condition, they called a general meeting of all their licentiates. They met our presiding elder, J. Page, and a number of Methodist ministers at a quarterly meeting in Logan County, and proposed to join the Methodist Episcopal Church as a body; but our aged ministers declined this offer, and persuaded them to rise up and embody themselves together, and constitute a Church. They reluctantly yielded to this advice, and, in due time and form, constituted what they denominated the "Cumberland Presbyterian Church;" and in their confession of faith split, as they supposed, the difference between the Predestinarians and the Methodists, rejecting a partial atonement or special election and reprobation, but retaining the doctrine of the final unconditional perseverance of the saints.

What an absurdity! While a man remains a sinner he may come, as a free agent, to Christ, if he will, and if he does not come his damnation will be just, because he refused offered mercy; but as soon as he gets converted his free agency is destroyed, the best boon of Heaven is then lost, and although he may backslide, wander away from Christ, yet he *shall* be brought in. He cannot finally be lost if he has ever been really converted to God.

They make a very sorry show in their attempt to support this left foot of Calvinism. But be it spoken to their credit, they do not often preach this doctrine. They generally preach Methodist doctrine, and have been the means of doing a great deal of good, and would have done much more if they had left this relic of John Calvin behind.

In this revival, usually termed in the West the Cumberland revival, many joined the different Churches, especially the Methodist and Cumberland Presbyterians. The Baptists also came in for a share of the converts, but not to any great extent. Infidelity quailed before the mighty power of God, which was displayed among the people. Universalism was almost driven from the land. The Predestinarians of almost all sorts put forth a mighty effort to stop the work of God.

Just in the midst of our controversies on the subject of the powerful exercises among the people under preaching, a new exercise broke out among us, called the *jerks*, which was overwhelming in its effects upon the bodies and minds of the people. No matter whether they were saints or sinners, they would be taken under a warm song or sermon, and seized with a convulsive jerking all over, which they could not by any possibility avoid, and the more they resisted the more they jerked. If they would not strive against it and pray in good earnest, the jerking would usually abate. I have seen more than five hundred persons jerking at one time in my large congregations. Most usually persons taken with the jerks, to obtain relief, as they said, would rise up and dance. Some would run, but could not get away. Some would resist; on such the jerks were generally very severe.

To see those proud young gentlemen and young ladies, dressed in their silks, jewelry, and prunella, from top to toe, take the *jerks*, would often excite my risibilities. The first jerk or so, you would see their fine bonnets, caps, and combs fly; and so sudden would be the jerking of the head that their long loose hair would crack almost as loud as a wagoner's whip.

At one of my appointments in 1804 there was a very large congregation turned out to hear the Kentucky boy, as they called me. Among the rest there were two very finely-dressed, fashionable young ladies, attended by two brothers with loaded horsewhips. Although the house was large, it was crowded. The two young ladies, coming in late, took their seats near where I stood, and their two brothers stood in the door. I was a little unwell, and I had a phial of peppermint in my pocket. Before I commenced preaching I took out my phial and swallowed a little of the peppermint. While I was preaching, the congregation was melted into tears. The two young gentlemen moved off to the yard fence, and both the young ladies took the jerks, and they were greatly mortified about it. There was a great stir in the congregation. Some wept, some shouted, and before our meeting closed several were converted.

As I dismissed the assembly a man stepped up to me, and warned me to be on my guard, for he had heard the two brothers swear they would horsewhip me when meeting was out, for giving their sisters the jerks. "Well," said I, "I'll see to that."

I went out and said to the young men that I understood they intended to horsewhip me for giving their sisters the jerks. One replied that he did. I undertook to expostulate with him on the absurdity of the charge against me, but he swore I need not deny it; for he had seen me take out a phial, in which I carried some truck that gave his sisters the jerks. As quick as thought it came into my mind how I would get clear of my whipping, and, jerking out the peppermint phial, said I, "Yes; if I gave your sisters the jerks I'll give them to you." In a moment I saw he was scared. I moved toward him, he backed, I advanced, and he wheeled and ran, warning me not to come near him, or he would kill me. It raised the laugh on him, and I escaped my whipping. I had the pleasure, before the year was out, of seeing all four soundly converted to God, and I took them into the Church.

While I am on this subject I will relate a very serious circumstance which I knew to take place with a man who had the jerks at a camp-meeting, on what was called the Ridge, in William

Magee's congregation. There was a great work of religion in the encampment. The jerks were very prevalent. There was a company of drunken rowdies who came to interrupt the meeting. These rowdies were headed by a very large drinking man. They came with their bottles of whisky in their pockets. This large man cursed the jerks, and all religion. Shortly afterward he took the jerks, and he started to run, but he jerked so powerfully he could not get away. He halted among some saplings, and, although he was violently agitated, he took out his bottle of whisky, and swore he would drink the damned jerks to death; but he jerked at such a rate he could not get the bottle to his mouth, though he tried hard. At length he fetched a sudden jerk, and the bottle struck a sapling and was broken to pieces, and spilled his whisky on the ground. There was a great crowd gathered round him, and when he lost his whisky he became very much enraged, and cursed and swore very profanely, his jerks still increasing. At length he fetched a very violent jerk, snapped his neck, fell, and soon expired, with his mouth full of cursing and bitterness.

I always looked upon the jerks as a judgment sent from God, first, to bring sinners to repentance; and, secondly, to show professors that God could work with or without means, and that he could work over and above means, and do whatsoever seemeth him good, to the glory of his grace and the salvation of the world.

There is no doubt in my mind that, with weakminded, ignorant, and superstitious persons, there was a great deal of sympathetic feeling with many that claimed to be under the influence of this jerking exercise; and yet, with many, it was perfectly involuntary. It was, on all occasions, my practice to recommend fervent prayer as a remedy, and it almost universally proved an effectual antidote.

There were many other strange and wild exercises into which the subjects of this revival fell; such, for instance, as what was called the running, jumping, barking exercise. The Methodist preachers generally preached against this extravagant wildness. I did it uniformly in my little ministrations, and sometimes gave great offense; but I feared no consequences when I felt my awful responsibilities to God. From these wild exercises, another great evil arose from the heated and wild imaginations of some. They professed to fall into trances and see visions; they would fall at meetings and sometimes at home, and lay apparently powerless and motionless for days, sometimes for a week at a time, without food or drink; and when they came to, they professed to have seen heaven and hell, to have seen God, angels, the devil and the damned; they would prophesy, and, under the pretense of Divine inspiration, predict the time of the end of the world, and the ushering in of the great millennium.

This was the most troublesome delusion of all; it made such an appeal to the ignorance, superstition, and credulity of the people, even saint as well as sinner. I watched this matter with a vigilant eye. If I opposed it, I would have to meet the clamor of the multitude; and if any one opposed it, these very visionists would single him out, and denounce the dreadful judgments of God against him. They would even set the very day that God was to burn the world, like the self-deceived modern Millerites. They would prophesy, that if any one did oppose them, God would send fire down from heaven and consume him, like the blasphemous Shakers. They would proclaim that they could heal all manner of diseases, and raise the dead, just like the diabolical Mormons. They professed to have converse with spirits of the dead in heaven and hell, like the modern spirit rappers. Such a state of things I never saw before, and I hope in God I shall never see again.

3

CHARLES G. FINNEY

Lectures on Revivals of Religion

TEXT.—O Lord, revive thy work in the midst of the years, in the midst of the years made known; in wrath remember mercy.—Hab. iii. 2.

IT is supposed that the prophet Habakkuk was contemporary with Jeremiah, and that this prophecy was uttered in anticipation of the Babylonish captivity. Looking at the judgments which were speedily to come upon his nation, the soul of the prophet was wrought up to an agony, and he cries out in his distress, "O Lord, revive thy work." As if he had said, "O Lord, grant that thy judgments may not make Israel desolate. In the midst of these awful years, let the judgments of God be made the means of reviving religion among us. In wrath remember mercy."

Religion is the work of man. It is something for man to do. It consists in obeying God with and from the heart. It is man's duty. It is true, God induces him to do it. He influences him by his Spirit, because of his great wickedness and reluctance to obey. If it were not necessary for God to influence men—if men were disposed to obey God, there would be no occasion to pray, "O Lord, revive thy work." The ground of necessity for such a prayer is, that men are wholly indisposed to obey; and unless God interpose the influence of his Spirit, not a man on earth will ever obey the commands of God.

A "Revival of Religion" presupposes a declension. Almost all the religion in the world has been produced by revivals. God has found it necessary to take advantage of the excitability there is in mankind, to produce powerful excitements among them, before he can lead them to obey. Men are so spiritually sluggish, there are so many things to lead their minds off from religion, and to oppose the influence of the Gospel, that it is necessary to raise an excitement among them, till the tide rises so high as to sweep away the opposing obstacles. They must be so excited that they will break over these counteracting influences, before they will obey God. Not that excited feeling is religion, for it is not; but it is excited desire, appetite and feeling that prevents religion. The will is, in a sense, enslaved by the carnal and worldly desires. Hence it is necessary to awaken men to a sense of guilt and danger, and thus produce an excitement of counter feeling and desire which will break the power of carnal and worldly desire and leave the will free to obey God.

Look back at the history of the Jews, and you will see that God used to maintain religion among *them* by special occasions, when there would be a great excitement, and people would turn to the Lord. And after they had been thus revived, it would be but a short time before there would be so many counteracting influences brought to bear upon them, that religion would decline, and keep on declining, till God could have time—so to speak—to convict them of sin by his Spirit and rebuke them by his providence, and thus so gain the attention of the masses to the great subject of salvation, as to produce a widespread awakening of religious interest, and consequently a revival of religion. Then the counteracting causes would again operate, and religion would decline, and the nation would be swept away in the vortex of luxury, idolatry, and pride.

There is so little *principle* in the church, so little firmness and stability of purpose, that unless the religious feelings are awakened and kept excited, counter worldly feeling and excitement will prevail, and men will not obey God. They have so little knowledge, and their principles are so weak, that unless they are excited, they will go back from the path of duty, and do nothing to promote the glory of God. The state of the world is still such, and probably will be till the millennium is fully come, that religion must be mainly promoted by means of revivals. How long and how often has the experiment been tried, to bring the church to act steadily for God, without these periodical excitements. Many good men have supposed, and still suppose, that the best way to promote religion, is to go along *uniformly*, and gather in the ungodly gradually, and without excitement. But however sound such reasoning may appear in the abstract, *facts* demonstrate its futility. If the church were far enough advanced in knowledge, and had stability of principle enough to *keep awake*, such a course would do; but the church is so little enlightened, and there are so many counteracting causes, that she will not go steadily to work without a special interest being awakened. As the millennium advances, it is probable that these periodical excitements will be unknown. Then the church will be enlightened, and the counteracting causes removed, and the entire church will be in a state of habitual and steady obedience to God. The entire church will stand and take the infant mind, and cultivate it for God. Children will be trained up in the way they should go, and there will be no such torrents of worldliness, and fashion, and covetousness, to bear away the piety of the church, as soon as the excitement of a revival is withdrawn.

It is very desirable it should be so. It is very desirable that the church should go on steadily in a course of obedience without these excitements. Such excitements are liable to injure the health. Our nervous system is so strung that any powerful excitement, if long continued, injures our health and unfits us for duty. If religion is ever to have a pervading influence in the world, it cannot be so; this spasmodic religion must be done away. Then it will be uncalled for. Christians will not sleep the greater part of the time, and once in a while wake up, and rub their eyes, and bluster about, and vociferate a little while, and then go to sleep again. Then there will be no need that ministers should wear themselves out, and kill themselves, by their efforts to roll back the flood of worldly influence that sets in upon the church. But as yet the state of the Christian world is such, that to expect to promote religion without excitements is unphilosophical and absurd. The great political, and other worldly excitements that agitate Christendom, are all unfriendly to religion, and divert the mind from the interests of the soul. Now these excitements can only be counteracted by *religious* excitements. And until there is religious principle in the world to put down irreligious excitements, it is vain to try to promote religion, except by counteracting excitements. This is true in philosophy, and it is a historical fact.

It is altogether improbable that religion will ever make progress among *heathen* nations except through the influence of revivals. The attempt is now making to do it by education, and other cautious and gradual improvements. But so long as the laws of mind remain what they are, it cannot be done in this way. There must be excitement sufficient to wake up the dormant moral powers, and roll back the tide of degradation and sin. And precisely so far as our own land approximates to heathenism, it is impossible for God or man to promote religion in such a state of things but by powerful excitements. This is evident from the fact that this has always been the way in which God has done it. God does not create these excitements, and choose this method to promote religion for nothing or without reason. Where mankind are so reluctant to obey God, they will not act until they are excited. For instance, how many there are who know that they ought to be religious, but they are afraid if they become pious they shall be laughed at by their companions. Many are wedded to idols, others are procrastinating repentance, until they are settled in life, or until they have secured some favorite worldly interest. Such persons will never give up their false shame, or relinquish their ambitious schemes, till they are so excited by a sense of guilt and danger that they cannot contain themselves any longer.

These remarks are designed only as an introduction to the

discourse. I shall now proceed with the main design, to show,
  I. What a revival of religion is not;
 II. What it is; and,
III. The agencies employed in promoting it.

I. A REVIVAL OF RELIGION IS NOT A MIRACLE.

1. A miracle has been generally defined to be, a Divine interference, setting aside or suspending the laws of nature. It is not a miracle in this sense. All the laws of matter and mind remain in force. They are neither suspended nor set aside in a revival.

2. It is not a miracle according to another definition of the term miracle—*something above the powers of nature.* There is nothing in religion beyond the ordinary powers of nature. It consists entirely in the *right exercise* of the powers of nature. It is just that, and nothing else. When mankind become religious, they are not *enabled* to put forth exertions which they were unable before to put forth. They only exert the powers they had before in a different way, and use them for the glory of God.

3. It is not a miracle, or dependent on a miracle, in any sense. It is a purely philosophical result of the right use of the constituted means—as much so as any other effect produced by the application of means. There may be a miracle among its antecedent causes, or there may not. The apostles employed miracles, simply as means by which they arrested attention to their message, and established its divine authority. But the miracle was not the revival. The miracle was one thing; the revival that followed it was quite another thing. The revivals in the apostles' days were connected with miracles, but they were not miracles.

I said that a revival is the result of the *right* use of the appropriate means. The means which God has enjoined for the production of a revival, doubtless have a natural tendency to produce a revival. Otherwise God would not have enjoined them. But means will not produce a revival, we all know, without the blessing of God. No more will grain, when it is sowed, produce a crop without the blessing of God. It is impossible for us to say that there is not as direct an influence or agency from God, to produce a crop of grain, as there is to produce a revival. What are the laws of nature according to which is is supposed that grain yields a crop? They are nothing but the constituted manner of the operations of God. In the Bible, the word of God is compared to grain, and preaching is compared to sowing seed, and the results to the springing up and growth of the crop. And the result is just as philosophical in the one case, as in the other, and is as naturally connected with the cause; or, more correctly, a revival is as naturally a result of the use of the appropriate means as a crop is of the use of its appropriate means. It is true that religion does not properly belong to the category of cause and effect; but although it is not *caused* by means, yet it has its occasion, and may as naturally and certainly result from its *occasion* as a crop does from its *cause*.

I wish this idea to be impressed on all your minds, for there has long been an idea prevalent that promoting religion has something very peculiar in it, not to be judged of by the ordinary rules of cause and effect; in short, that there is no connection of the means with the result, and no tendency in the means to produce the effect. No doctrine is more dangerous than this to the prosperity of the church, and nothing more absurd.

Suppose a man were to go and preach this doctrine among farmers, about their sowing grain. Let him tell them that God is a sovereign, and will give them a crop only when it pleases him, and that for them to plow and plant and labor as if they expected to raise a crop is very wrong, and taking the work out of the hands of God, that it interferes with his sovereignty, and is going on in their own strength; and that there is no connection between the means and the result on which they can depend. And now, suppose the farmers should believe such doctrine. Why, they would starve the world to death.

Just such results will follow from the church's being persuaded that promoting religion is somehow so mysteriously a subject of Divine sovereignty, that there is no natural connection between the means and the end. What *are* the results? Why, generation after generation has gone down to hell. No doubt more than five thousand millions have gone down to hell, while the church has been dreaming, and waiting for God to save them without the use of means. It has been the devil's most successful means of destroying souls. The connection is as clear in religion as it is when the farmer sows his grain.

There is one fact under the government of God, worthy of universal notice, and of everlasting remembrance; which is, that the most useful and important things are most easily and certainly obtained by the use of the appropriate means. This is evidently a principle in the Divine administration. Hence, all the *necessaries* of life are obtained with great *certainty* by the use of the simplest means. The luxuries are more difficult to obtain; the means to procure them are more intricate and less certain in their results; while things absolutely hurtful and poisonous, such as alcohol and the like, are often obtained only by torturing nature, and making use of a kind of infernal sorcery to procure the death-dealing abomination. This principle holds true in moral government, and as spiritual blessings are of surpassing importance, we should expect their attainment to be connected with *great certainty* with the use of appropriate means; and such we find to be the fact; and I fully believe that could facts be known, it would be found that when the appointed means have been *rightly* used, spiritual blessings have been obtained with greater uniformity than temporal ones.

II. I AM TO SHOW WHAT A REVIVAL IS.

It is the renewal of the first love of Christians, resulting in the awakening and conversion of sinners to God. In the popular sense, a revival of religion in a community is the arousing, quickening, and reclaiming of the more or less backslidden church and the more or less general awakening of all classes, and insuring attention to the claims of God.

It presupposes that the church is sunk down in a backslidden state, and a revival consists in the return of a church from her backslidings, and in the conversion of sinners.

1. A revival always includes conviction of sin on the part of the church. Backslidden professors cannot wake up and begin right away in the service of God, without deep searchings of heart. The fountains of sin need to be broken up. In a true revival, Christians are always brought under such convictions; they see their sins in such a light, that often they find it impossible to maintain a hope of their acceptance with God. It does not always go to that extent; but there are always, in a genuine revival, deep convictions of sin, and often cases of abandoning all hope.

2. Backslidden Christians will be brought to repentance. A revival is nothing else than a new beginning of obedience to God. Just as in the case of a converted sinner, the first step is a deep repentance, a breaking down of heart, a getting down into the dust before God, with deep humility, and forsaking of sin.

3. Christians will have their faith renewed. While they are in their backslidden state they are blind to the state of sinners. Their hearts are as hard as marble. The truths of the Bible only appear like a dream. They admit it to be all true; their conscience and their judgment assent to it; but their faith does not see it standing out in bold relief, in all the burning realities of eternity. But when they enter into a revival, they no longer see men as trees walking, but they see things in that strong light which will renew the love of God in their hearts. This will lead them to labor zealously to bring others to him. They will feel grieved that others do not love God, when they love him so much. And they will set themselves feelingly to persuade their neighbors to give him their hearts. So their love to men will be renewed. They will be filled with a tender and burning love for souls. They will have a longing desire for the salvation of the whole world. They will be in an agony for individuals whom they want to have saved—their friends, relations, enemies. They will not only be urging them to give their hearts to God,

but they will carry them to God in the arms of faith, and with strong crying and tears beseech God to have mercy on them, and save their souls from endless burnings.

4. A revival breaks the power of the world and of sin over Christians. It brings them to such vantage ground that they get a fresh impulse towards heaven. They have a new foretaste of heaven, and new desires after union with God; and the charm of the world is broken, and the power of sin overcome.

5. When the churches are thus awakened and reformed, the reformation and salvation of sinners will follow, going through the same stages of conviction, repentance, and reformation. Their hearts will be broken down and changed. Very often the most abandoned profligates are among the subjects. Harlots, and drunkards, and infidels, and all sorts of abandoned characters, are awakened and converted. The worst among human beings are softened, and reclaimed, and made to appear as lovely specimens of the beauty of holiness.

III. I AM TO CONSIDER THE AGENCIES EMPLOYED IN CARRYING FORWARD A REVIVAL OF RELIGION.

Ordinarily, there are three agents employed in the work of conversion, and one instrument. The agents are God,—some person who brings the truth to bear on the mind,—and the sinner himself. The instrument is the truth. There are *always two* agents, God and the sinner, employed and active in every case of genuine conversion.

1. The agency of God is two-fold; by his Providence and by his Spirit.

(1.) By his providential government, he so arranges events as to bring the sinner's mind and the truth in contact. He brings the sinner where the truth reaches his ears or his eyes. It is often interesting to trace the manner in which God arranges events so as to bring this about, and how he sometimes makes every thing seem to favor a revival. The state of the weather, and of the public health, and other circumstances concur to make every thing just right to favor the application of truth with the greatest possible efficacy. How he sometimes sends a minister along, just at the time he is wanted! How he brings out a particular truth, just at the particular time when the individual it is fitted to reach is in the way to hear!

(2.) God's special agency by his Holy Spirit. Having direct access to the mind, and knowing infinitely well the whole history and state of each individual sinner, he employs that truth which is best adapted to his particular case, and then sets it home with Divine power. He gives it such vividness, strength, and power, that the sinner quails, and throws down his weapons of rebellion, and turns to the Lord. Under his influence, the truth burns and cuts its way like fire. He makes the truth stand out in such aspects, that it crushes the proudest man down with the weight of a mountain. If men were *disposed* to obey God, the truth is given with sufficient clearness in the Bible; and from preaching they could learn all that is necessary for them to know. But because they are wholly *disinclined* to obey it, God clears it up before their minds, and pours in a blaze of convincing light upon their souls, which they cannot withstand, and they yield to it, and obey God, and are saved.

2. The agency of men is commonly employed. Men are not mere *instruments* in the hands of God. Truth is the instrument. The preacher is a moral agent in the work; he acts; he is not a mere passive instrument; he is voluntary in promoting the conversion of sinners.

3. The agency of the sinner himself. The conversion of a sinner consists in his obeying the truth. It is therefore impossible it should take place without his agency, for it consists in *his* acting right. He is influenced to this by the agency of God, and by the agency of men. Men act on their fellow-men, not only by language, but by their looks, their tears, their daily deportment. See that impenitent man there, who has a pious wife. Her very looks, her tenderness, her solemn, compassionate dignity, softened and moulded into the image of Christ are a sermon to him

all the time. He has to turn his mind away, because it is such a reproach to him. He feels a sermon ringing in his ears all day long.

Mankind are accustomed to read the countenances of their neighbors. Sinners often read the state of a Christian's mind in his eyes. If his eyes are full of levity, or worldly anxiety and contrivance, sinners read it. If they are full of the Spirit of God, sinners read it; and they are often led to conviction by barely seeing the countenance of Christians.

An individual once went into a manufactory to see the machinery. His mind was solemn, as he had been where there was a revival. The people who labored there all knew him by sight, and knew who he was. A young lady who was at work saw him, and whispered some foolish remark to her companion, and laughed. The person stopped and looked at her with a feeling of grief. She stopped, her thread broke, and she was so much agitated she could not join it. She looked out at the window to compose herself, and then tried again; again and again she strove to recover her self-command. At length she sat down, overcome with her feelings. The person then approached and spoke with her; she soon manifested a deep sense of sin. The feeling spread through the establishment like fire, and in a few hours almost every person employed there was under conviction, so much so, that the owner, though a worldly man, was astounded, and requested to have the works stop and have a prayer meeting; for he said it was a great deal more important to have these people converted than to have the works go on. And in a few days, the owner and nearly every person employed in the establishment were hopefully converted. The eye of this individual, his solemn countenance, his compassionate feeling, rebuked the levity of the young woman, and brought her under conviction of sin: and this whole revival followed, probably in a great measure, from so small an incident.

If Christians have deep feeling on the subject of religion themselves, they will produce deep feeling wherever they go.

And if they are cold, or light and trifling, they inevitably destroy all deep feeling, even in awakened sinners.

I knew a case, once, of an individual who was very anxious, but one day I was grieved to find that her convictions seemed to be all gone. I asked her what she had been doing. She told me she had been spending the afternoon at such a place, among some professors of religion, not thinking that it would dissipate her convictions to spend an afternoon with professors of religion. But they were trifling and vain, and thus her convictions were lost. And no doubt those professors of religion, by their folly, destroyed a soul, for her convictions did not return.

The church is required to use the means for the conversion of sinners. Sinners cannot properly be said to use the means for their own conversion. The church uses the means. What sinners do is to submit to the truth, or to resist it. It is a mistake of sinners, to think they are using means for their own conversion. The whole drift of a revival, and every thing about it, is designed to present the truth *to* your mind, for your obedience or resistance.

REMARKS.

1. Revivals were formerly regarded as miracles. And it has been so by some even in our day. And others have ideas on the subject so loose and unsatisfactory, that if they would only *think,* they would see their absurdity. For a long time, it was supposed by the church, that a revival was a miracle, an interposition of Divine power which they had nothing to do with, and which they had no more agency in producing, than they had in producing thunder, or a storm of hail, or an earthquake. It is only within a few years that ministers generally have supposed revivals were to be *promoted,* by the use of means designed and adapted specially to that object. Even in New England, it has been supposed that revivals came just as showers do, sometimes in one town, and sometimes in another, and that ministers and churches could do nothing more to produce

them than they could to make showers of rain come on their own town, when they were falling on a neighboring town.

It used to be supposed that a revival would come about once in fifteen years, and all would be converted that God intended to save, and then they must wait until another crop came forward on the stage of life. Finally, the time got shortened down to five years, and they supposed there might be a revival about as often as that.

I have heard a fact in relation to one of these pastors, who supposed revivals might come about once in five years. There had been a revival in his congregation. The next year, there was a revival in a neighboring town, and he went there to preach, and staid several days, till he got his soul all engaged in the work. He returned home on Saturday, and went into his study to prepare for the Sabbath. And his soul was in an agony. He thought how many adult persons there were in his congregation at enmity with God—so many still unconverted—so many persons *die* yearly—such a portion of them unconverted—if a revival does not come under five years, so many adult heads of families will be in hell. He put down his calculations on paper, and embodied them in his sermon for the next day, with his heart bleeding at the dreadful picture. As I understood it, he did not do this with any expectation of a revival, but he felt deeply, and poured out his heart to his people. And that sermon awakened *forty heads of families*, and a powerful revival followed; and so his theory about a revival once in five years was all exploded.

Thus God has overthrown, generally, the theory that revivals are miracles.

2. Mistaken notions concerning the sovereignty of God have greatly hindered revivals.

Many people have supposed God's sovereignty to be something very different from what it is. They have supposed it to be such an arbitrary disposal of events, and particularly of the gift of his Spirit, as precluded a rational employment of means for promoting a revival of religion. But there is no evidence from the Bible that God exercises any such sovereignty as that. There are no facts to prove it. But every thing goes to show that God has connected means with the end through all the departments of his government—in nature and in grace. There is no *natural* event in which his own agency is not concerned. He has not built the creation like a vast machine that will go on alone without his further care. He has not retired from the universe, to let it work for itself. This is mere atheism. He exercises a universal superintendence and control. And yet every event in nature has been brought about by means. He neither administers providence nor grace with that sort of sovereignty that dispenses with the use of means. There is no more sovereignty in one than in the other.

And yet some people are terribly alarmed at all direct efforts to promote a revival, and they cry out, "You are trying to get up a revival in your own strength. Take care, you are interfering with the sovereignty of God. Better keep along in the usual course, and let God give a revival when he thinks it is best. God is a sovereign, and it is very wrong for you to attempt to get up a revival, just because *you think* a revival is needed." This is just such preaching as the devil wants. And men cannot do the devil's work more effectually than by preaching up the sovereignty of God, as a reason why we should not put forth efforts to produce a revival.

3. You see the error of those who are beginning to think that religion can be better promoted in the world without revivals, and who are disposed to give up all efforts to produce religious awakenings. Because there are evils arising in some instances out of great excitements on the subject of religion, they are of opinion that it is best to dispense with them altogether. This cannot, and must not be. True, there is danger of abuses. In cases of great *religious* as well as all other excitements, more or less incidental evils may be expected of course. But this is no reason why they should be given up. The best things are always

liable to abuses. Great and manifold evils have originated in the providential and moral governments of God. But these *foreseen* perversions and evils were not considered a sufficient reason for giving them up. For the establishment of these governments was on the whole the best that could be done for the production of the greatest amount of happiness. So in revivals of religion, it is found by experience, that in the present state of the world, religion cannot be promoted to any considerable extent without them. The evils which are sometimes complained of, when they are real, are incidental, and of small importance when compared with the amount of good produced by revivals. The sentiment should not be admitted by the church for a moment, that revivals may be given up. It is fraught with all that is dangerous to the interests of Zion, is death to the cause of missions, and brings in its train the damnation of the world.

FINALLY.— I have a proposal to make to you who are here present. I have not commenced this course of Lectures on Revivals to get up a curious theory of my own on the subject. I would not spend my time and strength merely to give you instructions, to gratify your curiosity, and furnish you something to talk about. I have no idea of preaching *about* revivals. It is not my design to preach so as to have you able to say at the close, "We *understand* all about revivals now," while you do *nothing*. But I wish to ask you a question. What do you hear lectures on revivals for? Do you mean that whenever you are convinced what your duty is in promoting a revival, you will go to work and practise it?

Will you follow the instructions I shall give you from the Word of God, and put them in practise in your own lives? Will you bring them to bear upon your families, your acquaintance, neighbors, and through the city? Or will you spend the winter in learning *about* revivals, and do nothing *for* them? I want you, as fast as you learn any thing on the subject of revivals, to put it in practice, and go to work and see if you cannot promote a revival among sinners here. If you will not do this, I wish you to let me know at the beginning, so that I need not waste my strength. You ought to decide *now* whether you will do this or not. You know that we call sinners to decide on the spot whether *they* will obey the Gospel. And we have no more authority to let you take time to deliberate whether *you* will obey God, than we have to let sinners do so. We call on you to unite now in a solemn pledge to God, that you will do your duty as fast as you learn what it is, and to pray that He will pur out his Spirit upon this church and upon all the city this winter.

IV

THE MISSIONS ENTERPRISE

The Christian missionary imperative to "preach the gospel to all nations" served as an important impetus for colonization from the earliest days of exploration. Centuries before the actual discovery of America by Europeans, theologians had debated the existence of the "antipodes," unknown lands on the other side of the earth. If those lands actually existed, did the atonement of Christ apply to their human inhabitants? With the discoveries of new lands, Christians, both Catholic and Protestant, concluded that the "Indians" who lived there were indeed capable of receiving salvation. The missionary motivation thus added an evangelistic dimension to colonization efforts.

Catholic missionaries from various monastic orders sought to Christianize the Indians in the Southwest and in certain northern areas by bringing to them the sacraments of the Church, catechizing them in the faith, and seeking to improve their basic life-style. The friars did not always drastically alter the Indian way of life. Indigenous customs and rituals which were not in direct conflict with Catholic doctrine were often incorporated into the life of the newly established Indian missions.

The Protestants likewise were concerned with evangelizing the Indian population out of compassion and a desire to thwart Catholic influence. Protestants were less appreciative of Indian customs and rites, frequently suggesting that the Indians must first become "civilized" before they could fully realize the benefits of redemption.

The discovery of such an obviously pagan people also convinced many American Christians of the eschatological element behind evangelization of the Indian. If the return of Christ was contingent upon the proclamation of the gospel to all nations, then the missionary efforts among the Indians might hasten the second coming. Building upon this idea, others associated the Indians with the famous lost tribes of Israel to suggest that the conversion of the Indians was related to the conversion of the Jews, another factor in millennial fulfillment. Missionary activity among the Indians was often included in colonial charters as a motive for constructing settlements in the New World.

In spite of these lofty proclamations, only a minority of the colonists actually sought to implement such missionary endeavors. A few clergymen took the gospel directly to the Indians. Many of these men also sought to stem the tide of exploitation which increasingly became the policy of most colonial governments.

Missionary work was evident in the colony at Jamestown through such individuals as Alexander Whitaker, known to many as "the Apostle to the Indians." It was Whitaker who influenced Pocahontas to receive Christian conversion and baptism, officiating at her marriage to John Rolfe. Whitaker's "Good News From Virginia," published in 1613, vividly described Indian life. The treatise called on the English to contribute funds and workers for the task of evangelizing the Indians. By 1622, however, Indian uprisings had cost the lives of numerous Indians and settlers. The compassion of the English in Virginia toward Indian missions was sorely affected by these violent altercations.

Roger Williams was another of the early participants in the work with the Indians. Exiled from Massachusetts in the winter of 1636, Williams was sheltered by the Narraganset Indians and purchased from them the land on which he established Providence. He was a fervent champion of Indian claims to the land and an advocate of the fair treatment of Indians by the colonists. His *Key to the Language of the Natives in that part of America, Called New England*, published in 1643, was the earliest lexicon of Indian language in America.

Perhaps the most outstanding Puritan missionary to the Indians was John Eliot, pastor of the church at Roxbury, Massachusetts. Eliot devoted much of his life to the conversion and protection of the Indians. To protect Christian Indians from exploitation by whites and the wrath of other Indians, Eliot organized "Praying Towns" such as Natick where Indians could find community and instruction in the faith. He wrote a catechism in the language of the Indians and by the 1660s had published a translation of the entire Bible into Indian dialect.

During the 1700s missionary work with the Indians in New England was carried out by such well-known Puritans as Jonathan Edwards and David Brainerd. Expelled from his congregation at Northampton due to a controversy over church discipline and revival theology, Edwards moved to Stockbridge as pastor of the Congregational Church and minister to the Housatonic Indians. The invitation from the Society for the Propagation of the Gospel in New England was clearly a missionary appointment. During these years Edwards developed a close friendship with David Brainerd, an intense young preacher, deeply concerned for the Indians and engaged to Edwards' daughter, Jerusha. Following Brainerd's untimely death, Edwards published the young man's journal, a document which became one of the most influential works in the annals of American missions.

Brainerd, 1718–1747, humiliated by expulsion from Yale due to his zealous support of the revivals and his somewhat intemperate criticism of a tutor as having "no more grace than a chair," spent the final years of his brief life as a missionary to the Indians. A sickly man with a serious consumptive condition, he nonetheless determined to do his work in the harsh frontier areas of western Massachusetts. Deploring much of Indian life and religion as satanic, Brainerd sought to awaken the tribes to the miracle of grace and conversion. His journal is an account of his endeavors with the Indians, the hardships of his travels, and the morose dimensions of his own faith.

As the colonial population increased, the need for more land accelerated exploitation and warfare between Indians and whites. Diseases to which Europeans had long developed immunity decimated whole tribes of Indians. Missionary zeal toward the Indians, never really extensive, was limited to a few voices crying in the American wilderness for a Christian spirit of fairness and brotherhood.

The westward expansion of the early nineteenth century created another missionary response, however. Denominations acknowledged the urgent need for missionaries on the frontier who would win converts, build new churches, and extend Christian influence. Churches in the East united their efforts in order to raise funds for the support of traveling preachers who would do missionary work in the newly settled areas. Congregationalists, Baptists, and Presbyterians formed numerous state societies for the sponsorship of frontier missionaries.

In 1801 Presbyterians and Congregationalists formulated a Plan of Union, whereby members of those two denominations could unite in one frontier communion. Congregationalist or Presbyterian preachers served the churches interchangeably, and the form of church government was determined by majority vote of the congregation. Divisions within Congregationalism and a more structured system of the church order made the Plan of Union more advantageous for the Presbyterians. The Plan of Union endured for some thirty years.

As churches made a concerted effort to affect the religious life of the frontier, auxiliary mission societies were formed which provided materials and programs for evangelistic work. The American Bible Society was organized in 1816 as an interdenominational foundation for publication and circulation of the Scriptures. The American Tract Society, founded in 1825, provided printed materials for evangelism and teaching ministries. The Sunday School Union of 1824 sought to instruct new converts in the Bible and Christian living. The American Home Missionary Society, founded in 1826, was a source through which the religion and culture of the East was taken to frontier areas. Missionary societies also aimed at reaching particular groups or subjecting specific issues to the light of the gospel. Organizations promoting temperance, abolition, peace, and other social issues appeared in the early nineteenth century.

The concern of the churches ultimately extended beyond the boundaries of the American frontier in an effort to propagate the gospel throughout the world. In this endeavor Americans were profoundly influenced by the work of William Carey and the London Missionary Society founded in 1795. Word of Carey's activities in India reached America as the religious enthusiasm of the Second Great Awakening swept the churches. An increasing number of Americans felt compelled to follow Christ's command to preach the gospel to all nations.

One of the first expressions of missionary zeal was evident at Williams College in Massachusetts in a group of young men united to pray for missions. These individuals participated in the now famous "Haystack Prayer Meeting" of 1806, in which several of the men vowed to serve God as foreign missionaries. Several were actually sent out under the auspices of the Congregationalist society, the American Board of Commissioners for Foreign Missions, founded in 1810 as the first foreign missions board in America.

The sermon provided in this chapter was preached at a meeting of the American Board a few years after its founding. The sermon was delivered by Timothy Dwight, president of Yale and a prominent figure in the religious awakenings.

Dwight's discourse reveals the optimism of the early proponents of the foreign mission cause. In his mind, the missionary task would bring in a new day for the church and the world. Missionary endeavors would unite Christians in a common calling beyond sect, nationality, or color. They would spread Christian influence throughout the world. The false religions of Islam, infidelity, rationalism, and the "Romish Church" would be defeated by the proclamation of true Christian doctrine.

This effort to spread the gospel and defeat evil was a primary indication of the preparation for the millennium. Dwight suggested that while the millennium "in the full and perfect sense" would not begin until near the year 2000, the time for preparation was at hand. Thus the day of salvation was near, and Christians were to unite in the work of proclaiming the gospel, defeating the enemy, and preparing for the millennium.

Two of the first American missionaries sent out to India by the mission board were Adoniram Judson and Luther Rice. In the midst of their journey these two Congregationalists accepted Baptist views. Separating from the Congregational mission board, Judson moved on to Burma and Rice returned to the United States to secure the help of Baptists in the mission enterprise. By 1814 Baptists in America had formed the General Missionary Convention of the Baptist Denomination in the United States of America for Foreign Missions, soon known as the Triennial Convention. This represents the first national body unifying Baptists in a common evangelical task. Presbyterians formed a foreign mission agency in 1817 and Methodists a year later. Soon most major American denominations were raising funds and charting a course for world evangelization.

The missionary enterprise illustrates various qualities of American religion in the nineteenth century. The societies themselves were autonomous bodies constituted around carefully defined purposes, raising funds for specific types of work. Many were interdenominational efforts providing for cooperation between numerous ecclesiastical communions. The missionary and benevolence societies represent one of the first means for conducting large-scale charitable endeavors in American life. The missionary spirit was an outgrowth of American evangelism and revivalistic zeal. The awakening experienced in America was to be shared with the world. The missionary calling provided a means whereby the fervor of new converts could be channeled into a dramatic vocation. Hundreds of young men and women converted in the revivals responded to the call to mission fields, home and foreign.

At the same time, American millennial hopes were frequently related to missionary efforts. Many believed that the churches in the new land had an obligation to proclaim the gospel to all the earth and thereby hasten the day of Christ's return. Many nineteenth-century men and women were convinced that just as America had been chosen by God as a place where biblical, Reformation religion would be preserved and proliferated, it had also been called to share that message with the world.

Missionaries went out with a sense of divine destiny leading them to participate in bringing in the kingdom of God. For some early missionaries the kingdom was to be established in the hearts and lives of new believers and expressed in terms of the culture of each country and region on the mission field. For others, it was established within and without as the religion and civilization of America, capitalistic, Anglo-Saxon, and Protestant, to be transplanted throughout the earth. For these missionaries the cross and the flag were carried together. The tension between these two forces was a major issue for the Protestant missionary enterprise in the nineteenth and twentieth centuries.

Missions represents an important aspect of American religion. It was a source of both interdenominational cooperation and competition. The missionary enterprise nonetheless provided an important means for expressing the spirit of American evangelical Protestantism at home and abroad.

1

DAVID BRAINERD

The Diary of
David Brainerd[1]

THURSDAY, April 1, 1742. I seem to be declining with respect to my life and warmth in divine things; had not so free access to God in prayer as usual of late. Oh, that God would humble me deeply in the dust before Him! I deserve hell every day for not loving my Lord more, who has, I trust, loved me and given Himself for me. Every time I am enabled to exercise any grace renewedly, I am renewedly indebted to the God of all grace for special assistance. Where then is boasting? Surely it is excluded when we think how we are dependent on God for the being and every act of grace. Oh, if ever I get to heaven it will be because God wills, and nothing else; for I never did anything of myself but get away from God! My soul will be astonished at the unsearchable riches of divine grace when I arrive at the mansions, which the blessed Saviour is gone before to prepare.

Friday, April 2. In the afternoon I felt, in secret prayer, much resigned, calm, and serene. What are all the storms of this lower world, if Jesus by His Spirit does but come walking on the seas! Some time past, I had much pleasure in the prospect of the heathen being brought home to Christ, and desired that the Lord would employ me in that work. But now, my soul more frequently desires to die, to be with Christ. Oh, that my soul were rapt up in divine love, and my longing desires after God increased! In the evening, was refreshed in prayer, with the hopes of the advancement of Christ's kingdom in the world.

Saturday, April 3. Was very much amiss this morning and had a bad night. I thought, if God would take me to Himself now, my soul would exceedingly rejoice. Oh, that I may be always humble and resigned to God, and that He would cause my soul to be more fixed on Himself, that I may be more fitted both for doing and suffering!

Lord's Day, April 4. My heart was wandering and lifeless. In the evening God gave me faith in prayer, made my soul melt in some measure, and gave me to taste a divine sweetness. O my blessed God! Let me climb up near to Him, and love, and long, and plead, and wrestle, and stretch after Him, and for deliverance from the body of sin and death. Alas! my soul mourned to think I should ever lose sight of its Beloved again. "O come, Lord Jesus, amen."

> On the evening of the next day, he complains that he seemed to be void of all relish of divine things, felt much of the prevalence of corruption, and saw in himself a disposition to all manner of sin; which brought a very great gloom on his mind and cast him down into the depths of melancholy; so that he speaks of himself as amazed, having no comfort, but filled with horror, seeing no comfort in heaven or earth.—J. E.

Tuesday, April 6. I walked out this morning to the same place where I was last night, and felt as I did then; but was somewhat relieved by reading some passages in my diary, and seemed to feel as if I might pray to the great God again with freedom; but was suddenly struck with a damp [a sense of heaviness, making it hard to pray], from the sense I had of my own vileness.

Then I cried to God to cleanse me from my exceeding filthiness, to give me repentance and pardon. I then began to find it sweet to pray; and could think of undergoing the greatest sufferings, in the cause of Christ, with pleasure. *Found myself willing, if God should so order it, to suffer banishment from my native land, among the heathen, that I might do something for their salvation, in distresses and deaths of any kind.*

Then God gave me to wrestle earnestly for others, for the kingdom of Christ in the world, and for dear Christian friends. I felt weaned from the world and from my own reputation amongst men, willing to be despised and to be gazing stock for the world to behold. It is impossible for me to express how I then felt. I had not much joy, but some sense of the majesty of God, which made me as it were tremble. I saw myself mean and vile, which made me more willing that God should do what He would with me; it was all infinitely reasonable.

Wednesday, April 7. I had not so much fervency, but felt something as I did yesterday morning, in prayer. At noon I spent some time in secret, with some fervency, but scarce any sweetness; and felt very dull in the evening.

Thursday, April 8. *Had raised hopes today respecting the heathen. Oh, that God would bring in great numbers of them to Jesus Christ! I cannot but hope I shall see that glorious day.* Everything in this world seems exceeding vile and little to me: I look so on myself. I had some little dawn of comfort today in prayer; but especially tonight, I think I had some faith and power of intercession with God. I was enabled to plead with God for the growth of grace in myself; and many of the dear children of God then lay with weight upon my soul. Blessed be the Lord! It is good to wrestle for divine blessings.

Friday, April 9. Most of my time in morning devotion was spent without sensible sweetness; yet I had one delightful prospect of arriving at the heavenly world. I am more amazed than ever at such thoughts, for I see myself infinitely vile and unworthy. I feel very heartless and dull; and though I long for the presence of God and seem constantly to reach towards God in desires, yet I cannot feel that divine and heavenly sweetness that I used to enjoy. No poor creature stands in need of divine grace more than I, and none abuse it more than I have done, and still do.

Saturday, April 10. Spent much time in secret prayer this morning and not without some comfort in divine things. And, I hope, had some faith in exercise; but am so low and feel so little of the sensible presence of God that I hardly know what to call faith, and am made to possess the sins of my youth, and the dreadful sin of my nature. I am all sin; I cannot think, nor act, but every motion is sin. I feel some faint hopes, that God will, of His infinite mercy, return again with showers of converting grace to poor gospel-abusing sinners. My hopes of being employed in the cause of God, which of late have been almost extinct, seem now a little revived. Oh, that all my late distresses and awful apprehensions might prove but Christ's school to make me fit for greater service, by teaching me the great lesson of humility!

Lord's Day, April 11. In the morning, I felt but little life, excepting that my heart was somewhat drawn out in thankfulness to God for His amazing grace and condescension to me, in past influences and assistances of His Spirit. Afterwards, I had some sweetness in the thoughts of arriving at the heavenly world. Oh, for the happy day! After public worship God gave me special assistance in prayer. I wrestled with my dear Lord with much sweetness, and intercession was made a delightful employment to me. In the evening, as I was viewing the light in the north, I was delighted in contemplation on the glorious morning of the resurrection.

Monday, April 12. This morning the Lord was pleased to lift up the light of His countenance upon me in secret prayer, and made the season very precious to my soul. Though I have been so depressed of late, *respecting my hopes of future serviceableness in the cause of God,* yet now I had much encouragement respecting that matter. *I was especially assisted to intercede and plead for poor souls and for the enlargement of Christ's kingdom in the world, and for special grace for myself to fit me for special services.* I felt exceedingly calm and quite resigned to God, respecting my future employment, when and where He pleased. My faith lifted me above the world and removed all those mountains that I could not look over of late.

I wanted not the favor of man to lean upon; for I knew Christ's favor was infinitely better, and that it was no matter when, nor where, nor how Christ should send me, nor what trials He should still exercise me with, if I might be prepared for His work and will. I now found revived, in my mind, the wonderful discovery of infinite wisdom is all the dispensations of God towards me, which I had a little before I met with my great trial at college; everything appeared full of divine wisdom.

Tuesday, April 13. I saw myself to be very mean and vile and wondered at those that showed me respect. Afterwards I was somewhat comforted in secret retirement and assisted to wrestle with God with some power, spirituality, and sweetness. Blessed be the Lord, He is never unmindful of me but always sends me needed supplies. From time to time when I am like one dead, He raises me to life. Oh, that I may never distrust infinite goodness!

Lord's Day, April 18. I retired early this morning into the woods for prayer; had the assistance of God's Spirit and faith in exercise. Was enabled to plead with fervency for the advancement of Christ's kingdom in the world and to intercede for dear absent friends. At noon, God enabled me to wrestle with Him and to feel, as I trust, the power of divine love in prayer. At night I saw myself infinitely indebted to God, and had a view of my shortcomings. It seemed to me that I had done as it were nothing for God, and that I never had lived to Him but a few hours of my life.

Monday, April 19. I set apart this day for fasting and prayer to God for His grace; especially to prepare me for the work of the ministry, to give me divine aid and direction in my preparations for that great work, and in His own time to send me into His harvest. Accordingly, in the morning, I endeavored to plead for the divine presence for the day, and not without some life. In the forenoon, I felt the power of intercession for precious, immortal souls; for the advancement of the kingdom of my dear Lord and Saviour in the world; and withal, a most sweet resignation and even consolation and joy in the thoughts of suffering hardships, distresses, and even death itself, in the promotion of it. Had special enlargement in pleading for the enlightening and conversion of the poor heathen.

In the afternoon, God was with me of a truth. Oh, it was blessed company indeed! God enabled me so to agonize in prayer that I was quite wet with perspiration, though in the shade and the cool wind. My soul was drawn out very much for the world, for multitudes of souls. I think I had more enlargement for sinners than for the children of God, though I felt as if I could spend my life in cries for both. I enjoyed great sweetness in communion with my dear Saviour. I think I never in my life felt such an entire weanedness from this world and so much resigned to God in everything. Oh, that I may always live to and upon my blessed God! Amen, amen.

Tuesday, April 20. This day I am twenty-four years of age. Oh, how much mercy have I received the year past! How often has God caused His goodness to pass before me! And how poorly have I answered the vows I made this time twelve month to be wholly the Lord's, to be forever devoted to His service! The Lord help me to live more to His glory for the time to come. This has been a sweet, a happy day to me; blessed be God. I think my soul was never so drawn out in intercession for others as it has been this night. Had a most fervent wrestle with the Lord tonight for my enemies. I hardly ever so longed to live to God and to be altogether devoted to Him. I wanted to wear out my life in His service, and for His glory.

Wednesday, April 21. Felt much calmness and resignation, and God again enabled me to wrestle for numbers of souls, and had much fervency in the sweet duty of intercession. I enjoyed of late more sweetness in intercession for others than in any other part of prayer. My blessed Lord really let me come near to Him and plead with Him.

Lord's Day, April 25. This morning I spent about two hours in secret duties and was enabled more than ordinarily to agonize for immortal souls. Though it was early in the morning and the sun scarcely shined at all, yet my body was quite wet with sweat. I felt much pressed now, as frequently of late, to plead for the meekness and calmness of the Lamb of God in my soul; and through divine goodness felt much of it this morning. Oh, it is a sweet disposition heartily to forgive all injuries done us; to wish our greatest enemies as well as we do our own souls! Blessed Jesus, may I daily be more and more conformed to Thee.

At night I was exceedingly melted with divine love and had some feeling sense of the blessedness of the upper world. Those words hung upon me with much divine sweetness, Psalm 84:7: "They go from strength to strength, every one of them in Zion appeareth before God." Oh, the near access that God sometimes gives us in our addresses to Him! This may well be termed appearing before God: it is so indeed, in the true spiritual sense, and in the sweetest sense. I think I have not had such power of intercession these many months, both for God's children and for dead sinners as I have had this evening. I wished and longed for the coming of my dear Lord: I longed to join the angelic hosts in praises, wholly free from imperfections. Oh, the blessed moment hastens! All I want is to be more holy, more like my dear Lord. Oh, for sanctification! My very soul pants for the complete restoration of the blessed image of my Saviour, that I may be fit for the blessed enjoyments and employments of the heavenly world.

> Farewell, vain world; my soul can bid Adieu:
> My Saviour's taught me to abandon you.
> Your charms may gratify a sensual mind;
> Not please a soul wholly for God design'd.
> Forbear to entice, cease then my soul to call:
> 'Tis fix'd through grace; my God shall be my ALL.
> While He thus lets me heavenly glories view,
> Your beauties fade, my heart's no room for you.

The Lord refreshed my soul with many sweet passages of His Word. Oh, the new Jerusalem; my soul longed for it. Oh, the song of Moses and the Lamb! And that blessed song that no man can learn but they who are redeemed from the earth, and the glorious white robes that were given to the souls under the altar!

> Lord, I'm a stranger here alone;
> Earth no true comforts can afford:
> Yet, absent from my dearest one,
> My soul delights to cry, My Lord!
> Jesus, my Lord, my only love,
> Possess my soul, nor thence depart:
> Grant me kind visits, heavenly Dove;
> My God shall then have all My heart.

Monday, April 26. Continued in a sweet frame of mind, but in the afternoon felt something of spiritual pride stirring. God was pleased to make it a humbling season at first, though afterwards He gave me sweetness. Oh, my soul exceedingly longs for that blessed state of perfect deliverance from all sin! At night, God enabled me to give my soul up to Him, to cast myself upon Him, to be ordered and disposed of according to His sovereign pleasure; and I enjoyed great peace and consolation in so doing. My soul took sweet delight in God; my thoughts freely and sweetly centered in Him. Oh, that I could spend every moment of my life to His glory!

Tuesday, April 27. I retired pretty early for secret devotions; and in prayer God was pleased to pour such ineffable comforts into my soul that I could do nothing for some time but say over and over, "O my sweet Saviour! Oh my sweet Saviour! whom have I in heaven but Thee? and there is none upon earth, that I desire beside Thee." If I had had a thousand lives my soul would gladly have laid them all down at once to have been with Christ. My soul never enjoyed so much of heaven before. It was the most refined and most spiritual season of communion with God I ever yet felt. I never felt so great a degree of resignation in my life.

In the afternoon I withdrew to meet with my God; but found myself much declined, and God made it a humbling season to my soul. I mourned over the body of death that is in me. It grieved me exceedingly that I could not pray to and praise God with my heart full of divine heavenly love. Oh, that my soul might never offer any dead, cold services to my God! In the evening had not so much divine love as in the morning; but had a sweet season of fervent intercession.

Wednesday, April 28. I withdrew to my usual place of retirement in great peace and tranquillity; spent about two hours in secret duties and felt much as I did yesterday morning, only weaker and more overcome. I seemed to depend wholly on my dear Lord, wholly weaned from all other dependences. I knew not what to say to my God, but only lean on His bosom, as it were, and breathe out my desires after a perfect conformity to

Him in all things. Thirsting desires and insatiable longings possessed my soul after perfect holiness. God was so precious to my soul that the world with all its enjoyments was infinitely vile. I had no more value for the favor of men than for pebbles. The Lord was my ALL; and that He overruled all greatly delighted me. I think my faith and dependence on God scarce ever rose so high. I saw Him such a fountain of goodness that it seemed impossible I should distrust Him again, or be any way anxious about anything that should happen to me.

I now enjoyed great sweetness in praying for absent friends, and for the enlargement of Christ's kingdom in the world. Much of the power of these divine enjoyments remained with me through the day. In the evening my heart seemed to melt, and, I trust, was really humbled for indwelling corruption, and I mourned like a dove. I felt that all my unhappiness arose from my being a sinner. With resignation I could bid welcome to all other trials. But sin hung heavy upon me, for God discovered to me the corruption of my heart. I went to bed with a heavy heart because I was a sinner; though I did not in the least doubt of God's love. Oh, that God would purge away my dross, and take away my tin, and refine me seven times.

Saturday, May 1. I was enabled to cry to God with fervency for ministerial qualifications, that He would appear for the advancement of His own kingdom, and that He would bring in the heathen. Had much assistance in my studies. This has been a profitable week to me. I have enjoyed many communications of the blessed Spirit in my soul.

Monday, May 10. I rode to New Haven and saw some Christian friends there. Had comfort in joining in prayer with them and hearing of the goodness of God to them since I last saw them.

Friday, May 14. I waited on a council of ministers convened at Hartford, and spread before them the treatment I had met with from the rector and tutors of Yale College. They thought it advisable to intercede for me with the rector and trustees and to intreat them to restore me to my former privileges in college. [The application which was then made on his behalf, had not the desired success.—1817 edition.] After this, spent some time in religious exercises with Christian friends.

Saturday, May 15. I rode from Hartford to Hebron; was somewhat dejected on the road. Appeared exceeding vile in my own eyes, saw much pride and stubbornness in my heart. Indeed, I never saw such a week as this before; for I have been almost ready to die with the view of the wickedness of my heart. I could not have thought I had such a body of death in me. Oh, that God would deliver my soul!

Wednesday, May 19. (At Millington) I was so amazingly deserted this morning that I seemed to feel a sort of horror in my soul. Alas! when God withdraws, what is there that can afford any comfort to the soul!

> Through the eight days next following, he expresses more calm-
> ness and comfort, and considerable life, fervency, and sweetness in
> religion.—J.E.

Friday, May 28. (At New Haven) I think I scarce ever felt so calm in my life; I rejoiced in resignation and giving myself up to God, to be wholly and entirely devoted to Him forever.

Tuesday, June 1. Had much of the presence of God in family prayer, and had some comfort in secret. I was greatly refreshed from the Word of God this morning, which appeared exceeding sweet to me. Some things that appeared mysterious were opened to me. Oh, that the kingdom of the dear Saviour might come with power, and the healing waters of the sanctuary spread far and wide for the healing of the nations! Came to Ripton but was very weak. However, being visited by a number of young people in the evening, I prayed with them.

Lord's Day, June 6. I feel much deserted; but all this teaches me my nothingness and vileness more than ever.

Tuesday, June 15. Had the most ardent longings after God that ever I felt in my life. At noon in my secret retirement I could do nothing but tell my Lord, in a sweet calm, that He knew I longed for nothing but Himself, nothing but holiness; that He had given me these desires and He only could give me the thing desired. I never seemed to be so unhinged from myself and to be wholly devoted to God. My heart was swallowed up in God most of the day.

In the evening I had such a view of the soul being as it were enlarged, to contain more holiness, that it seemed ready to separate from my body. I then wrestled in an agony for divine blessings; had my heart drawn out in prayer for some Christian friends, beyond what I ever had before. I feel differently now from whatever I did under any enjoyments before; more engaged to live to God forever, and less pleased with my own frames. I am not satisfied with my frames, nor feel at all more easy after such strugglings than before; for it seems far too little, if I could always be so. Oh, how short do I fall of my duty in my sweetest moments!

Friday, June 18. Considering my great unfitness for the work of the ministry, my present deadness, and total inability to do anything for the glory of God that way, feeling myself very helpless and at a great loss what the Lord would have me to do; I set apart this day for prayer to God and spent most of the day in that duty, but amazingly deserted most of the day. Yet I found God graciously near, once in particular. While I was pleading for more compassion for immortal souls, my heart seemed to be opened at once and I was enabled to cry with great ardency for a few minutes. Oh, I was distressed to think that I should offer such dead, cold services to the living God! My soul seemed to breathe after holiness, a life of constant devotedness to God. But I am almost lost sometimes in the pursuit of this blessedness, and ready to sink, because I continually fall short and miss of my desire. Oh, that the Lord would help me to hold out, yet a little while, till the happy hour of deliverance comes!

Tuesday, June 22. In the morning, spent about two hours in prayer and meditation, with considerable delight.

Wednesday, June 30. Spent this day alone in the woods, in fasting and prayer; underwent the most dreadful conflicts in my soul that ever I felt, in some respects. I saw myself so vile that I was ready to say, "I shall now perish by the hand of Saul." I thought, and almost concluded, I had no power to stand for the cause of God, but was almost "afraid of the shaking of a leaf."

Spent almost the whole day in prayer, incessantly. I could not bear to think of Christians showing me any respect. I almost despaired of doing any service in the world. I could not feel any hope or comfort respecting the heathen, which used to afford me refreshment in the darkest hours of this nature. I spent the day in bitterness of my soul. Near night, I felt a little better; and afterwards enjoyed some sweetness in secret prayer.

Thursday, July 1. Had some sweetness in prayer this morning. Felt exceeding sweetly in secret prayer tonight, and desired nothing so ardently as that God should do with me just as He pleased.

Saturday, July 3. My heart seemed again to sink. The disgrace I was laid under at college seemed to damp me, as it opens the mouths of opposers. I had no refuge but in God. Blessed be His name that I may go to Him at all times and find Him a present help.

Wednesday, July 14. Felt a kind of humble resigned sweetness. Spent a considerable time in secret, giving myself up wholly to the Lord. Heard Mr. Bellamy preach towards night; felt very sweetly part of the time; longed for nearer access to God.

Thursday, July 22. Journeying from Southbury to Ripton, I called at a house by the way; where being very kindly entertained and refreshed, I was filled with amazement and shame that God should stir up the hearts of any to show so much kindness to such a dead dog as I. Was made sensible, in some measure, how exceeding vile it is not to be wholly devoted to God. I wondered that God would suffer any of His creatures to feed and sustain me from time to time.

Thursday, July 29. I was examined by the Association [The Association of Ministers of the Eastern District of Fairfield County, Conn.] met at Danbury, as to my learning and also my experiences in religion, and received a license from them to preach the gospel of Christ. Afterwards felt much devoted to God; joined in prayer with one of the ministers, my peculiar friend, in a convenient place; went to bed resolving to live devoted to God all my days.

TIMOTHY DWIGHT

A Sermon
for Foreign Missions[2]

JOHN x , 16.

AND OTHER SHEEP I HAVE, WHICH ARE NOT OF THIS FOLD. THEM ALSO
I MUST BRING; AND THEY SHALL HEAR MY VOICE; AND THERE SHALL
BE ONE FOLD, AND ONE SHEPHERD.

IN this discourse our Saviour, adopting the beautiful figurative
language of the prophets on the same subject, styles his followers
his sheep; and himself, the good Shepherd. Perhaps, no image
could have been selected with greater felicity. It is suggested by
the voice of nature. The object of allusion has ever been regarded
by mankind as one of the most striking exemplifications, found in
the natural world, of innocence, dependence, and amiableness.
How often do we hear the affectionate mother, smiling over her
beloved infant, utter all her tenderness and attachment in language derived from this source. How often has the poet selected
this interesting subject as the theme, on which he meant to lavish
in his most melodious numbers the utmost elegance of his conceptions, and the most gentle and amiable feelings of his heart. How
beautifully does the Prophet *Isaiah* present to us the same flock,
under the guidance of the same Shepherd, when he says, *"They
shall feed in the ways; and they shall be in all high places. They shall*

not hunger, nor thirst; neither shall the heat nor sun smite them: for he, that hath mercy on them shall lead them; even by the springs of water shall he guide them." Who, that has either piety, or taste, has not found these emotions kindled in a moment by this exquisite picture of the same unrivalled hand: *"He shall feed his flock like a shepherd: he shall gather the lambs with his arm, and carry them in his bosom."* With what inimitable tenderness, and elegance, does *David* exclaim, *"The Lord is my shepherd: I shall not want. He maketh me to lie down in green pastures: he leadeth me beside the still waters."*

It is hardly necessary to observe, that this allusion, so beautiful, and forcible, in our own view, must have had enhanced strength and beauty to the eye of a nation, extensively devoted to the pastoral life; and, therefore, realizing at once all its fine scenes, and all the gentle and tender emotions, to which they gave birth. Equally obvious is it to remark, that this discourse of our Saviour must be considered as singularly happy, and impressive, if we suppose it to have been delivered near the Sheep-gate, and in the confines of *Bethesda,* or the House of mercy.

In the text, after having displayed in his previous observations a tenderness, never exhibited by any other inhabitant of this world, Christ proceeds to inform us, that he had other sheep, beside those, of which he had been speaking; that he must bring, or collect, them; and that the two flocks should constitute one, be sheltered by one fold, and be led by one shepherd.

"Other sheep," says our Saviour, *"I have."* Other disciples, beside those of the Jewish nation, and the present age, I have, belonging to my family. They exist among the Gentiles in this age; and will exist in every future period. *The Gospel of the Kingdom,* which is to be *preached in all nations,* will every where find those, who will cordially receive, and obey, its dictates; those, who in the exercise of a living and affectionate confidence will hereafter give themselves up to me, and become mine. They are now mine; and were given to me from the beginning. *"Them I must bring."* To collect them from every part of the world is one of the great duties of my office; a part of *the* glorious *work, which* my Father gave me to do: and I shall not leave it unaccomplished. *"They shall hear*

my voice." When I call, they will know and acknowledge me as their Shepherd; and cheerfully obey the summons. *"There shall then be one fold:"* a single church; a single assembly of my disciples; one in name; one in their character, their life, and their destination: and I, the good, the only, Shepherd will lead them. *"They shall hunger no more, neither thirst any more; neither shall the sun light on them, nor any heat: but I will feed them, and lead them unto living fountains of waters."*

All real Christians, my brethren, belong to Christ; and were *chosen in him before the foundation of the world; that they should be holy, and without blame, before him in love. In him they have redemption through his blood; the forgiveness of sins; according to the riches of his grace.* In this world they are often hidden from each other; are separated by different names, forms of worship, and modes of discipline; and unhappily are in many instances, and in greater or less degrees, alienated from each other by unworthy and disgraceful contentions. The prophet *Elijah,* when he fled from *Jezebel* to *Horeb, the mount of* GOD, told his Maker, that *he, even he only, was left of the prophets; and that they sought his life, to take it away.* How must he have been astonished, when he heard that glorious Being answer, *"I have left me seven thousand in Israel, who have not bowed the knee unto Baal."* In a similar manner the Church is exhibited by the prophet *Isaiah,* as saying in her heart, after the general profligacy, which precedes the dawn of the Millennium, and the sudden multiplication of converts which shall follow; *"Who hath begotten me these? seeing I have lost my children, and am desolate; a captive, and moving to and fro: and who hath brought up these? Behold, I was left alone. These, where had they been?"* The answer to this complaint, also, is in the same spirit, as in that to *Elijah,* but immensely more delightful and glorious. *"Behold,"* saith the Lord GOD, *"I will lift up my hand to the Gentiles, and set up my standard to the people; and they shall bring thy sons in their arms, and shall carry thy daughters upon their shoulders. And kings shall be thy nursing fathers, and queens thy nursing mothers."* All these, strangers as they are to Zion, are still her children: and, however separated by distance, concealed by mutual ignorance, or arrayed against each other by unkind, uncharitable thoughts, are really, and will ultimately appear to be, possessed of one character. They will also constitute one visible church; having *one Lord, one faith, and one baptism.* The system of truth, revealed in the Gospel, is one: the Church formed by it, is one: and the scheme of worship, enjoined in it, is the same. He, whose *eye seeth not as man seeth,* discerns this *now,* with absolute certainty; and distinguishes every one of his children with an intuition, which cannot err, amid all the varieties of name and character which they assume, and the biasses, errours, and oppositions, by which they are often concealed from each other. The time will come, when among all, who *have put on the new man, which is renewed in knowledge after the image of him, who created him, there will be neither Greek nor Jew, circumcision nor uncircumcision, Barbarian nor Scythian, bond nor free; but Christ will be all and in all.*

This visible and glorious union of Christians will not, indeed, be perfectly accomplished, until *the heavens shall be no more.* Then the intercessory prayer of the Redeemer will be completely answered in the exact eventuation of the great purpose, which I have specified. *"Neither pray I for these alone, but for them also, who shall believe on me through their word: That they all may be one; as thou, Father, art in me, and I in thee, that they also may be one in us; that the world may believe, that thou hast sent me. And the glory which thou hast given me, I have given them; that they may be one, even as we are one.*

Still, the period is advancing; it is hastening; in which Christians will be most honourably united in the present world. The morning is even now approaching towards the horizon, and at no distant period will actually rise upon this dark world, when all distinctions of party and sect, of name and nation, of civilization and savageness, of climate and colour, will finally vanish. The day is approaching, when the traveller, who takes his circuit over the globe, will find Christians in every clime, inhabiting every city, and village, in his course. Churches will every where gladden his eye; and Hymns of praise vibrate upon his ear. From *Zembla* to *Cape Horn,* from *California* to *Japan,* the heralds of Salvation will repeat to astonished audiences with an enchanting voice the story, brought from heaven to the Shepherds of *Bethlehem*: *"Unto you is born in the city of David a Saviour, who is Christ, the Lord."* Throughout this vast extent, the happy race of *Adam*, united in a single, solemn response, will exclaim, *"How beautiful on the mountains are the feet of them, that bring good tidings; that publish peace; that bring good tidings of good; that publish salvation; and say unto Zion, 'Thy* GOD *reigneth!' "*

"Other sheep," saith our Saviour *"I have, which are not of this fold."* The sheep, which Christ then had, were *Jews*; inhabitants of a single country, and living at that single period. Nay, they were a little flock, gathered out of these. His other sheep, as he has taught us in his word, are *a great multitude, which no man can number, of all nations, kindreds, and tongues;* born in every future period; gathered from every distant land. *"Them I must bring, and they shall hear my voice."* He who took such effectual care of the *little flock* which followed him during his ministry, because *it was their Father's good pleasure to give them the kingdom,* will be easily believed, when he informs us, that he must, and will, bring into his fold a multitude, by their number, and character, of such immeasurable importance. For this very end *he hath ascended far above all heavens, that he might fill all things.* For this very end he is constituted *head over all things unto his Church.* This is the third great division of his employment, as Mediator. The first was to teach the will of GOD for our salvation; the second, to expiate our sins; the third is to gather us into his heavenly kingdom. It is in this employment, and in reference to the great subject, which we are contemplating, that he originally said, and that he is now saying, *"Look unto me, and be ye saved, all the ends of the earth: for I am* GOD; *and there is none else. I have sworn by myself; the word has gone out of my mouth in righteousness,* and shall not *return; that unto me every knee shall bow, and every tongue shall swear. Surely shall one say, "In* JEHOVAH *have I righteousness, and strength." "To him shall men come; and all that are incensed against him, shall be ashamed. In* JEHOVAH *shall all the seed of Israel be justified, and shall glory."* All the ends of the earth will hereafter actually look unto him, and be

saved. Every knee will bow to him. Every tongue will swear; or, as it is rendered by the Septuagint, and *St. Paul*, will confess; i. e. the reality, and glory, of his character, and a final devotion to his service. *"In* JEHOVAH *have I righteousness and strength,"* will resound wherever there is a heart to feel, and a tongue to speak. All these blessings he has promised, and promised with an oath. We need not ask whether they will be accomplished.

To a mind, solemnly examining this subject, equally astonishing and delightful, powerfully addressing itself to every expanded view of the intellect, and irresistibly engrossing every exalted affection of the heart, three questions present themselves, which involve every thing, necessary for the direction of our plans, purposes, and efforts. *What things are to be done, to complete this glorious end? In what manner are they to be done?* and *By whom are they to be done?* Concerning each of these particulars the following thoughts have presented themselves to my own mind.

In answer to the question, *What things are to be done for the completion of this end?* I observe,

1. *The Views of mankind concerning religious subjects, are to be extensively changed.*

It will not be questioned, that Truth is invariably an object of the Divine complacency; and Errour, of the Divine reprobation. As GOD *rejoices in his works;* so it is impossible, that he should not be pleased with truth; which is only a declaration of the state of those works, of his agency in accomplishing them, and of his character, displayed in that agency. Errour, which falsifies all these things, must, with equal evidence, be odious to him. As little can it be questioned, that truth is the instrument, through which we are *sanctified, and made free from the bondage of corruption.* Beside the passages of Scripture, to which I have directly alluded, there are others, too numerous to be mentioned at the present time, which are equally express, and decisive. *"The Gospel,"* says St. Paul, *"is the power of* GOD *unto salvation, to every one that believeth." "Of his own will begat he us,"* says St. James, *"by the Word of truth." "Who were born,"* says St. Peter, *"not of corruptible seed, but of incorruptible, by the Word of* GOD*."* Hence, *to know the truth, to walk in the* *truth, to be of the truth, to believe in the truth, to receive the love of the truth, and to abide in the truth,* are phrases, synonymous with the character of Christians, or good men; or, in other words, with Evangelical virtue: while the contrary phraseology is adopted every where in the Scriptures, to denote, in the same definite manner, the opposite character of sin. Nor can it be doubted, that truth, with respect to every subject, is one thing only; like its Author, *the same yesterday, to-day and forever.*

But the views, which mankind have hitherto entertained concerning religious subjects, and those of the highest importance, have been endlessly various and discordant. Among the western heathen Philosophers, *Themistius* declares, there were more than two hundred sects, widely differing from each other concerning these subjects. *Varro* was acquainted with two hundred and eighty-eight different opinions, adopted by these persons concerning the supreme Good; and with three hundred, concerning GOD. Many volumes have been written, and many more might be written without repetition, for the single purpose of reciting, and explaining, the different apprehensions of this class of mankind concerning things of high moment in the religious system. Among the various schemes, adopted by these men, with respect to each religious subject, it is mathematically certain, that one only can be true. The rest, beyond debate, are mere collections of errours. These errours, also, are in many instances radical: and those, who hold them, cannot, so long as they hold them, be united to the flock, or gathered into the fold, of the Redeemer. Into this flock, into this fold, no man, who is a worshipper of *Jupiter, Venus,* or *Bacchus,* can enter. It is impossible for man to make his way to Heaven by the oblation of human sacrifices; or by religious suicide. He, who prostrates himself, before a calf, or a cat, or finds his god in the stock of a tree, cannot, without an entire revolution in his character, be accepted by Him, who hath said, *"Confounded be all they that worship graven images."*

When *Pilate* proposed to the *Jewish* rulers and nation to release Christ to them; they said, *"Not this man, but Barabbas."* When he said again, *"What will ye then, that I shall do with him, whom ye call king of the Jews?"* they exclaimed, *"Crucify him; crucify him."* When *he washed his hands before the multitude, and said, "I am innocent of the blood of this just person;"* they all answered, *"His blood be on us, and on our children."* To this day, the same spirit is retained by their descendants. They are, still, more hostile to Christ than to any other person, and to Christianity than to any other religion. The very curse, which their ancestors invoked, appears still to rest upon them: and their hardness of heart is, according to the prediction of their great prophet, *a bye word, and an astonishment, to every nation, whither they have been driven.*

The glorious person, who was so furiously persecuted by this unhappy nation, declared to his persecutors, *"If ye believe not, that I am he; ye shall die in your sins."* It cannot be doubted, that this declaration extends its terrible efficacy, with equal certainty, to every subsequent generation. The *Jews*, therefore, can never be brought into the fold of Christ, until they renounce their unbelief, and essentially change their views concerning the Saviour of men.

The *Koran*, so far as it is not copied from the Jewish and Christian Scriptures, is a mass of falsehoods; and its author was by way of eminence *the false prophet*; the most successful, and the most mischievous, impostor, who has ever attempted to pervert the faith of mankind. Whenever men *are turned into fables, they turn away their ears from the truth.* Even the sound doctrines, which their leader derived from the Bible, and pronounced to be the word of GOD, *Mohammedans* appear, from the beginning, to have universally disregarded, and forgotten; and to have confined their faith to the miserable inventions of the deceiver. Christ, acknowledged by *Mohammed* to be a prophet from GOD, they have entirely disbelieved. His doctrines they have rejected from their creed, and his precepts from their moral code. Their faith, hope, and obedience, they have restricted to the instructions, promises, and precepts, of the Koran. This, indeed, is far from being strange. *The iron and the clay*, although they may seem to be parts of the same *image*, can never be united. The doctrines of *Mohammed* are only hostile to those of Christ. He, who receives the one class, will, therefore, certainly reject the other. Besides, a judicial sentence has gone out against the impostor, and his followers. *"If any man,"* says *St. John, "shall add unto these things; God shall add unto him the plagues, that are written in this book: and, if any man shall take away from the words of the book of this prophecy, God shall take away his part out of the book of life."* A change therefore, a mighty change, must be made in the views of the *Mohammedan* world, before its millions can be numbered in the flock of Christ.

Of the *Antichristian* doctrines it cannot be necessary to make a very particular mention at the present time. The idolatry of the *Romish* church is even more reprehensible than that of the heathen; and is infected with all the pollution, attributed in the Scriptures to that of the *Jews*. The idols are, here, set up in the temple of God; at the foot of the mercy seat; immediately before the Urim and Thummim; and in the very skirts of the Shechinah. The idolatry is practised beneath the cross; and openly insults the agonies of the Saviour. The endless train of external services also, in which the whole of Religion is placed; *the vain oblations; the incense,* that *is an abomination; the new moons, and sabbaths; the calling of assemblies,* which God *cannot away with; the solemn meeting,* which *is iniquity; the appointed feasts, which* his *soul hateth,* and is *weary to bear;* the absolutions, and indulgencies, in which the hierarchy *exalts its throne above the stars of* God, and says, *"I will be like the Most High;"* force upon us an irresistible conviction, that these *Augean* impurities must all be washed away, before the *Romish* world can become clean in the sight of the Creator.

Nor is it necessary to dwell, here, upon the *vain and deceitful philosophy of Infidels, which is after the traditions of men, and the rudiments of this world; and not after Christ.* The Atheist must believe, that there is a God; the Sceptic, that there is truth, of infinite importance to his future well-being; the Deist, that there is a Revelation; the Materialist, that he has a soul, accountable and immortal; the Animalist, that there is good, superiour to sensual enjoyment, which must be sought, and found, if he is ever to be happy beyond the grave; and the Practical unbeliever, that he must not only assent, but obey also, and obey with the heart;

before either can be blessed in this world, or accepted in that which is to come.

Finally, the same change of views must be found in Protestant nations. All the latitudinarian doctrines, which the ingenuity and labour of man, which the pride of Philosophy, the love of sin, the wish to perpetrate it with quiet and safety, and the earnest desire to blunt the stings of conscience here, and to escape from a terrible retribution hereafter, have forced reason to invent, or violently compelled the Scriptures to declare, will all vanish away; and with the *idols* of the Heathen, *be cast to the moles, and to the bats;* before those, who hold them, can be assembled in the fold of the Redeemer. Christ must be acknowledged, not only as a prophet, but as a Saviour; not only as our example, but as our propitiation; not only as our forerunner into the heavens, but as our intercessor, also, before the throne of GOD; not only as *come in the flesh,* but as *over all,* GOD, *blessed forever.* With *Paul,* men must *determine to know nothing,* as the way of salvation, *but Jesus Christ and him crucified;* and Ministers must feel the tremendous import of the anathema, denounced against him, *who preaches any other Gospel, than that which Paul preached.* Men must cease to create meanings for the Scriptures; and permit GOD to speak for himself. Universally, there must be throughout the world *one Lord* acknowledged, *one Mediator, and one faith.*

This change in the doctrines of men is indispensable to the great end, mentioned above, because the character will ultimately accord with the doctrines, which are actually believed, to such a degree, that no man is better, and almost every one worse, than the doctrines, which he embraces, declare; because truth, only, conducts the heart to righteousness, while errour leads it only to sin; and because truth is the sole instrument of our sanctification.

2. *A mighty change, also, must be wrought in the Disposition of man.*

To the accomplishment of the glorious purpose, announced in the text, that pride, which is the self-gratifying consciousness of superiority, and that ambition, which is the desire of it; both prime ingredients in the Apostasy of our first parents; that avarice, which substitutes gold for GOD, and is thus a prolific root of all kinds of evil; and that sensuality, which is the great brutalizing principle of our nature; must lose their seat in the heart, and cease to controul the life. Equally necessary is it, that that torpid insensibility to the sufferings of others, which winds its web around the soul, and prevents it from seeing, or feeling, any thing, which is not destined to be its prey; and that cruelty, which emulates the wolf and the tiger, and satiates itself only on suffering and slaughter; should return to those regions of eternal sin, from which they sprang. Nor is it less necessary, that the love of injustice, fraud, and falsehood, in which all these malignant passions, these *unclean spirits,* find the means of their efficacious operation, should, together with them, *go out of the man;* and no more find his heart *empty, swept,* and *garnished,* for their reception. Nor is it less indispensable, that impiety, and ingratitude to GOD, and distrust of his wisdom, goodness, and truth, should cease to form any part of the human character, and no longer interrupt the communication between earth and heaven.

To these attributes will succeed, whenever mankind shall be brought into the fold of Christ, that *Love* to GOD, and to man, which *is the fulfilling of the law,* that *Repentance towards* GOD, *and that faith in the Redeemer,* which are the primary obedience of the Gospel. In the train of these great Evangelical attributes will follow the meek and lowly virtues of Christianity, which so extensively occupied the instructions, and so beautifully adorned the life, of the Saviour: *Love, joy, peace, long-suffering, gentleness, goodness, faithfulness, meekness, and temperance:* all, glorious fruits of the Spirit of Grace; natives of Heaven; and, although for a time pilgrims in this melancholy world, destined to return to Heaven again.

3. *The change will not be less in the Conduct of men.*

On this copious topic I must necessarily be brief. To discuss it extensively would be to draw a picture of the world, and to delineate the character of man in all its endless varieties. Still, the nature of my design demands, that a few particulars should be mentioned.

Permit me, then, to observe, that *the private conduct of men* will experience a mighty and wonderful revolution. Profaneness will no longer pollute the tongue; nor pierce with anguish the ear of piety. The sabbath will be kept holy unto GOD; and beautifully resemble that first Sabbath, when the Creator *rested from his glorious work, and all the sons of* GOD *shouted for joy*. No longer will *the ways of Zion mourn, because few come to her solemn feasts. Strangers* innumerable will *be made joyful in the house of prayer*; and that house will to endless multitudes become, literally, *the gate of Heaven*. From the closet also, and the family altar, *incense, and a pure offering*, will rise every morning and every evening; and mingle in one vast exhalation, ascending to the throne of GOD.

Truth, at the same time, will resume her empire over the tongue, the pen, and the press. Slander will wound no man's good name; Sophistry cheat no man out of his salvation; Falsehood abuse no man's faith; and Perjury destroy no man's property, reputation, or life.

Honesty, also, will controul the dealings of men. The cheat will be lost out of human society; the name of fraud be forgotten; and a hard bargain boasted of no more.

In the same manner will unkindness vanish from the habitations of mankind. The fire side will show *how good, and how pleasant, it is for brethren to dwell together in unity:* and the neighbourhood will be only one great fireside. Parents will love their children. Children will honour their parents. No profligate father, no graceless son, no ruined daughter, will spread *lamentation, mourning, and woe,* over the domestic circle, destined by GOD to be happy. No litigation, no quarrel, will destroy the peace of neighbourhoods; and no duel hurry the impenitent wretch to a fearful retribution.

The stranger will every where find a home; and the wanderer, an asylum. The heart of charity will no longer be icy; nor her hand shut: nor will the cry of suffering ever plead in vain.

Uncharitableness, also, between those, who profess the religion of the Redeemer, will be found no more. Little things will be esteemed little; and only great things, great. Names will lose their fascination; realities will take their place; and all who love Christ, will love each other. In a world, men will be willing to walk to heaven together, although the colour, or the fashion, of their clothes should differ.

Nor will *the Public conduct* of mankind be less extensively inverted. The monarch will cease to oppress, the statesman to plunder; and the politician to sell his soul, to buy a place, or support a party. Throughout the haunts of man there will not be an electioneering trick, a cabal, or a demagogue. No candidate for office will proclaim his merits to the public; slander a rival; or solicit a suffrage. Wisdom and worth will then engross every man's vote; and take, as they ought, quiet possession of the hall of Legislation, and the chair of Magistracy.

On the Bench will then be seen those, and those only, who *shake their hands from holding bribes; stop their ears from hearing evil; and close their eyes from seeing blood.* At the bar of justice, prisoners will cease to be found: the deserted jail will crumble into dust: and the gibbet will be known only in the tales of other times.

Wars, also, will be no more. The monarch, and the Republic, will no longer summon their wretched subjects to the field of battle; the great slaughterhouse of mankind; for the purpose of adding to their dominions tracts, which they do not want and cannot govern; of sating their cannibal revenge on the flesh of man; of spangling a crown with another gem, or twisting into a wreath of laurel another twig; of being able to say, "I have vanquished one more enemy;" and of adding another cubit to the stature of pride. The sound of the trumpet will no more startle the sleep of the cradle; and the village will rise no more in flames to heaven: the name of glory will be no longer written in blood; nor the earth fattened with the corpses nor whitened with the bones, of men. The Angel Peace, will wave her olive branch over the nations; the tempest of six thousand years be hushed to silence; and the creation sigh, and *groan, and travail in pain,* no more.

Then *Religion* will resume her proper station; and no longer be subordinated to pleasure, gain, and glory; to frantic scrambles about place and power, and the aggrandizement of wretches, who steal into office by flattery and falsehood, in order to riot on peculation. From Heaven will she descend, *clothed with a cloud, and a rainbow upon her head: her face, as it were, the sun; and her feet, pillars of fire.* In her hand she will hold *a little book:* and that book will be opened to the eyes of all the nations of men. On its pages they will read, in lines of light, *"Now is come salvation, and strength, and the kingdom of our* GOD, *and the power of his Christ.* GOD *himself will dwell among* the great family of *Adam, and be their* GOD; *and they shall be his people.* The joy, which is kindled in heaven over repenting sinners, will be renewed, not over one solitary convert, but over *nations, born in a day.* The path to Heaven will become the great highway of mankind; not wandered over by now and then a lonely traveller, but crowded with hosts: while the broad road to perdition will be untrodden and desolate. *The skies will pour down righteousness; and the earth open, and bring forth salvation.* Above, all will be sunshine, and smiles: below, all will be a paradise. The Church *will be clothed with the sun; the moon will be under her feet; and upon her head a crown of twelve stars* will beam with immortal splendour.

To the second question; "In what manner are these things to be done?" I answer, They are to be accomplished, not by *miracles,* but by *means. St. Paul* has in the most express and decisive terms given us the law of procedure, by which the kingdom of GOD is to be established in every part of the habitable world. *"How,"* says that Apostle, *"shall they call on him, in whom they have not believed? and how shall they believe in him, of whom they have not heard? and how shall they hear without a preacher? So, then, faith cometh by hearing; and hearing, by the Word of* GOD." *The Gospel,* my brethren, *is the power of* GOD *unto salvation, to all them that believe.* Our course, therefore, is pointed out by the finger of Heaven. To the numerous votaries of idolatry, and superstition, are to be sent the Word of God, and the Ministers, by whom it is preached. To these are to be added, also, other books, less expensive and more numerous, into which the Word of GOD is transfused; together with Schoolmasters, and Catechists, to teach the children, while Ministers are instructing the Parents. In a word, the very means, by which men have become Christians here, are to spread Christianity through the world.

Permit me to add, that those, by whom these mighty things are to be done, are themselves to exhibit the spirit of the Gospel, as the great, controuling principle of their conduct. Common sense has proverbially declared, and all experience uniformly proved, that precept without example is vain. To the intended objects of this beneficence it would be worse than in vain. From men, who do not practise what they teach, instructions would be received, as the *Mexicans* received them from the *Spaniards*, only with contempt and indignation.

The process of this mighty work is, in this respect also, exactly marked out by *St. Paul. Salvation has come unto the Gentiles, to provoke the Jews to jealousy;* or, as in the *Greek, to excite them to emulation.* In other words, the Evangelical spirit of the Gentiles, as it will exist, and exhibit itself, at a period, which is still future, will convince the *Jews,* that the Gentiles are the chosen people of GOD; and awaken in them an emulous desire to obtain the same character, and the same blessings. This spirit, turning with abhorrence from all the hatred, scorn, and persecution, with which the *Jews* have been hunted down by the nations of Christendom, will hereafter treat them kindly, justly, and truly. In their exile, it will make their residence peaceful and pleasant; and, in their attempts to reestablish themselves in their own land, will furnish them every aid, which piety can prompt, or benevolence provide. Under this happy influence, enlightening, warming, and quickening, like the Sun, the *Jews* will feel a new conviction of the excellence of Christianity, and of the favor, with which it is regarded by GOD;

and new desires to possess the honourable character of their benefactors. The valley of death, the great receptacle of *the House of Israel*, will then begin to be reanimated with life from Heaven. *The bones,* with which it is *covered,* and whitened, will *with a noise, and a shaking, come together, bone to his bone. Sinews and flesh will come up upon them: and the skin will cover them above.* A voice will sound from Heaven; *"Thus said the Lord* GOD,*'Come from the four winds, O Breath; and breathe upon these slain that they may live.' "* At this command, the breath of life will enter these innumerable corpses; *and they will live, and stand upon their feet, an exceeding great army for multitude.*

The casting away of the Jews is the reconciling of the world: the receiving of them will be, to that same world, *life from the dead.* When *the voice of joy and gladness shall again be heard in the streets of Jerusalem; the voice of the bridegroom, and the voice of the bride; the voice of them that shall say,* "Praise the LORD *of hosts, for the* LORD *is good, and his mercy endureth for ever:"* the world will look on, and listen, with astonishment and rapture. This stupendous event, this wonder of wonders, will awaken in all nations a full conviction of the reality, and excellence, of Christianity; and force them to acknowledge, that *the truth of* GOD, *is as the great mountains, steadfast and immovable.* Life will every where spring up from the dead: and the world, a vast cemetery, in which souls are entombed, will be peopled with beings, spiritual and immortal.

It is hardly necessary to observe, that the measures, which will produce these mighty effects upon the *Jews,* will have a similar efficacy, wherever they are employed.

The third question; "By whom are these things to be done?" admits but of one answer. They are to be done by Protestant nations; and, extensively, by Us. In other words, they are to be done by those, to whom GOD has given the means, and the disposition.

On this subject there can be no debate. The time for doubt is past. The work is begun. Missionaries already in great numbers *run to and fro: and knowledge is,* even now, *greatly increased. The*

Gospel of the kingdom is already preached in *Greenland;* in *Labrador;* in *Tartary;* in *Hindostan;* in *China;* in *New Holland;* in the Isles of the *Pacific Ocean,* and the *Carribbean Sea;* in *Southern America;* and in the *African* deserts. *The voice of salvation, the song of praise to* JEHOVAH, echoes already from the sides of *Taurus,* and trembles over the waves of the Ganges. The Bible has travelled round the Globe. The *Esquimaux* now turns over the pages of the Gospel, written in his own tongue: the wild inhabitant of the *Cuban* has dropped the Koran; and reads with wonder, hope, and joy, the tidings of the Saviour: and the poor wanderer of *Caffraria* listens to the hymn, sung from heaven to the Shepherds of *Bethlehem.* From land to land, and from sea to sea, *the Word of* JEHOVAH *runs, and is glorified;* and throughout its divine career sheds, like its Author, light, and life, and happiness, on this benighted world.

In such an enterprise *all, who engage in it, must be united.* Consider how vast the work is; over what an extent of the earth it is to spread; what countless millions it is to reach; what a multitude of hands must be employed; what a multitude of hearts; what a multitude of prayers; what extensive contributions are necessary to supply the expense; and how many heralds of salvation must proclaim *the glad tidings of great joy.* In such a work, should all Protestant nations unite; and all the individuals, which those nations contain; how imperfectly sufficient would their labours appear, to the human eye, for the successful accomplishment of an enterprise so vast, a consummation so divine?

If Christians do not unite their hearts, and their hands, they will effectuate nothing. Solitary efforts will, here, be fruitless. Divided efforts will be equally fruitless. Clashing efforts will destroy each other.

It is a shame for those, who wear the name of Christians, not to unite with other Christians in such a purpose, as this. It is not the purpose of a sect, a party, or a name. It is not a purpose of superstition, bigotry, or enthusiasm. It is a purpose of GOD, an object of the highest complacency to Infinite wisdom. Shall not those, who *have been made to drink into one Spirit,* show themselves, while professing to aim at such an object, to *be of one accord, and one mind?* Shall not forms, and modes, here be forgotten; and, so far as the attainment of this mighty end is concerned, all names be lost in that of Christian, and all diversities amalgamated by the piety and benevolence of the Gospel? Shall not those, who profess to be Christians, prove by their harmony in this divine undertaking, that they are, indeed, the flock of Christ; that they belong to one fold; and that they are led by one Shepherd?

To enlist your hearts, and hands, my brethren, to engage your prayers, and labours, in this honorable enterprise, let me set before you the following motives.

1. *The work, to which you are summoned, is the Work of* GOD.

My brethren, it is the chief work of GOD, which has been announced to mankind. It is the end of this earthly creation. It is the end of this earthly Providence. It is the glorious end of Redemption. It is the subject of the first prophecy, ever delivered to man. It was repeated in the second. It was reiterated in the long train, which followed, in a thousand varieties of sublimity and rapture. The eye of the seer, extending a divinely enlightened vision down the vale of futurity, beheld, at an immense distance, this glorious object, dimly ascending above the horizon. Remote as it was; and obscurely as it was seen; it warmed his mind with wonder and transport. The prophet Isaiah, sublime beyond any other writer, accustomed to thoughts, fresh from heaven, and speaking with a tongue, which emulates that of Angels, rises, whenever this subject is presented to his view, above himself; and lifts his wing for a loftier flight towards the angelic world. And shall not we, to whom this dispensation *is nigh, even at the doors,* catch a portion of his fire, and glow with a share of his ecstasy? We profess to love GOD. Shall we not unite with all the heart, to further the divine purpose, for which he made the earth and the heavens?

We profess, that we have believed in Christ. Shall we not advance with our utmost powers the exalted end of his labours, and sufferings? Here, *He, for whom are all things, and by whom are all things,* is *bringing many sons unto glory.* Here the Redeemer is multiplying the trophies of his cross, and the many crowns of his final triumph. This is the great harvest of the world. He is now about to *send his angels, to gather his elect from the four winds.* Who would not unite himself with such labourers in such an employment?

2. *The present is the proper time for this glorious undertaking.*

It is the proper time, as it is marked out by the Spirit of prophecy. Almost all judicious commentators have agreed, that the Millennium, in the full and perfect sense, will begin at a period, not far from the year 2000. Christ, referring mediately at least, to this great event, says, "*Behold I come as a thief;*" i. e. suddenly; and sooner than the world will expect. By this declaration we are taught, that the duration of the two last vials will be comparatively short; and that the dawn of the succeeding day will be earlier than mankind have been accustomed to believe. But, should we fasten upon the year 2000, as the period in which there shall be a complete accomplishment of the predictions concerning this wonderful event, how evidently is it necessary, that all the measures, by which it is to be accomplished, should be now formed, and immediately begin to operate. Should we, should all Protestant nations, awake out of our long sleep; and *shake ourselves as mighty men;* should we bring every heart, and hand, to this vast work; should we pursue it with a firmness, which nothing can daunt, and an ardour, which nothing can extinguish; how uninterrupted, how rapid, how successful, must be our progress, in order to find its consummation at the date assigned? Think of the changes, which have been mentioned in this discourse: how numerous; how vast; how wonderful; how evidently indispensable. Think what it must be for so many millions of the human race to yield up their false systems of Religion: systems, gross and rank with corruption; hoary with the age of many centuries; bound to the soul with the chains of bigotry; and armed for their defence with the sword, the rack, and the faggot. Think what it must be for pride to bow; for the iron heart of avarice to dissolve; for ambition to feed no more upon blood; and for sensuality to wallow no longer in corruption. Think what it must be for private and public crimes to be no more, for falsehood and fraud, injustice and cruelty, to fly from the thrones of princes, and the habitations of men. How amazing must be the change, when the *Romish* cathedral, the mosque, and the pagoda, shall *not have one stone left upon another, which shall not be thrown down:* when the *Popish, Mohammedan, Hindoo, and Chinesian,* worlds shall be created anew; and the voice of angels exclaim concerning each, JEHOVAH *bless thee, O habitation of justice, O mountain of holiness:* when a pestilential Simoom shall no longer waft decay, and death over the moral wilds of *Africa;* and the soul throughout that vast continent be illumined by the beams of the Sun of Righteousness, and quickened with life from Heaven: when *Europe* shall no longer convert her wide domains into a stall of slaughter; nor offer herself as a voluntary holocaust upon the altar of *Moloch:* and when the human wolves, which have so long prowled around the *American* deserts, shall assume the innocence, and meekness, of the lamb. What a transmutation must man have undergone, when there shall not be a tyrant nor a slave, not a jail nor a gibbet, not a dram-shop nor a brothel, not a lie nor a theft, from *the rising of the sun to the going down of the same.* How astonished must the earth be, how delighted the heavens, to behold the Sabbath dawn with serenity and peace upon *Japan;* and, moving slowly, and solemnly, round this great world, shed its evening lustre upon *California;* and see the earth one vast altar, and the sky one magnificent temple, of JEHOVAH; perfumed with incense, offered up by the immense congregation of man? Who does not discern, that the centuries, which will expire before the specified date, will be a stinted period for the accomplishment of such a work as this? Who will not rejoice, and take courage, when he hears it proclaimed from heaven concerning this very work, "I, JEHOVAH, *will hasten it in its time.*"

The present is the proper time, also, because this work is actually begun; and begun upon an astonishing scale. How wonderful is it, that so many persons should have united in it; that such persons should have united in it; that they should have acted with so much Christian catholicism; that so many prejudices, which have hitherto been moles, and spots, on the divine aspect of Religion, should have disappeared; that contributions should have been so extensively, so liberally, so ardently, made; that prayers should have mingled in one strain of supplication from a thousand lands; that the Bible should have traversed the globe with the flight of an Eagle; and that Missionaries should already have proclaimed the tidings of eternal life to the four corners of the earth? The streamlet has already become a river: the river will soon expand into an ocean. Should these efforts cease; should this spirit expire: how many generations of men may pass, before the same mighty advantages will return; before even the attempt may be renewed?

There is a crisis in all human affairs. If seized, it almost ensures success: if lost, every thing is lost with it. Sow in season; and you will reap a rich harvest. Sow out of season; and you will reap nothing. For the great purpose before us *the present time is that crisis.* Look at these men. GOD summoned them together. Look at their efforts. GOD inspired them. Look at their success. The blessing which created it, descended from GOD. The voice of his Providence, *powerful and full of Majesty,* calls to us, *"Go forward."*

Regard no difficulty, which has hindered, and no disappointment, which has perplexed, this Evangelical enterprise. Difficulties are merely trials of our faith, and love. They exist, only to be surmounted. What would have become of the children of *Israel,* had they stopped between *Pi-hahiroth,* and *Baal-zephon?*

3. *The necessity of this work irresistibly demands every practicable effort.*

"*The whole world,*" says *St. John,* speaking of his own time, "*lieth in wickedness:* lieth, (for such is the indication of the original,) as a man slain lies weltering in his blood. How extensively is this strong picture a portrait of the world at the present moment? Cast your eyes abroad over this great globe; and mark how vast a portion of its surface is, in the moral sense, an immense field of death; a place of graves; a catacomb, where souls are buried, to wake no more. Look narrowly. Not a limb moves; not a bosom heaves. Listen. Not a sound trembles on the ear. Life has vanished: and solitude, and silence, brood over this receptacle of departed men. Who would not obey the voice, which commands, "*Take ye away the stone from this cave;*" while *the* Son of GOD stands before the entrance, ready to call to each of its slumbering inhabitants, "*Lazarus, come forth?*"

The gate, which in *Asia,* and *Africa,* was once opened wide at the head of the way to eternal life, has long since been barred; the path to Heaven forgotten; and the communication with that happy world finally cut off. Ignorance has benighted, sin bewildered, and misery broken down, their wretched inhabitants. Not an effort are they either disposed, or able, to make for themselves. Shall we, when we behold them *wounded,* and helpless, *pass by,* with the frozen hearted *priest* and *Levite, on the other side?* Shall we not infinitely rather, with the good *Samaritan, pour oil and wine into their wounds;* and provide effectually for their restoration to life and health?

Convey yourselves in thought, my brethren, to the regions of *Hindostan.* Behold there 20,000 wretched females annually offered up, as burnt-offerings, on the funeral piles of their deceased husbands; and thrice 20,000 orphans, in this manner bereaved, each of its surviving parent, thrown upon the world without a friend to protect, a hand to feed, or an eye to weep over them. Advance to the wild and desolate domain of *Juggernaut.* See a region, more than one hundred miles in diameter, white with the bones of men, who have perished in their devotion to this oriental *Moloch*. Mark the companies of dogs, jackals, and vultures, fattening themselves, throughout this wilderness of death, upon the flesh of men. See the wretched victims crushed beneath the chariot wheels of this gigantic idol, rolling over a path, paved with corpses. Enter the caverns of *Goa;* where a living *Moloch* sits on the tribunal of the Inquisition. Hear the chains clank; the groans murmur; and the shrieks burst the bosoms of the wretched prisoners, confined in this outer chamber of hell. Follow the barefooted victims, in their funeral habits, to the stakes, to which they are bound, and the flames, by which they are consumed to ashes.

To rescue man, poor, suffering, persecuted man, from these tremendous evils is one bright and glorious purpose of the work before you. The hearts, which will not feel these objects; the hands, which will not labor to sweep them from the earth; are the hearts and hands of friends. I will not insult my country with a suggestion, that such can be found here.

But we are not to be confined in our researches to *Hindostan*, to *Asia*, or to the Eastern Continent. We are to range the World. Whithersoever we go, we shall see ignorance, errour, and sin, sown every where; and every where producing misery, thirty, sixty, and an hundred fold. This rank and baneful crop is every where to be weeded out. Truth and righteousness are every where to be sown, and to produce their golden harvest of comfort, peace, and joy.

But, my brethren, all this is comparatively of small moment. The great duty before us is to rescue men from sin, and perdition. All numbers halt; all comprehension, beside that which is infinite, sits down in despair; when the worth of the soul, and the import of its eternal happiness or eternal woe, are to be estimated. Ascend on the wing of thought to the world of life. Station yourselves before the throne of infinite Greatness. Behold there an immortal mind, no longer a rebel against its Maker, no longer an outcast from his kingdom; but a child, *an heir of* GOD; *a joint heir with Jesus Christ* to the heavenly inheritance: its sins washed away in the blood of the Lamb: its conflicts ended: its victory achieved: its crown of glory won: and its career of transport commenced, to improve and brighten forever. Weigh this mind, and the blessings treasured up for its enjoyment, with the silver and the gold, the pains and the labours, which you, and all others, may be supposed to contribute for the accomplishment of its salvation: and you will pronounce them all *nothing, less than nothing, and vanity*. Weigh against such a mind, the world, which we inhabit. Weigh against it the universe, with all its worlds, and suns, and systems: and you will pronounce them *the drop of the bucket, and the small dust of the balance.*

But, my brethren, you are summoned, not to effectuate the salvation of one such mind; but of thousands, and millions. The whole earth waits, with ardent hope for *this manifestation of the sons of* GOD; this great jubilee of man; in which crimes and sufferings shall cease; in which *the boundage of corruption* shall terminate; and in which *from the uttermost parts of the earth are* to be *heard songs* of exultation and rapture; even *"Glory to the righteous!"* The everlasting Gospel is every where to be preached. Temples are every where to rise. Churches are every where to be gathered: and minds are every where to be born of God. Nay the world is to become one temple, and race of man to form one church, of the Redeemer. All these millions are destined to endless life; and will one day stretch their wings for the regions of immortality.

The day, in which these blessings are to be ushered in, has arrived. The day, in which the mighty work will be seen in its full completion, is at hand. *We must labour; that those, who come after us,* may *enter into our labours. We* must *sow: and in due time,* both we and our successors, if we *sow bountifully, shall reap* a divine harvest. With every faithful endeavour of ours the Spirit of Grace will co-operate. *As the earth bringeth forth her bud; and as the garden causeth the things, that are sown in it, to spring forth; so the Lord* GOD *will* speedily *cause righteousness and praise to spring forth before all the nations.* Into the divine kingdom sanctified minds will *fly as a cloud, and as doves to their windows.*

Forget, then, the little period, which intervenes between us, and this glorious day. Convey yourselves on the wings of anticipation to the dawn of this great Sabbath of time. Survey what the prophet beheld with exultation, at the distance of three thousand years. The way to eternal life is no longer narrow, and solitary. It has become a galaxy; ascending from the East, and from the West, and centering in midheaven. Up the broad and luminous path stars in endless multitudes rise from both skirts of the horizon: *stars, differing* from each other *in glory;* but all destined to shine with pure and eternal splendour.

But your interest in these things, my brethren, is not to terminate even here. You are not to rejoice merely in beholding the renovation, virtue, and happiness, of a world. You are not merely to follow in thought a single sanctified spirit, or millions of such spirits, to the realms of glory. The day is on the wing in which we, and they, shall *hear the voice of the Archangel, and the trump of* God, summoning *all, who are in their graves to come forth.* What thoughts will it then awake in the soul; with what emotions will the bosom heave; when the eye looks round upon the divine assembly of perfect minds, re-united to bodies, raised in incorruption, power, and glory; to be conscious, that even one immortal being has been rescued from the second death, and placed in the possession of endless life. How will the heart labour; how will the soul expand with vast conceptions; when it beholds, not one, but hundreds, thousands, millions, led by the efforts of ourselves, and our contemporaries, from the east and the west, from the north and the south, to the right hand of the Judge; and acknowledged before the universe as his friends and followers. And O, my brethren, with what ecstasy shall we accompany them to Heaven; seat ourselves by their side; learn from them the story of their salvation; and hear, pronounced by their own lips with a gratitude, which will increase forever, "The glory of this delightful world, the blessings of this immortal life, we owe first to GOD, and next to you?" *Unto Him, that loved us, and washed us from our sins in his own blood; and hath made us kings, and priests, unto GOD, even his Father: to him be glory, and dominion, forever and ever!* AMEN.

Notes

1. From *The Life and Diary of David Brainerd,* ed. Jonathan Edwards (Chicago: Moody Press, 1758).

2. Delivered in Boston on September 16, 1813, before the American Board of Commissioners for foreign missions at their fourth annual meeting.

V

CONTROVERSIES IN
AMERICAN RELIGION

From the beginning, controversy, dissent, and schism
have been characteristic of religion in America. Although
the early colonists might have wished to establish a holy
commonwealth of religious serenity and uniformity, they
could neither escape the debates of European churches nor
avoid new conflicts in America. The Puritans, for example,
quickly found themselves divided internally over matters
of theology and polity. Externally such abrasive voices as
those of the Quaker martyrs and the indomitable Roger
Williams brought upheaval and frustration to the "errand
in the wilderness." Throughout the colonies, as pluralism
became the actual "established" religion in America, it was
inevitable that churches would divide over theological and
practical matters great and small.

In this chapter, certain representative issues are discussed which illustrate theological, sectarian, and social
controversies within the churches. The theological conflicts
are evident in a series of challenges made by variant
ideologies to the prevailing orthodoxy of American religious life.

From the beginning of the American religious experience, the defenders of orthodoxy had attacked a variety of
heresies and heretics as destructive to true religion and,
more often than not, threats to the moral and spiritual fiber
of the New World. Often these ideologies were denounced
in terms that brought immediate negative response from
the faithful. One of the earliest American "heresies" was
known as "Arminianism" to Jonathan Edwards and other
divines, who criticized it vehemently. The term Arminian
was not used by these preachers to refer exclusively to the
classical theology of Jacob Arminius with its emphasis on a
general atonement, free will, and free grace. Rather, it
described those in the Puritan churches who, in contrast to
Calvinism, held a more optimistic view of human nature

and stressed the importance of human reason and the cooperation of the free will in salvation. This latter view led to their being called Arminians.

Arminianism was the subject of frequent attack by the more orthodox ministers as a threat to the true doctrine of Christ. In fact, many preachers of the First Great Awakening saw the Arminians as the major obstacle to revivals of religion. In reality, the Arminian trend represented a transition for many intellectuals seeking to make the traditional faith more compatible with the early stages of modern scientific and philosophical thought. They were generally opposed to the emotionalism and irrational qualities of the revivals, promoting a view of Christian experience based on spiritual growth through rational development.[1]

By the later 1700s the concern for rationalism in religion was further influenced by the deistic principles of the Enlightenment. Deism sought to apply the light of reason to the doctrines of revealed religion. It stressed the reasonableness of Christianity, the importance of natural revelation, and the superstitious folly of the supernatural.

Benjamin Franklin, Ethan Allen, Thomas Jefferson, and other leaders of the Republic were sympathetic toward Deism. Jefferson, in seeking to correct what he felt were irrational portions of Scripture, edited a copy of the New Testament, clipping out passages on the miraculous and the supernatural which he deemed an offense to reason. Deism caused little direct schism within the churches but provided the orthodox preachers with an obvious enemy for their scathing denunciation.

One of the earliest controversies which actually divided the Congregational churches was the Unitarian schism of the early nineteenth century. The initial stages of the movement were evident in certain antirevival forces of Arminian sentiment during the First Great Awakening. The desire for rational religion and the unity of God led many prominent Americans in the direction of Unitarianism.

In 1787 King's Chapel, the first Episcopal church in Massachusetts, ordained James Freeman, a young man of

Unitarian sentiments, as its pastor. The church then proceeded to remove all Trinitarian references from the *Book of Common Prayer*, which it continued to use in worship. In 1805 Henry Ware, a man of liberal theological tendencies, was named to the chair of divinity at Harvard. By 1815 an increasing number of Congregational churches around New England had begun to accept Unitarian doctrines. In 1819 William Ellery Channing, a noted Congregational minister, preached a sermon on the subject "Unitarian Christianity," which set forth the basic tenets of the movement. The sermon affirmed Jesus' work as mediator but denied his eternal equality with the Father. It stressed rationalism in religion and optimism regarding human nature. Unitarian doctrine was later summed up in the following statement: "The fatherhood of God, the brotherhood of man, the leadership of Jesus, salvation by character and the progress of mankind onward and upward forever."[2] In 1825 the American Unitarian Association was formed, and American Congregationalists had experienced their first major schism.

Those Unitarians who sought to bring new insight to Calvinistic churches were soon confronted by a schism of their own. A group of young idealists within the Unitarian ranks began to challenge the rationalism and impersonal religion which they observed in the churches. For these Transcendentalists the primary source of religious truth was the inner, intuitive authority. They believed that the divine presence could be observed and experienced in the natural world and that nature was filled with evidence of God's activity. External sources of religious authority were meaningless unless verified by inner response.

These romanticists formed the Transcendentalist Club in 1836 for the purpose of discussing and cultivating the truths of inner religion. The group was composed of such prominent individuals as Ralph Waldo Emerson, Margaret Fuller, Bronson Alcott, and Theodore Parker. Each of these persons gave to the movement certain unique expressions that were colorful and often eccentric.

In 1838 Emerson's address to the Harvard Divinity

School provided a basic statement of Transcendentalist philosophy. Religion, he insisted, cannot be known second-hand. It must be verified within the experience of every individual, not from outside authority. Not even the Scriptures could provide a substitute for the reality of direct encounter with God.

The Transcendentalists were an esoteric minority within Unitarianism. In their diversity members made outstanding literary contributions, participated in communitarian experiments, and promoted the importance of experience as vital to religion.

Another source of controversy and divisiveness within American religion is evident in the proliferation of sectarian Christianity. Millennialism influenced many in the belief that the new land provided an environment in which new revelations could be implemented for hastening the establishment of the kingdom of God. From the millennial hopes of the Shakers to the social utopia of New Harmony to the Church of Jesus Christ of Latter-Day Saints, America provided a place where the wildest utopian dreams could be attempted.

One geographic area particularly susceptible to sectarian fervor was a large section of western New York which earned the name the "Burned Over District." This term described a region which had been swept repeatedly by the fires of revival, each movement bringing a great outburst of religious zeal, additional revelations, and accompanying sectarian response. Here the great revivalist Charles G. Finney was converted and began preaching; the Oneida community attempted its strange communitarian experiment; and American Spiritualism thrived. Here Joseph Smith claimed to have translated golden tablets into the *Book of Mormon*. Across the Burned Over District, the United Society of Believers in Christ's Second Appearing, or the Shakers, attracted some of their earliest converts.

The Shakers began in England as a young woman named Ann Lee gained ascendancy over a small group of "Shaking Quakers." Lee was an illiterate whose difficulties in marriage and loss of four infant children influenced her belief that sexual intercourse was the source of human sin. Her visions and other ecstatic revelations convinced her followers that she represented the second appearance of Christ, calling them to enter the millennial kingdom.

Persecution led Ann and eight others to leave England for America, arriving in 1774 and establishing the first community at Watervliet, New York, near Albany. Here they welcomed all who would accept the Shaker life founded on a willingness to confess all sin and assume the cross of celibacy.

The Shakers created something of a Protestant monastic environment, living communally in chastity and obedience to their recognized elders, both male and female. They were resourceful and creative, constructing communities as beautiful as they were simple from Maine to the frontier areas of Ohio and Kentucky. Inventive people, the Shakers were known for their seeds, spices, and farm implements. They invented such common utensils as the flat-sided broom, the clothespin, and the circular saw. Their worship, the source of the name Shaker, was at once a communal expression and an outlet for individual religious energies. Dances were synchronized with the simple songs of heart religion and communal devotion. Perhaps the most famous refrain begins:

> 'Tis the gift to be simple
> 'tis the gift to be free
> 'tis the gift to come down
> where we ought to be
> And when we find ourselves
> in the place just right
> 'Twill be in the valley
> of love and delight.

With the modern era the Shaker agricultural base declined, as did membership. The order was officially closed in 1957, but a small group of Shaker women remain in two communities, Canterbury, New Hampshire, and Sabbath-day Lake, Maine. They are the remnant of the most enduring of the utopian sects of eighteenth- and nineteenth-century America.

Other such sects have nonetheless left a continuing imprint on American religion and culture. The perfectionist community founded by John Humphrey Noyes at Oneida, New York, in the 1840s lasted as a community barely forty years; yet its name continues in the well-known Oneida Company, Ltd.

Noyes' view of Christian perfection involved confession of sin and community of goods. True Christian love was not "exclusive" to one man or woman but was to be shared freely with all persons. Thus Oneida's sexual practice, regulated in the community, but in which sexual contact could be experienced with numerous individuals, brought them under the legal and moral scrutiny of the larger society. Their efforts at birth control, feminine equality, and eugenics were much in advance of their time.

Other communities such as Fruitlands in Massachusetts were founded by idealists like Bronson Alcott who wrote and dreamed, but had few practical resources for economic success. Fruitlands, founded in 1844, collapsed in less than a year because the idealistic members would not work the farm or care for the physical needs of the community.

Whatever the specific sectarian expression, these nineteenth-century groups had several similar traits. They represented a reaction against institutional religion and were often founded by a charismatic leader with some new revelation or ideal. They generally purchased land in remote areas where they could develop their unique life-style without harassment from the outside world. Most groups were built on utopian concepts as well as certain millennial and communitarian influences. They represent an optimism regarding the American experience and the millennial age which would be established through their work as the chosen people of God. Hundreds of faithful souls left homes and traditional denominations for these latter-day groups. The sects served as colorful and controversial forces in American religious life in the nineteenth century.

Perhaps the most divisive issue in American life, however, was slavery, that "peculiar institution" of the American South. As no other controversy, its effects brought tragedy to persons both black and white, to the churches, and to the nation. The slavery controversy is a dramatic illustration of the unending tension between culture and religion in America. It demonstrates the way in which religion may be utilized to support the cultural, economic, and social traditions of a particular way of life.

The first blacks, twenty in number, arrived at Jamestown as indentured servants in 1619. Soon the slave ships were bringing thousands of Africans to bondage in the new world. Almost one million blacks were transported to America as slaves, and by 1860 the twenty at Jamestown had become several million.

One of the earliest concerted efforts at evangelizing the slaves was carried out by the Anglican Church through its missionary agency, the Society for Propagation of the Gospel. Lest evangelization pose a threat to the status of blacks as enslaved persons, missionaries were required to assure the slave owners that salvation of the slaves' souls did not change their position as bonded servants.

In many areas of the South, blacks were received as members of white churches but relegated to slave galleries or the back pews of the churches. Fearing that separate gatherings might provide occasions for insurrection, the masters generally demanded that any separate services by blacks be supervised by white observers. Black religion developed some of its unique and liberating qualities, however, in the "hush arbors" or secret services held in secluded areas by blacks themselves. In these gatherings the spiritual qualities, the preaching, and the congregational response took on unique expressions. The themes of liberation that whites frequently sought to obscure were sounded for those who knew little of, but desperately desired, freedom and deliverance.

Antislavery sentiments were strong in the North and portions of the South during the late eighteenth and early nineteenth centuries. Antislavery societies were formed in several states; and journals promoting antislavery causes abounded, many published in the South. Numerous denominations attacked slavery as a deplorable situation. Most of these groups refused to advocate the immediate or violent emancipation of the blacks, preferring instead a variety of plans for gradual manumission.

One proposal came from the American Colonization Society, founded in 1814. James Madison, John Marshall, and Henry Clay and other prominent humanitarians proposed to raise private funds in order to purchase young slaves and send them back to Africa. The colony known as Liberia was chosen to receive the immigrants. The idea was to remove the problems of slavery by removing the blacks. It was an impractical and basically racist approach that ignored the social and regional problems of slavery. The Society was never able to send enough blacks back to Africa and was sometimes used as a means for deporting free blacks whose freedom was seen as a threat to the slave system.

By 1830 the economic and political situation in America was changing rapidly. The invention of the cotton gin made cotton the backbone of Southern economy. Blacks were thought to be the most economical means of labor in the hot Southern climate. Slavery was believed necessary to keep the blacks working efficiently. As slaveholders became more prominent in those denominations which had earlier opposed slavery, the denominations increasingly modified their antislavery stance to avoid schism.

The development of abolitionist groups in the North, demanding immediate emancipation of slaves, served to polarize the opinions of Southerners. As abolitionists denounced Southern slavery, along with the religion and traditions that supported and defended it, the Southerners refined their own arguments for slavery as acceptable to God, sanctioned by the Bible, and beneficial to the conversion of the slaves.

In 1830 William Lloyd Garrison founded *The Public Liberator*, a periodical dedicated to destroying slavery. A variety of books also became useful in promoting the abolitionist crusade, among them Harriet Beecher Stowe's

Uncle Tom's Cabin and the collection of essays by Theodore D. Weld utilized in this chapter. Through accounts such as the one provided here, abolitionists sought to awaken the indifferent to the plight of the slave and the conditions of slave life.

Weld, an evangelical abolitionist, attacked the contentions of the Southerners that slaves were treated lovingly and gently by producing certain "case studies" written by various Northerners who had witnessed the slave experience in the South. These accounts are provided as a dramatic contradiction to Southern claims of kind treatment, adequate housing, and moderate labor. The blacks, these witnesses observed, were kept in bondage through punishment and fear, not by just and loving treatment. Obviously, such descriptions produced indignation in the North and in the South as slaveholders reacted to "outside agitators" whom they felt caricatured Southern life.

In response, Southerners promoted arguments such as those of Dr. Richard Furman. Furman, a prominent Southern clergyman, served as president of the South Carolina Baptist Convention and the Triennial Convention of the Baptist Missionary Society. His arguments were based on biblical precedents and were intended to demonstrate that a literal interpretation of Scripture would verify the claims of slaveholders. Furman could find no clear statement in biblical material which explicitly condemned slavery. Indeed, he suggested that slavery was a blessing since it led to the conversion of the blacks who otherwise would not have heard the gospel.

With the beginning of the Civil War, American churches were badly divided both spiritually and regionally. Baptists and Methodists, North and South, split in 1845; and Presbyterians did so in 1860. Others divided less formally but were nonetheless affected by the agony of the nation. The wounds of slavery and the war provided a deep and enduring influence on American religion.

This chapter on controversies in American religion thus ends as the entire volume began, with the assertion that pluralism is basic to the religion of America. This pluralistic quality is evident in the variant orthodoxies, the sectarian experiments, the ethical debates, and the denominational schisms that occurred in the years between 1607 and 1840. During this period American religion was at once prophetic and compromising, magnanimous and bigoted, responding to American society while reflecting that society in the life of the churches.

1

Schism
in the Churches

RALPH WALDO EMERSON

Transcendentalism: An Address[3]

IN THIS refulgent summer, it has been a luxury to draw the breath of life. The grass grows, the buds burst, the meadow is spotted with fire and gold in the tint of flowers. The air is full of birds, and sweet with the breath of the pine, the balm-of-Gilead, and the new hay. Night brings no gloom to the heart with its welcome shade. Through the transparent darkness the stars pour their almost spiritual rays. Man under them seems a young child, and his huge globe a toy. The cool night bathes the world as with a river, and prepares his eyes again for the crimson dawn. The mystery of nature was never displayed more happily. The corn and the wine have been freely dealt to all creatures, and the never-broken silence with which the old bounty goes forward has not yielded yet one word of explanation. One is constrained to respect the perfection of this world in which our senses converse. How wide; how rich; what invitation from every property it gives to every faculty of man! In its fruitful soils; in its navigable sea; in its mountains of metal and stone; in its forests of all woods; in its animals; in its chemical ingredients; in the powers and path of light, heat, attraction and life, it is well worth the pith and heart of great men to subdue and enjoy it. The planters, the mechanics, the inventors, the astronomers, the builders of cities, and the captains, history delights to honor.

But when the mind opens and reveals the laws which traverse the universe and make things what they are, then shrinks the great world at once into a mere illustration and fable of this mind. What am I? and What is? asks the human spirit with a curiosity new-kindled, but never to be quenched. Behold these outrunning laws, which our imperfect apprehension can see tend this way and that, but not come full circle. Behold these infinite relations, like, so unlike; many, yet one. I would study, I would know would admire forever. These works of thought have been the entertainments of the human spirit in all ages.

A more secret, sweet, and overpowering beauty appears to man when his heart and mind open to the sentiment of virtue. Then he is instructed in what is above him. He learns that his being is without bound; that to the good, to the perfect, he is born, low as he now lies in evil and weakness. That which he venerates is still his own, though he has not realized it yet. *He ought*. He knows the sense of that grand word, though his analysis fails to render account of it. When in innocency or when by intellectual perception he attains to say—"I love the Right; Truth is beautiful within and without for evermore. Virtue, I am thine; save me; use me; thee will I serve, day and night, in great, in small, that I may be not virtuous, but virtue;" then is the end of the creation answered, and God is well pleased.

The sentiment of virtue is a reverence and delight in the presence of certain divine laws. It perceives that this homely game of life we play, covers, under what seem foolish details, principles that astonish. The child amidst his baubles is learning the action of light, motion, gravity, muscular force; and in the game of human life, love, fear, justice, appetite, man, and God, interact. These laws refuse to be adequately stated. They will not be written out on paper, or spoken by the tongue. They elude our persevering thought; yet we read them hourly in each other's faces, in each other's actions, in our own remorse. The moral traits which are all globed into every virtuous act and thought—in speech we must sever, and describe or suggest by painful enumeration of many particulars. Yet, as this sentiment is the essence of all religion, let me guide your eye to the precise objects of the sentiment, by an enumeration of some of those classes of facts in which this element is conspicuous.

The intuition of the moral sentiment is an insight of the perfection of the laws of the soul. These laws execute themselves. They are out of time, out of space, and not subject to circumstance. Thus in the soul of man there is a justice whose retributions are instant and entire. He who does a good deed is instantly ennobled. He who does a mean deed is by the action itself contracted. He who puts off impurity, thereby puts on purity. If a man is at heart just, then in so far is he God; the safety of God, the immortality of God, the majesty of God do enter into that man with justice. If a man dissemble, deceive, he deceives himself, and goes out of acquaintance with his own being. A man in the view of absolute goodness, adores, with total humility. Every step so downward, is a step upward. The man who renounces himself, comes to himself.

See how this rapid intrinsic energy worketh everywhere, righting wrongs, correcting apperances, and bringing up facts to a harmony with thoughts. Its operation in life, though slow to the senses, is at last as sure as in the soul. By it a man is made the Providence to himself, dispensing good to his goodness, and evil to his sin. Character is always known. Thefts never enrich; alms never impoverish; murder will speak out of stone walls. The least admixture of a life—for example, the taint of vanity, any attempt to make a good impression, a favorable appearance—will instantly vitiate the effect. But speak the truth, and all nature and all spirits help you with unexpected furtherance.

Speak the truth, and all things alive or brute are vouchers, and the very roots of the grass underground there do seem to stir and move to bear you witness. See again the perfection of the Law as it applies itself to the affections, and becomes the law of society. As we are, so we associate. The good, by affinity, seek the good; the vile, by affinity, the vile. Thus of their own volition, souls proceed into heaven into hell.

These facts have always suggested to man the sublime creed that the world is not the product of manifold power, but of one will, of one mind; and that one mind is everywhere active, in each ray of the star, in each wavelet of the pool; and whatever opposes that will is everywhere balked and baffled, because things are made so, and not otherwise. Good is positive. Evil is merely privative, not absolute: it is like cold, which is the privation of heat. All evil is so much death or nonentity. Benevolence is absolute and real. So much benevolence as a man hath, so much life hath he. For all things proceed out of this same spirit, which is differently named love, justice, temperance, in its different applications, just as the ocean receives different names on the several shores which it washes. All things proceed out of the same spirit, and all things conspire with it. Whilst a man seeks good ends, he is strong by the whole strength of nature. In so far as he roves from these ends, he bereaves himself of power, or auxiliaries; his being shrinks out of all remote channels, he becomes less and less, a mote, a point, until absolute badness is absolute death.

The perception of his law of laws awakens in the mind a sentiment which we call the religious sentiment, and which makes our highest happiness. Wonderful is its power to charm and to command. It is a mountain air. It is the embalmer of the world. It is myrrh and storax, and chlorine and rosemary. It makes the sky and the hills sublime, and the silent song of the stars is it. By it is the universe made safe and habitable, not by science or power. Thought may work cold and intransitive in things, and find no end or unity; but the dawn of the sentiment of virtue on the heart, gives and is the assurance that Law is sovereign over all natures; and the worlds, time, space, eternity, do seem to break out into joy.

This sentiment is divine and deifying. It is the beatitude of man. It makes him illimitable. Through it, the soul first knows itself. It corrects the capital mistake of the infant man, who seeks to be great by following the great, and hopes to derive advantages *from another*—by showing the fountain of all good to be in himself, and that he, equally with every man, is an inlet into the deeps of Reason. When he says, "I ought;" when love warms him; when he chooses, warned from on high, the good and great deed; then, deep melodies wander through his soul from Supreme Wisdom. Then he can worship, and be enlarged by his worship; for he can never go behind this sentiment. In the sublimest flights of the soul, rectitude is never surmounted, love is never outgrown.

This sentiment lies at the foundation of society, and successively creates all forms of worship. The principle of veneration never dies out. Man fallen into superstition, into sensuality, is never quite without the visions of the moral sentiment. In like manner, all the expressions of this sentiment are sacred and permanent in proportion to their purity. The expressions of this sentiment affect us more than all other compositions. The sentences of the oldest time, which ejaculate this piety, are still fresh and fragrant. This thought dwelled always deepest in the minds of men in the devout and contemplative East; not alone in Palestine, where it reached its purest expression, but in Egypt, in Persia, in India, in China. Europe has always owed to oriental genius its divine impulses. What these holy bards said, all sane men found agreeable and true. And the unique impression of Jesus upon mankind, whose name is not so much written as ploughed into the history of this world, is proof of the subtle virtue of this infusion.

Meantime, whilst the doors of the temple stand open, night and day, before every man, and the oracles of this truth cease never, it is guarded by one stern condition; this, namely, it is an intuition. It cannot be received at second hand. Truly speaking, it is not instruction, but provocation, that I can receive from another soul. What he announces, I must find true in me, or reject; and on his word, or as his second, be he who he may, I can accept nothing. On the contrary, the absence of this primary faith is the presence of degradation. As is the flood, so is the ebb. Let this faith depart, and the very words it spake and the things it made become false and hurtful. Then falls the church, the state, art, letters, life. The doctrine of the divine nature being forgotten, a sickness infects and dwarfs the constitution. Once man was all; now he is an appendage, a nuisance. And because the indwelling Supreme Spirit cannot wholly be got rid of, the doctrine of it suffers this perversion, that the divine nature is attributed to one or two persons, and denied to all the rest, and denied with fury. The doctrine of inspiration is lost; the base doctrine of the majority of voices usurps the place of the doctrine of the soul. Miracles, prophecy, poetry, the ideal life, the holy life, exist as ancient history merely; they are not in the belief, nor in the aspiration of society; but, when suggested, seem ridiculous. Life is comic or pitiful as soon as the high ends of being fade out of sight, and man becomes near-sighted, and can only attend to what addresses the senses.

These general views, which, whilst they are general, none will contest, find abundant illustration in the history of religion, and especially in the history of the Christian church. In that, all of us have had our birth and nurture. The truth contained in that, you, my young friends, are now setting forth to teach. As the Cultus, or established worship of the civilized world, it has great historical interest for us. Of its blessed words, which have been the consolation of humanity, you need not that I should speak. I shall endeavor to discharge my duty to you on this occasion, by pointing out two errors in its administration, which daily appear more gross from the point of view we have just now taken.

Jesus Christ belonged to the true race of prophets. He saw with open eye the mystery of the soul. Drawn by its severe harmony, ravished with its beauty, he lived in it, and had his being there. Alone in all history he estimated the greatness of man. One man was true to what is in you and me. He saw that God incarnates himself in man, and evermore goes forth anew to take possession of his World. He said, in this jubilee of sublime emotion, I am divine. Through me, God acts; through me, speaks. Would you see God, see me; or see thee, when thou also thinkest as I now think. But what a distortion did his doctrine and memory suffer in the same, in the next, and the following ages! There is no doctrine of the Reason which will bear to be taught by the Understanding. The understanding caught this high chant from the poet's lips, and said, in the next age, 'This was Jehovah come down out of heaven. I will kill you, if you say he was a man.' The idioms of his language and the figures of his rhetoric have usurped the place of his truth; and churches are not built on his principles, but on his tropes. Christianity became a Mythus, as the poetic teaching of Greece and of Egypt, before. He spoke of miracles; for he felt that man's life was a miracle, and all that man doth, and he knew that this daily miracle shines as the character ascends. But the word Miracle, as pronounced by Christian churches, gives a false impression; it is Monster. It is not one with the blowing clover and the falling rain.

He felt respect for Moses and the prophets, but no unfit tenderness at postponing their initial revelations to the hour and the man that now is to the eternal revelation in the heart. Thus was he a true man. Having seen that the law in us is commanding, he would not suffer it to be commanded. Boldly, with hand, and heart, and life, he declared it was God. Thus is he, as I think, the only soul in history who has appreciated the worth of man.

1. In this point of view we become sensible of the first defect of historical Christianity. Historical Christianity has fallen into the error that corrupts all attempts to communicate religion. As it appears to us, and as it has appeared for ages, it is not the doctrine of the soul, but an exaggeration of the personal, the positive, the ritual. It has dwelt, it dwells, with noxious exag-

geration about the *person* of Jesus. The soul knows no persons. It invites every man to expand to the full circle of the universe, and will have no preferences but those of spontaneous love. But by this eastern monarchy of a Christianity, which indolence and fear have built, the friend of man is made the injurer of man. The manner in which his name is surrounded with expressions which were once sallies of admiration and love, but are now petrified into official titles, kills all generous sympathy and liking. All who hear me, feel that the language that describes Christ to Europe and America is not the style of friendship and enthusiasm to a good and noble heart, but is appropriated and formal—paints a demigod, as the Orientals or the Greeks would describe Osiris or Apollo. Accept the injurious impositions of our early catechetical instruction, and even honesty and self-denial were but splendid sins, if they did not wear the Christian name. One would rather be

"A pagan, suckled in a creed outworn,"

than to be defrauded of his manly right in coming into nature and finding not names and places, not land and professions, but even virtue and truth foreclosed and monopolized. You shall not be a man even. You shall not own the world; you shall not dare and live after the infinite Law that is in you, and in company with the infinite Beauty which heaven and earth reflect to you in all lovely forms; but you must subordinate your nature to Christ's nature; you must accept our interpretations, and take his portrait as the vulgar draw it.

That is always best which gives me to myself. The sublime is excited in me by the great stoical doctrine, Obey thyself. That which shows God in me, fortifies me. That which shows God out of me, makes me a wart and a wen. There is no longer a necessary reason for my being. Already the long shadows of untimely oblivion creep over me, and I shall decease forever.

The divine bards are the friends of my virtue, of my intellect, of my strength. They admonish me that the gleams which flash across my mind are not mine, but God's; that they had the like, and were not disobedient to the heavenly vision. So I love them. Noble provocations go out from them, inviting me to resist evil; to subdue the world; and to Be. And thus, by his holy thoughts, Jesus serves us, and thus only. To aim to convert a man by miracles is a profanation of the soul. A true conversion, a true Christ, is now, as always, to be made by the reception of beautiful sentiments. It is true that a great and rich soul, like his, falling among the simple, does so preponderate, that, as his did, it names the world. The world seems to them to exist for him, and they have not yet drunk so deeply of his sense as to see that only by coming again to themselves, or to God in themselves, can they grow forevermore. It is a low benefit to give me something; it is a high benefit to enable me to do somewhat of myself. The time is coming when all men will see that the gift of God to the soul is not a vaunting, overpowering, excluding sanctity, but a sweet, natural goodness, a goodness like thine and mine, and that so invites thine and mine to be and to grow.

The injustice of the vulgar tone of preaching is not less flagrant to Jesus than to the souls which it profanes. The preachers do not see that they make his gospel not glad, and shear him of the looks of beauty and the attributes of heaven. When I see a majestic Epaminondas, or Washington; when I see among my contemporaries a true orator, an upright judge, a dear friend; when I vibrate to the melody and fancy of a poem; I see beauty that is to be desired. And so lovely, and with yet more entire consent of my human being, sounds in my ear the severe music of the bards that have sung of the true God in all ages. Now do not degrade the life and dialogues of Christ out of the circle of this charm, by insulation and peculiarity. Let them lie as they befell, alive and warm, part of human life and the landscape and the cheerful day.

2. The second defect of the traditionary and limited way of using the mind of Christ is a consequence of the first; this, namely; that the Moral Nature, that Law of laws whose revelations introduce greatness—yea, God himself—into the open soul, is not explored as the fountain of the established teaching

in society. Men have come to speak of the revelation as some-what long ago given and done, as if God were dead. The injury to faith throttles the preacher; and the goodliest of institutions becomes an uncertain and inarticulate voice.

It is very certain that it is the effect of conversation with the beauty of the soul, to beget a desire and need to impart to others the same knowledge and love. If utterance is denied, the thought lies like a burden on the man. Always the seer is a sayer. Somehow his dream is told; somehow he publishes it with solemn joy: sometimes with pencil on canvas, sometimes with chisel on stone, sometimes in towers and aisles of granite, his soul's worship is builded; sometimes in anthems of indefinite music; but clearest and most permanent, in words.

The man enamored of this excellency becomes its priest or poet. The office is coeval with the world. But observe the condition, the spiritual limitation of the office. The spirit only can teach. Not any profane man, not any sensual, not any liar, not any slave can teach, but only he can give, who has; he only can create, who is. The man on whom the soul descends, through whom the soul speaks, alone can teach. Courage, piety, love, wisdom, can teach; and every man can open his door to these angels, and they shall bring him the gift of tongues. But the man who aims to speak as books enable, as synods use, as the fashion guides, and as interest commands, babbles. Let him hush.

To this holy office you propose to devote yourselves. I wish you may feel your call in throbs of desire and hope. The office is the first in the world. It is of that reality that it cannot suffer the deduction of any falsehood. And it is my duty to say to you that the need was never greater of new revelation than now. From the views I have already expressed, you will infer the sad conviction, which I share, I believe, with numbers, of the universal decay and now almost death of faith in society. The soul is not preached. The Church seems to totter to its fall, almost all life extinct. On this occasion, any complaisance would be criminal which told you, whose hope and commission it is to preach the faith of Christ, that the faith of Christ is preached.

It is time that this ill-suppressed murmur of all thoughtful men against the famine of our churches; this moaning of the heart because it is bereaved of the consolation, the hope, the grandeur that come alone out of the culture of the moral nature—should be heard through the sleep of indolence, and over the din of routine. This great and perpetual office of the preacher is not discharged. Preaching is the expression of the moral sentiment in application to the duties of life. In how many churches, by how many prophets, tell me, is man made sensible that he is an infinite Soul; that the earth and heavens are passing into his mind; that he is drinking forever the soul of God? Where now sounds the persuasion, that by its very melody imparadises my heart, and so affirms its own origin in heaven? Where shall I hear words such as in elder ages drew men to leave all and follow—father and mother, house and land, wife and child? Where shall I hear these august laws of moral being so pronounced as to fill my ear, and I feel ennobled by the offer of my uttermost action and passion? The test of the true faith, certainly, should be its power to charm and command the soul, as the laws of nature control the activity of the hands—so commanding that we find pleasure and honor in obeying. The faith should blend with the light of rising and of setting suns, with the flying cloud, the singing bird, and the breath of flowers. But now the priest's Sabbath has lost the splendor of nature; it is unlovely; we are glad when it is done; we can make, we do make, even sitting in our pews, a far better, holier, sweeter, for ourselves.

Whenever the pulpit is usurped by a formalist, then is the worshipper defrauded and disconsolate. We shrink as soon as the prayers begin, which do not uplift, but smite and offend us. We are fain to wrap our cloaks about us, and secure, as best we can, a solitude that hears not. I once heard a preacher who sorely tempted me to say I would go to church no more. Men go, thought I, where they are wont to go, else had no soul entered the temple in the afternoon. A snow-storm was falling around us. The snow-storm was real, the preacher merely spectral, and the eye felt the sad contrast in looking at him, and then out of the window behind him into the beautiful meteor of the snow. He had lived in vain. He had no one word intimating that he had laughed or wept, was married or in love, had been commended, or cheated, or chagrined. If he had ever lived and acted, we were none the wiser for it. The capital secret of his profession, namely, to convert life into truth, he had not learned. Not one fact in all his experience had he yet imported into his doctrine. This man had ploughed and planted and talked and bought and sold; he had read books; he had eaten and drunken; his head aches, his heart throbs; he smiles and suffers; yet was there not a surmise, a hint, in all the discourse, that he had ever lived at all. Not a line did he draw out of real history. The true preacher can be known by this, that he deals out to the people his life—life passed through the fire of thought. But of the bad preacher, it could not be told from his sermon what age of the world he fell in; whether he had a father or a child; whether he was a freeholder or a pauper; whether he was a citizen or a countryman; or any other fact of his biography. It seemed strange that the people should come to church. It seemed as if their houses were very unentertaining, that they should prefer this thoughtless clamor. It shows that there is a commanding attraction in the moral sentiment, that can lend a faint tint of light to dulness and ignorance coming in its name and place. The good hearer is sure he has been touched sometimes; is sure there is somewhat to be reached, and some word that can reach it. When he listens to these vain words, he comforts himself by their relation to his remembrance of better hours, and so they clatter and echo unchallenged.

I am not ignorant that when we preach unworthily, it is not always quite in vain. There is a good ear, in some men, that draws supplies to virtue out of very indifferent nutriment.

There is poetic truth concealed in all the commonplaces of prayer and of sermons, and though foolishly spoken, they may be wisely heard; for each is some select expression that broke out in a moment of piety from some stricken or jubilant soul, and its excellency made it remembered. The prayers and even the dogmas of our church are like the zodiac of Denderah and the astronomical monuments of the Hindoos, wholly insulated from anything now extant in the life and business of the people. They mark the height to which the waters once rose. But this docility is a check upon the mischief from the good and devout. In a large portion of the community, the religious service gives rise to quite other thoughts and emotions. We need not chide the negligent servant. We are struck with pity, rather, at the swift retribution of his sloth. Alas for the unhappy man that is called to stand in the pulpit, and *not* give bread of life. Everything that befalls, accuses him. Would he ask contributions for the missions, foreign or domestic? Instantly his face is suffused with shame, to propose to his parish that they should send money a hundred or a thousand miles, to furnish such poor fare as they have at home and would do well to go the hundred or the thousand miles to escape. Would he urge people to a godly way of living; and can he ask a fellow-creature to come to Sabbath meetings, when he and they all know what is the poor uttermost they can hope for therein? Will he invite them privately to the Lord's Supper? He dares not. If no heart warm this rite, the hollow, dry, creaking formality is too plain, than that he can face a man of wit and energy and put the invitation without terror. In the street, what has he to say to the bold village blasphemer? The village blasphemer sees fear in the face, form, and gait of the minister.

Let me not taint the sincerity of this plea by any oversight of the claims of good men. I know and honor the purity and strict conscience of numbers of the clergy. What life the public worship retains, it owes to the scattered company of pious men, who minister here and there in the churches, and who, sometimes accepting with too great tenderness the tenet of the elders, have not accepted from others, but from their own heart, and genuine impulses of virtue, and so still command our love and awe, to the sanctity of character. Moreover, the exceptions are not so much to be found in a few eminent preachers, as in the better hours, the truer inspirations of all—nay, in the sincere moments of every man. But, with whatever exception, it is still true that tradition characterizes the preaching of this country; that it comes out of the memory, and not out of the soul; that it aims at what is usual, and not at what is necessary and eternal; that thus historical Christianity destroys the power of preaching, by withdrawing it from the exploration of the moral nature of man; where the sublime is, where are the resources of astonishment and power. What a cruel injustice it is to that Law, the joy of the whole earth, which alone can make thought dear and rich; that Law whose fatal sureness the astronomical orbits poorly emulate; that it is travestied and depreciated, that it is behooted and behowled, and not a trait, not a word of it articulated. The pulpit in losing sight of this Law, loses its reason, and gropes after it knows not what. And for want of this culture the soul of the community is sick and faithless. It wants nothing so much as a stern, high, stoical, Christian discipline, to make it know itself and the divinity that speaks through it. Now man is ashamed of himself; he skulks and sneaks through the world, to be tolerated, to be pitied, and scarcely in a thousand years does any man dare to be wise and good, and so draw after him the tears and blessings of his kind.

Certainly there have been periods when, from the inactivity of the intellect on certain truths, a greater faith was possible in names and persons. The Puritans in England and America found in the Christ of the Catholic Church and in the dogmas inherited from Rome, scope for their austere piety and their longings for civil freedom. But their creed is passing away, and none arises in its room. I think no man can go with his thoughts about him into one of our churches, without feeling that what hold the public worship had on men is gone, or going. It has lost its grasp on the affection of the good and the fear of the bad. In the country, neighborhoods, half parishes are *signing off,* to use the local term. It is already beginning to indicate character and religion to withdraw from the religious meetings. I have heard a devout person, who prized the Sabbath, say in bitterness of heart, "On Sundays, it seems wicked to go to church." And the motive that holds the best there is now only a hope and a waiting. What was once a mere circumstance, that the best and worst men in the parish, the poor and the rich, the learned and the ignorant, young and old, should meet one day as fellows in one house, in sign of an equal right in the soul, has come to be a paramount motive for going thither.

My friends, in these two errors, I think, I find the causes of a decaying church and a wasting unbelief. And what greater calamity can fall upon a nation than the loss of worship? Then all things go to decay. Genius leaves the temple to haunt the senate or the market. Literature becomes frivolous. Science is cold. The eye of youth is not lighted by the hope of other worlds, and age is without honor. Society lives to trifles, and when men die we do not mention them.

And now, my brothers, you will ask, What in these desponding days can be done by us? The remedy is already declared in the ground of our complaint of the Church. We have contrasted the Church with the Soul. In the soul then let the redemption be sought. Wherever a man comes, there comes revolution. The old is for slaves. When a man comes, all books are legible, all things transparent, all religions are forms. He is religious. Man is the wonderworker. He is seen amid miracles. All men bless and curse. He saith yea and nay, only. The stationariness of religion; the assumption that the age of inspiration is past, that the Bible is closed; the fear of degrading the character of Jesus by representing him as a man; indicate with sufficient clearness the falsehood of our theology. It is the office of a true teacher to show us that God is, not was; that He speaketh, not spake. The true Christianity—a faith like Christ's in the infinitude of men—is lost. None believeth in the soul of man, but only in some man or person old and departed. Ah me! no man goeth alone. All men go in flocks to this saint or that poet, avoiding the God who seeth in secret. They cannot see in secret; they love to be blind in public. They think society wiser than their soul, and know not that one soul, and their soul is wiser than the whole world. See how nations and races flit by on the sea of time and leave no ripple to tell where they floated or sunk, and one good soul shall make the name of Moses or of Zeno, or of Zoroaster, reverend forever. None assayeth the stern ambition to be the Self of the nation and of nature but each would be an easy secondary to some Christian scheme or sectarian connection, or some eminent man. Once leave your own knowledge of God, your own sentiment, and take secondary knowledge, as St. Paul's, or George Fox's, or Sedenborg's and you get wide from God with every year this secondary form lasts, and if, as now, for centuries—the chasm yawns to that breadth, that men can scarcely be convinced there is in them anything divine.

Let me admonish you, first of all, to go alone; to refuse the good models, even those which are sacred in the imagination of men, and dare to love God without mediator or veil. Friends enough you shall find who will hold up to your emulation Wesleys and Oberlins, Saints and Prophets. Thank God for the good men, but say, 'I also am a man.' Imitation cannot go above its model. The imitator dooms himself to hopeless mediocrity. The inventor did it because it was natural to him, and so in him it has a charm. In the imitator something else is natural, and he bereaves himself of his own beauty, to come short of another man's.

Yourself a newborn bard of the Holy Ghost, can behind you all conformity, and acquaint men at first hand with Deity. Look to it first and only, that fashion, custom, authority, pleasure, and money, and nothing to you—are not bandages over your eyes, that you cannot see—but live with the privilege the immeasurable mind. Not too anxious to visit periodically all families and each family in your parish connection—when you meet one of these men or women, be to them a divine man; be to them thought and virtue; let their timid aspirations find in you a friend; let their trampled instincts be genially tempted out in your atmosphere; let their doubts know that you have doubted, and their wonder feel that you have wondered. By trusting your own heart, you shall gain more confidence in other men. For all our penny-wisdom, for all our soul-destroying slavery to habit, it is not to be doubted that all men have sublime thoughts; that all men value the few real hours of life; they love to be heard; they love to be caught up into the vision of principles. We mark with light in the memory the few interviews we have had, in the dreary years of routine and of sin, with souls that made our souls wiser; that spoke what we thought; that told us what we knew; that gave us leave to be what we inly were. Discharge to men the priestly office, and, present or absent, you shall be followed with their love as by an angel.

And, to this end, let us not aim at common degrees of merit. Can we not leave, to such as love it, the virtue that glitters for the commendation of society, and ourselves pierce the deep solitudes of absolute ability and worth? We easily come up to the standard of goodness in society. Society's praise can be cheaply secured, and almost all men are content with those easy merits; but the instant effect of conversing with God will be to put them away. There are persons who are not actors, not speakers, but influences; persons too great for fame, for display; who disdain eloquence; to whom all we call art and artist, seems too nearly allied to show and by-ends, to the exaggeration of the finite and selfish, and loss of the universal. The orators, the poets, the commanders encroach on us only as fair women do, by our allowance and homage. Slight them by preoccupation of mind, slight them, as you can well afford to do, by high and universal aims, and they instantly feel that you have right, and that it is in lower places that they must shine. They also feel your right; for they with you are open to the influx of the all-knowing Spirit, which annihilates before its broad noon the little shades and gradations of intelligence in the compositions we call wiser and wisest.

In such high communion let us study the grand strokes of rectitude: a bold benevolence, an independence of friends, so that not the unjust wishes of those who love us shall impair our freedom, but we shall resist for truth's sake the freest flow of kindness, and appeal to sympathies far in advance; and—what is the highest form in which we know this beautiful element—a certain solidity of merit, that has nothing to do with opinion, and which is so essentially and manifestly virtue, that it is taken for granted that the right, the brave, the generous step will be taken by it, and nobody thinks of commending it. You would compliment a coxcomb doing a good act, but you would not praise an angel. The silence that accepts merit as the most natural thing in the world, is the highest applause. Such souls, when they appear, are the Imperial Guard of Virtue, the perpetual reserve, the dictators of fortune. One needs not praise their courage—they are the heart and soul of nature. O my friends, there are resources in us on which we have not drawn. There are men who rise refreshed on hearing a threat; men to whom a crisis which intimidates and paralyzes the majority—demanding not the faculties of prudence and thrift, but comprehension, immovableness, the readiness of sacrifice—comes graceful and beloved as a bride. Napoleon said of Massena, that he was not himself until the battle began to go against him; then, when the dead began to fall in ranks around him, awoke his powers of combination, and he put on terror and victory as a robe. So it is in rugged crises, in unweariable endurance, and in aims which put sympathy out of question that the angel is shown. But these are heights that we can scarce remember and look up to without contrition and shame. Let us thank God that such things exist.

And now let us do what we can to rekindle the smouldering,

nigh quenched fire on the altar. The evils of the church that now is are manifest. The question returns, What shall we do? I confess, all attempts to project and establish a Cultus with new rites and forms, seem to me vain. Faith makes us, and not we it, and faith makes its own forms. All attempts to contrive a system are as cold as the new worship introduced by the French to the goddess of Reason—to-day, pasteboard and filigree, and ending to-morrow in madness and murder. Rather let the breath of new life be breathed by you through the forms already existing. For if once you are alive, you shall find they shall become plastic and new. The remedy to their deformity is first, soul, and second, soul, and evermore, soul. A whole popedom of forms one pulsation of virtue can uplift and vivify. Two inestimable advantages Christianity has given us; first the Sabbath, the jubilee of the whole world, whose light dawns welcome alike into the closet of the philosopher, into the garret of toil, and into prison-cells, and everywhere suggests, even to the vile, the dignity of spiritual being. Let it stand forevermore, a temple, which new love, new faith, new sight shall restore to more than its first splendor to mankind. And secondly, the institution of preaching—the speech of man to men—essentially the most flexible of all organs, of all forms. What hinders that now, everywhere, in pulpits, in lecture-rooms, in houses, in fields, wherever the invitation of men or your own occasions lead you, you speak the very truth, as your life and conscience teach it, and cheer the waiting, fainting hearts of men with new hope and new revelation?

I look for the hour when that supreme Beauty which ravished the souls of those Eastern men, and chiefly of those Hebrews, and through their lips spoke oracles to all time, shall speak in the West also. The Hebrew and Greek Scriptures contain immortal sentences, that have been bread of life to millions. But they have no epical integrity; are fragmentary; are not shown in their order to the intellect. I look for the new Teacher that shall follow so far those shining laws that he shall see them come full circle; shall see their rounding complete grace; shall see the world to be the mirror of the soul; shall see the identity of the law of gravitation with purity of heart; and shall show that the Ought, that Duty, is one thing with Science, with Beauty, and with Joy.

2

The Sects

THE SHAKERS

Sketches of the Life of Mother Ann Lee

1. ANN LEE was the daughter of John Lee, of Manchester, in England. She was born February 29th, 1736. Her father was by occupation a blacksmith, and tho' poor, he was respectable in character, moral in principle, honest and punctual in his dealings, and industrious in business. Her mother was esteemed as a religious and very pious woman. They had eight children, five sons and three daughters. Their children, as was then common with poor people in manufacturing towns, were brought up to work instead of being sent to school. By this means Ann acquired a habit of industry, but could neither read nor write. During her childhood and youth, she was employed in a cotton factory, and was afterwards a cutter of hatter's fur. She was also, for some time, employed as a cook in the Manchester infirmary, and was peculiarly distinguished for her faithfulness, neatness, prudence and economy.

2. In her childhood she discovered a very bright and active genius, was remarkably sagacious, but serious and thoughtful,

and never addicted to play like other children. In early child-hood she was the subject of religious impressions, and was peculiarly favored with heavenly visions. As she advanced in years, she was strongly impressed with a sense of the great depravity of human nature, and of the odiousness of sin, and especially of the impure and indecent nature of sexual coition. She often experessed her feelings to her mother concerning these things, and earnestly desired that she might be kept from the snares of sin, and from those abominations which her soul abhorred.

3. But not having attained that knowledge of God which she early desired, and finding no one to strengthen and assist her in the pursuit of that true holiness which she sought after, nor even to encourage her to withstand the powerful example of a lost world, (her mother having deceased while she was yet young,) she grew up in the same fallen nature with the rest of mankind, and through the importunities of her relations, was married to Abraham Stanley, a blacksmith by trade. By him she had four children who all died in infancy; one only, which was a daughter, attained to the age of about six years. They lived together at her father's house, in peace and harmony, and procured a comfortable living. But the convictions of her youth often returned upon her with great force, which at length brought her under excessive tribulation of soul. In this situation she sought earnestly for deliverance from the bondage of sin, and gave herself no rest, day nor night, but often spent whole nights in laboring and crying to God for deliverance from sin.

4. While under these exercises of mind, she became ac-quainted with James and Jane Wardley, and the society under their care. As these people were favored with a greater degree of divine light, and a more clear and pointed testimony against the nature of sin than had hitherto been made manifest, Ann readily embraced their testimony, and united herself to the society in the month of September 1758, being then in the 23d year of her age. The light of these people led them to an open

confession of every sin which they had committed, and to a full and final cross against every thing which they knew to be evil: hence they were endowed with great power over sin: and hence Ann found that protection which she had so long desired, and which, for the time being, was answerable to her faith.

5. By her faithful obedience to the counsel and instruction of her leaders, she was baptized into the same spirit, and, by degrees, attained to the full knowledge and experience in spiritual things which they had found. As she occasionally related to the American believers some of her experience and sufferings in England, it may not be improper to give the following short sketch concerning the early part of her faith, in her own words.

6. "Soon after I set out to travail in the way of God, I labored anights in the works of God. Sometimes I labored all night, continually crying to God for my own redemption; sometimes I went to bed and slept; but in the morning I could not feel that sense of the work of God which I did before I slept. This brought me into great tribulation. Then I cried to God, and promised him that if he would give me the same sense that I had before I slept I would labor all night. This I did many nights; and in the day time I put my hands to work and my heart to God; and when I felt weary and in need of rest, I labored for the power of God, and the refreshing operations of the power of God would release me, so that I would feel able to go to my work again.

7. "Many times when I was about my work, I felt my soul overwhelmed with sorrow; and I used to work as long as I could keep it concealed, and then run to get out of sight, lest some one should pity me with that pity which God did not. In my travail and tribulation, my sufferings were so great, that my flesh consumed upon my bones, and bloody sweat pressed through the pores of my skin, and I became as helpless as an infant. And when I was brought through, and born into the spiritual kingdom, I was like an infant just brought into the world. They see colors and objects; but they know not what they see; and so it was with me when I was born into the spiritual world. But

before I was twenty-four hours old, I saw, and I knew what I saw."

8. John Hocknell, who was well acquainted with her in the time of her experience and sufferings in England, used frequently to speak of them, with many peculiar circumstances that came under his knowledge. According to this account, as well as that of her own, and others who came from England with her, it appears that in watchings, fastings, tears and incessant cries to God, she labored day and night, for deliverance from the very nature of sin; and that, under the most severe tribulation of mind, and the most violent temptations and buffetings of the enemy, the agony of her soul was often so extreme as to occasion a perspiration of blood. Sometimes, for whole nights together, her cries, screeches and groans were such as to fill every soul around with fear and trembling.

9. By these painful sufferings and deep mortifications her flesh sometimes wasted away, like that of a person in a consumption, till she became so weak and emaciated that her friends were obliged to support and nourish her like a helpless infant; altho' she possessed by nature a sound and strong constitution, and an invincible fortitude of mind. Tho' Ann was wrought upon in this manner; more or less, for the space of nine years; yet she often had intervals of releasement, in which her bodily strength and vigor was sometimes miraculously renewed, and her soul was at times filled with heavenly visions and divine revelations. By these means the way of God and the nature of his work gradually opened upon her mind with increasing light and understanding. The divine manifestations which she received, from time to time, were communicated to the society, and tended greatly to enlighten the understandings, and encourage the faith of the members, and to increase and confirm their testimony.

10. Her mind, ever intent on the great work of salvation was deeply affected concerning the lost state of mankind, which she clearly saw in all their works. But the real foundation of that loss

was still concealed from her view; nor could she see any prospect of recovery under existing circumstances: for she had long been convinced that there was nothing in all their religious professions nor practices that could save them from sin here, or furnish any reasonable hope of salvation hereafter. Hence she spent much time in earnest and incessant cries to God, to shew her the real foundation of man's loss, what it was, and wherein it consisted; how the way of salvation could be effectually opened to a lost world in its present state; and how the great work of redemption was to be accomplished.

11. While in deep exercise of mind concerning these things, she was brought into a state of excessive tribulation of soul, in which she felt her way hedged up, seemingly, on every side, and was constrained to cry mightily to God to open some way of deliverance. In the midst of her sufferings and earnest cries to God, her soul was filled with divine light, and the mysteries of the spiritual world were brought clearly to her understanding. She saw the Lord Jesus Christ in his glory, who revealed to her the great object of her prayers, and fully satisfied all the desires of her soul. The most astonishing visions and divine manifestations were presented to her view in so clear and striking a manner, that the whole spiritual world seemed displayed before her. In these extraordinary manifestations, she had a full and clear view of the mystery of iniquity, of the root and foundation of human depravity, and of the very act of transgression, committed by the first man and woman in the garden of Eden. Here she saw whence and wherein all mankind were lost from God, and clearly realized the only possible way of recovery. This revelation she received in the summer of 1770, in prison, where she was confined on account of her religious principles, under a pretence of her having profaned the sabbath.

12. Tho' Ann had before received many extraordinary manifestations of God, tho' she had received great light concerning the depravity of human nature, and the effects of man's loss

from God, and tho' she had taken up her cross against the carnal gratifications of the flesh, and had testified her faith to the society on this subject, many of whom, in consequence of her testimony, had walked in the same faith; yet, not having then received a clear revelation of the root of human depravity, and the cause of man's fall, she had continued to yield obedience to James and Jane Wardley, as her superiors, and was eminently useful to them in leading, teaching, strengthening and protecting the society.

13. But when she was released from her imprisonment, and came to reveal to the society these last extraordinary manifestations, so great was the display of divine light with which her soul was filled, and so mighty the power of God which accompanied her testimony, and so keen the searching power of her spirit in discovering and bringing to light the hidden works of darkness, that every soul present was struck with astonishment and filled with fear and trembling.—They saw at once that the candle of the Lord was in her hand, and that she was able by the light thereof, to search every heart and try every soul among them. From this time she was received and acknowledged as the first visible leader of the church of God upon earth.

14. The preceding work in this society, under the ministration of James and Jane Wardley, was evidently preparatory to the ushering in of the second coming of Christ; and it may with propriety be compared to the work of John the Baptist, or the spirit of Elias, the forerunner of the Lord Jesus. When therefore Ann was baptised into the fulness of the spirit and work of that society, she was then prepared for the Baptism of the Holy and Divine nature,* and was made a fit vessel to receive the true Spirit of Christ, and to revive and bring to light his perfect law of righteousness for the direction and salvation of all souls who were willing to obey her testimony; and here commenced the real manifestation of Christ's second appearance.

15. From this time the light and power of God revealed in Ann, and through her administered to those who received her

testimony, had such sensible effect in giving them power over all sin, and filling them with visions, revelations and other gifts of God, that she was readily acknowledged as their spiritual *Mother in Christ.*—Hence she received the title of *Mother;* and hence those of the society who received and obeyed her testimony, found a great increase in the power and gifts of God; while on the other hand, those who rejected it, lost all their former light and power, and fell back into a state of darkness, and into the common course of the world.

16. By the immediate revelation of Christ, she henceforth bore an open testimony against the lustful gratifications of the flesh, as the source and foundation of human corruption; and testified, in the most plain and pointed manner, that no soul could follow Christ in the regeneration, while living in the works of natural generation, or in any of the gratifications of lust. Her testimony was often delivered with such mighty power of God, accompanied with such a heart-searching and soul-quickening spirit, that it seemed to penetrate every secret of the heart. By this means the most hidden abominations were often brought to light; and these secret acts of wickedness, which had been deceitfully covered under a fair outside profession of sanctity, were many times brought to view in such a manner as to make every guilty soul fear and tremble in her presence . . . .

24. These are but a part of the outward afflictions which Mother Ann endured from her enemies in England. Besides many circumstances of less note, there were several other instances of abuse which must inevitably have deprived her of life, had she not been protected by that Almighty Being in whom she always trusted; and it is worthy of remark, that nothing short of Divine Power could have supported her through all these trying scenes, and enabled her to maintain her testimony in the midst of a crooked and perverse generation.

25. But in consequence of the sudden and untimely death of some of her most bitter persecutors, and the conviction of

others, these cruel abuses finally ceased. Her enemies saw that she was evidently protected and supported, and her life preserved, by some interposing power, notwithstanding all their attempts to destroy it; and hence, for more than two years previous to her leaving England, she and her little band enjoyed their faith in peace. And tho' there was no important addition to their number, yet the faith and substance of the gospel continued to increase in the hearts of the faithful. But their public testimony ceased in England about a year before they embarked for America.

26. Mother Ann, whose mind was ever intent on the work of God, and who always stood ready to obey any call of God to her, was at length, by a special revelation, directed to repair to America; and at the same time, she received a divine promise, that the work of God would greatly increase, and the millennial church would be established in that country. This revelation was communicated to the society, and was soon confirmed by signs, visions and extraordinary manifestations, to many individual members; and permission was given for all those of the society to accompany her, who were able, and who felt any special impressions on their own minds so to do. Accordingly those who became the companions of Mother Ann, in her voyage to America, and who were all at that time, professedly members of the society, were Abm. Stanley, her husband, Wm. Lee, her brother, James Whittaker, John Hocknell, Richard Hocknell, son of John Hocknell, James Shepherd, Mary Partington, and Nancy Lee, a niece of Mother Ann. These eight were all that accompanied Mother Ann in her voyage to America.

27. Having settled their affairs and made arrangements for the voyage, they embarked at Liverpool, on board the ship Mariah, Captain Smith, of New-York, and sailed on the 19th of May, 1774. Before they embarked, Mother Ann told the captain that he should not have whereof to accuse them, except it were concerning the law of their God. While on their passage, they went forth, in obedience to their inward feelings, to praise God

in songs and in dances. This offended the captain to such a degree, that he threatened to throw them overboard, if they attempted the like exercise again. But as Mother Ann had put her trust in God, whom she feared, she was not willing to be restrained in her duty by the fear of mortals; she therefore chose to obey God rather than man, and accordingly went forth again, in obedience to the divine influences which she felt.

28. At this the captain became greatly enraged, and attempted to put his threats in execution. But that God in whom they trusted, and who had sent them to do his will, had power to protect them. This he did in a marvelous manner. It was in the evening, in time of a storm; and the ship suddenly sprung a leak, occasioned by the starting of a plank between wind and water. The water now flowed in so rapidly, that notwithstanding all their exertions at the pumps, it gained upon them so fast, that the whole ship's crew were greatly alarmed. The captain turned pale as a corpse, and said they must all perish before morning; for he saw no possible means to save the ship from sinking.

29. But Mother Ann maintained her confidence in God, and said, "Captain be of good cheer; there shall not a hair of our heads "perish; we shall all arrive safe to America. I just now saw "two bright angels of God standing by the mast, through whom I "received this promise." She then encouraged the seamen, and she and her companions zealously assisted at the pumps. Shortly after this, a large wave struck the ship with great violence, and the loose plank was instantly closed to its place.

30. Whether this remarkable incident was effected by the violent force of the wave against the plank, or by some other unaccountable means, it was then viewed by all on board, as a miraculous interposition of Divine Providence in their favor. They were soon in a great measure released from the pumps; and the captain, after this, gave them free and full liberty to worship God according to the dictates of their own consciences, and promised that he would never molest them again. He was faithful to his promise, and treated them with kindness and

respect during the remainder of the voyage, and was afterwards free to declare, that had it not been for these people, he should have been sunk in the sea, and never reached America.

31. Thus, after enduring the storms and dangers of the sea, in an old leaky ship, which had been condemned as unfit for the voyage, and which came very near foundering at sea, they all arrived safe in New-York on the 6th of August following.

3

Slavery

RICHARD FURMAN

An Exposition[4]

Charleston,24th, December, 1822.

SIR,

WHEN I had, lately, the honour of delivering to your Excellency an Address, from the Baptist Convention in this State, requesting that a Day of Public Humiliation and Thanksgiving might be appointed by you, as our Chief Magistrate, to be observed by the Citizens of the State at large, in reference to two important recent events, in which the interposition of Divine Providence has been conspicuous, and in which the interests and feelings of our Citizens have been greatly concerned—viz: The protection afforded them from the horrors of an intended Insurrection; and the affliction they have suffered from the ravages of a dreadful Hurricane—I took the liberty to suggest, that I had a further communication to make on behalf of the Convention, in which their sentiments would be disclosed respecting the policy of the measure proposed; and on the lawfulness of holding slaves—the subject being considered in a moral and religious point of view.

You were pleased, sir, to signify, that it would be agreeable to you to receive such a communication. And as it is incumbent on me, in faithfulness to the trust reposed in me, to make it, I now take the liberty of laying it before you.

The Political propriety of bringing the intended Insurrection into view by publicly acknowledging its prevention to be an instance of the Divine Goodness, manifested by a providential, gracious interposition, is a subject, which has employed the serious attention of the Convention; and, if they have erred in the judgment they have formed upon it, the error is, at least, not owing to a want of consideration, or of serious concern. They cannot view the subject but as one of great magnitude, and intimately connected with the interests of the whole State. The Divine Interposition has been conspicuous; and our obligations to be thankful are unspeakably great. And, as principles of the wisest and best policy leads nations, as well as individuals, to consider and acknowledge the government of the Deity, to feel their dependence on him and trust in him, to be thankful for his mercies, and to be humbled under his chastening rod; so, not only moral and religious duty, but also a regard to the best interests of the community appear to require of us, on the present occasion, that humiliation and thanksgiving, which are proposed by the Convention in their request. For a sense of the Divine Government has a meliorating influence on the minds of men, restraining them from crime, and disposing them to virtuous action. To those also, who are humbled before the Heavenly Majesty for their sins, and learn to be thankful for his mercies, the Divine Favour is manifested. From them judgments are averted, and on them blessings are bestowed.

The Convention are aware, that very respectable Citizens have been averse to the proposal under consideration; the proposal for appointing a Day of Public Thanksgiving for our preservation from the intended Insurrection, on account of the influence it might be supposed to have on the Black Population—by giving publicity to the subject in *their view*, and by affording them excitements to attempt something further of the same nature. These objections, however, the Convention view as either not substantial, or overbalanced by higher considerations. As to publicity, perhaps no fact is more generally known by the persons referred to; for the knowledge of it has been communicated by almost every channel of information, public and private, even by documents under the stamp of Public Authority; and has extended to every part of the State. But with the knowledge of the conspiracy is united the knowledge of its frustration; and of that, which Devotion and Gratitude should set in a strong light, *the merciful interposition of Providence,* which produced that frustration. The more rational among that class of men, as well as others, know also, that our preservation from the evil intended by the conspirators, is a subject, which should induce us to render thanksgivings to the Almighty; and it is hoped and believed, that the truly enlightened and religiously disposed among them, of which there appear to be many, are ready to unite in those thanksgivings, from a regard to their own true interests: if therefore it is apprehended, that an undue importance would be given to the subject in their view, by making it the matter of public thanksgiving; that this would induce the designing and wicked to infer our fear and sense of weakness from the fact, and thus induce them to form some other scheme of mischief: Would not our silence, and the omission of an important religious duty, under these circumstances, undergo, at least, as unfavourable a construction, and with more reason?

But the Convention are persuaded, that publicity, rather than secrecy is the true policy to be pursued on this occasion; especially, when the subject is taken into view, in connexion with other truths, of high importance and certainty, which relate to it, and is placed in a just light; the evidence and force of which truths, thousands of this people, when informed, can clearly discern and estimate. It is proper, the Convention conceives, that the Negroes should know, that however numerous they are in some parts of these Southern States, they, yet, are not, even including all descriptions, bond and free, in the United States, but little more than one sixth part of the whole number of inhabitants, estimating that number which it probably now is, at Ten Millions; and the Black and Coloured Population, according to returns made at 1,780,000: That their destitution in respect to arms, and the knowledge of using them, with other disabilities, would render their physical force, were they all united in a common effort, less than a tenth part of that, with which they would have to contend. That there are multitudes of the best informed and truly religious among them, who, from principle, as well as from prudence, would not unite with them, nor fail to disclose their machinations, when it should be in their power to do it: That, however in some parts of our Union there are Citizens, who favour the idea of general emancipation; yet, were they to see slaves in our Country, in arms, wading through blood and carnage to effect their purpose, they would do what both their duty and interest would require; unite under the government with their fellow-citizens at large to suppress the rebellion, and bring the authors of it to condign punishment: That it may be expected, in every attempt to raise an insurrection (should other attempts be made) as well as it was in that defeated here, that the prime movers in such a nefarious scheme, will so form their plan, that in a case of exigency, they may flee with their plunder and leave their deluded followers to suffer the punishment, which law and justice may inflict: And that, therefore, there is reason to conclude, on the most rational and just principles, that whatever partial success might at any time attend such a measure at the onset, yet, in this country, it must finally result in the discomfiture and ruin of the perpetrators; and in many instances pull down on the heads of the innocent as well as the guilty, an undistinguishing ruin.

On the lawfulness of holding slaves, considering it in a moral and religious view, the Convention think it their duty to exhibit their sentiments, on the present occasion, before your Excellency, because they consider their duty to God, the peace of the State, the satisfaction of scrupulous consciences, and the welfare of the slaves themselves, as intimately connected with a right view of the subject. The rather, because certain writers on politics, morals and religion, and some of them highly respectable, have advanced positions, and inculcated sentiments, very unfriendly to the principle and practice of holding slaves; and by some these sentiments have been advanced among us, tending in their nature, *directly* to disturb the domestic peace of the State, to produce insubordination and rebellion among the slaves, and to infringe the rights of our citizens; and *indirectly*, to deprive the slaves of religious privileges, by awakening in the minds of their masters a fear, that acquaintance with the Scriptures, and the enjoyment of these privileges would naturally produce the aforementioned effects; because the sentiments in opposition to the holding of slaves have been attributed, by their advocates, to the Holy Scriptures, and to the genius of Christianity. These sentiments, the Convention, on whose behalf I address your Excellency, cannot think just, or well founded: for the right of holding slaves is clearly established in the Holy Scriptures, both by precept and example. In the Old Testament, the Israelites were directed to purchase their bond-men and bond-maids of the Heathen nations; except they were of the Canaanites, for these were to be destroyed. And it is declared, that the persons purchased were to be their "bond-men forever;" and an "inheritance for them and their children." They were not to go out free in the year of jubilee, as the Hebrews, who had been purchased, were: the line being clearly drawn between them. In example, they are presented to our view as existing in the families of the Hebrews as servants, or slaves, born in the house, or bought with money: so that the children born of slaves are here considered slaves as well as their parents. And to this well known state of things, as to its reason and order, as well as to special privileges, St. Paul appears to refer, when he says, "But I was free born."

In the New-Testament, the Gospel History, or representation of facts, presents us with a view correspondent with that, which is furnished by other authentic ancient histories of the state of the world at the commencement of Christianity. The powerful Romans had succeeded, in empire, the polished Greeks; and, under both empires, the countries they possessed and governed were full of slaves. Many of these with their masters, were converted to the Christian Faith, and received, together with them into the Christian Church, while it was yet under the ministry of the inspired Apostles. In things purely spiritual, they appear to have enjoyed equal privileges; but their relationship, as masters and slaves, was not dissolved. Their respective duties are strictly enjoined. The masters are not required to emancipate their slaves; but to give them the things that are just and equal, forbearing threatening; and to remember, they also have a master in Heaven. The "servants under the Yoke" (bond-servants or slaves) mentioned by Paul to Timothy, as having "believing masters," are not authorized by him to demand of them emancipation, or to employ violent means to obtain it; but are directed to "account their masters worthy of all honour," and "not to despise them, because they were brethren" in religion; "but the rather to do them service, because they were faithful and beloved partakers of the Christian benefit." Similar directions are given by him in other places, and by other Apostles. And it gives great weight to the argument, that in this place, Paul follows his directions concerning servants with a charge to Timothy, as an Evangelist, to teach and exhort men to observe this doctrine.

Had the holding of slaves been a moral evil, it cannot be supposed, that the inspired Apostles, who feared not the faces of men, and were ready to lay down their lives in the case of their God, would have tolerated it, for a moment, in the Christian Church. If they had done so on a principle of accommodation, in cases where the masters remained heathen, to avoid offences and civil commotion; yet, surely, where both master and servant were Christian, as in the case before us, they would have enforced the law of Christ, and required, that the master should liberate his slave in the first instance. But, instead of this, they let the relationship remain untouched, as being lawful and right, and insist on the relative duties.

In proving this subject justifiable by Scriptural authority, its morality is also proved; for the Divine Law never sanctions immoral actions.

The Christian golden rule, of doing to others, as we would they should do to us, has been urged as an unanswerable argument against holding slaves. But surely this rule is never to be urged against that order of things, which the Divine government has established; nor do our desires become a standard to us, under this rule, unless they have a due regard to justice, propriety and the general good.

A father may very naturally desire, that his son should be obedient to his orders: Is he, therefore, to obey the orders of his son? A man might be pleased to be exonerated from his debts by the generosity of his creditors; or that his rich neighbour should equally divide his property with him; and in certain circumstances might desire these to be done: Would the mere existence of this desire, oblige him to exonerate *his* debtors, and to make such division of his property? Consistency and generosity, indeed, might require it of him, if he were in circumstances which would justify the act of generosity; but, otherwise, either action might be considered as the effect of folly and extravagance.

If the holding of slaves is lawful, or according to the Scriptures; then this Scriptural rule can be considered as requiring no more of the master, in respect of justice (whatever it may do in point of generosity) than what he, if a slave, could, consistently, wish to be done to himself, while the relationship between master and servant should be still continued.

In this argument, the advocates for emancipation blend the ideas of injustice and cruelty with those, which respect the existence of slavery, and consider them as inseparable. But, surely, they may be separated. A bond-servant may be treated with justice and humanity as a servant; and a master may, in an important sense, be the guardian and even father of his slaves.

They become a part of his family, (the whole, forming under him a little community) and the care of ordering it and of providing for its welfare, devolves of him. The children, the aged, the sick, the disabled, and the unruly, as well as those, who are capable of service and orderly, are the objects of his care: The labour of these, is applied to the benefit of those, and to their own support, as well as to that of the master. Thus, what is effected, and often at a great public expense, in a free community, by taxes, benevolent institutions, bettering houses, and penitentiaries, lies here on the master to be performed by him, whatever contingencies may happen; and often occasions much expense, care and trouble, from which the servants are free. Cruelty, is, certainly, inadmissible; but servitude may be consistent with such degrees of happiness as men usually attain in this imperfect state of things.

Some difficulties arise with respect to bringing a man, or class of men, into a state of bondage. For crime, it is generally agreed, a man may be deprived of his liberty. But, may he not be divested of it by his own consent, directly, or indirectly given: And, especially, when this assent, though indirect, is connected with an attempt to take away the liberty, if not the lives of others? The Jewish law favours the former idea: And if the inquiry on the latter be taken in the affirmative, which appears to be reasonable, it will establish a principle, by which it will appear, that the Africans brought to America were, in general, slaves, by their own consent, before they came from their own country, or fell into the hands of white men. Their law of nations, or general usage, having, by common consent the force of law, justified them, while carrying on their petty wars, in killing their prisoners or reducing them to slavery; consequently, in selling them, and these ends they appear to have proposed to themselves; the nation, therefore, or individual, which was overcome, reduced to slavery, and sold would have done the same by the enemy, had victory declared on their, or his side. Consequently, the man made a slave in this manner, might be said to be made so by his own consent, and by the indulgence of barbarous principles.

That Christian nations have not done all they might, or should have done, on a principle of Christian benevolence, for the civilization and conversion of the Africans: that much cruelty has been practised in the slave trade, as the benevolent Wilberforce, and others have shown; that much tyranny has been exercised by individuals, as masters over their slaves, and that the religious interests of the latter have been too much neglected by many cannot, will not be denied. But the fullest proof of these facts, will not also prove, that the holding men in subjection, as slaves, is a moral evil, and inconsistent with Christianity. Magistrates, husbands, and fathers, have proved tyrants. This does not prove, that magistracy, the husband's right to govern, and parental authority, are unlawful and wicked. The individual who abuses his authority, and acts with cruelty, must answer for it at the Divine tribunal; and civil authority should interpose to prevent or punish it; but neither civil nor ecclesiastical authority can consistently interfere with the possession and legitimate exercise of a right given by the Divine Law.

If the above representation of the Scriptural doctrine, and the manner of obtaining slaves from Africa is just; and if also purchasing them has been the means of saving human life, which there is great reason to believe it has; then, however the slave trade, in present circumstances, is justly censurable, yet might motives of humanity and even piety have been originally brought into operation in the purchase of slaves, when sold in the circumstances we have described. If, also, by their own confession, which has been made in manifold instances, their condition, when they have come into the hands of humane masters here, has been greatly bettered by the change; if it is, ordinarily, really better, as many assert, than that of thousands of the poorer classes in countries reputed civilized and free; and, if, in addition to all other considerations, the translation from their native country to this has been the means of their mental and religious improvement, and so of obtaining salvation, as many of themselves have joyfully and thankfully confessed—then may the just and humane master, who rules his slaves and provides for them, according to Christian principles, rest satisfied, that he is not, in holding them, chargeable with moral evil, nor with acting, in this respect, contrary to the genius of Christianity.—It appears to be equally clear, that those, who by reasoning on abstract principles, are induced to favour the scheme of general emancipation, and who ascribe their sentiments to Christianity, should be particularly careful, however benevolent their intentions may be, that they do not by a perversion of the Scriptural doctrine, through their wrong views of it, not only invade the domestic and religious peace and rights of our Citizens, on this subject; but, also by an intemperate zeal, prevent indirectly, the religious improvement of the people they design, professedly, to benefit; and, perhaps, become, evidently, the means of producing in our country, scenes of anarchy and blood; and all this in a vain attempt to bring about a state of things, which, if arrived at, would not probably better the state of that people; which is thought, by men of observation, to be generally true of the Negroes in the Northern States, who have been liberated.

To pious minds it has given pain to hear men, respectable for intelligence and morals, sometimes say, that holdings slaves is indeed indefensible, but that to us it is necessary, and must be supported. On this principle, mere politicians, unmindful of morals, may act. But surely, in a moral and religious view of the subject, this principle is inadmissible. It cannot be said, that theft, falsehood, adultery and murder, are become necessary and must be supported. Yet there is reason to believe, that some of honest and pious intentions have found their minds embarrassed if not perverted on this subject, by this plausible but unsound argument. From such embarrassment the view exhibited above affords relief.

The Convention, Sir, are far from thinking that Christianity fails to inspire the minds of its subjects with benevolent and generous sentiments; or that liberty rightly understood, or enjoyed, is a blessing of little moment. The contrary of these positions they maintain. But they also consider benevolence as consulting the truest and best interests of its objects; and view the happiness of liberty as well as of religion, as consisting not in the name or form, but in the reality. While men remain in the chains of ignorance and error, and under the dominion of tyrant lusts and passions, they cannot be free. And the more freedom of action they have in this state, they are but the more qualified by it to do injury, both to themselves and others. It is, therefore, firmly believed, that general emancipation to the Negroes in this country, would not, in present circumstances, be for their own happiness, as a body; while it would be extremely injurious to the community at large in various ways: And, if so, then it is not required even by benevolence. But acts of benevolence and generosity must be free and voluntary; no man has a right to compel another to the performance of them. This is a concern, which lies between a man and his God. If a man has obtained slaves by purchase, or inheritance, and the holding of them as such is justifiable by the law of God; why should he be required to liberate them, because it would be a generous action, rather than another on the same principle, to release his debtors, or sell his lands and houses, and distribute the proceeds among the poor? These also would be generous actions: Are they, therefore obligatory? Or, if obligatory, in certain circumstances, as personal, voluntary acts of piety and benevolence, has any man or body of men, civil or ecclesiastic, a right to require them? Surely those, who are advocates for compulsory, or strenuous measures to bring about emancipation, should duly weigh this consideration.

Should, however, a time arrive, when the Africans in our country might be found qualified to enjoy freedom; and, when they might obtain it in a manner consistent with the interest and peace of the community at large, the Convention would be happy in seeing them free: And so they would, in seeing the state of the poor, the ignorant and the oppressed of every description, and of every country meliorated; so that the reputed free might be free indeed, and happy. But there seems to be just reason to conclude that a considerable part of the human race, whether they bear openly the character of slaves or are reputed freemen, will continue in such circumstances, with mere shades of variation, while the world continues. It is evident, that men are sinful creatures, subject to affliction and to death, as the consequences of their nature's pollution and guilt: That they are now in a state of probation; and that God as a Righteous, All-wise Sovereign, not only disposes of them as he pleases, and bestows upon them many unmerited blessings and comforts, but subjects them also to privations, afflictions and trials, with the merciful intention of making all their afflictions, as well as their blessings, work finally for their good; if they embrace his salvation, humble themselves before him, learn righteousness, and submit to his holy will. To have them brought to this happy state is the great object of Christian benevolence, and of Christian piety; for this state is not only connected with the truest happiness, which can be enjoyed in time, but is introductory to eternal life and blessedness in the future world: And the salvation of men is intimately connected with the glory of their God and Redeemer.

And here I am brought to a part of the general subject, which, I confess to your Excellency, the Convention, from a sense of their duty, as a body of men, to whom important concerns of Religion are confided, have particularly at heart, and wish it may be seriously considered by all our Citizens: This is the religious interests of the Negroes. For though they are slaves, they are also men; and are with ourselves accountable creatures; having immortal souls, and being destined to future eternal award. Their religious interests claim a regard from their masters of the most serious nature; and it is indispensible. Nor can the community at large, in a right estimate of their duty and happiness, be indifferent on this subject. To the truly benevolent it must be pleasing to know, that a number of masters, as well as ministers and pious individuals, of various Christian denominations among us, do conscientiously regard this duty; but there is great reason to believe, that it is neglected and disregarded by many.

The Convention are particularly unhappy in considering, that an idea of the Bible's teaching the doctrine of emancipation as necessary, and tending to make servants insubordinate to proper authority, has obtained access to any mind; both on account of its direct influence on those, who admit it; and the fear it excites in others, producing the effects before noticed. But it is hoped, it has been evinced, that the idea is an erroneous one; and, that it will be seen, that the influence of a right acquaintance with that Holy Book tends directly and power-fully, by promoting the fear and love of God, together with just and peaceful sentiments toward men, to produce one of the best securities to the public, for the internal and domestic peace of the State.

It is also a pleasing consideration, tending to confirm these sentiments, that in the late projected scheme for producing an insurrection among us, there were very few of those who were, as members attached to regular Churches, (even within the sphere of its operations) who appear to have taken a part in the wicked plot, or indeed to whom it was made known; of some Churches it does not appear, that there were any. It is true, that a considerable number of those who were found guilty and executed, laid claim to a religious character; yet several of these were grossly immoral, and, in general, they were members of an irregular body, which called itself the *African Church*, and had intimate connection and intercourse with a similar body of men in a Northern City, among whom the supposed right to emancipation is strenuously advocated.

The result of this inquiry and reasoning, on the subject of slavery, brings us, sir, if I mistake not, very regularly to the following conclusions:—That the holding of slaves is justifiable by the doctrine and example contained in Holy writ; and is, therefore consistent with Christian uprightness, both in sentiment and conduct. That, all things considered, the Citizens of America have in general obtained the African slaves, which they possess, on principles, which can be justified; though much cruelty has indeed been exercised towards them by many, who have been concerned in the slave-trade, and by others who have held them here, as slaves in their service; for which the authors of this cruelty are accountable. That slavery, when tempered with humanity and justice, is a state of tolerable happiness; equal, if not superior, to that which many poor enjoy in countries reputed free. That a master has a scriptural right to govern his slaves so as to keep them in subjection; to demand and receive from them a reasonable service; and to correct them for the neglect of duty, for their vices and transgressions; but that to impose on them unreasonable, rigorous services, or to inflict on them cruel punishment, he has neither a scriptural nor a moral right. At the same time it must be remembered, that, while he is receiving from them their uniform and best services, he is required by the Divine Law, to afford them protection, and such necessaries and conveniencies of life as are proper to their condition as servants; so far as he is enabled by their services to afford them these comforts, on just and rational principles. That it is the positive duty of servants to reverence their master, to be obedient, industrious, faithful to him, and careful of his interests; and without being so, they can neither be the faithful servants of God, nor be held as regular members of the Christian Church. That as claims to freedom as a *right*, when that right is forfeited, or has been lost, in such a manner as has been represented, would be unjust; and as all attempts to obtain it by violence and fraud would be wicked; so all representations made to them by others, on such censurable principles, or in a manner tending to make them discontented; and finally, to produce such unhappy effects and consequences, as have been before noticed, cannot be friendly to them (as they certainly are not to the community at large,) nor consistent with righteousness: Nor can the conduct be justified, however in some it may be palliated by pleading benevolence in intention, as the motive. That masters having the disposal of the persons, time and labour of their servants, and being the heads of families, are bound, on principles of moral and religious duty, to give these servants religious instruction; or at least, to afford them opportunities, under proper regulations to obtain it: And to grant religious privileges to those, who desire them, and furnish proper evidence of their sincerity and uprightness: Due care being at the same time taken, that they receive their instructions from right sources, and from their connexions, where they will not be in danger of having their minds corrupted by sentiments unfriendly to the domestic and civil peace of the community. That, where the life, comfort, safety and religious interest of so large a number of human beings, as this class of persons is among us, are concerned; and, where they must necessarily, as slaves, be so much at the disposal of their masters; it appears to be a just and necessary concern of the Government, not only to provide laws to prevent or punish insurrections, and other violent and villanous conduct among them (which are indeed necessary) but, on the other hand, laws, also, to prevent their being oppressed and injured by unreasonable, cruel masters, and others; and to afford them, in respect of morality and religion, such privileges as may comport with the peace and safety of the State, and with those relative duties existing between masters and servants, which the word of God enjoins. It is, also, believed to be a just conclusion, that the interest and security of the State would be promoted, by allowing, under proper regulations, considerable religious privileges, to such of this class, as know how to estimate them aright, and have given suitable evidence of their own good principles, uprightness and fidelity; by attaching them, from principles of gratitude and love, to the interests of their masters and the State; and thus rendering their fidelity firm and constant. While on the other hand, to lay them under an interdict, as some have supposed necessary, in a case where reason, conscience, the genius of Christianity and salvation are concerned, on account of the bad conduct of others, would be felt as oppressive, tend to sour and alienate their minds from their masters and the public, and to make them vulnerable to temptation. All which is, with deference, submitted to the consideration of your Excellency.

With high respect, I remain, personally, and on behalf of the Convention,

Sir, your very obedient and humble servant,
RICHARD FURMAN.
President of the Baptist State Convention.

His Excellency GOVERNOR WILSON.

THEODORE D. WELD

American Slavery As It Is

Introduction

READER, you are empanelled as a juror to try a plain case and bring in an honest verdict. The question at issue is not one of law, but of fact—"What is the actual condition of the slaves in the United States?" A plainer case never went to a jury. Look at it. TWENTY-SEVEN HUNDRED THOUSAND PERSONS in this country, men, women, and children, are in SLAVERY. Is slavery, as a condition for human beings, good, bad, or indifferent? We submit the question without argument. You have common sense, and conscience, and a human heart;—pronounce upon it. You have a wife, or a husband, a child, a father, a mother, a brother or a sister—make the case your own, make it theirs, and bring in your verdict. The case of Human Rights against Slavery has been adjudicated in the court of conscience times innumerable. The same verdict has always been rendered—"Guilty;" the same sentence has always been pronounced, "Let it be accursed;" and human nature, with her million echoes, has rung it round the world in every language under heaven, "Let it be accursed. Let it be accursed." His heart is false to human nature, who will not say "Amen." There is not a man on earth who does not believe that slavery is a curse. Human beings may be inconsistent, but human *nature* is true to herself. She has uttered her testimony against slavery with a shriek ever since the monster was begotten; and till it perishes amidst the execrations of the universe, she will traverse the world on its track, dealing her bolts upon its head, and dashing against it her condemning brand. We repeat it, every man knows that slavery is a curse. Whoever denies this, his lips libel his heart. Try him; clank the chains in his ears, and tell him they are for *him*. Give him an hour to prepare his wife and children for a life of slavery. Bid him make haste and get ready their necks for the yoke, and their wrists for the coffle chains, then look at his pale lips and trembling knees, and you have *nature's* testimony against slavery.

Two millions seven hundred thousand persons in these States are in this condition. They were made slaves and are held such by force, and by being put in fear, and this for no crime! Reader, what have you to say of such treatment? Is it right, just, benevolent? Suppose I should seize you, rob you of your liberty, drive you into the field, and make you work without pay as long as you live, would that be justice and kindness, or monstrous injustice and cruelty? Now, everybody knows that the slaveholders do these things to the slaves every day, and yet it is stoutly affirmed that they treat them well and kindly, and that their tender regard for their slaves restrains the masters from inflicting cruelties upon them. We shall go into no metaphysics to show the absurdity of this pretence. The man who *robs* you every day, is, forsooth, quite too tenderhearted ever to cuff or kick you! True, he can snatch your money, but he does it gently lest he should hurt you. He can empty your pockets without qualms, but if your *stomach* is empty, it cuts him to the quick. He can make you work a life time without pay, but loves you too well to let you go hungry. He fleeces you of your *rights* with a relish, but is shocked if you work bareheaded in summer, or in winter without warm stockings. He can make you go without your *liberty*, but never without a shirt. He can crush, in you, all hope of bettering your condition, by vowing that you shall die his slave, but though he can coolly torture your feelings, he is too compassionate to lacerate your back—he can break your heart, but he is very tender of your skin. He can strip you of all protection and thus expose you to all outrages, but if you are exposed to the *weather*, half clad and half sheltered, how yearn his tender bowels! What! Slaveholders talk of treating men well, and yet not only rob them of all they get, and as fast as they get it, but rob them of *themselves*, also; their very hands and feet, all their muscles, and limbs, and senses, their bodies and minds, their time and liberty and earnings, their free speech and rights of conscience, their right to acquire knowledge, and property, and reputation;—and yet they, who plunder them of all these, would fain make us believe that their soft hearts ooze out so lovingly toward their slaves that they always keep them well housed and well clad, never push them too hard in the field, never make their dear backs smart, nor let their dear stomachs get empty.

But there is no end to the absurdities. Are slaveholders dunces, or do they take all the rest of the world to be, that they think to bandage our eyes with such thin gauzes? Protesting their kind regard for those whom they hourly plunder of all they have and all they get! What! When they have seized their victims, and annihilated all their *rights*, still claim to be the special guardians of their *happiness!* Plunderers of their liberty, yet the careful suppliers of their wants? Robbers of their earnings, yet watchful sentinels round their interests, and kind providers for their comfort? Filching all their time, yet granting generous donations for rest and sleep? Stealing the use of their muscles, yet thoughtful of their ease? Putting them under *drivers*, yet careful that they are not hard-pushed? Too humane forsooth to stint the stomachs of their slaves, yet force their *minds* to starve, and brandish over them pains and penalties, if they dare to reach forth for the smallest crumb of knowledge, even a letter of the alphabet!

It is no marvel that slaveholders are always talking of their *kind treatment* of their slaves. The only marvel is, that men of sense can be gulled by such professions. Despots always insist that they are merciful. The greatest tyrants that ever dripped with blood have assumed the titles of "most gracious," "most clement," "most merciful," &c., and have ordered their crouching vassals to accost them thus. When did not vice lay claim to those virtues which are the opposites of its habitual crimes? The guilty, according to their own showing, are always innocent, and cowards brave, and drunkards sober, and harlots chaste, and pickpockets honest to a fault. Everybody understands this. When a man's tongue grows thick, and he begins to hiccough and walk cross-legged, we expect him, as a matter of course, to protest that he is not drunk; so when a man is always singing the praises of his own honesty, we instinctively watch his movements and look out for our pocketbooks. Whoever is simple enough to be hoaxed by such professions, should never be trusted in the streets without somebody to take care of him. Human nature works out in slaveholders just as it does in other men, and in American slaveholders just as in English, French, Turkish, Algerine, Roman and Grecian. The Spartans boasted of their kindness to their slaves, while they whipped them to death by thousands at the altars of their gods. The Romans lauded their own mild treatment of their bondmen, while they branded their names on their flesh with hot irons, and when old, threw them into their fish ponds, or like Cato "the Just," starved them to death. It is the boast of the Turks that they treat their slaves as though they were their children, yet their common name for them is "dogs," and for the merest trifles, their feet are bastinadoed to a jelly, or their heads clipped off with the scimitar. The Portugese pride themselves on their gentle bearing toward their slaves, yet the streets of Rio de Janeiro are filled with naked men and women yoked in pairs to carts and wagons, and whipped by drivers like beasts of burden.

Slaveholders, the world over, have sung the praises of their tender mercies towards their slaves. Even the wretches that plied the African slave trade, tried to rebut Clarkson's proofs of their cruelties, by speeches, affidavits, and published pamphlets, setting forth the accommodations of the "middle passage," and their kind attention to the comfort of those whom they had stolen from their homes, and kept stowed away under hatches, during a voyage of four thousand miles. So, according to the testimony of the autocrat of the Russias, he exercises great clemency towards the Poles, though he exiles them by thousands to the snows of Siberia, and tramples them down by millions, at home. Who discredits the atrocities perpetrated by Ovando in Hispaniola, Pizarro in Peru, and Cortez in Mexico,—because they filled the ears of the Spanish Court with protestations of their benignant rule? While they were yoking the enslaved natives like beasts to the draught, working them to death by thousands in their mines, hunting them with bloodhounds, torturing them on racks, and broiling them on beds of coals, their representations to the mother country teemed with eulogies of their parental sway! The bloody atrocities of Philip II, in the expulsion of his Moorish subjects, are matters of imperishable history. Who disbelieves or doubts them? And yet his courtiers magnified his virtues and chanted his clemency and his mercy, while the wail of a million victims, smitten down by a tempest of fire and slaughter let loose at his bidding, rose above the *Te Deums* that thundered from all Spain's cathedrals. When Louis XIV revoked the edict of Nantes, and proclaimed two millions of his subjects free plunder for persecution,—when from the English channel to the Pyrenees the mangled bodies of the Protestants were dragged on reeking hurdles by a shouting populace, he claimed to be "the father of his people," and wrote himself "His most *Christian* Majesty."

But we will not anticipate topics, the full discussion of which more naturally follows than precedes the inquiry into the actual condition and treatment of slaves in the United States.

As slaveholders and their apologists are volunteer witnesses in their own cause, and are flooding the world with testimony that their slaves are kindly treated; that they are well fed, well clothed, well housed, well lodged, moderately worked, and bountifully provided with all things needful for their comfort, we propose—first, to disprove their assertions by the testimony of a multitude of impartial witnesses, and then to put slaveholders themselves through a course of cross-questioning which shall draw their condemnation out of their own mouths. We will prove that the slaves in the United States are treated with barbarous inhumanity; that they are overworked, underfed, wretchedly clad and lodged, and have insufficient sleep; that they are often made to wear round their necks iron collars armed with prongs, to drag heavy chains and weights at their feet while working in the field, and to wear yokes, and bells, and iron horns; that they are often kept confined in the stocks day and night for weeks together, made to wear gags in their mouths for hours or days, have some of their front teeth torn out or broken off, that they may be easily detected when they run away; that they are frequently flogged with terrible severity, have red pepper rubbed into their lacerated flesh, and hot brine, spirits of turpentine, &c., poured over the gashes to increase the torture; that they are often stripped naked, their backs and limbs cut with knives, bruised and mangled by scores and hundreds of blows with the paddle, and terribly torn by the claws of cats, drawn over them by their tormentors; that they are often hunted with bloodhounds and shot down like beasts, or torn in pieces by dogs; that they are often suspended by the arms and whipped and beaten till they faint, and when revived by restoratives, beaten again till they faint, and sometimes till they die; that their ears are often cut off, their eyes knocked out, their bones broken, their flesh branded with red hot irons; that they are maimed, mutilated and burned to death over slow fires. All these things, and more, and worse, we shall PROVE. Reader, we know whereof we affirm, we have weighed it well; *more and worse* WE WILL PROVE. Mark these words, and read on; we will establish all these facts by the testimony of scores and hundreds of eye witnesses, by the testimony of *slaveholders* in all parts of the slave states, by slaveholding members of Congress and of state legislatures, by ambassadors to foreign courts, by judges, by doctors of divinity, and clergymen of all denominations, by merchants, mechanics, lawyers and physicians, by presidents and professors in colleges and *professional* seminaries, by planters, overseers and drivers. We shall show, not merely that such deeds are committed, but that they are frequent; not done in corners, but before the sun; not in one of the slave states, but in all of them; not perpetrated by brutal overseers and drivers merely, but by magistrates, by legislators, by professors of religion, by preachers of the gospel, by governors of states, by "gentlemen of property and standing," and by delicate females moving in the "highest circles of society." We know, full well, the outcry that will be made by multitudes, at these declarations; the multiform cavils, the flat denials, the charges of "exaggeration" and "falsehood" so often bandied, the sneers of affected contempt at the credulity that can believe such things, and the rage and imprecations against those who give them currency. We know, too, the threadbare sophistries by which slaveholders and their apologists seek to evade such testimony. If they admit that such deeds are committed, they tell us that they are exceedingly rare, and therefore furnish no grounds for judging of the general treatment of slaves; that occasionally a brutal wretch in the *free* states barbarously butchers his wife, but that no one thinks of inferring from that, the general treatment of wives at the North and West.

They tell us, also, that the slaveholders of the South are proverbially hospitable, kind, and generous, and it is incredible that they can perpetrate such enormities upon human beings; further, that it is absurd to suppose that they would thus injure their own property, that self-interest would prompt them to treat their slaves with kindness, as none but fools and madmen wantonly destroy their own property; further, that Northern visitors at the South come back testifying to the kind treatment of the slaves, and that the slaves themselves corroborate such representations. All these pleas, and scores of others, are bruited in every corner of the free States; and who that hath eyes to see, has not sickened at the blindness that saw not, at the palsy of heart that felt not, or at the cowardice and sycophancy that dared not expose such shallow fallacies. We are not to be turned from our purpose by such vapid babblings. In their appropriate places, we propose to consider these objections and various others, and to show their emptiness and folly.

The foregoing declarations touching the inflictions upon slaves, are not haphazard assertions, nor the exaggerations of fiction conjured up to carry a point; nor are they the rhapsodies of enthusiasm, nor crude conclusions, jumped at by hasty and imperfect investigation, nor the aimless outpourings either of sympathy or poetry; but they are proclamations of deliberate, well-weighed convictions, produced by accumulations of proof, by affirmations and affidavits, by written testimonies and statements of a cloud of witnesses who speak what they know and testify what they have seen, and all these impregnably fortified by proofs innumerable, in the relation of the slaveholder of his slave, the nature of arbitrary power, and the nature and history of man.

Of the witnesses whose testimony is embodied in the following pages, a majority are slaveholders, many of the remainder have been slaveholders, but now reside in free States.

Another class whose testimony will be given, consists of those who have furnished the results of their own observation during periods of residence and travel in the slave States.

Narrative and Testimony of Rev. Horace Moulton

MR. MOULTON is an esteemed minister of the Methodist Episcopal Church, in Marlborough, Mass. He spent five years in Georgia, between 1817 and 1824. The following communication has been recently received from him.

MARLBOROUGH, MASS., FEB. 18, 1839

DEAR BROTHER-

Yours of Feb. 2d, requesting me to write out a few facts on the subject of slavery, as it exists at the south, has come to hand. I hasten to comply with your request. Were it not, however, for the claims of those "who are drawn unto death," and the responsibility resting upon me, in consequence of this request, I should forever hold my peace. For I well know that I shall bring upon myself a flood of persecution, for attempting to speak out for the dumb. But I am willing to be set at nought by men, if I can be the means of promoting the welfare of the oppressed of our land. I shall not relate many particular cases of cruelty, though I might a great number; but shall give some general information as to their mode of treatment, their food, clothing, dwellings, deprivations, &c.

Let me say, in the first place, that I spent nearly five years in Savannah, Georgia, and in its vicinity, between the years 1817 and 1824. My object in going to the south, was to engage in making and burning brick; but not immediately succeeding, I engaged in no business of much profit until late in the winter, when I took charge of a set of hands and went to work. During my leisure, however, I was an observer, at the auctions, upon plantations, and in almost every department of business. The next year, during the cold months, I had several two-horse teams under my care, with which we used to haul brick, boards, and other articles from the wharf into the city, and cotton, rice, corn, and wood from the country. This gave me an extensive acquaintance with merchants, mechanics and planters. I had slaves under my control some portions of every year when at the south. All the brick-yards, except one, on which I was engaged, were connected either with a corn field, potato patch, rice field, cotton field, tan-works, or with a wood lot. My business, usually, was to take charge of the brick-making department. At those jobs I have sometimes taken in charge both the field and brick-yard hands. I have been on the plantations in South Carolina, but have never been an overseer of slaves in that state, as has been said in the public papers.

I think the above facts and explanations are necessary to be connected with the account I may give of slavery, that the reader may have some knowledge of my acquaintance with *practical* slavery: for many mechanics and merchants who go to the South, and stay there for years, know but little of the dark side of slavery. My account of slavery will apply to *field hands*, who compose much the largest portion of the black population, (probably nine-tenths,) and not to those who are kept for kitchen maids, nurses, waiters, &c., about the houses of the planters and public hotels, where persons from the north obtain most of their knowledge of the evils of slavery. I will now proceed to take up specific points.

I. The Labor of the Slaves

Males and females work together promiscuously on all the plantations. On many plantations *tasks* are given them. The best working hands can have some leisure time; but the feeble and unskilful ones, together with slender females, have indeed a hard time of it, and very often answer for non-performance of tasks at the *whipping-posts*. None who worked with me had tasks at any time. The rule was to work them from sun to sun. But when I was burning brick, they were obliged to take turns, and *sit up all night* about every other night, and work all day. On one plantation, where I spent a few weeks, the slaves were called up to work long before daylight, when business pressed, and worked until late at night; and sometimes some of them *all night*. A large portion of the slaves are owned by masters who keep them on purpose to hire out—and they usually let them to those who will give the highest wages for them, irrespective of their mode of treatment; and those who hire them, will of course try to get the greatest possible amount of work performed, with the least possible expense. Women are seen bringing their infants into the field to their work, and leading others who are not old enough to stay at the cabins with safety. When they get there, they must set them down in the dirt, and go to work. Sometimes they are left to cry until they fall asleep. Others are left at home, shut up in their huts. Now, is it not barbarous, that the mother, with her child or children around her, half starved, must be whipped at night if she does not perform her task? But so it is. Some who have very young ones, fix a little sack, and place the infants on their backs, and work. One reason, I presume is, that they will not cry so much when they can hear their mother's voice. Another is, the mothers fear that the poisonous vipers and snakes will bite them. Truly, I never knew any place where the land is so infested with all kinds of the most venomous snakes, as in the low lands round about Savannah. The moccasin snakes, so called, and water rattlesnakes—the bites of both of which are as poisonous as our upland rattle-snakes at the north,—are found in myriads about the stagnant waters and swamps of the South. The females, in order to secure their infants from these poisonous snakes, do, as I have said, often work with their infants on their backs. Females are sometimes called to take the hardest part of the work. On some brick-yards where I have been, the women have been selected as the *moulders* of brick, instead of the men.

II. The Food of the Slaves

It was a general custom, wherever I have been, for the master to give each of his slaves, male and female, *one peck of corn per week* for their food. This at fifty cents per bushel, which was all that it was worth when I was there, would amount to twelve and a half cents per week for board per head.

It cost me upon an average, when at the south, one dollar per day for board. The price of fourteen bushels of corn per week. This would make my board equal in amount to the board of *forty-six slaves!* This is all that good or bad masters allow their slaves round about Savannah on the plantations. One peck of gourd-seed corn is to be measured out to each slave once every week. One man with whom I labored, however, being desirous to get all the work out of his hands he could, before I left, (about fifty in number), bought for them every week, or twice a week, a beef's head from market. With this, they made a soup in a large iron kettle, around which the hands came at meal-time, and dipping out the soup, would mix it with their hominy, and eat it as though it were a feast. This man permitted his slaves to eat twice a day while I was doing a job for him. He promised me a beaver hat and as good a suit of clothes as could be bought in the city, if I would accomplish so much for him before I returned to the north; giving me the entire control over his slaves. Thus you may see the temptations overseers sometimes have, to get all the work they can out of the poor slaves. The above is an exception to the general rule of feeding. For in all other places where I worked and visited; the slaves had *nothing from their masters but the corn,* or its equivalent in potatoes or rice, and to this, they were not permitted to come but *once a day*. The custom was to blow the horn early in the morning, as a signal for the hands to rise and go to work, when commenced; they continued work until about eleven o'clock, A.M., when, at the signal, all hands left off, and went into their huts, made their fires, made their corn-meal into hominy or cake, ate it, and went to work again at the signal of the horn, and worked until night, or until their tasks were done. Some cooked their breakfast in the field while at work. Each slave must grind his own corn in a hand-mill after he has done his work at night. There is generally one hand-mill on every plantation for the use of the slaves.

Some of the planters have no corn, others often get out. The substitute for it is, the equivalent of one peck of corn either in rice or sweet potatoes; neither of which is as good for the slaves as corn. They complain more of being faint, when fed on rice or potatoes, than when fed on corn. I was with one man a few weeks who gave me his hands to do a job of work, and to save time one cooked for all the rest. The following course was taken,—Two crotched sticks were drived down at one end of the yard, and a small pole being laid on the crotches, they swung a large iron kettle on the middle of the pole; then made up a fire under the kettle and boiled the hominy; when ready, the hands were called around this kettle with their wooden plates and spoons. They dipped out and ate standing around the kettle, or sitting upon the ground, as best suited their convenience. When they had potatoes they took them out with their hands, and ate them. As soon as it was thought they had had sufficient time to swallow their food they were called to their work again. *This was the only meal they ate through the day.* Now think of the little, almost naked and half-starved children, nibbling upon a piece of cold Indian cake, or a potato! Think of the poor female just ready to be confined, without anything that can be called convenient or comfortable! Think of the old toil-worn father and mother, without anything to eat but the coarsest of food, and not half enough of that! Then think of *home.* When sick, their physicians are their masters and overseers, in most cases, whose skill consists in bleeding and in administering large portions of Epsom salts, when the whip and *cursing* will not start them from their cabins.

III. Houses

The huts of slaves are mostly of the poorest kind. They are not as good as those temporary shanties which are thrown up beside railroads. They are erected with posts and crotches, with but little or no framework about them. They have no stoves or chimneys; some of them have something like a fireplace at one end, a board or two off at that side, or on the roof, to let off the smoke. Others have nothing like a fireplace in them; in these the fire is sometimes made in the middle of the hut. These buildings have but one apartment in them; the places where they pass in and out, serve both for doors and windows; the sides and roofs are covered with coarse, and in many instances with refuse boards. In warm weather, especially in the spring, the slaves keep up a smoke, or fire and smoke, all night, to drive away the gnats and mosquitos, which are very troublesome in all the low country of the south; so much so that the whites sleep under frames with nets over them, knit so fine that the mosquitos cannot fly through them.

Some of the slaves have rugs to cover them in the coldest weather, but I should think *more have not*. During driving storms they frequently have to run from one hut to another for shelter. In the coldest weather, where they can get wood or stumps, they keep up fires all night in their huts, and lay around them, with their feet towards the blaze. Men, women and children all lie down together, in most instances. There may be exceptions to the above statements in regard to their houses but so far as my observations have extended, I have given a fair description, and I have been on a large number of plantations in Georgia and South Carolina up and down the Savannah river. Their huts are generally built compactly on the plantations, forming villages of huts, their size proportioned to the number of slaves on them. In these miserable huts the poor blacks are herded at night like swine, *without any conveniences of bedsteads, tables or chairs.* O misery to the full! To see the aged sire beating off the swarms of gnats and mosquitos in the warm weather, and shivering in the straw, or bending over a few coals in the winter, clothed in rags. I should think males and females, both lie down at night with their working clothes on them. God alone knows how much the poor slaves suffer for the want of convenient houses to secure them from the piercing winds and howling storms of winter, especially the aged, sick and dying. Although it is much warmer there than here, yet I suffered for a number of weeks in the winter, almost as much in Georgia as I do in Massachusetts.

IV. Clothing

The masters [in Georgia] make a practice of getting two suits of clothes for each slave per year, a thick suit for winter, and a thin one for summer. They provide also one pair of northern made sale shoes for each slave in *winter*. These shoes usually begin to rip in a few weeks. The Negroes' mode of mending them is, to *wire* them together, in many instances. Do our northern shoemakers know that they are augmenting the sufferings of the poor slaves with their almost good for nothing sale shoes? Inasmuch as it is done unto one of those poor sufferers it is done unto our Saviour. The above practice of clothing the slave is customary to some extent. How many, however, fail of this, God only knows. The children and old slaves are, I should think, *exceptions* to the above rule. The males and females have their suits from the same cloth for their winter dresses. These winter garments appear to be made of a mixture of cotton and wool, very coarse and *sleazy*. The whole suit for the men consists of a pair of pantaloons and short sailor-jacket, *without shirt, vest, hat, stockings, or any kind of loose garments!* These, if worn steadily when at work, would not probably last more than one or two months; therefore, for the sake of saving them, many of them work, especially in the summer, with no clothing on them except a cloth tied around their waist, and *almost all* with nothing more on them than pantaloons, and these frequently so torn that they do not serve the purposes of common decency. The women have for clothing a short petticoat, and a short loose gown, something like the male's sailor-jacket, *without any undergarment, stockings, bonnets, hoods, caps, or any kind of overclothes.* When at work in warm weather, they usually strip off the loose gown, and have nothing on but a short petticoat with some kind of covering over their breasts. Many children may be seen in the summer months *as naked as they came into the world*. I think, as a whole, they suffer more for the want of comfortable bedclothes, than they do for wearing apparel. It is true, that some by begging or buying, have more clothes than above described, but the *masters provide them with no more*. They are miserable objects of pity. It may be said of many of them, "I was *naked* and ye clothed me not." It is enough to melt the hardest heart to see the ragged mothers nursing their almost naked children, with but a morsel of the coarsest food to eat. The Southern horses and dogs have enough to eat and good care taken of them, but Southern Negroes, who can describe their misery?

V. Punishments

The ordinary mode of punishing the slaves is both cruel and barbarous. The masters seldom, if ever, try to govern their slaves by moral influence, but by whipping, kicking, beating, starving, branding, *cat-hauling*, loading with irons, imprisoning, or by some other cruel mode of torturing. They often boast of having invented some new mode of torture, by which they have "tamed the rascals." What is called a moderate flogging at the south is horribly cruel. Should we whip our horses for any offence as they whip their slaves for small offences, we should expose ourselves to the penalty of the law. The masters whip for the smallest offences, such as not performing their tasks, being caught by the guard or patrol by night, or for taking anything from the master's yard without leave. For these, and the like crimes, the slaves are whipped thirty-nine lashes, and sometimes seventy or a hundred, on the bare back. One slave, who was under my care, was whipped. I think one hundred lashes, for getting a small handful of wood from his master's yard without leave. I heard an overseer boasting to this same master that he gave one of the boys seventy lashes, for not doing a job of work just as he thought it ought to be done. The owner of the slave appeared to be pleased that the overseer had been so faithful. The apology they make for whipping so cruelly is, that it is to frighten the rest of the gang. The masters say, that what we call an ordinary flogging will not subdue the slaves; hence the most cruel and barbarous scourgings ever witnessed by man are daily and *hourly* inflicted upon the naked bodies of these miserable bondmen; not by masters and Negro-drivers only, but by the constables in the common markets and jailors in their yards.

When the slaves are whipped, either in public or private, they have their hands fastened by the wrists, with a rope or cord prepared for the purpose: this being thrown over a beam, a limb of a tree, or something else, the culprit is drawn up and stretched by the arms as high as possible, without raising his feet from the ground or floor: and sometimes they are made to stand on tip-toe; then the feet are made fast to something prepared for them. In this distorted posture the monster flies at them, sometimes in great rage, with his implements of torture, and cuts on with all his might, over the shoulders, under the arms, and sometimes, over the head and ears, or on parts of the body where he can inflict the greatest torment. Occasionally the whipper, especially if his victim does not beg enough to suit him, while under the lash, will fly into a passion, uttering the most horrid oaths; while the victim of his rage is crying, at every stroke, "Lord have mercy! Lord have mercy!" The scenes exhibited at the whipping post are awfully terrific and frightful to one whose heart has not turned to stone; I never could look on but a moment. While under the lash, the bleeding victim writhes in agony, convulsed with torture. Thirty-nine lashes on the bare back, which tear the skin at almost every stroke, is what the South calls a *very moderate punishment!* Many masters whip until they are tired—until the back is a gore of blood—then rest upon it: after a short cessation, get up and go at it again; and after having satiated their revenge in the blood of their victims, they sometimes *leave them tied, for hours together, bleeding at every wound.*—Sometimes, after being whipped, they are bathed with a brine of salt and water. Now and then a master, but more frequently a mistress who has no husband, will send them to jail a few days, giving orders to have them whipped, so many lashes, once or twice a day. Sometimes, after being whipped, some have been shut up in a dark place and deprived of food, in order to increase their torments: and I have heard of some who have, in such circumstances, died of their wounds and starvation.

Such scenes of horror as above described are so common in Georgia that they attract no attention. To threaten them with death, with breaking in their teeth or jaws, or cracking their heads, is *common talk,* when scolding at the slaves.—Those who run away from their masters and are caught again generally fare the worst. They are generally lodged in jail, with instructions from the owner to have them cruelly whipped. Some order the constables to whip them publicly in the market. Constables at the south are generally savage, brutal men. They have become so accustomed to catching and whipping Negroes, that they are as fierce as tigers. Slaves who are absent from their yards, or plantations, after eight o'clock P.M., and are taken by the guard in the cities, or by the patrols in the country, are, if not called for before nine o'clock A.M. the next day, secured in prisons, and hardly ever escape, until their backs are torn up by the cowhide. On plantations, the *evenings* usually present scenes of horror. Those slaves against whom charges are preferred for not having performed their tasks, and for various faults, must, after work-hours at night, undergo their torments. I have often heard the sound of the lash, the curses of the whipper, and the cries of the poor Negro rending the air, late in the evening, and long before day-light in the morning.

It is very common for masters to say to the overseers or drivers, "Put it on to them," "don't spare that fellow," "give that scoundrel one hundred lashes," &c. Whipping the women when in delicate circumstances, as they sometimes do, without any regard to their entreaties or the entreaties of their nearest friends, is truly barbarous. If Negroes could testify, they would tell you of instances of women being whipped until they have miscarried at the whipping-post. I heard of such things at the south—they are undoubtedly facts. Children are whipped unmercifully for the smallest offences, and that before their mothers. A large proportion of the blacks have their shoulders, backs, and arms all scarred up, and not a few of them have had their heads laid open with clubs, stones, and brick-bats, and with the butt-end of whips and canes—some have had their jaws broken, others their teeth knocked in or out; while others have had their ears cropped and the sides of their cheeks gashed out. Some of the poor creatures have lost the sight of one of their eyes by the careless blows of the whipper, or by some other violence.

But punishing of slaves as above described, is not the only mode of torture. Some tie them up in a very uneasy posture, where they must stand *all night,* and they will then work them hard all day—that is, work them hard all day and torment them all night. Others punish by fastening them down on a log, or something else, and strike them on the bare skin with a board paddle full of holes. This breaks the skin, I should presume, at every hole where it comes in contact with it. Others, when other modes of punishment will not subdue them, *cat-haul* them— that is, take a cat by the nape of the neck and tail, or by the hind legs, and drag the claws across the back until satisfied. This kind of punishment poisons the flesh much worse than the whip, and is more dreaded by the slave. Some are branded by a hot iron, others have their flesh cut out in large gashes, to mark them. Some who are prone to run away, have iron fetters riveted around their ankles, sometimes they are put only on one foot, and are dragged on the ground. Others have on large iron collars or yokes upon their necks, or clogs riveted upon their wrists or ankles. Some have bells put upon them, hung upon a sort of frame to an iron collar. Some masters fly into a rage at trifles and knock down their Negroes with their fists, or with the first thing that they can get hold of. The whiplash knots, or rawhide, have sometimes by a reckless stroke reached round to the front of the body and cut through to the bowels. One slaveholder with whom I lived, whipped one of his slaves one day, as many, I should think, as one hundred lashes, and then turned the *butt end* and went to beating him over the head and ears, and truly I was amazed that the slave was not killed on the spot. Not a few slaveholders whip their slaves to death, and then say they died under a "moderate correction." I wonder that ten are not killed where one is! Were they not much hardier than the whites many more of them must die than do. One young mulatto man, with whom I was acquainted, was killed by his master in his yard with *impunity*. I boarded at the same time near the place where this glaring murder was committed, and knew the master well. He had a plantation, on which he enacted, almost daily, cruel barbarities, some of them, I was informed, more terrific, if possible, than death itself. Little notice was taken of this murder, and it all passed off without any action being taken against the murderer. The masters used to try to make me whip their Negroes. They said I could not get along with them without flogging them—but I found I could get along better with them by coaxing and encouraging them than by beating and flogging them. I had not a heart to beat and kick about those beings; although I had not grace in my heart the first three years I was there, yet I sympathised with the slaves. I was never guilty of having but one whipped, and he was whipped but eight or nine blows. The circumstances were as follows: Several Negroes were put under my care, one spring, *who were fresh from Congo and Guinea*. I could not understand them, neither could they me, in one word I spoke. I therefore pointed to them to go to work; all obeyed me willingly but one—he refused. I told the driver that he must tie him up and whip him. After he had tied him, by the help of some others, we struck him eight or nine blows, and he yielded. I told the driver not to strike him another blow. We untied him, and he went to work, and continued faithful all the time he was with me. This one was not a sample, however—many of them have such exalted views of freedom that it is hard work for the masters to whip them into brutes, that is to subdue their noble spirits. The

Negroes being put under my care, did not prevent the masters from whipping them when they pleased. But they never whipped much in my presence. This work was usually left until I had dismissed the hands. On the plantations, the masters chose to have the slaves whipped in the presence of all the hands, to strike them with terror.

VI. Runaways

Numbers of poor slaves run away from their masters; some of whom doubtless perish in the swamps and other secret places, rather than return back again to their masters; others stay away until they almost famish with hunger, and then return home rather than die, while others who abscond are caught by the Negro-hunters, in various ways. Sometimes the master will hire some of his most trusty Negroes to secure any stray Negroes, who come on to their plantations, for many come at night to beg food of their friends on the plantations. The slaves assist one another usually when they can, and not be found out in it. The master can now and then, however, get some of his hands to betray the runaways. Some obtain their living in hunting after lost slaves. The most common way is to train up young dogs to follow them. This can easily be done by obliging a slave to go out into the woods, and climb a tree, and then put the young dog on his track, and with a little assistance he can be taught to follow him to the tree, and when found, of course the dog would bark at such game as a poor Negro on a tree. There was a man living in Savannah when I was there, who kept a large number of dogs for no other purpose than to hunt runaway Negroes. And he always had enough of this work to do, for hundreds of runaways are never found, but could he get news soon after one had fled, he was almost sure to catch him. And this fear of the dogs restrains multitudes from running off.

When he went out on a hunting excursion, to be gone several days, he took several persons with him, armed generally with rifles and followed by the dogs. The dogs were as true to the track of a Negro, if one had passed recently, as a hound is to the track of a fox when he has found it. When the dogs draw near to their game, the slave must turn and fight them or climb a tree. If the latter, the dogs will stay and bark until the pursuers come. The blacks frequently deceive the dogs by crossing and recrossing the creeks. Should the hunters who have no dogs, start a slave from his hiding place, and the slave not stop at the hunter's call, he will shoot at him, as soon as he would at a deer. Some masters advertise so much for a runaway slave, dead or alive. It undoubtedly gives such more satisfaction to know that their property is dead, than to know that it is alive without being able to get it. Some slaves run away who never mean to be taken alive. I will mention one. He run off and was pursued by the dogs, but having a weapon with him he succeeded in killing two or three of the dogs; but was afterwards shot. He had declared, that he never would be taken alive. The people rejoiced at the death of the slave, but lamented the death of the dogs, they were such ravenous hunters. Poor fellow, he fought for life and liberty like a hero; but the bullets brought him down. A Negro can hardly walk unmolested at the south.—Every colored stranger that walks the streets is suspected of being a runaway slave, hence he must be interrogated by every Negro hater whom he meets, and should he not have a pass, he must be arrested and hurried off to jail. Some masters boast that their slaves would not be free if they could. How little they know of their slaves! They are all sighing and groaning for freedom. May God hasten the time!

VII. Confinement at Night

When the slaves have done their day's work, they must be herded together like sheep in their yards, or on their plantations. They have not as much liberty as northern men have, who are sent to jail for debt, for they have liberty to walk a larger yard than the slaves have. The slaves must all be at their homes precisely at eight o'clock P.M. At this hour the drums beat in the cities, as a signal for every slave to be in his den. In the country, the signal is given by firing guns, or some other way by which they may know the hour when to be at home. After this hour, the guard in the cities, and patrols in the country, being well armed, are on duty until daylight in the morning. If they catch any Negroes during the night without a pass, they are immediately seized and hurried away to the guard-house, or if in the country to some place of confinement, where they are kept until nine o'clock, A.M., the next day; if not called for by that time, they are hurried off to jail, and there remain until called for by their master and his jail and guard-house fees paid. The guards and patrols receive one dollar extra for every one they can catch, who has not a pass from his master, or overseer, but few masters will give their slaves passes to be out at night unless on some special business: notwithstanding, many venture out, watching every step they take for the guard or patrol, the consequence is, some are caught almost every night, and some nights many are taken; some, fleeing after being hailed by the watch, are shot down in attempting their escape, others are crippled for life. I find I shall not be able to write out more at present. My ministerial duties are pressing, and if I delay this till the next mail, I fear it will not be in season. Your brother for those who are in bonds.

HORACE MOULTON

Notes

1. Sydney Ahlstrom, *A Religious History of the American People* (New Haven: Yale University Press, 1972), pp. 390-391.
2. Winthrop S. Hudson, *Religion in America* (New York: Charles Scribner's Sons, 1965), p. 161.
3. Delivered to the senior class of Harvard Divinity School, July 15, 1838.
4. "Rev. Dr. Richard Furman's Exposition of the Views of the Baptists Relative to the Coloured Population in the United States in a Communication to the Governor of South Carolina, 1822."

ABOUT THE EDITOR

Bill J. Leonard is Associate Professor of Church History at The Southern Baptist Theological Seminary, Louisville, Kentucky. Dr. Leonard is a graduate of Texas Wesleyan College (B.A.), Southwestern Baptist Theological Seminary (M.Div.) and Boston University (Ph.D.). He has served churches in Texas and Massachusetts. Dr. Leonard is a member of the American Society of Church History and the Southern Baptist Historical Society. He has written extensively in the area of church history in America.